Preface

I SPENT thirty-six years living among the Arabs. During the first nineteen of these years, I lived almost entirely with them, rarely meeting Europeans and sometimes not speaking a word of English for weeks on end. I originally went to Iraq in 1920 as a regular officer of the British Army, seeking fresh fields of adventure and a wider knowledge of the many different forms of modern soldiering. But when I had spent five years amongst the Arabs, I decided to change the basis of my whole career. I made up my mind to resign my commission in the British Army and devote my life to the Arabs. My decision was largely emotional. I loved them.

Fourteen years later, in April 1939, I was called to assume command of the Arab Legion—the army of the little State of Trans-Jordan. It was a tiny army and a little State, but even so, it was a "State", which possessed its own government. And this government had relations with other governments—that is to say, it moved on the international level. By becoming the principal military officer to a government, I began for the first time to gain an insight into international affairs. I was able to devote less and less of my time to living completely amongst Arabs, and working at their parochial affairs. I was obliged to live in the capital, to meet with royalties, presidents, cabinet ministers and ambassadors, and to consider the policies and actions of other governments. For it was now my first responsibility to be ready to defend Trans-Jordan. The present book deals primarily with this second period of my life among the Arabs.

As my field of action widened and we plunged into the dark uncertainties of the Second World War, I began to think of wider and more distant objectives. The West, it seemed to me, had become too dominant over Asia. Western peoples had not done this intentionally. Their industrial progress, on the one hand, had produced immense wealth. They had also experienced a period of tremendous energy, initiative and enthusiasm. In the case of Britain, at least, her world-wide power and interests had been built up by adventurous individuals, not by Machiavellian state planning. But now this tide of energy and enthusiasm, like all tides, had partly spent itself. Asia would now slowly reassert herself until a fair equilibrium was established. Such were the processes of history. We had no right to object to this; indeed, we had not planned to seize this power—it "just happened".

But I strenuously opposed any idea that East was East and West was West and that the two could never agree. I had experienced in myself, as I thought, the feasibility of living simultaneously as an Arab amongst Arabs and as an Englishman amongst Europeans. Why should not the two work hand in hand? There were, of course, many differences in outlook and temperament. But differences do not necessarily mean rivalry; on the contrary, they can be a means of harmony, for one becomes the complement of the other.

It was my idea to help the Arabs by introducing to their country those skills and methods and products in which Europe excelled. I hoped that the Arabs would remain basically Arabs, clinging to and priding themselves on the many fine qualities and traditions inherited by them from their past. But I hoped simultaneously to be able to help them to hold their own in the modern world. Such close co-operation presupposed a high degree of friendship, sympathy and mutual confidence between Europe and Asia—that is to say, in my limited sphere, between Arabs and British.

From 1921 to 1951, while Jordan was under the wise rule of King Abdulla, the country seemed to be making appreciable strides in that direction. There was a perfectly genuine feeling of friendship and confidence between the two countries. But to a considerable extent, these sentiments were limited to Trans-Jordan. The remainder of the Arab countries, and indeed the greater part of Asia, was becoming increasingly poisoned with hatred and distrust for the West.

In July 1951, King Abdulla was murdered. Gradually the foundations of Jordan, which had stood like a rock amid the streams of hatred and emotion, were undermined.

The people dwelling east of the Jordan were my people. I had grown old amongst them, and my home was in their midst. But the union of Trans-Jordan with Arab Palestine introduced into the country a new population—a population which had suffered an immense injustice as a result of Western policy. Gradually the Trans-Jordanians were partially submerged, and the rock of Jordan, with its wise moderation and its broadminded comprehension of East and West, disintegrated in the flood of hate. The tides of mistrust and hatred were constantly rising. Finally, on February 29th, 1956, the King and government of Jordan, whom I had served for twenty-six years, ordered me to leave their country in two hours. My departure did not lead to a better understanding between them and Britain. The tides of suspicion and resentment continued to rise.

I had failed hopelessly in the task to which I had devoted nearly all my life—to promote ever closer co-operation and understanding between East and West. When I left Jordan, mistrust and hate seemed to hold the field.

In the course of this narrative, I have voiced a number of criti-

A Soldier with the Arabs

Lieutenant-General
SIR JOHN BAGOT GLUBB
K.C.B., C.M.G., D.S.O., O.B.E., M.C.

"Fool!" said my Muse to me,
"Look in thy heart, and write."
Sir Philip Sidney

LONDON
HODDER AND STOUGHTON

MADE AND PRINTED IN GREAT BRITAIN FOR
HODDER AND STOUGHTON LTD., LONDON, BY
HAZELL WATSON AND VINEY LTD., AYLESBURY AND LONDON

A Soldier with the Arabs

THE STORY OF THE ARAB LEGION

"Glubb Pasha tells his exhilarating story of adventure and achievement—a story made more vivid by a real gift for the portrayal of the desert scene, by excellent illustrations and by many revealing little anecdotes and excursions into history. I find it entrancing."

GENERAL SIR JOHN BURNETT-STUART, *Sunday Times*

"Informative, adventurous, comprehensive and modest. A stimulating, curiously moving book." HAROLD NICOLSON, *Daily Telegraph*

"A story crowded with living men, exciting scenes, daring expeditions, desolate and majestic landscapes. The prose rises naturally to a simple nobility when swayed by a mood or a scene."

SIR JOHN SQUIRE, *Illustrated London News*

"If one wanted to have an idea of what the Arabs are today from a single book, this would be the book to choose."

EDWARD SHANKS, *Daily Graphic*

"A fascinating book." PETERBOROUGH, *Daily Telegraph*

King Abdulla of Jordan

PLATE 1

cisms of the actions of various governments, notably those of Britain, the United States, France, the Arab countries and Israel. I should like to emphasize that I have done so with all humility. I have been deeply impressed, as a result of my own experience, with the complexities of the modern world, and with the immense resulting difficulty which confronts statesmen in making their decisions. I have made so many mistakes myself that I hesitate to give voice to condemnation of other people's actions. Moreover, such criticisms, being external, are necessarily superficial. I cannot know all the considerations which impelled any particular government to follow a certain course of action. In view of these factors I at first decided to avoid every form of comment which might be construed as criticism.

When I attempted to carry out this plan, however, the result seemed to be dull and colourless. As a result, I decided to include my opinions. It would be wearisome to prefix every opinion with remarks such as: "as far as I can judge" or "I may be wrong." I have preferred, therefore, to make this apology once and for all. I have put forward my opinions sincerely but humbly, realizing my inadequacy to lay down the law in matters of State policy.

Criticism of the Israeli government does, however, require a particular explanation. A number of people, both Jews and Gentiles, are apt to refer to any criticism of Israeli policy as "offensive anti-Semitism", an accusation implying a definite moral lapse. I wish to defend myself against such a charge. "Anti-Semitism", I assume, is an emotion of hatred or dislike towards Jews as a whole, whether considered from the point of view of race or religion. I can state categorically and with all sincerity that I feel no such emotion. But it is of the essence of Western democracy to allow free criticism of the government, a right freely exercised against the governments of the U.S.A., Britain, France and other free countries. It does not seem to me to be either just or expedient that similar criticisms directed against the Israeli government should brand the speaker with the moral stigma generally associated with anti-Semitism.

Perhaps I should here make my position clear once and for all. I believe that the creation and maintenance of the State of Israel by armed force was a mistake. That the result has been disastrous for the British and the Arabs alike is only too obvious. It seems to me not improbable that it will ultimately prove to be disastrous for the Jews also. This is purely an intellectual opinion on my part, devoid of any emotion.

In the end, as I have said, I appear to have failed hopelessly in the task to which I devoted nearly all my working life.

" 'Tis not in mortals to command success," said Joseph Addison, two hundred and fifty years ago, and I might perhaps claim this line as the epitaph on my career. But Addison completed his couplet with words in which the speaker expressed his resolve to deserve success, even if he could not command it. I cannot claim to have done this. I am no judge of what I deserved. Rather would I borrow the phrase with which Gordon, besieged in Khartoum, concluded his diary:

"I have done my best."

J. B. G.

West Wood St. Dunstan,
   Mayfield,
     Sussex.

AUTHOR'S NOTE

In transliterating Arabic words and names, I have endeavoured as far as possible to help the English reader to pronounce the word correctly. As a result I have not followed any regular system. In cases where there is already a well-known anglicized form, however, I have preferred to adhere to that.

Acknowledgments

THIS book is only a personal narrative. It does not aspire to the dignity of history. I have accordingly not overloaded it with footnotes or references, as I do not imagine that students will ever refer to it for facts or figures. I have read a great many books about the Middle East, and I suppose I have digested some of the information therein, though I have not quoted from them. The greater part of the contents of this book is based on private contemporary papers of my own, and on my memory.

Many friends have helped me in the preparation of this book— their names are too numerous to mention, and so I hope that they will accept this general expression of my gratitude to them all. I owe a special debt to Sir Alec Kirkbride who devoted so great a part of his life to work in Jordan. He has most kindly read all the proofs and assisted me with advice and suggestions.

I already owe so much to my wife in every department of my life that it seems unnecessary to mention that she gave me invaluable help in this book also. My secretary, Miss Angela Besant, bore with me patiently while she did the typing.

Finally, I should like here to acknowledge my gratitude to the Hashemite royal family, in whose dominions I served for so many years, and from whom I received innumerable kindnesses. I shall never be able to repay what I owe to the good people of Jordan, amongst whom I lived with so much happiness. But, above all, I am indebted to the officers, N.C.O.s and men of the Arab Legion, to whose gallantry and devotion any credit I have won is solely due.

For the moment, politics, the bane of soldiers, have built an impenetrable barrier between my comrades and myself. I pray God that these clouds may pass, that old friendships may once more be renewed and that one day the nightmare of hatreds in which we live will be succeeded by a wiser, happier, more tolerant and more charitable age.

Contents

Contents

List of Illustrations

A number of the illustrations in this book are from photographs in the author's possession and it has not been possible in every case to trace the owner. If any readers should find their pictures reproduced without their permission, the author hopes that they will believe him that the discourtesy has been involuntary.

List of Maps

For Hashemite genealogical table see page 25

I

Background Setting

The singular part of their history is this, that though willing aliens from their native Palestine, they remained Jews in character and religion; they continued to be a separate people and refused to mingle themselves with the population of the country in which they were domiciled. . . . The Temple became . . . the object of the profoundest reverence; but the land of their fathers had lost its hold of their affections.   MILMAN, *History of the Jews*

Force is not a remedy.   JOHN BRIGHT (1880)

I

BACKGROUND SETTING

THE royal palace in Amman stands on a hill, overlooking the closely packed houses of the town, crammed into a narrow valley at its feet. The palace is surrounded by plantations of pine-trees, in one of which, nestling in to the hillside behind the palace, lies a little three-roomed cottage. Here, in his later years, the Amir (afterwards King) Abdulla loved to sit and work in seclusion.

On a cloudless early morning in April 1939, I walked across the little garden and under the vine-covered trellis to the door of the cottage. An officer met me and led me to a door opening off the tiny entrance-hall.

"Our lord is waiting for you," he said.

His Highness the Amir Abdulla was sitting behind his desk in the little sitting-room of the cottage. Ever since the State of Trans-Jordan had come into existence seventeen years before, the Amir's army, known in English as "The Arab Legion", had been commanded by Colonel Peake Pasha. Now Peake had resigned, and I had been appointed to take his place. It seemed to me that His Highness was concerned at the departure of Peake, who had served him so long.

"You are English," said the Amir, motioning me to sit down, "and this is an Arab country, and an Arab army. Before you take over command, I want you to pledge me your word, that, as long as you remain in this appointment, you will act always as if you had been born a Trans-Jordanian.

"I know you would not wish to fight your own countrymen. If it should ever come to fighting between us and the English, I will hold you excused. You may leave us then and stand aside. But if, by God's will, this does not happen, I want you to be one of the people of Trans-Jordan."

"Sir," I answered, "I give you my word of honour. From now onwards I am a Trans-Jordanian, except under the conditions you mentioned, and which I pray God may never come."

*　　　*　　　*　　　*　　　*

The Middle East is the very hub and centre of the Old World. Through it passes the oldest and busiest of the world's trade routes, connecting Europe and North Africa with Asia, East Africa and

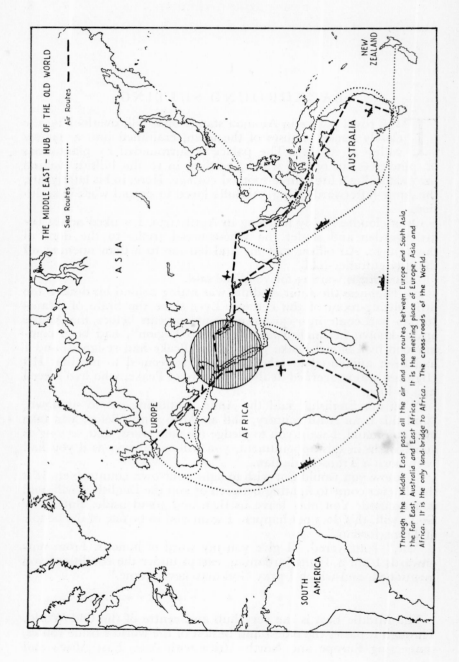

THE MIDDLE EAST – HUB OF THE OLD WORLD

Sea Routes .... Air Routes ━ ━ ━

Through the Middle East pass all the air and sea routes between Europe and South Asia, the Far East, Australia and East Africa. It is the meeting place of Europe, Asia and Africa. It is the only land-bridge to Africa. The cross-roads of the World.

Australasia. It influences, and is influenced by, Europe, Africa and Asia alike. It is the only land-bridge to the continent of Africa. It is the land of origin of Judaism, Islam and Christianity. Being principally Muslim today, its affairs arouse lively concern wherever Muslims are to be found, from Morocco and Nigeria to China and Malaya. It was not Britain who first invented or opened this channel for commerce—it was as important in Roman times as it is today— Persia and Rome fought for its possession. We must not imagine that this trade is profitable to Europe alone, much less to Britain only. Trade is always two-way. Southern Asia, Australia and the Far East profit no less than does Europe. Political passion and prejudice may for a time appear to submerge economics, but sooner or later economic factors must reassert themselves.

Let us not imagine that the peoples of the Middle East must be made the victims of the economic needs of Western Europe and Southern Asia. The exact reverse is the case. The importance and the prosperity of the inhabitants of Egypt and Arabia have, through-out the ages, depended on the fact that they live on this trade route. Until the discovery of oil, Arabia was one of the poorest areas in the world. But the stream of commerce which flowed across it provided prosperity and employment, attracted merchants and business. Rich and flourishing cities, often in arid surroundings, sprang up where the trade flowed through—Petra, Palmyra, Basra, Damascus, Port Said. The coming and going of merchants and sailors of many nations brought culture and ideas. The Arabs themselves took part in the trade. Those of the south sailed to India, Malaya and East Africa. Those of the interior carried the merchandise on their caravans. Those of the Mediterranean sailed with it to Greece, Rome and Gaul. Where, two thousand years ago, the products of India were borne across Arabia by caravans of camels, today oil flows in pipe-lines. Geography has made Arabia a corridor.

In war, the power established in the Middle East can maintain ships and submarines in the Mediterranean and the Indian Ocean. The immense plains of Northern Arabia form great natural aero-dromes, from which Europe, Asia and Africa can be attacked by air. It owes this vitally important situation to geography, irrespective of the nature or capabilities of its inhabitants. Napoleon called it the crossroads of the world. Others have said that the Power which dominates it can rule the world—and the statement is scarcely an exaggeration.

*　　*　　*　　*　　*

The pilot of an aircraft flying in eastward over the bright blue Mediterranean to Palestine first sees below him a narrow coastal plain, and then the rugged chain of the Palestine mountains, lying

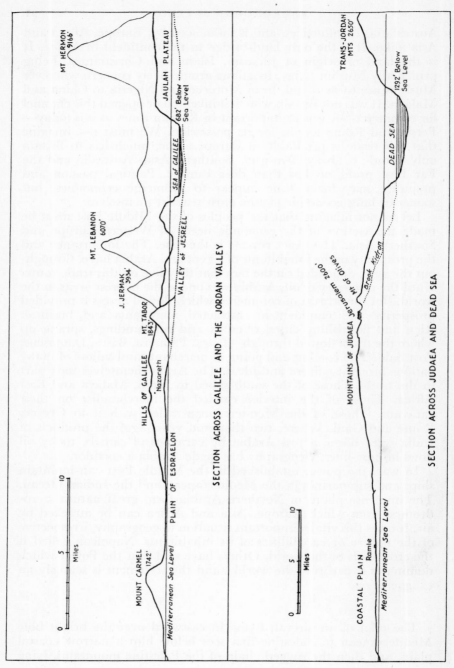

SECTION ACROSS GALILEE AND THE JORDAN VALLEY

MOUNT CARMEL 1742'

Mediterranean Sea Level

PLAIN OF ESDRAELON

Nazareth

HILLS OF GALILEE

MT TABOR 1843'

J. JERMAK 3934'

MT. LEBANON 6070'

MT HERMON 9166'

JAULAN PLATEAU

602' Below Sea Level

SEA OF GALILEE

VALLEY of JESREEL

0   5   10
Miles

SECTION ACROSS JUDAEA AND DEAD SEA

COASTAL PLAIN
Ramle

Mediterranean Sea Level

MOUNTAINS OF JUDAEA
Jerusalem 2600'
Mt of Olives

Brook Kidron

TRANS-JORDAN MTS 2650'

1292' Below Sea Level

DEAD SEA

0   5   10
Miles

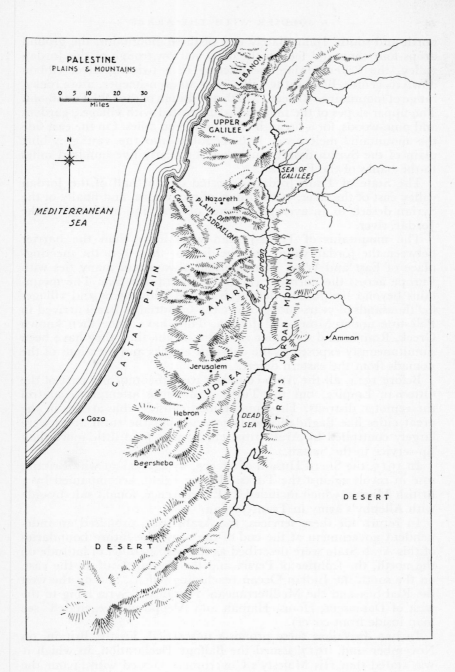

PALESTINE
PLAINS & MOUNTAINS

0 5 10   20   30
        Miles

N

MEDITERRANEAN
SEA

LEBANON

UPPER
GALILEE

SEA OF
GALILEE

COASTAL PLAIN

Mt Carmel

Nazareth

PLAIN OF
ESDRAELON

R. Jordan

JORDAN MOUNTAINS

Amman

SAMARIA

Jerusalem

TRANS

JUDAEA

Gaza

Hebron

DEAD
SEA

Beersheba

DESERT

DESERT

23

north and south. Immediately east of these mountains, the ground drops four thousand feet to the deep, narrow trough of the Jordan valley, the River Jordan meandering in a twisting silver ribbon down its centre. Behind the valley rises an even steeper, more rocky, range of mountains—Gilead, Moab and Edom of the Old Testament. The upper slopes of the mountains are dotted with villages, gardens and pine-woods, for a breadth of about fifteen miles. On the east side the mountains melt away imperceptibly into the vast grey-blue plain of the Syrian desert, unbroken for nearly five hundred miles to the banks of the Euphrates.

The State of Trans-Jordan consisted of that half of the Jordan valley east of the river, of the range of mountains, and finally of the Syrian desert, to an average distance of some 150 miles east of the Jordan river.

The mountains of Trans-Jordan were more than the barrier between the Jordan valley and the desert—they were the meeting-place of East and West. Palestine had always had many ties with Europe across the narrow eastern Mediterranean Sea. The mountains beyond the Jordan had been dotted with towns and villages for thousands of years—long before the Children of Israel arrived in Palestine under Moses and Joshua. They have since then known Greek, Roman and Crusader rule. But all the time they have been simultaneously exposed to the constant attacks and invasions of the nomads from the eastern desert.

Before 1914, all the Arab countries were theoretically part of the Ottoman Empire, but the Turks made little attempt to control the remoter districts. They maintained considerable armies in the great cities like Baghdad and Damascus, but the rural areas were largely controlled by Arab tribal chiefs, who paid little more than lip-service to the Sultan.

In 1915, the Sherif Husain of Mecca, by agreement with Britain, rose in revolt against the Turks. His son Feisal, accompanied by a British Mission which included T. E. Lawrence, fought side-by-side with Allenby's army in Trans-Jordan.

In return for these services, the Arabs were promised an independent government at the end of the war. The future boundaries of this Arab State were described as the 37th parallel of latitude on the north, the frontier of Persia and the Persian Gulf on the east, on the south the Indian Ocean (excluding Aden), and on the west the Red Sea and the Mediterranean. Portions of Syria lying to the west of Damascus, Homs, Hamah and Aleppo were excluded (see map inside front cover).

In two directions these promises miscarried. Firstly, Britain, on November 2nd, 1917, issued the Balfour Declaration, in which it was stated that His Majesty's Government viewed with favour the

A GENEALOGY OF THE HASHEMITE FAMILY

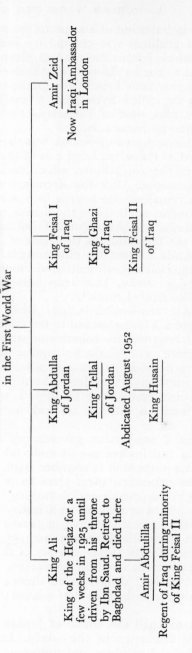

Sherif Husain of Mecca
(Later King Husain of the Hejaz)

It was with him that the British Government negotiated an agreement in 1915, which resulted in the Arab rebellion against the Turks in the First World War

King Ali
King of the Hejaz for a few weeks in 1925 until driven from his throne by Ibn Saud. Retired to Baghdad and died there

Amir Abdulilla
Regent of Iraq during minority of King Feisal II

King Abdulla
of Jordan

King Tellal
of Jordan
Abdicated August 1952

King Husain

King Feisal I
of Iraq

King Ghazi
of Iraq

King Feisal II
of Iraq

Amir Zeid
Now Iraqi Ambassador in London

The Hashemite family trace their descent directly from the Prophet Muhamad, who died in A.D. 632

Note: *Persons still alive are underlined*

establishment in Palestine of a national home for the Jewish people.

The second problem was created by France. The area west of Damascus, excluded from the pledges given to Sherif Husain, had been promised to her by Britain. The hinterland was to be an Arab State ruled by the Amir Feisal from Damascus, and including what were later to be called Syria and Trans-Jordan. But soon after occupying the area west of Damascus (now known as Lebanon), France occupied all Syria also.

The area thus occupied by France was the hinterland of Lebanon. The hinterland of Palestine, lying east of the Jordan, had originally formed part of the Arab State, which had been created with its capital in Damascus. After the French occupation of Damascus, Trans-Jordan remained for a year in a state of anarchy, with no central government at all. Then the British government agreed with the Amir Abdulla, brother of Amir Feisal and son of Sherif Husain of Mecca, to the formation of the State of Trans-Jordan. In 1921, the Amir Abdulla formed his government. Captain Peake, of the Duke of Wellington's Regiment, undertook to serve the Amir as commander of his army. This army was called Al Jeish al Arabi, in English "The Arab Legion".

I was not in Trans-Jordan in 1921, when Peake Pasha raised the first Arab Legion. I had gone out to Iraq in 1920 as a British officer, and in 1926 I resigned my commission and took service under the Iraqi government. The Turks had never attempted to control the desert, and its nomadic tribes had always waged war upon one another with impunity. A modern administration could not tolerate private wars, and from 1926 to 1930 I was engaged under the Iraqi government in putting an end to desert raiding in that country.

In 1930, the Trans-Jordan government also decided to put an end to raiding and invited me to undertake the task. I arrived in Amman for this purpose in November 1930. By the simple device of employing the tribesmen themselves to police their own deserts, we succeeded in putting an end to raiding in Trans-Jordan, almost without firing a shot or making an arrest.

The last bedouin raid occurred in June 1932. I spent nine of the happiest years of my life, from 1930 to 1939, as officer commanding the desert area. Nearly three-quarters of the area of Trans-Jordan was desert, though the bedouin population amounted only to some fifty thousand souls. I deeply loved these poor simple people, and became so intimate with them that among them I felt as if I were at home.

From 1932 to 1948 the whole of Jordan was indeed one of the happiest little countries in the world. In spite of poverty and drought, in spite of troubles and upheavals in neighbouring countries, in spite even of a world war, Trans-Jordan seemed to lead a charmed life. The people acquired an almost superstitious confidence—and a fond pride—in the happiness of their country. With the rest of the world in agony, with the neighbouring Arab countries in constant upheaval, in Trans-Jordan for sixteen years nothing could go wrong. How many Trans-Jordanians have said to me since then with a sigh—"We were so happy until 1948."

In 1939, when I assumed command of the Arab Legion and made my promise to the Amir Abdulla that thenceforward I would behave like a Trans-Jordanian by birth, gangs of Palestine Arab rebels were endeavouring to penetrate the mountains of northern Trans-Jordan. It was the first occasion on which this tragic Palestine problem had erupted violently into Trans-Jordan. Henceforward we were to plunge deeper and deeper into that slough of despond. So before proceeding with this narrative, we must take at least a cursory glance at the history of the problem.

*   *   *   *   *

At the time of Moses, about one thousand five hundred years before Christ, Palestine was already inhabited by a settled people with a comparatively high culture. The Habiru, or Hebrews, were a backward nomadic tribe by comparison when they crossed the River Jordan and invaded Palestine. It is noticeable that the Children of Israel are still described as living in tents, as late as the time of Solomon and his son Rehoboam, though the original peoples were already living in cities before the time of Abraham. At the time of the arrival of the Israelites, the people of Palestine were divided into many tribes—that long list of Canaanites, Hittites, Perizzites, Girgashites, Amorites and Jebusites which we found such tongue-twisters at school.

We make the mistake of attributing to Biblical Palestine our own modern and Western European ideas of nationality. In reality, the Israelites were a tribal group, which forced its way into the richer and more cultured agricultural area and eventually settled down there. The original inhabitants, of course, remained, and the various groups intermingled and sometimes intermarried. The Philistines became dominant in the coastal plain.

Eventually the Kingdom of Israel was destroyed by Assyria. In 722 B.C., its people were carried away captive to Mesopotamia. The Kingdom of Judah survived for another 136 years, until it was overthrown by Babylon in 586 B.C. Some historians believe that, until the captivity of Judah, the Hebrew tribes dwelt in peace and often in co-operation and intermarriage with the other inhabitants of Palestine. But a number of men of the tribe of Judah returned, after only sixty years in exile. The remaining tribes, other than Judah,

remained in Iraq. Some continued a separate community as prac-
tising Jews, while others probably intermarried with and disappeared
into the population of Iraq.

The members of the tribe of Judah who returned from Babylon
laid the foundation of Jewish separatism. They denounced all intermixture with the other races or tribes of Palestine. They fostered in
their companions (now called Jews—that is, the tribe of Judah) that
aloofness which has served to keep them a peculiar people until the
present day. Ever since then, two rival trends have divided Jewry.
One party consisted of the cosmopolitan, international men of the
world, liberal, tolerant and cultured. The other was insular, iso-
lationist and opposed to admixture with Gentiles.

In 332 B.C., Alexander the Great conquered Palestine and planted
in it a number of Greek colonies. Thenceforward, until the destruction of the Temple in A.D. 70, Greek culture played a leading role
in Palestine. The country was far from being entirely Jewish. The
coastal plain was largely Gentile, Greek and subsequently Roman.
Galilee, in the New Testament, is referred to as "Galilee of the
Gentiles". It was only in Jerusalem and its immediate surroundings,
the territory of Judah, that the Jews were in supreme control. Our
Lord, it will be remembered, when the Jewish leaders became incensed against Him, was in danger only in Jerusalem. In the freer,
more cosmopolitan atmosphere of Galilee, He was safe. The mountain country north of Jerusalem was inhabited by the Samaritans,
with whom the Jews were at bitter enmity.

"We must not indeed conceive the Jews of those days as like the
Jews of Mediaeval Europe, an unwarlike people given to sedentary
pursuits and the handling of money. It was the policy of the Christian
Roman Empire which barred to the Jews the profession of arms, and
produced the type commonly regarded in later times as Jewish. The
Jews of Palestine in the second century B.C. were not distinguished
by any marked aptitude for trade or finance. Even at the end of the
first century A.D. Josephus could write: 'We are not a commercial
people.' In Palestine the main occupation of the Jewish people was
agriculture and stockbreeding. Jews were also in demand as good
soldiers; we hear of a Jewish garrison in Upper Egypt in the fifth
century B.C. The Ptolemies settled Jewish military allotment-holders
in different parts of the country; Antiochus III had done the same
in Asia Minor."[1]

Meanwhile, Jews were already spreading over the world. Many
Jews of the Captivity had settled permanently in Iraq. There were
great and wealthy Jewish settlements in Egypt. In the reign of
Caligula, Philo claims that there were one million Jews in Egypt.
The dispersion cannot, it would appear, be attributed to the destruc-

---

[1] *Cambridge Ancient History*, Volume VIII, Chapter XVI.

tion of Jerusalem by Titus. In the accounts of St. Paul's missionary journeys, we find Jewish communities in the cities of Asia Minor and Greece, and as far west as Rome.

In A.D. 70, Jerusalem was captured and destroyed by Titus. Many Jews were massacred, deported or fled into exile. A final Jewish revolt in A.D. 135 resulted in the virtual extinction of the Jews in Palestine, which became a Roman province until the Arab conquest in A.D. 636. Following the conversion of the Roman Empire to Christianity, Palestine became a Christian country. After the Arab conquest, the greater part of the inhabitants were gradually converted to Islam, though a strong Christian minority has survived to this day.

These facts were unknown to the general public in Britain and America in 1917. Knowledge of Palestine was to a great extent limited to Bible study. The Bible narrative ends before the fall of Jerusalem in A.D. 70. As the teaching of history in England fifty years ago normally began at the year 1066, many people were ignorant of the history of the Middle East from A.D. 60 until modern times. There was little realization that Palestine had ceased to be the land of the Jews nearly nineteen hundred years ago, and indeed had never been populated by Jews alone.

Western Europeans are familiar with the conception of one country inhabited by one race, as are England and France. But such has never hitherto been the state of affairs in the Middle East, where a given area of territory has almost always been shared by a number of different races, communities and religions. Each of these groups is normally distinct, possessing its own rights, laws, schools, judges and headmen. This state of affairs has historically been the normal rather than the exceptional, but it is a conception entirely foreign to modern European nations.

I believe that many British people in 1917 imagined Palestine to be still the land of the Jews, and it never occurred to them to doubt that the vast majority of its people were of that faith. They would have been surprised to hear that they formed only seven per cent of the inhabitants, the remaining ninety-three per cent being Muslims or Christians.

A further illusion prevailed, arising from indiscriminate use of the word "Arab", that the non-Jewish inhabitants of Palestine were nomads from the desert.

"Why cannot the Arabs return to their desert?" was a question which used frequently to be asked. In reality, Palestine, so near the junction of Europe, Asia and Africa, has always been a crucible in which many elements have melted and fused. The "Arabs" of Palestine are the descendants of the Philistines, the Canaanites, the other tribes of three thousand years ago, Greeks, Romans, Jews converted to Christianity, Arabs, Crusaders, Mongols and Turks. The fact that they now speak Arabic, and that Muslim culture has been a powerful influence amongst them, has resulted in their being loosely termed "Arabs".

*   *   *   *   *

When the idea of a homeland for the Jews was mooted at the end of the nineteenth century, several alternative sites were suggested, Kenya being one of them. But in the end, it was agreed that only Palestine would be equally acceptable to all Jews. But Palestine was already populated. The Turkish Empire showed no great enthusiasm for a return of the Jews, although a few colonies were established before 1914.

In the First World War, the Zionists saw and seized their opportunity. Confused thinking, a neglect to ascertain the facts, and the concentration of all thought in 1917 on the conduct of the war, caused the British government to issue the vaguely worded Balfour Declaration. In it, they stated that His Majesty's Government "viewed with favour" (not "would establish by force") "a national home for the Jews in Palestine". The word "national" is here significant, for the Jews are not, in the commonly accepted sense, a nation, but a religion.

The second paragraph of the Balfour Declaration qualified the first:

"It being clearly understood that nothing should be done which might prejudice the civil and religious rights of existing non-Jewish communities in Palestine."

Whatever the British government meant by this confused document, the Zionists were in no doubt what they wanted. Dr. Weizmann, himself a moderate Zionist, had no illusions. He stated the object to be: "to make Palestine as Jewish as England is English."

This, it will be seen, is the modern European conception of the homogeneous nation living in one country. It has never been a Middle Eastern conception. Even at the time of the Kingdom of David, the Golden Age of Israelite political power, Palestine was not inhabited solely by Israelites, as England is today by English.

The Zionists were perfectly clear about what they were trying to do. They had at their disposal world-wide means of publicity, through Jews resident in every country. Their object, from 1920 to 1939, was to force more and more Jews into Palestine. The British, harassed and confused and with no clear idea of what they were trying to do, found themselves using armed force against the Arabs, who rose in revolt against this influx of foreigners. From 1936 to 1939, the Arabs of Palestine were in rebellion against the British mandatory government.

It was in the course of this rebellion that gangs of Palestine rebels had overflowed into Trans-Jordan in the spring of 1939, at the moment when I pledged my faith to the Amir Abdulla to consider myself henceforward as a born Trans-Jordanian.

Everyone in Trans-Jordan sympathized profoundly with the Arabs of Palestine. Nevertheless, the Arab Legion drove the rebel gangs from Trans-Jordan without hesitation. If Palestine were to be ruined, nothing was to be gained by ruining Trans-Jordan also.

The practical question today is whether the Zionists are likely to succeed. For they have fallen into the trap of seeking a short-cut to the achievement of their hopes by the use of force. They have forgotten that those who take the sword are liable to perish by the sword. Will they be able, twenty, fifty or a hundred years hence, to maintain themselves as a foreign element on a beach-head on the shores of Asia? Can they become Arabicized and thus come to terms with their neighbours, without sacrificing the distinctiveness of the "Jewish nation", which it is their whole object to preserve?

The position of Britain is scarcely less problematical. For the Arabic-speaking belt, extending from Persia to Morocco, lies across our line of communications to the East and to our sister nations in Australia and New Zealand. Freedom of transit across the Middle East is thus vital to Britain, but it is vital to no-one else. Russia has no sister nations to reach which she must pass through Syria or Egypt.

If Britain had limited herself, as she had promised, to "viewing with favour" the Jewish home, instead of supporting it by force of arms, she might have retained that traditional friendship with the Arab and Muslim world which is so essential to her interests. If the Jews had been more patient and less aggressive, they might have achieved their spiritual home in Jerusalem, while retaining citizenship of those Western countries where they can lead a free and democratic life. But they would have done so, perhaps, at the risk of absorption by other races.

To a great extent the trouble arose from the application of the modern European conception of a single "nation" in one country. If the Jews had been willing to "share" Palestine, they might have secured a "national home" there without provoking intense Arab hostility. In such a case, the use of force on a large scale might have been avoided, and Jews and Arabs alike need not have been caught in the endless succession of acts of violence from which they cannot break free.

The Gentile observer may appreciate the fear felt by the Jews lest their religion and culture disappear by being submerged in other races. Others may believe that their "return" to Palestine is a fulfilment of prophecy. But it can never be right to do evil that good may come. To drive a million Arabs from their homes and country cannot be justified by any consideration.

*　　*　　*　　*　　*

Jews and Arabs alike have fallen victims to unscientific modern theories of race. The Jews, as I have already stated, are not a race, but a religion. In fact, the "Arabs" are scarcely less mixed. At the moment, the Egyptians receive most of the publicity, partly because they are the most vocal and partly owing to the fact that the Suez Canal passes through their territory.

When the Arabs burst forth from the Arabian peninsula in the seventh century A.D. and swept as conquerors across Egypt and North Africa to Morocco, they were still to a great degree in a nomadic state of development. They did not relish the damp and the mud of the Nile delta, but moved on to the higher desert lands of Libya or southwards towards the Sudan. Here tribes related to those of Arabia are still in existence. The dwellers in the delta of the Nile adopted the language and (to a great extent) the religion of the Arab conquerors. But racially they remained distinct—the direct descendants of the Egyptians of the Pharaohs. Thus, even today, they are a people very different from the Arabs of Arabia.

As a race, the Egyptians are physically inclined to be lethargical, a quality doubtless to be attributed to their climate. After middle age they tend to obesity, though in youth they may be agile. They prefer to settle their problems by intellectual means, rather than by physical action. They are extremely expert at intrigue, politics, demagogy and subtle argument, but rarely meet with success in war. Physical lethargy combined with intellectual acuteness naturally causes people to sit and argue, and the Egyptians are notorious for their volubility. The people of Egypt are in many ways attractive, and have a pleasant sense of humour. The cartoons in the Egyptian press are often extremely clever. In their rulers, volubility may at times degenerate into arrogance.

The peoples of Arabia proper are of mixed origin. Here geography has also played its part. The centre of Arabia is largely desert and inhabited by nomads. The wealth and civilization of the peninsula are principally confined to the outer circumference. Palestine, Lebanon, Syria, Iraq, a few places on the Persian Gulf, Oman, Had-hramaut, Aden and the Yemen are the countries with sedentary populations. The centre is a wilderness.

Ever since the beginning of history, the desert has been a formidable barrier to intercourse. Thus Palestine and the Lebanon have always had more connection with Europe than with Iraq, the Persian Gulf or the Yemen. Similarly northern Syria was in closer contact with Anatolia than with Arabia, while Iraq was for cen-

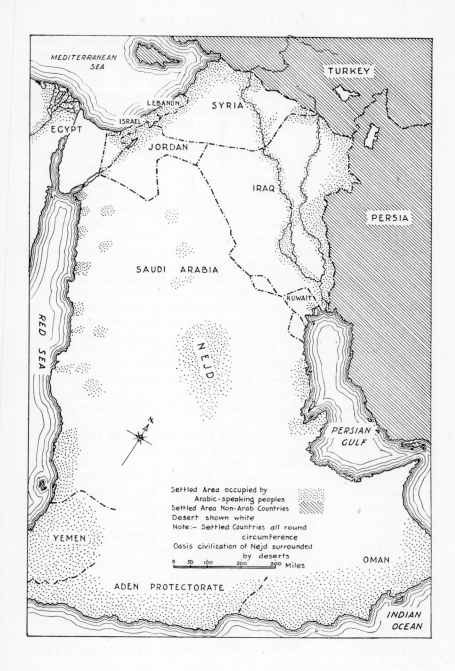

MEDITERRANEAN
SEA

TURKEY

LEBANON

ISRAEL

SYRIA

EGYPT

JORDAN

IRAQ

PERSIA

SAUDI ARABIA

KUWAIT

RED SEA

NEJD

PERSIAN
GULF

Settled Area occupied by
    Arabic-speaking peoples
Settled Area Non-Arab Countries
Desert shown white
Note:— Settled Countries all round
        circumference
Oasis civilization of Nejd surrounded
        by deserts
0   50   100   200   300 Miles

YEMEN

OMAN

ADEN PROTECTORATE

INDIAN
OCEAN

turies a part of Persia, and since then has been closely associated
with that country. In the same manner, Oman has old connections
with both India and East Africa, and the Hadhramaut with Malaya.
This extraordinary peripheral arrangement, with the desert barrier
in the middle, has resulted in a centrifugal development—certain
Arab countries being at times more closely associated with non-
Arab neighbours than with the other Arab countries across the
desert.

But in the very centre of the desert interior is a land of towns
and oases, surrounded by a belt of desert in every direction. This
central inhabited area is called Nejd. Here what may be called a
purely Arab culture was evolved, until recently little affected by
outside influences, but to a great extent permeated with the spirit
of the tribes that surround it on all sides. These live in the desert
belt which divides Nejd from the peripheral countries.

We are, for our present purposes, more concerned with the
northern Arab countries than with those which face the Indian
Ocean. The northern peoples may be divided into three classes.

Firstly the Levantines—Palestine, Lebanon and western Syria—
secondly the tribes of the desert and thirdly the people of Iraq. The
Levantines enjoy a warm and equable climate, cooler and less
enervating than that of Egypt, but imposing the minimum of hard-
ships on its inhabitants. Unused, as a result, to severe physical
endurance, the Mediterranean Arabs are subtle and intellectual,
in a way resembling the Greeks. Indeed there is doubtless no little
Greek blood in their veins. Syria has always been a land with a
tendency to fanaticism, a breeding-place of plots, secret societies
and esoteric religious sects.

The Lebanon is more European than Arab. Here still lie Tyre
and Sidon from which the ancient Phoenicians set out to colonize
the Mediterranean as far as Spain and France. She is the only
Arabic-speaking nation in which Christians equal Muslims in
numbers. Lebanon maintains a surprisingly free democratic form
of government, which the intrigues of Egypt, Syria and Saudi
Arabia have hitherto been unable to overthrow.

Science corroborates experience and confirms that the Arabs
of the Mediterranean countries differ racially from those of the
interior. Many people with round heads are found in Syria, Lebanon
and among Palestine Arabs. The people of Central Arabia are all
long-headed.

From history we can learn the explanation of these differences.
Romans, Greeks, Mongols, Turks, Armenians and Circassians have
all swept into Syria and Lebanon from the north, within the last
two thousand years. None of these invasions penetrated Central
Arabia.

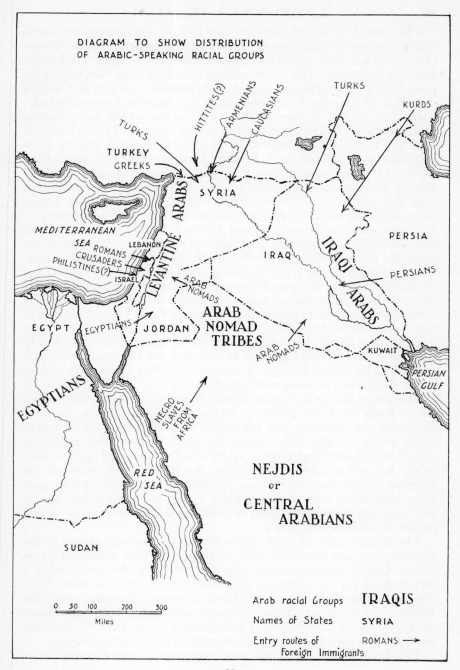

DIAGRAM TO SHOW DISTRIBUTION
OF ARABIC-SPEAKING RACIAL GROUPS

TURKS

KURDS

HITTITES(?)

ARMENIANS

CAUCASIANS

TURKS

TURKEY
GREEKS

SYRIA

PERSIA

MEDITERRANEAN
SEA ROMANS
CRUSADERS
PHILISTINES(?)

LEBANON

LEVANTINE ARABS

IRAQ

IRAQI ARABS

ISRAEL

PERSIANS

ARAB NOMADS

EGYPT

EGYPTIANS

JORDAN

ARAB
NOMAD
TRIBES

ARAB
NOMADS

KUWAIT

PERSIAN
GULF

EGYPTIANS

NEGRO SLAVES FROM AFRICA

RED
SEA

NEJDIS
or
CENTRAL
ARABIANS

SUDAN

0 50 100   200   300
Miles

Arab racial Groups   IRAQIS

Names of States   SYRIA

Entry routes of   ROMANS ⟶
Foreign Immigrants

35

The desert tribes of the interior live in circumstances which differ strikingly from those of the Mediterranean coast. Desert climatic conditions are so severe that the mere struggle for human survival is intense. The surroundings in which they live have here produced a hardy race, endowed with martial qualities and with a practical, as opposed to an intellectual or theoretical turn of mind.

Central Arabia is one of those arid areas which have always produced more inhabitants than they can support. Throughout the ages the hardy inhabitants of Nejd and the central deserts have migrated to the fertile lands around them, particularly those of the north. At times whole tribes have burst into the border lands to pillage and conquer. At other periods, individuals have infiltrated into and settled in the more fertile agricultural countries. Today most of the nomadic tribes in the desert between Syria, Jordan and Iraq can trace their origin from Central Arabia a few centuries ago. Thus the culture and mentality of the northern desert tribes resemble those of Central Arabia more than those of the Mediterranean seaboard. As a result, along the borders of the desert and the fertile regions, the people are of mixed origin. Here the inhabitants of the Mediterranean seaboard mingle with invaders from the central deserts to form a hybrid race and culture. Trans-Jordan and east Syria are of this kind.

Central or Saudi Arabia produces an intensely virile race, but in education and technology she is still behind the northern Arab countries, let alone Europe. Farther south, the Yemen is still in spirit mediaeval, isolated and fanatical.

The Iraqis live in a climate hotter than that of Egypt, but which differs from the latter owing to its distance from the sea. Its temperatures are extreme, but the air is dry, whereas that of Egypt tends to be humid. The Iraqis are rugged, curt and practical, rather than subtle and refined as are the Levantines. Iraq is wisely using her oil royalties to develop the natural resources of the country. Large sums are being invested in irrigation, social progress, education and housing. While Egypt is spending her energy and emotion on politics, Iraq is building up her future by caring for the welfare of her people.

The racial origin of the Iraqis is probably as mixed as that of the Syrians, but not identical with it. Three or four thousand years before Christ, southern Iraq was inhabited by the Sumerians, a non-Semitic race of unknown origin but thought to have come from the East. From 539 B.C., when Cyrus captured Babylon, until the Islamic conquests nearly one thousand years later, Iraq was almost continuously part of Persia. Throughout a great part of the same period, Syria and Palestine formed part of the Roman Empire.

This brief sketch of a complicated subject may suffice to emphasize how deceptive is the view that the "Arabs" are all one race. Arabia, in reality, is not a country but a subcontinent. The Yemenis are as different from the Lebanese, or the Palestinians from the inhabitants of Oman, as are the Scandinavians from the Greeks—perhaps more different. It is an involved and complicated pattern. Glib generalizations about "the Arabs" are usually wrong. If we cannot understand all the intricacies of the Middle East, we shall at least have gained something if we realize how complicated are the many problems to be solved.

Although, however, the "Arabs" are not by any means one race, it is possible to trace one or two broad characteristics, which most of them share, and which differentiate them from Europeans.

The Arabs in general are hot-headed, hasty and volatile. They are proud and touchy, ready to suspect an insult and hasty to avenge it. To hate their enemies is to them not only a natural emotion but a duty. Should any man claim to forgive an enemy, they find it difficult to believe in his sincerity and suspect a trap. Politically they tend, like the proverbial Irishman, to be against the government. Of whatever form or complexion it may be, they are usually ready to change it, though they may later on regret their action and wish to return to their former state. It is easy to conquer any Arab country, but their natural inclination to rebellion makes it difficult and expensive for the invader to maintain his control. Their mutual jealousies, however, provide their rulers with the means of playing them off against one another, an art which they themselves consider to be of the very essence of politics.

But while their hot-bloodedness makes the Arabs good haters, it makes them also cordial friends. No race can be more pleasant or charming. They are delightful company, with a ready sense of humour.

In one quality, the Arabs lead the world—it is the virtue of hospitality, which some of them carry to a degree which becomes almost fantastic.

I went to the Arab countries in 1920 as an ordinary regimental officer in the British Army. I stayed there for thirty-six years because I loved them. To this day I have more friends in Arabia than I have in England.

II

War, Peace and Terrorism

The great soldier of today is not a romantic animal . . . but a quiet grave man, busied in charts, exact in sums, occupied in trivial detail; thinking, as the Duke of Wellington was said to do, most of the shoes of his soldiers.

WALTER BAGEHOT

II

WAR, PEACE AND TERRORISM

THE Arab rebellion in Palestine was already petering out when I assumed command of the Arab Legion in April 1939. The leader of that revolt had been a member of one of the principal land-owning families of Jerusalem, Haj Ameen al Husaini. To a great extent the British themselves had built up the position of Ameen al Husaini, which they finally established by appointing him Mufti of Jerusalem, a post which virtually carried with it the religious leadership of the Muslims of Palestine.

Haj Ameen was nominally a religious leader, but in reality a fanatical politician. Basically there was considerable justice in the cause he served—resistance to the armed suppression of the people of Palestine, who objected to the mass immigration of Jews against the will of the majority of the inhabitants. But the Mufti's methods were both unwise and immoral—utter intransigence, a complete refusal to compromise and terrorist murders of Palestinians who differed from him.

During the course of the rebellion, Haj Ameen escaped from Palestine and took refuge in Beirut and subsequently in Baghdad.

When the Second World War began in September 1939, the Arab Legion was about 1,350 strong. Of this force, however, one thousand officers and men were the civil police of the country. A small force of about 350 all ranks was organized on para-military lines. It had been created a year before to prevent incursions by Arab rebel gangs from Palestine into Trans-Jordan.

On the outbreak of war, the Amir Abulla immediately cabled the full support of his country and its resources for Britain. For the ensuing seven months, however, everything remained normal in Trans-Jordan. Then, with the fall of France, we suddenly found ourselves in the front line. German and Italian commissions arrived in Beirut and Damascus, to supervise the French army and administration in Syria and Lebanon.

Meanwhile Haj Ameen al Husaini was in Baghdad, where he was busily fomenting trouble. Partly owing to his activities a *coup d'état* took place in Iraq in April 1941, and the young king and the regent of Iraq arrived as fugitives in Amman. Iraq declared war on Britain. With enemies now in control of Lebanon, Syria and Iraq, and with the Germans and Italians advancing on Egypt from the Western Desert, Trans-Jordan, with her mobile force of 350 men, seemed almost certain soon to be overrun. In the whole world, Britain had no ally. Yet at this desperate moment, the Amir Abdulla reiterated his open support of Britain and his readiness to fight at her side. It was an act of heroism, when even the giants like the United States and Russia were seeking to gain time and to find some means of avoiding hostilities with a triumphant Germany.

A tiny column of British troops set out across five hundred miles of desert from Palestine to relieve the R.A.F. station at Habbaniya, on the Euphrates (see map inside front cover). The Arab Legion mobile force accompanied it. Habbaniya was relieved, and columns consisting of the Household Cavalry Regiment, a battalion of the Essex Regiment, a battery of field artillery and the Arab Legion invaded a country of five million inhabitants and possessing an army (on paper at least) of three divisions. It was one of the most remarkable examples of military daring in history. Fortunately, the Iraqis were not themselves united behind the military junta which had seized power. On May 31st, 1941, Baghdad surrendered, and this brief campaign was at an end. Haj Ameen escaped to Berlin, where he passed the remainder of the war.

At this time, Syria was still garrisoned by a Vichy French army, supervised by an Italo-German armistice commission. It was feared that Germany, having occupied Greece, might attack Turkey, which would be encircled if the Germans were also in power in Syria. On June 8th, the British Army invaded Syria and the Lebanon, assisted by a small force of Free French. The Arab Legion once more marched with the British Army, accompanying a column which carried out an outflanking movement through the desert. After taking Palmyra, it turned west towards Homs, thereby cutting the communications of the main Vichy French army, which was still resisting, just north of Damascus.

On July 11th, 1941, an armistice was signed, and the British Army occupied the whole of Syria.

During these two brief campaigns, the Arab Legion received its baptism of fire in a real war. The British Army was impressed, and the Amir was asked to increase his 350-man mobile force into a brigade of lorried infantry. This task was to occupy us day and night for many months. Perhaps it would have been better to employ the now seasoned veterans of the mobile force as long-range desert raiders against the German communications in the Western Desert. They were splendid men and the desert was their home. The process of changing them into a regular brigade was too long. They were almost ready for action when the battle of Alamein brought desert warfare to an end.

The Arab Legion had meanwhile developed another sphere of activity. Russia had been invaded by Germany and one of the principal routes for the despatch of war material was by the port of Haifa, across the desert to Baghdad and up into Persia. The Middle East was covered with vital points, roads, harbours, camps and depots of military stores, all choked with war material of priceless value. To guard it all would have absorbed a British division. The Arab Legion raised a force for the purpose. It consisted of independent infantry companies which assumed responsibility for static guard duties all over the Middle East. It was often an exhausting duty, requiring a high standard of discipline, vigilance and integrity.

During these years of war, the Arab Legion established an extraordinary relationship with the British Army. As an allied army, high-level plans were of course co-ordinated. But in the lower ranks, the comradeship was more intimate. Arab Legion N.C.O.s and men had the freedom of all British canteens and camps. Considering that scarcely any men of either army could speak the language of the other, this understanding seemed all the more remarkable. Any man of the Arab Legion who appeared in a British canteen was sure to be welcomed, greeted and supplied with tea. Arab Legion officers exchanged entertainments with British messes—sheep were slaughtered on one side, lunch parties arranged on the other. Everywhere an extraordinary spirit of comradeship showed itself. Politics have since then destroyed all these ties. Nevertheless, in a world so dominated by hate, it is worthy of record that two such diverse armies should have been on such cordial terms.

*　　*　　*　　*　　*

I have an intense love for Jerusalem, a city saturated in history and religion. In and around it (see the maps on pages 112 and 122), the Bible still lives before our eyes. The Old City is still completely surrounded by its ancient walls. Those standing today were indeed built by the Turkish Sultan, Saleem the Grim, but part of them are still on the site of the walls in the time of Christ. Within the walls are the Holy Sepulchre, the Temple area, the coloured tiles on the Dome of the Rock, the Via Dolorosa, and the sword and spurs of Godfrey de Bouillon. The Citadel is on the site of Herod's Palace, and of the castle where Godfrey refused to be crowned.

"I will not wear a crown of gold," he said, "where my Saviour wore a crown of thorns."

Outside the walls, Bethany still clings to the arid hillside. The path still runs to Jerusalem from Bethany, over the shoulder of the Mount of Olives, where the crowd strewed branches on the path and called "Hosanna!" To the north, Mount Scopus still overlooks the city, as it did when Titus with his army camped there. This indeed is living history.

During the Second World War, Jerusalem had many attractions. The Holy City had a pleasant cosmopolitan atmosphere. There were of course the British Army and the officials of the mandatory government. A Polish army corps was in training nearby. A number of charming White Russians added a slightly different touch. The Churches produced an endless variety of nuns and clerics—English, Irish, French, Italian, American, Arab, Spanish. The consular corps and a selection of Protestant missionaries increased the choice of society. There was a sprinkling of Free French, and the German nuns were still working at the German Hospice. There are always Greeks in the Middle East, and Armenians almost monopolized the photography business. The Austrian Jews kept the most delightful shops. Some had brought furniture and antiques from Vienna, when they were, I think, forbidden to take money away. Others kept excellent bookshops, one of them with many rare and old editions.

For obvious reasons, being known as the servant of an Arab government, I came little in contact with the Jewish leaders, but I was fortunate in being able to visit Doctor Magnes. He was a man whose character inspired profound respect. He represented the small, but quite influential, group of Jews, who wished to live in peace and brotherhood with the Arabs. He died soon afterwards, and the voices of his followers were silenced in the torrent of hate and violence.

*   *   *   *   *

A Nazi victory would probably have been fatal to Jewish aspirations in Palestine. When Germany appeared to be winning and while the issue still hung in doubt, both Arabs and Jews in Palestine remained inactive, watching, as it were fascinated, the battle of the giants. As soon, however, as it became obvious that the final result was no longer in question, violence and bloodshed recommenced. But whereas, from 1920 to 1939, it had been the Arabs who had been in revolt against the mandatory government, henceforward it was Jewish terrorism which went over to the attack. It was directed solely against Britain, the Arabs being neglected as though they did not exist. The principal Jewish underground organization was the Irgun Zvai Leumi under Menachim Begin, a Polish Jew who arrived in Palestine only in 1942.

The Irgun devoted itself to attacks on British forces. Not only were British soldiers and police murdered, but some were kidnapped, flogged, ill-treated and hanged. Mass murders were carried out, such as the blowing up of the King David Hotel, which was in use as the secretariat of the Palestine government. British, Arab and Jewish officials alike were buried in the ruins.

The Irgun developed its own propaganda machine, particularly in the United States. It depicted the Jews as living in their "home-land" in Palestine, groaning under the oppression of a foreign military occupation. The Arabs, who still formed two-thirds of the population, were hardly ever mentioned. This propaganda met with no small success in the United States, where stories of British oppression of the weak always seem to find ready listeners.

"As a result of World War Two," wrote Menachim Begin, "the Power which was oppressing us was confronted with a hostile Power in the East and not a very friendly Power in the West. . . . It is noteworthy that the American, Warren Austin, in supporting the demand for the replacement of British rule in Eretz Israel by a new régime, used language almost identical with that of the Russian Gromyko."

This pattern has indeed since then been repeated again and again. The United States has frequently associated herself with Russia in attacking Britain's policy in the Middle East. Only too often, the resulting weakening of Britain's position has given Russia her opportunity.

To the indifferent spectator (if any can be indifferent in so small a world) it must be of interest to note that Britain wrecked all her position in the Middle East by protecting Jewish immigration into Palestine, only to be denounced by no less a person than Mr. Ben Gurion as the Jews' "public enemy No. 1" and that this outburst of Jewish hate was supported by Britain's two closest allies in the war still scarcely ended—the U.S.A. and Russia.

This bitter Anglo-Jewish feud, however, did nothing to alleviate Arab resentment. Arab politicians and publications did not cease, then and for years to come, to picture Britain as the devoted friend and servant of Jewry.

It cannot indeed be denied that British forces alone made possible the mass immigration of Jews into Palestine from 1920 to 1939. But the skill of Jewish policy and the mistakes of Palestine Arab leaders must, in all fairness, share the responsibility. Indeed, a marked contrast was noticeable throughout this period between the policies followed by the Jewish and Arab leaders respectively. The Jews invariably accepted every promise or concession which they could obtain, even if it were much less than they had hoped for. Having secured any such concession, they then proceeded to demand more, and to enlarge the meaning of the promise which they had received. The Arabs persistently followed the exactly opposite course. They demanded their full programme and rejected categorically any concession which abated by one jot or one tittle from the text of their full demands. The result was catastrophic. The Jews went from strength to strength, securing one partial concession after another, and every time growing more powerful. The Arabs always demanded all or nothing—and obtained nothing. If the Arabs had been as skilful as the Jews, the tragedy of the Arab refugees need never have occurred.

I do not consider, however, that this consideration can be held to exonerate the British government, which had accepted the mandate for Palestine. For a mandate was described in the Covenant of the League of Nations as a trusteeship over "peoples not yet able to stand by themselves". If the Jews were too clever for the Arab leaders, the trustee should herself have intervened to prevent the disaster which resulted.

*   *   *   *   *

I had been married in November 1938, in the little English Church on the shore of the blue Mediterranean in Beirut. My father had died a few months earlier, and both my mother and my mother-in-law came to live with us. In fact they both accompanied us on our honeymoon!

Munich was just past. In Amman, the world seemed to me all joy. I was happily married, and in April 1939 I had become commander of the Arab Legion. So much happiness seemed to me scarcely credible. I had a superstitious feeling that it could not last.

Then in September began the Second World War. Our son was born in October, a month after war began.

In my family, illness often seems to coincide with disasters in the outside world. My wife was lying in hospital, between life and death, at the moment when the German army invaded Belgium and Holland. One evening I returned to the house alone, leaving her delirious in the hospital. By some malevolent chance, I switched on the wireless, to be greeted by the sneering voice of Lord Haw-Haw, instinct with hate. The Germans were attacking, while the remnants of the British Army embarked in the "little ships" at Dunkirk. At the end of a long account of German triumphs, he concluded in a voice vibrating with vindictive hatred: "Good-night to everybody in England, and pleasant dreams!" Even if it had not been speaking of the German victories, there would have been something repulsive in that voice—something revolting, that human nature could fall so low.

After Alamein, and even more after the landings in Europe, we were far better off than people in Britain. The active fighting had moved away and the final issue was no longer in doubt. We had henceforward no black-out, no rationing, and indeed felt not a little ashamed of ourselves for being so comfortable.

Just as the world seemed to be smiling on us again, a private tragedy overtook us. Our second son died at birth. My wife was taken ill at home one evening after dinner. There were no facilities, and no doctors at hand. Frenzied telephoning eventually produced a British doctor, and two hours later an ambulance with two army orderlies, who carried her down the garden on a stretcher. In the Italian Hospital, she went straight to the theatre and received an anaesthetic. I was given a chair in the passage outside, where a dim light shone. I could hear whispered talking in the theatre. I sat with cold terror in my heart. There were more whisperings within. The door opened and the doctor slipped out in his white apron. He lifted up the mask from his mouth.

"Your wife ought to pull through, but the child's dead. It was a boy," he said, and disappeared into the theatre again.

I sat gripping my chair and repeating mechanically to myself: "O God help us! O God help us!" There were sounds from inside the theatre. I supposed she was coming round after the anaesthetic. I heard my wife's voice crying:

"Oh, doctor! Is the baby all right?"

"Yes! Yes!" he said. "He's all right!"

There was a pause of a few minutes. Then she cried again in an anguished voice:

"Oh, doctor! Is he *really* all right?"

"Yes! Yes! Take it easy. He's all right!"

I could not stand it any longer. I jumped up and began to walk up and down. Suddenly the doors opened and they brought her out. She was very white and seemed to be unconscious again. They carried her into a room.

"You'd better leave her to sleep if off. Come back at nine," said the doctor.

I drove home through the dark streets. A pale light was beginning to appear in the east. At the house, our cook and my orderly were waiting on the garden path.

"Good news, if Allah wills!" they said anxiously.

"The lady is well, but my son is dead," I managed to answer. I ran past them into the house and shut the door.

I buried him on the dusty hill across the valley opposite our house. It was a primitive little cemetery for Arab Christians. There were no British mourners. Not that they would have been unsympathetic, but there were few of them then in Amman. Besides, I did not feel as if I wanted to tell anyone. Two Arab Christian priests read the burial service. My Arab orderly and my driver stood by the grave.

* * * * *

During the last year of the Second World War, the strength of the military units of the Arab Legion had risen to eight thousand. This force consisted of:

(*a*) The mechanized brigade including brigade headquarters and three regiments. This was in reality an infantry brigade, but without supporting arms or services. It had no artillery, engineers, or supply and transport. It included one medical officer per regiment but no field ambulance.

(*b*) Sixteen garrison companies, scattered over Syria, Iraq, Jordan and Palestine. These were guard units with very little tactical training and no battalion or brigade organization.

We also commanded the civil police force, which was two thousand strong. It will be seen that Arab Legion headquarters was incapable of being an operational headquarters. On the military side, it resembled the War Office, being responsible for budget provisions, contracts, purchases and policy, in addition to discipline, training and administration. The fact that it also commanded the civil police was both an advantage and a disadvantage. I was also still directly responsible for the desert and its tribes, and for frontier liaison with the Saudi government.

With the end of the World War, the economy axe began to be applied, though the speed of reduction was modified owing to the increasing disorder in Palestine, where the British Army was badly in need of troops to guard stores, depots and vital points. The wide dispersion of units involved me in a considerable amount of touring. I had for many years imposed upon myself a rough-and-ready system, according to which I worked one day in the office and then spent one day on tour, or roughly three days each week in the office and three days in the field.

Some ministers seemed surprised at my constant mobility. A number of them expressed wonder and admiration at such energy, but others were slightly annoyed. In particular Taufiq Pasha abu al Huda, who was several times Prime Minister, used to say to me often, almost irritably:

"I could not get you yesterday on the telephone. Where were you? You never seem to be in your office." On another occasion he looked at me and said:

"You have read about Sindbad the Seaman, who went on so many journeys? I am going to call you Sindbad the Landman—you seem to travel quite as much as the original Sindbad."

Travelling in Palestine was not always enjoyable, particularly in 1947 and onwards. We had companies stationed all up the coastal plain—in Gaza and Sarafand, at Aqir, Jaffa and Haifa (see the map on page 61). The area was covered with Jewish colonies, and month after month their attitude became more hostile. There was something peculiarly unpleasant in this type of domestic stab-in-the-back struggle. Life was by way of being normal and the streets of the cities were crowded with Jews, Arabs, British and many other

nationalities. Then suddenly a loud explosion and a burst of
shooting—and something had happened.

Unfortunately the Arab Legion was not unpopular with the Jews
alone. I remember well an officer of the garrison companies telling
me bitterly how he had met some Arabs of the Mufti's party in
Haifa, and how they had said:

"We reckon the Arab Legion to be a greater danger to us than
are the Jews!"

Such pettiness seemed almost incredible. The Mufti personally
had doubtless hoped one day to be himself the ruler of Palestine,
and the entry of the Amir Abdulla into the field perhaps weakened
his chances. But surely he should have preferred any Arab to
control Palestine rather than his alleged sworn enemies, the Jews.
This little incident was, however, only a foretaste of what was to
come. For Jordan and the Arab Legion were for many years to
represent the moderate, practical defence of the Arab cause, and
as a result they were to be anathema to Jews and Arabs alike. The
Jews saw in them the principal obstacle to their complete victory.
The Arabs always believed them to be but half-hearted in their
cause.

*   *   *   *   *

In the spring of 1946, the Amir Abdulla visited England. A new
treaty was negotiated with Britain, as a result of which the mandate
for Trans-Jordan was terminated and the Amir assumed the royal
title. On his return, he was inaugurated as King, and a ceremonial
review of the Arab Legion was held, amid great popular enthusiasm.
That day was the climax of twenty-five years of labour. In 1921, the
Amir Abdulla had arrived in a wild tribal land, never before regularly administered. He was without a government, without an
army, without money, without police or any of the attributes of a
modern State. On this day, twenty-five years later, he was proclaimed King of a loyal, happy, proud and contented country. A
simple people, united behind the throne, had stood like a rock while
rebellion followed rebellion in Palestine, Syria, Iraq and Saudi
Arabia.

I remember an American journalist who spent several days alone
touring Trans-Jordan in 1944. At the end he called on me to say
good-bye.

"This," he said to me, "is the only country in the world I have
ever visited where everybody without exception praises the government."

Where formerly nomadic tribes had terrorized the villages, a
modern State had been built up—a State which had gained the
respect of the world. Although it contained less than half a million

inhabitants, it was regarded as almost in the same category as Egypt, with forty times that number. On that happy coronation day, the future of Trans-Jordan seemed to be all hope, the prospects all propitious.

There can be no doubt that these twenty-five happy years in Trans-Jordan were principally due to the personality of King Abdulla. He alone was able to appreciate the need of his country for the assistance and advice of a Great Power, while at the same time he was firm enough to be able to hold his own on terms of equality. There was never any British domination of Trans-Jordan or of the Arab Legion. That country alone achieved this ideal state. There alone, the energy and affection of the people of the country were reinforced by the technical and financial help of a Great Power, in cordial co-operation.

Little did we dream that the happy little country we served was so soon to be destroyed—not by any mistakes on the part of Trans-Jordan, but by the overwhelming disaster of Palestine.

*   *   *   *   *

King Abdulla liked to adhere to old Muslim customs. Some of them were derived from the court of Sultan Abdul Hamid of Turkey. We were less enthusiastic, for we were often deprived thereby of our rare chances of a holiday.

Friday is the Muslim day of rest, and it was a holiday for us, whereas Sunday was a working day. But every Friday morning the King held a levee, and senior officials and officers had to attend. We were obliged to don our best blue uniforms, with Wellington boots and stiff high collars, and be up at the palace at eight o'clock in the morning (King Abdulla always rose at dawn). The visitors were always received in batches. The Prime Minister and the Cabinet went in first. Then came the senior officers of the army, who were later followed by judges, officials, merchants, notables or whoever else had come.

When shown into His Majesty's presence, we each in turn saluted and shook hands. There were usually eight or ten of us, and when all had paid their respects, the King motioned us to chairs. In the East, great importance is (or used to be) attached to seniority. Consequently the senior officer present was the only man entitled to speak. The remainder sat in silence unless spoken to. For twelve years of King Abdulla's reign, I was the senior officer, and was obliged to provide the necessary small talk, or to give vent to suitably intelligent comments, if His Majesty chose to speak.

When the King had had enough of our company, he pressed a bell on his desk, and a negro entered with coffee. As soon as he had dispensed a cup to all those present, I rose and said: "Will you permit us, sir?" The process of shaking hands and saluting was then repeated and we withdrew. Having bowed and saluted our way through the other visitors in the ante-room, we could at last go home, throw off our stiff uniforms, pull on an old pair of trousers and sit with a book in the garden.

The King always prayed the midday prayer in public on Fridays, in the Great Mosque in Amman. The procedure was ceremonious. The Arab Legion provided a guard of honour with a band and a colour outside the mosque. The guard of honour with their band used to march through the streets to the mosque with bayonets fixed—a nice little piece of military ceremony. Then the King would drive through the town to the prayers with a mounted escort, the guard of honour would present arms, the band would play, the crowd would cheer and the King would walk into the mosque.

The customs which we found most irksome were those connected with the Muslim feasts. There are two such in the year—the Great Feast or Feast of Sacrifice, and the Feast of Ramadhan, at the end of the month of fasting. Each feast was celebrated by five days official holiday, which consisted of one day before the feast, the day of the feast itself, and three days afterwards. The day of the feast, however, involved official ceremonies for us, so that we could not go away for the five days. By the time the ceremonies of the feast day were over, there were only three days left.

Muslim law prescribes that the morning prayer should be offered when the sun is one lance's length above the horizon. This description was doubtless satisfying for the Prophet Muhamad, who probably rose before dawn and had ample leisure in which to observe the exact moment when the sun was a lance's length above the horizon. But in our case it was more difficult. Reveille had to be fixed, trucks had to parade to transport the troops, who had to debus, fall in, march to their various positions and so on. All this necessitated quite long and detailed orders. The only man who ought to have been able to tell us at what time the sun would be a lance's length above the horizon on the morning of the feast was the chief qadhi. This venerable worthy always made himself extremely elusive before the feast day—perhaps because he himself did not know. As the Muslim feasts are reckoned according to the lunar months, they come on a different date, and dawn is therefore at a different time each year.

When the day came, I had to be ready in front of the Great Mosque in Amman before sunrise, in full dress with sword and decorations. The streets were lined with troops, and a guard of honour with colours and band was drawn up outside the mosque. Members of the Cabinet, general officers and senior officials awaited the King's arrival.

When the sun was a lance's length above the horizon (in theory at least), His Majesty would arrive with a sovereign's escort of his lancers on white horses. The mosque was usually packed, with an overflow congregation praying on the flat roof above. I have sometimes seen some of the worshippers praying in the street outside when they were unable to find room within.

After prayers, the King drove back in state to the palace, along the streets lined with troops. An hour later, a reception was held in the throne room, on the first floor of the old palace. His Majesty would stand at one end of the room. First members of the royal family entered, kissed his hand and then stood on the King's right. Then the Prime Minister and Cabinet shook hands and lined up on the King's left. Then senior officers of the Arab Legion came next. We formed up on his right. The remainder of the visitors filed past, shaking hands and bowing—officials, judges, qadhis, doctors, Christian religious dignitaries, merchants, and finally the general public. It always seemed to me a delightful relic of the old Arab patriarchy to see shopkeepers, shaikhs, bedouins, farmers and mechanics all filing past in the throne room to say the Muslim equivalent of "Happy Christmas" to their King. Now that Western democratic organization has been introduced—or perhaps it would be wiser to say, with the increase of sophistication—these simple relations between ruler and people no longer exist.

The floor of the throne room was in polished parquet and very slippery. At one time, a small Persian carpet used to be spread in front of the King. This carpet slid all too easily across the parquet, and was liable to shoot away beneath the feet of an unwary courtier, causing him to sit down in a highly undignified manner at the feet of his sovereign. We used to find these prolonged ceremonies rather wearisome, especially as we had to remain standing to attention at the King's right hand. We diverted ourselves by observing the advancing dignitaries and wondering which of them would come to grief on the magic carpet. Abdul Qadir Pasha al Jundi, for many years my deputy, and Ahmed Sudqi Pasha were usually standing on my right. We did not dare to move or nudge one another, but used to try to exchange a furtive wink out of the corners of our eyes.

At the end of the palace ceremony, the three of us set out together to pay formal calls. We started with the Prime Minister, then the Minister of Defence, the King's cousin the Amir Shakir ibn Zeid, then the Amir Tellal, former Prime Ministers, the chief qadhi and the head of the Circassian community. At each house we gave the greeting: "A blessed feast! May you every year be happy!" "Welcome! Welcome! May you every year be happy!" the host would answer. We sat down, and the inevitable cup of coffee, tray of sweets, or sticky lemonade would follow. After five minutes' polite conversation, we would rise, saying: "Will you permit us? May you every year be happy!" and move on to the next port of call.

In the town, the children would be running excitedly about, dressed in new clothes for the feast. The little girls especially would be resplendent in gay colours, red or yellow satins or bright blue silk dresses. In the early days, there would be swings rigged up for the occasion in the ruined Roman amphitheatre, where the children could shout and play, and buy sweetmeats and toffee apples. But with the spoil-sport officiousness of modern governments, the municipal engineer one day reported that the swings were unsafe, and put an end to the children's fun.

Looking back now, those happy days seem to have been in a past life—almost even another universe.

* * * * *

Meanwhile, however, the instability introduced by the war, the construction of airports and roads connecting one Arab country to another, and the increasing intermixture of the peoples of the different Arab countries, had greatly intensified the tendency towards Arab unity. The Arab Legion itself had contributed its share to this process, by the operations and subsequent garrison duties, which it carried out in the other Arab countries. The British government were in favour of increased Arab unity. As early as 1941, Mr. (later Sir Anthony) Eden had said:

"Many Arab thinkers desire for the Arab peoples a greater degree of unity than they now enjoy. In reaching out for this unity, they hope for our support. No such appeal from our friends should go unanswered."

A great Arab State extending from Anatolia to the Indian Ocean had been the vision of the British government in 1916, but had subsequently been obscured by the rival claims of the French and the Zionists. Now, in a different form, the proposal was revived. Britain's traditional need in the Middle East was for freedom of passage. She needed nothing from the peoples of those countries except their friendship. Even now, since oil has been found there, this basic consideration is unchanged. Britain, and with her all the maritime and commercial nations of the West, needs free passage for her ships and trade in peace time. In war, Britain needs the right to pass through with her forces. In return she would give every possible diplomatic, technical and financial support to the Arabs in peace, and she would guarantee to come to their assistance in the event of their being attacked by any other Power in war. There would be here material for a perfectly fair and honourable agreement to the mutual benefit of both.

As the end of the war drew near, Britain attempted once more to return to the statesmanlike plan of 1915, by concluding an agreement with an Arab group friendly to her and strong enough to stand alone with her help. In the thirty years which had elapsed since 1915, many Arab governments had been formed, and had acquired individual peculiarities. It was no longer possible to dream of a single Arab government. Thus emerged the plan for the Arab League.

It is ironical now to remember that Britain played a leading part in the creation of the Arab League. At least two Arab States were unwilling to join, and only did so as a result of British advice. The members of the Arab League were Egypt, Iraq, Saudi Arabia, Syria, Lebanon, Trans-Jordan and the Yemen.

All unperceived, a major innovation had here occurred. In the thirty years from 1915 to 1945, Egypt had not entered into plans for Arab political development. In the pledges to Sherif Husain, the western boundary of the Arab government-to-be was defined as the Red Sea and the Mediterranean. Egypt had played no part in the Versailles negotiations or the subsequent troubles. The Egyptians indeed were not regarded as Arabs, nor did they consider themselves to be such. The great majority of Egyptians who gave the subject any thought at all looked upon Egypt as a separate nation, the heir of the Pharaohs and of one of the most ancient civilizations of the world. They considered the Arabs to be a backward and ignorant race. The inclusion of Egypt in the list of Arab States was profoundly to modify the position of the Arabs in subsequent times.

The formation of the Arab League, and the inclusion of Egypt as "an Arab State", was to prove to be the beginning of a new era in the relations of the Arabs and the West. Immediately after the war, however, the Arabs and the British enjoyed a brief honeymoon. Iraq had declared war on Britain in 1941, but the latter had occupied the country with no sign of resentment or vindictiveness, a generosity appreciated by many Iraqis. The French and British had simultaneously evacuated Syria and Lebanon. Britain had supported, and assisted in, the formation of the Arab League. Trans-Jordan, as always, was happy in her alliance with Britain. Two factors were to destroy the rosy prospects of 1945—the struggle in Palestine and Egypt's ambition to lead the Arab world.

In the summer of 1945, a general election had taken place in Britain, and the Labour Party had been returned to power; Mr. Ernest Bevin, the new Foreign Secretary, prepared to deal with the thorny problem of Palestine.

III

The Insoluble Problem

How much easier it is to be critical than to be correct.   DISRAELI

We have all enough strength to endure the misfortunes of other people.   LA ROCHEFOUCAULD, *Maximes*

THE INSOLUBLE PROBLEM

WHEN the Labour government took office in Britain, the old process recommenced. A committee of inquiry arrived, toured round Palestine, took evidence and asked advice. The power and prestige of the United States had been greatly enhanced by the war, and that country had been voicing increasingly loud criticisms of the British administration in Palestine. These criticisms were the result of Jewish propaganda. In 1946 and 1947, no voice was raised in America in support of the Arabs.

The British government presumably hoped to quieten American criticism by inviting the United States to share in the task of settlement. The new committee of inquiry, therefore, was Anglo-American. Half the members were British and the other half from the United States. It was a curious and unsatisfactory arrangement, because the Americans were invited to give their views but their government would not be responsible for the execution of the proposals submitted. As a result, the United States government was given the opportunity to make political capital by its recommendations, but would be free of responsibility for failure in their application.

Jewish influence was strong in American internal politics. Mr. Truman, unfortunately, chose this critical moment to demand the admission of 100,000 Jewish refugees into Palestine. It was doubtless an astute move in America, and, had it been adopted, the United States would not have been responsible for the suppression of the ensuing Arab revolt. It was unfortunate also that the Anglo-American committee adopted Mr. Truman's proposal in its report, a fact which enabled the uncharitable to remark that the committee was merely a tool of American party politics.

In addition to the immediate admission of 100,000 Jews to Palestine, the committee recommended that neither an Arab nor a Jewish State be set up. It suggested that the mandate (or a similar trusteeship organization) should continue until the establishment of a Palestine State, in which both Jews and Arabs would agree to cooperate. To obtain this object, the committee pointed out, it was essential first to establish friendly relations between Jews and Arabs. The report omitted to explain how the two sides were to be persuaded to be friends. Meanwhile, Jewish terrorism was on the increase, and the Arabs were likewise considering plans for a resort to violence.

The committee's report paid little attention to any difficulties which might be encountered in implementing their proposals. The only reference to this subject seemed to be contained in one sentence.

"Receiving so large a number," said the report, referring to the 100,000 Jewish immigrants, "will be a heavy burden on Palestine. We feel sure that the authorities will shoulder it."

This one sentence alone was sufficient to reveal the failure of the committee to grasp the nature of the problem. It was not a matter of the authorities shouldering the responsibility. It was a question of how many divisions of troops would have been necessary to fight a three-cornered civil war against Jews and Arabs simultaneously.

The report of the Anglo-American committee was dead almost as soon as it was issued. It seemed obvious that both Jews and Arabs would resist its implementation by force.

It seemed to me that the committee had omitted to consider two vital factors. The first of these was the intense resentment felt by the Arabs that neither America nor Britain seemed to be anxious to admit Jewish refugees to their countries. "America," said an Arab politician to me, "is intensely distressed at the tragic fate of the Jews of Europe. She is ready to assist them, by giving them the country of the Arabs to live in."

A sub-committee of the Anglo-American committee visited Trans-Jordan. I was present at a reception given in their honour. A number of Trans-Jordanians (including a former Prime Minister) were talking to one of the American members. One of the Arabs enquired why the United States did not herself accept some of the 100,000 Jewish immigrants of whom Mr. Truman had spoken. "There are limits to kindness," replied the American drily. The cynicism of this answer infuriated the Trans-Jordanians. The United States is the most generous of nations. He could truly have quoted the immense benefits which America had already conferred, as an excuse for her inability to do more.

"If there are limits to American kindness, there are presumably no limits to Arab patience," retorted one of the Jordanians hotly.

The second aspect of the situation which the committee appeared to have overlooked was the existence of the Arab League. They seemed to envisage that they were dealing only with the people of Palestine.

"It is one of the peculiarities of the Palestine problem," I wrote at the time, "that it has come to outweigh all other political questions in the eyes of the Arabs. British help in Iraq, British intervention to secure the independence of Syria and Lebanon, thirty-five years of alliance with Ibn Saud, the grant of independence to Trans-Jordan —gratitude for all these benefits will be swept away in a moment.

All friendship and co-operation will be turned into hatred—if things go wrong in Palestine." My prophecy was, alas! to prove only too true.

We in Trans-Jordan produced our own solution. We favoured partition, but we considered it essential to retain British garrisons in Jerusalem and Haifa. If such a plan had been adopted, fighting would have been avoided. Any necessary exchanges of population could have been carried out without unnecessary hardship, and there would have been no destitute refugees. Such parts of Palestine as were allotted to the Arabs would have been incorporated in the neighbouring Arab States. Galilee would have joined Lebanon; Samaria and Judaea would have been united to Trans-Jordan; and the Gaza–Beersheba district to Egypt. Lord Moyne, British Minister of State in the Middle East, to whom I explained the idea, professed himself to be keenly interested. But before he could take up the scheme, he was assassinated in Cairo by Jewish terrorists sent down from Palestine for the purpose. In any case, it is unlikely that our proposal would have been considered. For it appears to be a principle of modern democracy that policy on any subject should be laid down by a committee of persons who know nothing of the subject under discussion. It is felt that such individuals will be impartial. They are also ignorant.

As a result of the failure of the Anglo-American committee, representatives of all the Arab States and of the Jews were summoned to London. They failed to agree. They refused even to meet, or sit together in the same room. Finally, however, they agreed on one subject only. Jemal al Husaini, nephew of Haj Ameen, the ex-Mufti of Jerusalem, was alleged to have remarked:

"The Arabs agreed with the Jews on one point only, and that was that British troops should withdraw, and allow the Arabs and the Jews to fight it out."

Both the U.S.A. and Russia were still attacking the British administration in Palestine. Mr. Bevin, the British Secretary of State for Foreign Affairs, acknowledged defeat. He notified the United Nations that Britain would hand back the mandate. It was a decision pregnant with human tragedy.

* * * * *

Not only did Britain decide to abandon the mandate. She fixed May 15th, 1948, as the day on which she would withdraw. There was at first a feeling almost amounting to consternation in Lake Success. It had been easy to tease Britain for the manner in which she had conducted the mandate. It was less easy to find an alternative régime to replace hers.

The first visible result of Britain's resignation of the mandate was the arrival of yet another committee. This one was called UNSCOP—United Nations Special Committee on Palestine. It did the usual tour, it heard the same old evidence, and it disappeared again. On August 31st, 1947, UNSCOP submitted its report. It was not unanimous. Seven members recommended partition. Three voted for a Federal State with Jewish and Arab cantons. One member wished the committee to report the facts to the General Assembly without recommendations. The General Assembly appointed an *ad hoc* committee to study the report. By 25 votes to 18, with 11 abstentions, the committee rejected an Arab proposal that the Balfour Declaration be submitted to the International Court of Justice. By only 21 votes to 20, the committee dismissed the question of the competency of UNO to enforce partition without the consent of the majority of the inhabitants of Palestine. A resolution on the subject of the absorption of Jewish displaced persons in countries other than Palestine was defeated by 18 votes to 15.

Eventually a proposal to adopt the UNSCOP report in favour of partition was adopted by 25 votes to 13, with 17 abstentions. In other words, in a committee of 55 members, only 25 voted for the proposal. The statement made by the Canadian representative was typical of the feelings of most of the members. "We support the plan," he said, "with heavy hearts and many misgivings."

The Pakistani Foreign Minister, Sir Muhamad Zafrullah, uttered a prophetic warning to the Western Powers when he said:

"Remember that you may need friends tomorrow, that you may need allies in the Middle East. I beg of you not to ruin and blast your credit in those lands."

A vote in the General Assembly requires a two-thirds majority. The vote was to be taken on November 26th, 1947, but was postponed. The supporters of the partition plan feared that they would not achieve the required majority. The Zionists were engaged in frenzied lobbying. The White House lent its support to the plan. The Zionists acknowledged the invaluable aid of Mr. Truman. The General Assembly met again on November 28th, but voting was once more postponed for twenty-four hours. On November 29th, partition was accepted by 33 votes to 13, with 10 abstentions. But many of the delegates witnessed the conclusion of the debates with heavy hearts.

A striking fact throughout all this struggle was that the United States and Soviet Russia worked hand in hand. They were unanimous, firstly, in decrying the British mandatory administration, secondly, in lobbying in favour of the partition plan, and finally, in May 1948, in a race to be the first to recognize the new State of Israel.

It is doubtful whether either Russia or America was acting from

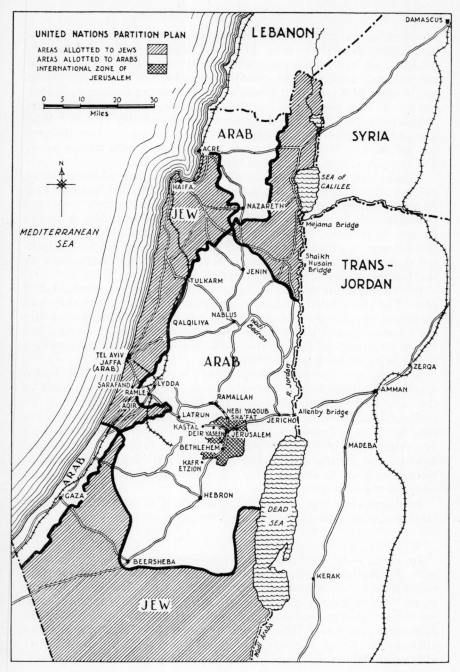

UNITED NATIONS PARTITION PLAN

AREAS ALLOTTED TO JEWS
AREAS ALLOTTED TO ARABS
INTERNATIONAL ZONE OF
      JERUSALEM

0   5 10   20   30
      Miles

N

MEDITERRANEAN
        SEA

LEBANON

DAMASCUS

ARAB

SYRIA

ACRE

SEA of
GALILEE

HAIFA

JEW

NAZARETH

Mejama Bridge

TULKARM

JENIN

Shaikh
Husain
Bridge

TRANS-
JORDAN

NABLUS

QALQILIYA

Wadi Bedran

ARAB

R. Jordan

ZERQA

TEL AVIV
JAFFA
(ARAB)

AMMAN

SARAFAND

RAMLE

LYDDA

AQIR

RAMALLAH

LATRUN

NEBI YAQOUB
SHA'FAT

Allenby Bridge

JERICHO

KASTAL

DEIR YASEEN

JERUSALEM

ARAB

BETHLEHEM

MADEBA

KAFR
ETZION

GAZA

HEBRON

DEAD
SEA

BEERSHEBA

KERAK

JEW

Wadi Araba

61

idealistic motives. The White House had its eye on the Jewish vote in the Presidential election. From the Russian point of view, the Middle East had been a preserve of the Western Powers. To support any measure which would destroy the prestige of the United States and Britain in a vital part of the world was to the Russians an obvious move. Had not Lenin, thirty years before, announced the policy of destroying the West by overthrowing its position in Asia? Here was the West itself committing suicide—of its own volition destroying its ancient bonds with Asia. What more could Russia wish? She happily seized the hand of her American ally.

Britain had stood aloof from all the debates, had abstained from voicing any opinion, had absented herself from the voting. Like Achilles, she was sulking in her tent. But was she thereby innocent of the result? It was she who had accepted the mandate from the League of Nations. It was she whose administration had produced the impasse in which UNO found itself, though it must be admitted that she had, all along, been encouraged in her fatal course by the League of Nations and by the U.S.A.

But the ultimate result was to be far worse even than the UNO plan. For the United Nations could pass resolutions, but they had no power to enforce them. A great part of the ensuing tragedy could have been avoided if the United Nations, or Britain, or some other Power or group of Powers had been willing to contribute armed forces to supervise implementation.

Some form of partition was probably inevitable. The UNO plan was unjustly biased in favour of the Jews. It gave sixty per cent of the area of Palestine, including the fertile coastal plain and the plain of Esdraelon, to one-third of the inhabitants. If a garrison belonging to one Power or to a group of Powers could have held Jerusalem and Haifa, supervised the execution of the plan, prevented fighting and arranged a gradual and peaceful exchange of populations, much of the tragedy, hatred, bloodshed and suffering could have been avoided.

In this gloomy and despairing mood, the United Nations Organization drifted into a blood-soaked tragedy.

*   *   *   *   *

In 1946, King Abdulla had personally negotiated a new treaty with the British government. But in the ensuing two years, certain unsatisfactory aspects of the new agreement had become apparent to the Trans-Jordan government. In the spring of 1948, a Trans-Jordan delegation went to London to negotiate a number of modifications to the treaty. The delegation consisted of Taufiq Pasha abu al Huda, the Prime Minister, and Fawzi Pasha al Mulqi, the Minister of Foreign Affairs. I accompanied the party as their military adviser.

The treaty modifications were negotiated with no great difficulty. When the negotiations were finished, Taufiq Pasha requested a private interview with the British Foreign Secretary, Mr. Ernest Bevin. The Trans-Jordan Prime Minister spoke no English, and consequently he asked me to accompany him as interpreter. The meeting took place in the Secretary of State's room in the Foreign Office, where the tall windows looked out on the Horse Guards' Parade and the black leafless trees in St. James's Park.

Taufiq Pasha explained the reason for his request for an interview, while I translated for him, sentence by sentence. The British mandate for Palestine, he said, was about to come to an end. The Jews had prepared a government which would be able to assume power as soon as the mandate was terminated on May 15th. But the Palestine Arabs had made no preparations to govern themselves. They had no leaders in the country capable of organizing an administration. In the same way, the Jews had prepared a police force from the Jewish members of the Palestine Police. But, what was more important still, the Jews had an army in the form of the Hagana. The Arabs had no armed forces, and no means of creating an army. Consequently, Taufiq Pasha explained, if the situation were left as it was, one of two things would happen. Either the Jews would neglect the United Nations partition plan and would seize the whole of Palestine up to the River Jordan; or else the Mufti would return and endeavour to make himself ruler of Arab Palestine. Neither of these alternatives would suit either Britain or Trans-Jordan. The Mufti was the bitterest enemy of Britain and had spent the war with Hitler in Berlin. He was also an irreconcilable enemy of Trans-Jordan and considered himself to be the personal rival of King Abdulla.

During recent weeks, King Abdulla and the government of Trans-Jordan had received, and were still receiving, many requests and petitions from Palestine Arab notables. In all these communications, the Palestinians begged for the help and protection of the Arab Legion as soon as the British forces withdrew. The Trans-Jordan government accordingly proposed to send the Arab Legion across the Jordan when the British mandate ended, and to occupy that part of Palestine awarded to the Arabs which was contiguous with the frontier of Trans-Jordan.

I can to this day almost see Mr. Bevin sitting at his table in that splendid room. When I had finished my translation thus far, he interrupted Taufiq Pasha's statement by saying:

"It seems the obvious thing to do."

I reminded Taufiq Pasha, speaking in Arabic, that the Arab Legion could not occupy the Gaza area or upper Galilee, which had also been allotted to the Arabs. Taufiq Pasha accordingly made a

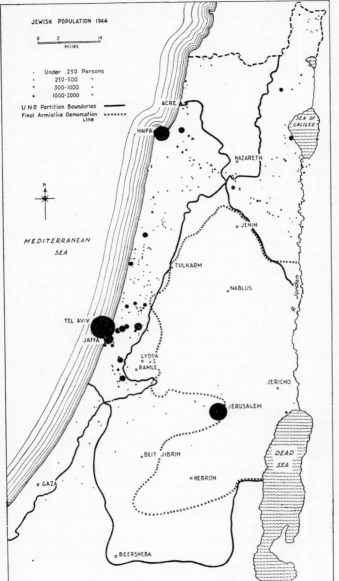

JEWISH POPULATION 1944

0   5   10
Miles

· Under 250 Persons
· 250-500 ·
· 500-1000 ·
· 1000-2000 ·

U N O Partition Boundaries ————
Final Armistice Demarcation ×××××××
Line

ACRE

SEA OF
GALILEE

HAIFA

NAZARETH

N

MEDITERRANEAN
SEA

JENIN

TULKARM

NABLUS

TEL AVIV
JAFFA

LYDDA
RAMLE

JERICHO

JERUSALEM

BEIT JIBRIN

DEAD
SEA

HEBRON

GAZA

BEERSHEBA

It will be noted that the UNO partition boundary in the north includes almost all the Jewish settlements in the proposed Jewish State. With the exception of two Jewish colonies north of Jerusalem and a few others west of the city, nearly all Jewish settlements were in the coastal plain or in the strip running north of Jenin and west of the Sea of Galilee, up to Lebanon. The UNO boundary was drawn on this basis.

The worst injustice in the UNO plan was that the Neqeb running southwards from Beersheba for 200 miles to Aqaba was given to the Jews, whereas there were none living there, nor had it ever in history been inhabited by Jews.

Note the large concentrations of Jews in the cities of Tel Aviv, Haifa and Jerusalem, as opposed to the small number in the rural districts.

Compare the UNO boundary with the armistice demarcation line on the maps of the Jewish and Arab populations. Notice that the additional areas conquered by the Jews in the fighting were nearly entirely Arab areas—namely the Lydda–Ramle area, and the "corridor" west and south-west of Jerusalem. There were scarcely any Jews in either of these areas before 1948.

ARAB POPULATION 1944

It will be seen that, although the UNO boundary in the north included nearly all the Jewish settlements, it also contained great numbers of Arab towns and villages. If the UNO plan had been implemented, the Jewish State would have contained as many Arabs as Jews. In the rural districts, the Arabs would have outnumbered the Jews, but the cities of Tel Aviv and Haifa sufficed to even up the numbers of the two races. If the Arab League States had not intervened, and the UNO partition plan had been implemented peacefully, the Jews would have found it extremely difficult to organize their State. The hostilities enabled them to rid themselves of the Arabs.

This map is deceptive in that it makes the Beersheba area appear uninhabited. This is due to the fact that it was compiled on the basis of villages and towns. Nearly all the inhabitants of the Beersheba area and the Neqeb lived in tents, and therefore do not appear. This does not mean that they were nomadic. In southern Palestine and Trans-Jordan there are tens of thousands of farmers and cultivators who still live in tents. They own their land and farm it, but they prefer to live in tents rather than houses. The area between Beersheba and Gaza was cultivated with wheat and barley by Arabs, who owned the land, but lived in tents. Farther south, in the two hundred miles from Beersheba to Aqaba, lived also nomadic tribes, who bred sheep, goats and camels, as they have done for thousands of years. Nearly all of them have been driven out by Israel.

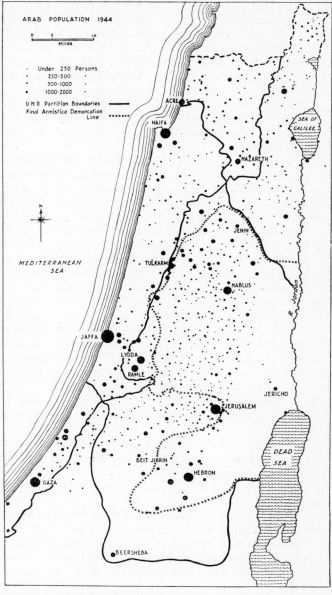

There does not seem necessarily to be any justification for depriving men of their country merely because they prefer to live in tents rather than brick or stone houses.

Note the fact that most of the Arab population were rural and lived in villages, in contrast to the city-dwelling majority of Jews.

statement to that effect, which I duly translated into English.

"It seems the obvious thing to do," repeated Mr. Bevin, "but do not go and invade the areas allotted to the Jews."

"We should not have the forces to do so, even if we so desired," replied the Jordan Prime Minister. He then continued his statement by pointing out that the Anglo-Trans-Jordan treaty made it incumbent on the two contracting parties to consult one another whenever a critical situation threatened to arise. It was in accordance with this paragraph of the treaty that he had explained the intentions of the Trans-Jordan government to the British Foreign Secretary.

Mr. Bevin thanked Taufiq Pasha for his frank exposition of the position of Trans-Jordan, and expressed his agreement with the plans put forward. We rose, shook hands cordially and took our leave.

It should be recollected that, when this conversation took place, neither the British nor the Trans-Jordanians had any idea that the Arab League would intervene—much less that the Arab States would send troops to Palestine. At the time when we visited London, we anticipated that the Arab Legion would occupy Arab Palestine (less Gaza and Galilee), would establish internal security there, form an administration and patrol the frontier with the Jewish areas.

In the end these plans were to be frustrated by two factors.

Firstly, the British authorities lost control of internal security before the mandate ended. The Palestine Arabs attempted to close the Jerusalem road and the Jewish forces invaded the Arab area in order to keep the road open. Perhaps also the Jews had already decided to occupy Jerusalem as their capital, in spite of its international status under the partition plan.

Secondly, the Arab League under Egyptian leadership decided to call upon its members to attack the Jews as soon as the mandate ended.

These two factors were fundamentally to alter the mental picture which was visualized when we discussed our proposals with Mr. Bevin.

*   *   *   *   *

I returned to Amman by air as soon as the negotiations were over, leaving Taufiq Pasha to follow. He proposed to travel overland to Marseilles and thence by sea to Beirut. The situation in Palestine was already deteriorating and I was in some anxiety concerning the Arab Legion units still in that country, co-operating with the British Army.

A few days after my return, I was in Ramallah, when an orderly informed me that I was wanted on the telephone. When I picked up the receiver, I heard a voice speaking in English, which said:

"Glubb Pasha? Is that you, sir?"

"Yes, Glubb speaking."

"Please don't be alarmed, sir," it said. "Your family are safe, but your house has been blown up."

"What happened?" I asked.

"A bomb went off just outside your house at eleven o'clock this morning, sir," said the voice. "None of your family was injured, but all the windows were shattered. The house is no longer habitable. Mrs. Glubb has gone to stay with her mother."

"Thank you very much, Broadhurst," I said. "I'll be back this afternoon."

Broadhurst, an officer seconded from the Palestine Police, was in charge of the training and administration of the police wing of the Arab Legion. It would have been impossible to find a more loyal, simple and devoted officer or friend.

When I arrived home, I found indeed that the house was not habitable. Every window had been shattered by the explosion, all the rooms were strewn with broken glass, and the wind and rain were blowing in.

My wife had been suffering from an attack of influenza and was in bed. Our bedroom was on the ground floor, and it appeared that a time-bomb had been placed in the garden, immediately outside our bedroom window. The bomb exploded at eleven o'clock in the morning. Perhaps the perpetrator intended only to frighten us and not to kill us. Perhaps he did not know how to set the time device.

My wife, as I have said, was in bed, but by an extraordinarily fortunate coincidence, she was lying on her side with her back to the window. She was stunned by the explosion, but when she recovered her presence of mind, she found that her pillow and her hair were full of splinters of glass. If she had been lying on her other side, she would have received this hail of broken glass in her face and eyes. The door of our bedroom was on the opposite side of the room to the window under which the bomb had exploded. The door was scratched and splintered all over with fragments, as also were two wooden wardrobes. Anyone standing up in the room would have been killed. As it was, our bedroom furniture remained pitted and torn with splinters until we left Amman eight years later. Our little girl, aged four, was fortunately at a kindergarten school a hundred yards from our house.

No arrests were made. The police finally reported that the bomb had been placed by a young man who had come down for that purpose from Damascus. If he placed the bomb at night in the dark, and set the time device for eleven o'clock next morning, he was probably back in Damascus before the explosion occurred. But in any case, the police report did not strike me as convincing.

In those days, I had no guard on my house. Thereafter I always had a guard and an escort.

The police alleged that the motive of the crime was to protest against the signature of the Anglo-Trans-Jordan treaty. Happily, in this direction, I felt no qualms of conscience. The treaty was extremely favourable to Trans-Jordan. Indeed, the country could not survive without it. The Trans-Jordanians were perfectly satisfied with their King and their government, and felt a genuine and cordial friendship for Britain. In the Second World War, they had stood magnificently by Britain, and indeed they fully deserved the generous treatment which they received.

Indirectly, the conduct of Britain was less commendable, for by surrendering the Palestine mandate to the United Nations without reserving any rights to Trans-Jordan, she virtually condemned that country to death. Trans-Jordan had lived hitherto by exporting cheap and bulky agricultural produce, principally wheat, barley and wool. All her imports and exports had passed through Haifa port, which was free to her as long as Britain held the mandate for Palestine. But the partition plan had awarded the port of Haifa to the Jews. Henceforward any Trans-Jordanian exports or imports would either be at the mercy of the Jews, or would have to be sent through Damascus to Beirut, passing *en route* through two other independent countries—Syria and Lebanon. In the case of such bulky and low-priced exports as wheat and barley, such a long overland haul was prohibitive. As soon as the UNO partition plan was published, I wrote the following words:

"The proposal may or may not settle the problem of Palestine. But one thing is certain—it will certainly be the death of Britain's most loyal ally—Trans-Jordan."

The implementation of the partition plan did not immediately lead to the extinction of Trans-Jordan, as I had foreseen. The fighting qualities shown by the Arab Legion in 1948 impressed Britain with the idea that the new Jordan was a worth-while ally. Thus, although Trans-Jordan (and then the new Jordan) was to bear nearly all the burden of the disaster impending, Britain was to keep her alive by subsidies for several years to come.

But it was not Trans-Jordan's impending economic death which was worrying the young man who tried to blow up my house. In Syria there were already bitterly anti-Western parties, to whom the idea of any Anglo-Trans-Jordan treaty was unacceptable, whether it were to be benefit of Trans-Jordan or not.

IV

The Slide to Chaos

If, therefore, war should ever come between these two countries, it will not, I think, be due to irresistible laws, it will be due to the want of human wisdom.

ARTHUR BONAR LAW, House of Commons, 1911

IV

THE SLIDE TO CHAOS

AS May 1948 and the end of the mandate drew nearer, fighting and confusion in Palestine increased. Battles took place in the very streets of Jerusalem. The Jews began slowly and methodically to conquer and occupy the Arab quarters of the city (see the map on page 112). Several predominantly Arab residential areas, such as Katamon and the so-called Greek and German colonies, lay in the southern suburbs. While these house-to-house battles were in progress, British Army units were only a few hundred yards away. Yet they intervened slowly and deliberately only if a particular battle lasted too long, or if heavy casualties seemed to be likely. In Palestine, Jews and Arabs alike were agreed in demanding the withdrawal of Britain from the country. Perhaps the British were to be excused if they desired to avoid the loss of further British lives in keeping Jews and Arabs apart, when they knew that, a month or so later, the two sides intended in any case to fight it out.

It so happened, early in April, that the Jews were attacking the suburb of Katamon. The Iraqi Consulate was situated in this area, and the Jewish forces, advancing from house to house, were drawing near to it. The Iraqis appealed to the Trans-Jordan government, as one Arab State to another, and asked them to place a guard on their Consulate.

The proposal was a somewhat delicate one, because the Arab Legion in Palestine was operating as an allied army with the British Army. The arrangement was a relic of the war, when other allied armies, Free French and Poles for example, were also present. Since the war had ended, nobody had been so rash as to attempt any definition of what the role of the Arab Legion had become. They remained in Palestine provisionally. The British Army, however, never called upon the Arab Legion to take part in active operations, whether against Jews or Arabs. They were still guarding those accumulations of warlike stores which had grown up during the war, when Palestine was on one of the main supply routes for aid to Russia. Whether it was proper for the Arab Legion to defend the Iraqi Consulate from a Jewish attack might have been made the subject of diplomatic controversy for days. The Trans-Jordan government were unwilling to see the Consulate of an allied Arab government captured by the Jews. I was ordered to send a guard forthwith.

Meanwhile, the Hagana—the embryo Jewish army—were advancing. They were resisted by an improvised collection of Arab irregulars, without training or leadership. Katamon was a comparatively wealthy quarter, consisting of residential houses, each in its own garden. As the Jews captured one house after another, the well-do-do Arab residents began to abandon their homes. Soon the Iraqi Consulate also moved out, and the Arab Legion guard was left in an empty building. The house next to it on one side, and then that on the other side of the road, were occupied by the Jews. The Arab Legion guard improvised loopholes on the roof and in the windows. There was a good deal of shooting. The Jews withdrew. Next day they returned. Miniature battles developed.

I was sitting in my house, working at some papers in the evening, when the telephone rang. It was from the Arab Legion in Jerusalem. They reported that the Jews had by-passed the house held by our guard, and had taken another house behind it. Our men would soon be cut off. In view of the fact that the Iraqi Consulate had moved out, and the building had only been rented by it, was it necessary for the Arab Legion guard to remain?

I rang up the Prime Minister for orders, as it was he who had instructed us to guard the building. Taufiq Pasha was highly strung and he was feeling the strain of these events. He was a quiet, neat, methodical little man, who should have spent his life as an auditor or a chartered accountant. Before I could complete my account of developments in Jerusalem, he burst out in an excited torrent of speech.

"You British," he began, "let the country fall into chaos and then you take no action to restore order, and ring me up and ask me. . . ." A storm of indignant protest overwhelmed me.

I remained silent and allowed his nervous excitement to run its course. Eventually he paused, and I seized the opportunity.

"Sir," I said, "you seem to forget that I am not a servant of the British. I am your servant. The representative of Britain is the British Minister. It was your Excellency who ordered me, four days ago, to place a guard on the Iraqi Consulate. I am asking your Excellency's orders as to whether that guard is to be withdrawn or to remain."

His tone changed immediately.

"I am sorry," he said. "I forgot myself. You are one of us." He spoke quietly and calmly. "If the Iraqis have all left and taken their documents with them, the guard may be withdrawn."

"As your Excellency orders," I replied, replacing the receiver. I could not prevent myself from leaning back in my chair with a sigh. It was difficult entirely to blame Taufiq Pasha. A situation had arisen which might almost be called "authorized anarchy". With the machinery of the Palestine government still in position, with officials still going to their offices every morning, with the police still in the streets and a considerable army still in its barracks, raging battles were going on in the country almost unhindered. Poor Taufiq Pasha! He loved a life of routine. He went to the office at the same minute every morning and returned to his house at precisely the same time every afternoon. He enjoyed detail, particularly financial detail. He delighted in finding some minor irregularity in financial procedure. He loathed all things military, as if by instinct. He detested emergencies, he loathed hasty improvisations. He even disliked people. He lived between his house and his office. He enjoyed handling impersonal problems, minuting files, looking up regulations and checking accounts. Few men could have been more unsuited to rule the storms of a world rapidly sliding into chaos.

I could not myself avoid the feeling that the British in Palestine should have done more to keep order until the mandate ended. And yet—could we blame them? They had been through an unparalleled ordeal. For one glorious year, they had challenged the world alone, while the Russian and American giants looked on. Now it was all over—and in what an anti-climax! Now nothing Britain could do was right. Jews and Arabs, Russians and Americans vied with one another in their condemnations. Even the stolid Mr. Bevin—stout heart that he was—could scarcely be blamed for giving up.

"Well, if you don't like us," the British were saying, "you can sort yourselves out as best you can." Their critics perhaps deserved such a reply, but the tragedy was not to be borne by them, but by the poor, the ignorant and the simple—the common folk of Palestine.

A month before the end of the mandate the British High Commissioner succeeded in arranging a truce between the Jews and the Arabs in the Holy City. The truce applied to the city only. Outside Jerusalem, battles continued. But inside it life, for a few weeks, seemed by comparison to return to normal.

*　　*　　*　　*　　*

One of the main foundations on which Zionist policy in Palestine had been built was the purchase of land. From 1918 to 1938, Jewish funds had been spent on the purchase of land all over Palestine, the economic aspect being the consideration which received priority. That is to say, the best land obtainable was bought, looked at as a financial investment. With effect from 1938, however, this policy was changed. The 1936–1938 Arab rebellion had convinced the Zionists that their conflict with the Arabs would ultimately be decided by force. Thenceforward, the emphasis shifted to the political and strategic importance of the areas to be acquired.

In the spring of 1948, as Palestine descended more and more into anarchy, the strategic locations of many Jewish colonies became increasingly obvious. The Jews had established one group of colonies immediately north of Jerusalem, and another south of the Holy City, between Bethlehem and Hebron. Thus the chief Arab cities—Jerusalem, Hebron and Nablus—could be cut off from one another and isolated, whenever the Jewish command so desired.

Of these road-block colonies, the most awkward was that at Nebi Yaqoub—in Hebrew, Nevi Yaacov (see the map on page 61). This colony was only three miles north of Jerusalem and consisted of a small village with a considerable frontage on the main Jerusalem–Ramallah road. The Jews had built a concrete blockhouse only about twenty feet from the edge of the road. From the end of 1947 until May 15th, 1948, this blockhouse was continually manned by armed Jewish "soldiers". When British control began to relax, these men, whenever the spirit moved them, would enter their blockhouse, shut the door and man the loopholes. They would then fire at a few yards' range at any Arab vehicle attempting to pass. Many Arab buses and taxis suffered casualties in this manner, often to women and children. When the Jews tired of this sport, they would open the door of their blockhouse, walk out, sit beside the road, light their cigarettes and watch the Arabs.

I remember on one occasion driving up from Jerusalem and finding an Arab Legion vehicle halted exactly opposite the Jewish blockhouse. A little Arab Legion bedouin corporal called Auda Dhuweihi, rather a friend of mine, was standing in the road. On his left, an Arab taxi was overturned in the ditch, the Jews having shot the driver as the car drove past. Pinned underneath the overturned taxi were an Arab woman and child. A few yards away, the Jews had come out of their blockhouse and were smoking and laughing.

The little corporal was trembling with rage and swearing under his breath, "God curse the father of an army where a man has to stand by and see women shot." We extricated the woman and child, while the Jews were standing only a few yards away. Presumably they did not wish to antagonize the Arab Legion as yet. We had strict orders not to retaliate whatever happened.

On another occasion soon afterwards, I was coming down the road in the opposite direction from Ramallah to Jerusalem and drove safely past the Nebi Yaqoub blockhouse, but when we approached the Arab village of Sha'fat, a mile farther on, we heard firing. Just before reaching Sha'fat, we found the G.O.C., General Sir Gordon MacMillan, standing in the road with a military police sergeant. The General's car was parked close by. Heavy firing was going on in the village.

"So damned stupid, infernally annoying!" the General was saying.

It appeared that a convoy of Jewish vehicles had left Jerusalem to carry supplies to Nebi Yaqoub; the Arabs had blocked the road and were attacking the convoy. An Arab came up and explained excitedly that, the day before, a Jewish convoy had driven through the village, run over and killed a little Arab girl, and driven straight on. We did not know if this was true or not.

A bend in the road prevented us from seeing what was happening in the village street. There was heavy firing, and it was not easy to hear oneself speak. A few stray bullets passed by—*wheut—wheut—wheut*! The military police sergeant ducked his head. We advanced down the road on foot as far as the bend. A Jewish lorry was lying half in the ditch. A dead Jew, a young, fair-haired man, was lying beside the road. His trousers were torn and blood-soaked, and the white skin of his back could be seen stained with red. Colonel Ahmed Sudqi Beg, commander of the garrison companies in Palestine, was with me.

"How horrible is a dead human body," he said. We looked into the lorry. Another dead Jew was slumped across the driving wheel.

When we rounded the bend in the road, we saw a large Jewish armoured car halted in the middle of the village street. The street was wide, and the houses on each side had small gardens in front of them. The houses and gardens were full of Arabs firing their rifles at the armoured car. Every now and then, the muzzle of an automatic was thrust through a loophole in the side of the armoured car and fired a few bursts at the Arabs, and was then withdrawn. There were obviously living Jews inside the armoured car, but we could not tell how many. The noise of firing was deafening.

The General had a wireless set with him, and had sent several signals to Jerusalem to call for troops, but none had come. The battle raged on. Suddenly we saw an armoured car coming up the road from Jerusalem beyond the village.

"It must be from the Household Cavalry Regiment," said General MacMillan. "Now we can stop this nonsense."

The armoured car halted two hundred yards beyond the village, and then opened up with a machine gun into the village. It appeared to be spraying Jews and Arabs indiscriminately.

"Get him on your wireless set. Tell him not to fire," shouted the General. "We want to stop this battle, not add to it."

An orderly ran back to the set. Meanwhile, the armoured car continued to fire bursts into the village, increasing the noise and general pandemonium.

As we watched the battle, we saw an Arab crawl out of a garden and across the road and slip under the back axle of the Jewish armoured car. He was dragging with him a sack, presumably soaked in petrol or paraffin. He crouched under the armoured car, struck a match, and set the sack alight.

"He's going to set fire to the car," said the General. "Damn it! We can't stand here and see them roasted alive!"

A thin column of smoke rose from the sack underneath the armoured car. Suddenly a loophole in the armoured car opened and a bomb dropped out and burst with a crack on the road. The Arab rolled out from underneath the vehicle and into the ditch.

"Glubb! Can't you stop these Arabs firing?" shouted the General.

The din was appalling. Everybody in the village seemed to be shooting—the Jewish armoured car was shooting back. The Household Cavalry armoured car was still firing bursts.

"I'll have a try," I said, "but it's not easy to get in touch, with all these people shooting."

I slipped across the road and through a small garden to the back of a house. Two Arab Legion soldiers followed me. We began to work our way through the back gardens behind the houses. We got our breath behind each house, then ran across the gap between it and the next house. Then we repeated the process. The Jewish armoured car was only twenty yards away now. The British armoured car fired a long burst which whistled over our heads.

"God curse their fathers!" growled one of the soldiers beside me. "They want to kill us." He gave me a grin. We ran forward again and jumped over a low wall, in full view of the Jews at about fifteen yards range. Fortunately their loopholes were closed, or they would have thought we were attacking them. Now we were behind the house in front of which the Jewish vehicle was stuck. A crowd of excited Arabs was lining the garden wall, shooting at the Jews. I came up to them from behind. "Stop shooting!" I shouted. They did not hear. I seized one man by his collar. "*Ya walad, la tirmi.* Stop shooting, my lad." He looked round at me. "Why?" he shouted. I thumped the other Arabs on the back. "Stop shooting!" I yelled. Just at that moment, a loophole in the Jewish vehicle opened. We ducked in time. A burst of what seemed to be Sten-gun fire went over. "If you stop shooting and let us take over the Jews, you can have the car and everything in it," I shouted. "Why get killed? You can have the armoured car and all the contents for nothing."

Some of them were listening now. We crouched behind the low wall.

"We want the arms and ammunition," one man said.

"All right! You can have it," I said. "Stop your men firing."

"Who is he?" asked another man. "He is the father of Faris,"[1]

---

[1] It is a compliment among Arabs to address a man in this way by the name of his eldest son: "O father of Ahmed!" for example. My eldest son was christened Godfrey, but the Amir Abdulla (as he then was) said that he must also have an Arab name, and called him Faris, meaning "Knight". I therefore became "the father of Faris".

shouted one of our men. "By Allah! They say he is a good man."
said one of the villagers.

It took us nearly a quarter of an hour to stop all the villagers
shooting. We waved the British armoured car up until it was right
against the Jewish car. Then we battered on the Jewish armoured
car.

"Come out!" shouted the sergeant in the British car. "Come out!
We're British!" They suspected a trap, and indeed I thought if they
did come out, the Arabs might shoot them before they could enter
the British vehicle. A British 15 cwt. truck had also arrived. I now
had Ahmed Sudqi Beg and six men of the Arab Legion. We closed
round the two vehicles, making a wall on each side with our bodies.
At last the Jews ventured to open a crack of the door. The sight of
the Household Cavalry sergeant reassured them. One by one we
got them out, passing them between us into the British vehicle. Two
could hop. Several were dead. It was difficult to see whether some
were dead or alive. Their clothes were torn, they were little more
than a heap of lacerated meat. It was like a butcher's shop—so
much torn flesh and pools of blood. Dragging, carrying, pushing, and
covering them with our bodies, we thrust them into the British
vehicles, which drove off. I called our soldiers to one side. I waved
to the villagers—"It's all yours," I shouted.

*   *   *   *   *

While the Jewish colony of Nebi Yaqoub was so sited as to block
the main road out of Jerusalem on the north, another group of
colonies could close the road on the south between Bethlehem and
Hebron. There were four Jewish colonies in this locality, the principal of which was Kafr Etzion. Unlike Nebi Yaqoub, this village
was not actually on the main road; indeed, it was out of range of the
road to small-arms fire. Within three hundred yards of the road,
however, was an almost empty building belonging to the Orthodox
Church. This building, which stood on an eminence, completely
commanded the main road for a length of about a quarter of a mile.
The Jews from Kafr Etzion occupied this building and proceeded to
fire on all traffic using this road. The exact similarity between the
Jewish action at Nebi Yaqoub and Kafr Etzion proved that all these
strategic colonies were acting under orders.

Throughout 1947 and until immediately before the end of the
mandate in 1948, the Arab Legion had a garrison company in Gaza
and Rafah. The line of communication of this company lay through
Beersheba and Hebron to Jerusalem and thence to Amman. In
addition, the Arab Legion was still drawing stores from the Suez
Canal Zone from the British Army. Thus Arab Legion traffic up
and down the Hebron–Jerusalem road was considerable. As time

passed, vehicles on the road were more and more frequently held up. Soon it was impossible for single vehicles to pass. Convoys had to be used. Then escorts were necessary, to engage the Jews with fire while the unarmed trucks made a dash for it.

By April 1948, the British had virtually given up any attempt to keep the roads open, except for their own columns evacuating their troops and stores. Complete battles developed along the roads, like that at Sha'fat in which I had been involved with General Mac-Millan.

In the first half of May—the last fortnight before the end of the mandate—the British instructed us to draw a quantity of stores and vehicles from Egypt. It was our last chance to do so. With the end of the mandate, it was unlikely we should ever again be able to come and go to Egypt by road. Meanwhile, however, Kafr Etzion was in a position completely to block the road.

Moreover, according to the United Nations partition plan, the Kafr Etzion colonies were in the centre of a purely Arab area. They were in a position to cut off Hebron from Jerusalem after the end of the mandate. Our convoy from Egypt was due back two days before the end of the mandate. Jewish forces were already in many places operating inside the area allotted to the Arabs. We accordingly decided to remove the Kafr Etzion colonies before they could destroy our convoy and cut us off from Hebron.

Two days before the end of the mandate, the Arab Legion attacked Kafr Etzion with two companies, supported by four three-inch mortars. The colonies had been surrounded by belts of barbed wire and fairly extensive fields of mines. During the operation, Jewish troops from the coastal plain were dropped by parachute to reinforce the colony. Eventually all four colonies were captured and their garrisons transferred to Trans-Jordan. The Arab Legion treated all Jews as prisoners of war. As soon as the Arab Legion withdrew, the villagers of the Hebron district looted the Jewish colonies, leaving not one stone upon another. These colonies had been so aggressive that they had deliberately compelled Arab retaliation.

* * * * *

The United Nations partition plan had been announced on November 29th, 1947. The Mufti had returned from Germany to the Middle East. The Jordan government was not admitted to the inner councils of the Egyptian and Syrian governments, or of the Mufti, who was in Damascus. It would appear, however, that these Arab leaders, together with Abdul Rahman Pasha Azzam, Secretary-General of the Arab League, had already decided to use force. The Arabs had to a great extent been deluded by their own enthusiasm. Fond of studying and retailing in public the story of the Arab conquests of thirteen centuries ago, they believed themselves to be a great military people, and regarded the Jews as a nation of shopkeepers. The Egyptians, the Syrians and the Iraqis, out of touch with the situation in Palestine and too inexperienced to realize the necessity to find out the facts, assumed that they would find no difficulty in defeating the Jews. The Arabs of Palestine, familiar with the Jews but knowing little of the Arab governments, were confident that the Egyptians, Syrians and Iraqis would be amply strong. The Arab governments did immense harm to the cause of the Palestine Arabs, because they encouraged them to be defiant, and when it came to violence, they failed.

Only King Abdulla and Jordan were in a position to take a balanced view. They were near enough to know the extent and thoroughness of the Jewish preparations. They were in sufficiently close touch with the Arabs to know their inefficiency. One of the major causes of the Arab failure in 1948 was their unwillingness to face facts. Not only did they neglect to study the potential military strengths of both sides, but they accused of treachery any man with the courage to speak the unpalatable truth. King Abdulla always possessed the moral courage to say what he thought. He deprecated the idea of fighting and was immediately covered with bitter reproaches, and charged with treachery in the most opprobrious terms.

The Mufti, the Egyptians and the Syrians did not at first believe that it would be necessary to use their regular forces. They were persuaded that a force of irregulars would be sufficient. In December 1947, recruitment of irregulars was started in Syria and a motley force was collected under the title of the "Arab Liberation Army". (The interpreter in Arab Legion headquarters rather ineptly translated their Arabic title as "The Salvation Army".) To those with even the slightest knowledge of the immense labour, organization, training and equipment necessary to build up an army, the idea that a mob of bandits and enthusiasts could, in three or four weeks, be made into an army was ludicrous in the extreme. But the Arab governments were utterly ignorant of military matters, and had never waged a war of their own.

Early in January. the first detachments of the Arab Liberation Army began to infiltrate into Palestine from Syria. Some came through Jordan and even through Amman, but such was the exaltation and enthusiasm of the Arab world that it would have been impossible to prevent them. They were in reality to strike the first blow in the ruin of the Arabs of Palestine.

The greater part of the Liberation Army established itself in the Nablus area. The commander, a Lebanese soldier of fortune, Fawzi al Kaukji, arrived on February 12th, passing through Amman *en route*. Three days later, the Liberation Army attempted an attack on a Jewish colony in the Jordan valley, five miles south of Beisan. The Arabs, almost completely untrained, embarked on a frontal attack which ended in fiasco. Fawzi did nothing more until April 4th, when he attacked the Jewish colony of Mishmar Haemek, east of Haifa. Again the operation was a fiasco. As their morale and enthusiasm waned, the Liberation Army became more interested in looting—often from the Arabs of Palestine.

The fighting around Jerusalem was more determined, perhaps because the Palestinians themselves played a greater part in it—and they were fighting for their land and their homes.

Ever since January 1948, the Arabs had been endeavouring to cut the main road from Tel Aviv to Jerusalem, and thereby isolate the Jewish inhabitants of the Holy City. Where the road from Jaffa and Tel Aviv left the coastal plain to climb the mountains of Judaea to Jerusalem it entered a narrow ravine, the rocky sides of which had been planted with trees. In this narrow defile, known as Bab al Wad, the local Arabs placed obstacles on the road below and then sat on the wooded slopes above, ready to shoot down on Jewish convoys on the road. The peasants of Palestine were joined in this task by parties of bedouins from Trans-Jordan, and later also by detachments from the Liberation Army. Nearly every Jewish convoy to Jerusalem fought a battle. Some were completely turned back—others fought their way through. By March 1948, the British Army had given up the attempt to keep this road open. They themselves proposed, at the end of the mandate, to retire northwards through Ramallah, and this road they kept open while abandoning the direct road to Jaffa and Tel Aviv.

Farther east, the road emerged from the gorge on to the plateau, where it was commanded by the Arab village of Kastal (see the map on page 61). Here fierce fighting took place. The Arabs were led by Abdul Qadir Husaini, a cousin of the exiled Mufti, and a capable and courageous leader. His men were villagers, totally without military training, as was Abdul Qadir himself, and with very few weapons and still less ammunition. I was standing in the street in Ramallah one day in April 1948, when a man arrived in the town in a taxi. He jumped out in the street and shouted:

"The men fighting in Kastal have no ammunition. Has anyone got any rifle ammunition for sale? I will pay cash." He ran through the streets until he had collected about two hundred rounds of miscellaneous ammunition—Turkish, German, British and French. The Arabs, unorganized and undisciplined, fought doggedly. Then Abdul Qadir Husaini was killed and no other leader arose to replace him.

While the battle of the Jerusalem road was in progress, the Irgun and the Stern Gang were invited by the Hagana to capture the village of Deir Yaseen. This village was regarded with suspicion by many Arabs, because it was alleged to be one which co-operated with the Jews. It was not far west of Jerusalem and most of the men worked in the city, rather than as real peasants or farmers. It is claimed that all the young men were away at work when the Jewish terrorists approached Deir Yaseen, but the Jews themselves stated that they suffered casualties when approaching the village. They may have made contact with a party of Arab irregulars—not the villagers. The fact remains that when the terrorists entered the village, they found in it only old men, women and children. These were massacred apparently without exception, and without regard to age or sex. Two hundred and fifty dead bodies were thrown down the village well. The Irgun and Stern at first openly claimed the credit for this massacre. The Jewish Agency officially expressed its horror.

The exact relations between the Jewish Agency (later to become the first Israeli government) and the Irgun and Stern are difficult for a Gentile to unravel. The Agency at this stage was undoubtedly afraid that the terrorists would compete with them for the government of the country after the end of the mandate, and to that extent disliked and feared them. Where, however, the question was one of massacring Gentiles, their relations were more complicated. While the mandate lasted, the Jewish Agency regularly registered its horror at the terrorists' outrages, but it never took action against them for terrorist activities against non-Jews.

In December 1947, a senior British officer in the Arab Legion was one day visiting a British district commissioner in Palestine. A Jewish district officer employed under the district commissioner was also present. They were having drinks in the evening. The UNO partition plan had recently been published. The British officer asked the Jewish official whether the new Jewish State would not have many internal troubles, in view of the fact that the Arab inhabitants of the Jewish State would be equal in number to the Jews.

"Oh, no!" replied the Jewish officer. "That will be fixed. A few calculated massacres will soon get rid of them!" The speaker was not a terrorist—he was a respectable moderate Jewish official, employed in the mandatory government.

Later on, when the problem of the Arab refugees became a tragedy which drew the attention of the world, Jewish apologists claimed that the Arabs had voluntarily become refugees, and that they had not been driven out. It is certainly true that if the Arabs had not left, the Jewish State would have been unworkable. To what extent they were intentionally driven out by "a few calculated massacres", no Gentile will probably ever know.

Two or three years later, I was discussing these events with a prominent English Jew. He expressed incredulity. "You cannot be right," he said. "No Jew would do such things. You have been de-deceived by anti-Semitic propaganda." He was deeply shocked and unable to credit my account.

Most of the terrorists, and a high proportion of the people of Israel, were Eastern European Jews. They were doubtless accustomed to violence. Many of their compatriots had been massacred by the Nazis. Others had been sent to Siberian labour camps by the Russians. They meted out to their Arab victims the same treatment as they had suffered from their persecutors in Eastern Europe.

Although nearly a year elapsed between Britain's announcement of her intention to abandon the mandate and her actual withdrawal on May 15th, 1948, it was only at the last moment that it became clear that the Arab States proposed to fight. The pressure to do so came from Egypt, seconded by Syria.

As soon as it became obvious that fighting would be inevitable, I called on Taufiq Pasha, to ask what financial arrangements the Trans-Jordan government proposed to make to pay for the war. The Press had already reported that the Egyptian Parliament had voted a supplementary sum of £45,000,000 to pay for the impending military operations. To my amazement, the Prime Minister replied that no additional sums could be made available.

"You have your budget allotment for the Arab Legion," he said. "You will have to make the most of that."

"But, sir," I replied, "it is not possible to fight a war on a no-cost basis. The money allotted to pay for an army in peace-time cannot possibly be enough for a war. Egypt has already voted £45,000,000. It just cannot be done without money."

"The people who insist on making this war had better pay for it," said Taufiq Pasha bitterly. He did not specify to whom he was referring. My protests were of no avail.

"It is not that I have the money and refuse to give it to you," he said. "The money does not exist. The Trans-Jordan government has no reserve funds."

I was defeated. I came away perplexed and anxious. What was to be done? The Trans-Jordan government was ordering me to engage in military operations with no money. It simply was not possible.

Meanwhile, only a matter of days remained before May 15th. For the thirty years of the British Palestine mandate—from 1918 to 1948—Palestine and Trans-Jordan had always been entirely distinct countries. There were extremely few roads connecting them. Only three bridges over the Jordan were crossed by metal roads. Of these, the northern two—the Mejama and Shaikh Husain bridges—now led straight into Israeli territory. Allenby Bridge alone was available to enable the Arab Legion to cross into Palestine on May 15th.

Unfortunately, the main road which crossed the Allenby Bridge led straight up into the city of Jerusalem. The only road access either to Ramallah or to Hebron lay through the centre of Jerusalem city where a battle between the Jews and the Arabs would probably be raging. There was, however, a narrow third-class road leading from Jericho up the Jordan valley to Jiftlik, and thence up the gorge of the Wadi Bedran to Nablus. (It was when retiring down this narrow Wadi Bedran track in 1918 that the Turkish army had been caught by the Royal Flying Corps—one of the earliest examples of effective air action against ground troops.) This road up the Wadi Bedran was only wide enough for one vehicle. Moreover it meant that the distance from Zerqa to Ramallah would be 140 miles, instead of 90 miles *via* Jerusalem.

I drove down to Jericho to study this road problem. It would be impossible to operate in Palestine depending only on the Wadi Bedran track for our communications. As I drove up from the banks of the Jordan towards Jericho, the long range of the Palestine mountains faced me like an immense wall four thousand feet high. Throughout most of its length, it consisted of rocky cliffs, slashed through by deep ravines and precipitous stony valleys. Then, as I stared at this mighty wall, I noticed that a spur of the mountains ran down to the plain immediately behind Jericho. I followed this spur with my eye. I thought that I could trace it distinctly, sometimes little more than a knife-edge—a little water-shed between two ravines and their tributaries. As I looked westwards over the little town of Jericho, I could see on the left the rocky, narrow gash in the mountains where the brook Kerith emerged—where Elijah had been fed by the ravens. Slightly to the right, the Mount of the Temptation towered above the palm-trees of Jericho—the mountain which was reputed to be the site of Our Lord's forty days in the wilderness. Between the brook Kerith and the Mount of Temptation, this low spur ran down from the mountains to the plain. Further reconnaissance confirmed that this spur was neither cut by a ravine nor blocked by a vertical cliff, but a good deal of work would be required to make an earth track up it, which would be passable to wheeled vehicles. It emerged on the crest of the mountains at Beiteen, the Bethel of the Bible, where Jacob had laid his head on a stone and had seen his vision of angels ascending and descending the ladder which reached to Heaven.

The budget which had come into operation on April 1st, 1948, had of course been prepared the previous August, when there had been no suggestion of war in Palestine. There was no item in that budget which could possibly be construed as covering expenditure on making tracks up the mountains in Palestine. And Taufiq Pasha had insisted that—war or no war—the Arab Legion must adhere to its peace-time expenditure and financial regulations. Here indeed was a fresh dilemma—but where there is a will, there is proverbially a way. The Arab Legion canteen fund was £4,000 in credit. The money, of course, should have been spent on amenities for the troops—"Christmas" dinners on Muslim feast days, or the purchase of wireless sets for unit canteens. But necessity knows no law. I drew out that £4,000.

There was still the difficulty that Palestine was a separate country until May 15th. The Arab Legion had no right to commence opening roads while the British mandate was still in force. I gave the £4,000 to an Arab officer and sent him over to the mountain villages below Beiteen. The villagers willingly set to work, and two earth tracks from Jericho up to the crest of the mountains were just passable on May 15th. These earth tracks are marked on the map on page 160.

It was only some months later that the Director of Archaeology, Gerald Harding, told me that it was up this same mountain spur that Joshua led the Children of Israel to the invasion of Palestine, after the capture of Jericho. In these days of mechanical warfare and lethal weapons, there seemed to be something extraordinary in the fact that I had chosen for our trucks and armoured cars the same spur of the hills that Joshua had selected nearly four thousand years ago for the migrating tribes and flocks of Israel. *"Plus ça change, plus c'est la même chose."*

Two days before the mandate ended, the Arab League arrived in Amman with the Secretary-General, Abdul Rahman Pasha Azzam. They held various meetings at which I was not present. I was, however, summoned to two interviews with Azzam Pasha. He asked me how many men the Arab Legion had. When I told him that we could send about 4,500 all ranks to Palestine, he expressed disappointment. He said he thought we had far more. He then asked me how many I thought the Jews had. I replied that intelligence reports had spoken of 65,000 men as having received training. I thought they varied considerably in quality. Azzam Pasha again expressed great surprise. He said that he had no idea there were so many.

"However," he added, "I expect it will be all right. I have arranged to get up seven hundred men from Libya."

"Seven hundred is not very many," I remarked. "How are they armed?"

"I have sent a man to buy seven hundred rifles from Italy," replied he.

The conversation passed to the Syrian army. I hazarded the remark that their standard of training was not reputed to be high. The Pasha brushed the remark aside as being trivial.

"Perhaps not," he said, "but what is more important is that they are very enthusiastic."

I was far more surprised, however, when he remarked casually that he would be willing to accept me as commander-in-chief of all the Arab armies. I could not help laughing.

"No, thank you, sir," I answered. "I am unfit to command the Arab Legion—much less several different armies."

I could not understand this amazing remark. Later on, Egypt offered the title of supreme commander to King Abdulla, but when His Majesty requested an order of battle of the Egyptian army, his request met with no reply, nor did he ever receive or despatch a single official letter in his capacity as commander-in-chief. In spite of this, however, the Egyptians (after the *débâcle*) on various occasions attributed the failure of the operations to the incapacity of the royal commander-in-chief. It was only then, more than a year later, that it dawned upon me that Azzam Pasha's extraordinary offer to me was perhaps intended for the same purpose. A foreign commander-in-chief could have been disregarded if the operations went well, but might have proved a useful scapegoat if the war ended in defeat.

In one respect, however, Azzam Pasha's visit gave me immense satisfaction. He told us we need not worry about money. The Arab League, he said, had a war chest of nearly £4,000,000. Trans-Jordan being so poor and so intimately involved in the war, deserved, he thought, to receive all—or nearly all—this sum. At any rate, he said, we could count on him for anything up to £3,000,000. As earnest of his desire to help, he made us an immediate payment of £250,000. This indeed was a load off my mind.

V

On The Brink of War

War is a Divine Institution.   MOLTKE

They who defend war, must defend the dispositions that lead to war, and these are clean against the Gospel.   ERASMUS

V

ON THE BRINK OF WAR

THE fighting in Palestine in the summer of 1948 was a curious imitation of a war, artificially limited by political considerations. The greater part of the military units of the Arab Legion were already in Palestine before the British mandate came to an end, having remained there at the end of the Second World War. The British government, however, decided that they must all leave before the end of the mandate, and the greater part of the three mechanized regiments crossed the Jordan and camped near Zerqa before the end of April. The infantry garrison companies, however, could not all be spared, as some of them were guarding Haifa right up to May 15th. Some of them withdrew from Palestine only a few hours before the end. A weak company of infantry was actually cut off in the Hebron area, where it had been keeping open the road from Egypt. The Jews closed the road from Hebron through Jerusalem to Jericho and this company remained completely cut off from Trans-Jordan and the rest of the Arab Legion until an earth track over the mountains could be opened to establish contact with it once more. The remainder of the Arab Legion, except for a few men in Ramallah, were back east of the Jordan by May 14th.

Yet although the British Army insisted on the withdrawal of the Arab Legion, war had already been in progress in Palestine for several weeks. The Jewish forces were already well across the United Nations partition line and were in occupation of considerable areas allotted to the Arabs, even while British troops were still in nominal control.

The withdrawal of the Arab Legion to the east of the Jordan and the termination of British control left the Arabs of Palestine alone, heavily engaged with the Jewish forces on the morning of May 15th, until the Arab Legion could get back. It was an opportunity of which the Jews failed to take advantage, except in the city of Jerusalem itself. In the rest of the country, the critical three or four days after the end of the mandate passed without any major incidents. Perhaps the Jews were too disorganized, or perhaps all their thoughts and preoccupations were centred on the city of Jerusalem.

*　　*　　*　　*　　*

The problem confronting the Arab Legion on May 14th was a difficult one. The strength provided for in the 1948 budget was

6,000 all ranks, apart from civil police. Of these, about 4,500 were available for operations in Palestine, consisting of the following units:

(a) Four "mechanized regiments" or, in other words, lorried infantry battalions.

(b) Two twenty-five-pounder batteries, each of four guns.

(c) Seven garrison companies. These units were to have been all disbanded by April 1st, 1948, and there was no provision for them in the 1948 budget. We had kept them on, hoping somehow or other to be able to pay for them.

The garrison companies had received no tactical training, and had been employed as guards on camps, stores and vital points, during the Second World War. They were armed with rifles and one Bren gun per platoon. They had no mortars or other weapons.

This was the total of our expeditionary force.

The Arab Legion had hitherto included no "services". It had grown in the period from 1941 to 1948 from a strength of 1,350 to 8,000 in 1945 and back to 6,000 in 1948. Throughout the whole of this period, it was entirely rationed by the British Army, which also provided all medical services, except unit medical officers. Workshops and ordnance services were also carried out by the British Army. On May 14th, therefore, the Arab Legion for the first time commenced to maintain its own services. Supply and transport, hospitals and M.T. workshops all had to be improvised at short notice, in most cases without the necessary tools.

The four regiments (or battalions) were divided into two brigades, each of two battalions. It will be recollected that, during the war, only one so-called mechanized brigade of three regiments was in existence. In February 1948, however, we stopped four garrison companies which were about to be disbanded, and gave them an improvised battalion organization. They camped for three months in Trans-Jordan, but owing to lack of equipment and support weapons, they never really succeeded in doing any regimental training. They were not shown in the 1948 budget, and they also were kept on in the hope that somehow money would be found later on.

A second brigade headquarters was improvised when the four regiments were divided into two brigades. Over the two brigades was an improvised divisional headquarters, which, however, consisted of less than twelve officers. It was a purely tactical headquarters and was commanded by Brigadier N. O. Lash. Arab Legion headquarters was not an operational formation, being a kind of Ministry of Defence plus War Office. It was stationary in Amman.

The eight twenty-five-pounder guns had only been received in

February 1948, and the artillery had three months to form and train. Each battery was commanded by a British officer, and there was one warrant officer, who was an assistant instructor in gunnery. These three officers alone could act as O.P. officers and direct the fire of the guns.

A very weak point in the Arab Legion organization was that it had no reserve. All the men were long-service regular volunteers, but when they left, they did so with no reserve obligations. In its twenty-eight years of life, it had never been contemplated that the Arab Legion would fight an independent war. The British Army had always been in Palestine, and there was, moreover, no potential enemy, the country being surrounded by other Arab States. In 1947, as soon as Britain declared her intention of surrendering the Palestine mandate, the formation of a reserve had been sanctioned and thereafter men were enlisted with a six-year reserve obligation after their colour service. But no such men had as yet completed their colour service when the fighting began in 1948; as a result, every man killed or wounded left a gap in the ranks, which there was no reserve and no reinforcements to fill.

In the same manner, the Arab Legion had never held reserve stocks of ammunition. The British Army had large stocks and was ready to issue to the Arab Legion (on repayment) whenever required. This system was extremely economical from the Arab Legion point of view. It saved us the considerable cost of erection and guarding storage accommodation for ammunition, a costly commitment. The initial cost of buying and building up a reserve of ammunition was also beyond our financial resources.

As soon as it became clear that Britain intended to abandon Palestine, the question of operational reserves of ammunition for the Arab Legion became urgent, but as late as March 1948, it was not foreseen that any war with the Jews would result from partition. The budget for 1947 had of course not included any large capital item for the purchase of ammunition. It did not occur to anyone then that Britain might leave Palestine. The British Army were unable to "give" it without repayment.

When, however, hostilities in Palestine became inevitable, I sent a personal signal direct to the Commander-in-Chief, Middle East, asking him to dispatch immediately to Aqaba, a ship containing certain specified types of ammunition. The C.-in-C. rose to the occasion and the ship was duly loaded and steamed out of Suez for Aqaba. But before it left the Gulf of Suez, an Egyptian launch overtook the vessel and brought it back to port. A convoy of Egyptian army trucks had already lined up on the quay. The ammunition was rapidly unloaded from the ship and loaded into the trucks, which drove off.

I received a signal from the British Commander-in-Chief, informing me that our allies the Egyptian army had seized and confiscated our ammunition. I replied imploring him to send another ship and at the same time urged the Jordan government to protest. The British Army duly loaded another ship, but before it sailed the United Nations had issued a prohibition against the sale of warlike stores to either side. The British Army consequently unloaded the ship once more.

When fighting began, the Arab Legion had a reasonable stock of ·303 ammunition for rifles and Bren guns. In the evacuation, the British Army were unable to clear all their small-arms ammunition and were glad to dispose of it to us. But for mortars and guns we had only first-line ammunition, enough in theory for one battle only. More than a year was to elapse before we again received any ammunition. This one-battle supply of ammunition for guns and mortars had to last us for a year and four months.

As against 4,500 men of the Arab Legion, the State of Israel, proclaimed on May 15th, 1948, was believed to have some 65,000 armed men. Of these, some 300 officers and (presumably) about 4,000 other ranks, had formed part of the Jewish Brigade raised by the British Army during the Second World War. This brigade had taken only a very slight part in the actual fighting in Europe, as its training was only just completed when the war ended. But it had been trained up to a standard at which it was ready to enter battle in Europe. The total number of officers in the Israeli army who had seen previous service in other armies is not known, but many had served in the British, American and French forces. Great numbers of other ranks had also served in the Russian and Polish armies. Their number has been estimated at 20,000.[1] In 1941, when a German invasion of Palestine seemed possible, a number of Jews had also been trained by the British. They were to remain in Palestine as a resistance movement if the enemy were to occupy the country.

The organization of the Jewish forces was complicated. Generally speaking, they consisted of the Palmach and the Hagana. The Palmach ("Spearhead") was the regular army. It was 3,500 or 4,000 strong and consisted of full-time regular soldiers. All, or nearly all, of its members had served in European regular armies, or had received commando training from the British Army. The Palmach was raised in 1941, like the military units of the Arab Legion. Indeed, the two forces were in numbers not unequally balanced. The Palmach consisted of five battalions, the Arab Legion of four, with seven independent garrison companies. Behind the Palmach spearhead came the main Israeli army, which, in

[1] O'Ballance, *The Arab-Israeli War*.

May 1948, may have been 55,000 strong. Its training, quality and armament varied considerably in different units.

Of heavier weapons, the Arab Legion, as already stated, had eight twenty-five-pounders, the use of which was limited by lack of training and ammunition. In the four infantry regiments, obsolete Marmon Harrington armoured cars replaced the Bren-carriers, which are used in British infantry battalions. About fifty of these armoured cars were operational. The Jews had very little artillery to begin with, but a great many mortars. As many of the mortars were made in Israel, they had large quantities of ammunition. The Arab Legion possessed sixteen three-inch mortars with little ammunition. The Israeli forces had perhaps five to six hundred armoured cars, most of them locally made.

In addition to "government forces", there existed the two terrorist organizations in Israel, the Irgun and the Stern. They may have totalled three or four thousand all together. Begin, commander of the Irgun, claims that they were short of weapons, and that otherwise they could have placed many battalions in the field. In 1948, the terrorists "co-operated" with the regular Israeli army. They were not very effective in the field. They distinguished themselves as murderers and raiders rather than as war soldiers.

On the whole, the Israeli forces in May 1948 were probably fourteen times as great as the Arab Legion in numbers. In their heavier armament, the Arab Legion had a few British weapons, with very little ammunition. The Israelis had many locally made weapons with ample ammunition.

The other Arab armies were almost unknown to us. There had been no joint planning of any kind. The Israelis subsequently claimed knowledge of an Arab master plan, combining the strategy of all the Arab armies. No such plan existed, nor had any attempt been made to prepare one.

Before the end of the mandate, an Iraqi staff officer had visited Palestine on a secret reconnaissance. He is alleged to have reported that the task would be a very formidable one, and to have opposed the idea of using force. The Jordan government, aware of the true facts, urged a political solution. But the politicians, the demagogues, the Press and the mob were in charge—not the soldiers. Warnings went unheeded. Doubters were denounced as traitors. It would be wrong to state that no one foresaw the result. A senior British officer from Egypt, who came to Jordan at this time and knew the facts, gave the Arabs a five per cent chance of victory—but all to no avail. The Egyptians, led by Abdul Rahman Pasha Azzam, Secretary-General of the Arab League, were the most insistent on war.

The Iraqi army, in May 1948, committed only one armoured

car regiment and one battalion of infantry. They did their own reconnaissance and decided to cross the Jordan opposite Beisan, in an independent operation.

No information was available to Arab Legion headquarters as to what the other Arab armies proposed to do or the strengths which they had available. The Syrians were believed to be ready to use one brigade. The Lebanese a little more than one battalion. Saudi Arabia was rumoured to have contributed two hundred or three hundred men, who joined the Egyptians.

The Egyptian appeared to be the largest of the Arab armies, but no information on its strength, operations or intentions was ever made available to the Arab Legion. An Egyptian liaison officer, Brigadier Saboor, joined Arab Legion headquarters. He was a charming man and most helpful. He saw all our operational reports, knew our order of battle and visited our front whenever he wished. But not one word regarding the Egyptian operations was ever made available to us, in spite of many requests.

The force used by the Egyptians in May 1948 has been estimated at one armoured unit, six battalions and a regiment of twenty-five-pounders[1]—perhaps ten thousand men. Thus the total Arab forces which took the field on May 15th, 1948, may be estimated as follows:

Egypt	10,000
Arab Legion	4,500
Syria	3,000
Lebanon	1,000
Iraq	3,000

This gives a total of 21,500, as against the Jewish figure of 65,000. All these figures, however, are unreliable. Not only have no official figures been published, but the various protagonists have themselves at different times decreased or increased their numbers, in accordance with their propaganda at any given time, or in any particular country.

It may, however, be worth while to draw attention to certain fallacies. For example, it is the common practice to add up the total strengths of all the Arab armies at home, and compare this with that of the Israeli forces, taking no account of distance.

It is not realized that the distance from Baghdad to Haifa is seven hundred miles, as far as from Calais to Vienna, or London to Berlin. Moreover, by far the greater part of this distance is across waterless desert. To maintain even a brigade group at this long range would be no mean task for an Eastern army, most of which

[1] O'Ballance.

are weak in administrative units. The Egyptian army had a line of communications of two hundred and fifty miles, also mostly desert. Even the Arab Legion had an average of eighty or ninety miles of communication to its front units, and the journey included a descent and a climb of four thousand feet in crossing the Jordan valley.

In addition to the transport difficulties, these distances necessitated the retention of a considerable part of each army at home. Particularly did this apply to the Iraqi army. The mountains of Kurdistan are an unending commitment for the Iraqis. About half their army consisted of mountain units on mules, and could not be used at a considerable distance from home and in flat plains. The Egyptian and Syrian armies also were obliged to leave a considerable part of their forces at home for internal security reasons.

The Jews, on the contrary, were operating in a tiny area, itself criss-crossed by a network of excellent roads built by the British. Most units were operating at only ten or fifteen miles from their depots and homes. This gave ideal conditions for the rapid transfer of forces from one front to another, to strike different enemies in succession. The fact that the Arab armies were converging from widely different directions and from far countries would in any case have made close liaison difficult. In practice, however, not the least attempt at liaison or co-operation was made.

Another common form of comparison was between the civilian populations. Forty million Arabs, it was stated, were attacking less than a million Jews. The parallel is deceptive, for, at any given moment, it was armed strength that counted rather than civilians. No less an authority than Field Marshal Smuts once likened Israel fighting against the Arabs to Britain in 1940 standing up to Germany. The comparison was misleading. Britain in 1940 had virtually no army left, while Germany had several millions of men under arms. In 1948, the number of armed Israelis in the field was always much greater than that of the combined Arab armies attacking them.

But these facts do not justify the lamentable inefficiency of the Arab governments. If the task were so difficult, they should have known this and used other methods. And the facts were known to such soldiers as had taken the trouble to find them out. But the Arab governments were in the hands of politicians, who had never experienced war, and, in the case of Syria and Lebanon, had only two years before received their independence.

When the first independent Syrian government was formed, the President engaged a British Army officer to advise him. He asked for an estimate of cost of a regiment of tanks. To his surprise, the British officer included an estimate for workshops. The President crossed it out. "But, sir," remonstrated the British officer, "your tanks will not long remain in the field if you have no means of maintaining or repairing them." "In the field?" replied the President. "I don't want them in the field! I want them to drive down the Boulevard on Independence Day!"

*　　*　　*　　*　　*

When the Arab Legion originally planned to enter Palestine on the termination of the mandate, no war with the Jews had been visualized. It was proposed only to occupy the central and largest area of Palestine allotted to the Arabs by the 1947 partition. The Jews were most likely aware of this proposal and did not appear to object to it, although they were probably anxious to secure Jerusalem for themselves. But two factors subsequently transformed all these plans. Firstly, the fighting in Jerusalem during the mandate, the arrival of the Liberation Army and the Arab attempts to cut the road to Jerusalem, and eventually the outbreak of Jew-Arab fighting over the whole area—while the British Army was still in the country and the mandatory government in charge. The second factor was the insistence of Egypt and the other Arab governments on invading. These two factors together made the execution of the UNO partition plan impossible, even before the mandate ended.

On the face of it, the Arab governments were largely responsible for the ruin of the Palestine Arabs. By raising the hopes of the latter, they made them intransigent. Had they, on the contrary, restrained the Palestinians and used their considerable influence in UNO to secure a modification of the partition plan, the result for the Palestine Arabs would have been far better.

On the other hand, Jewish forces were already well into Arab territory west of Jerusalem. The commander of the Jewish forces in Jerusalem had proposed the evacuation of Jewish colonies in Arab territory, but the Jewish Agency had refused and had told him to defend them at all costs. It is doubtful, moreover, if the Jews would long have been satisfied with an international Jerusalem. And, finally, even if the Israeli government had decided to abide by the UNO plan, the Irgun and Stern would almost certainly have made trouble. If the Israeli forces had moved forwards on May 15th and the Arab Legion had not crossed into Palestine, the Jews in a very short time would have conquered all Palestine up to the Jordan.

On May 16th, 1948, the day after the Arab Legion crossed the Jordan, the Belgian Consul-General in Jerusalem called on King Abdulla in Amman. He came in the name of the Security Council to protest to King Abdulla against the "unilateral aggression" committed by the Arab armies by their entry into Palestine.

This was the first time since their establishment that the United Nations had denounced an aggressor. With commendable promptitude, they issued their denunciation within a few hours. The only doubt which might have been raised was whether they denounced the right aggressor.

To the Arabs, indeed, Britain appeared to be the original aggressor, for she had introduced the Jews into Palestine by force of arms, against the will of the people. Perhaps an illustration may help to present this viewpoint.

Let us imagine that Hitler won the Second World War and that there were then still two million Jews in Europe. He decided to transfer these to England and ordered the establishment of a national home for them in Kent and Sussex. The German army landed in Britain, imported the two million Jews and protected them by armed force for twenty-five years. The Germans then withdrew. If the British had tried to return to Kent and Sussex by force, would they have been guilty of unilateral aggression?

The problem of the Arab Legion was more complicated, however. Let us assume that Hitler had chosen Kent, Surrey and Sussex as the Jewish national home, but that when the German army evacuated, it was decided that Kent and Sussex would remain to the Jews, but that Surrey would after all remain to the British. It would, however, be an independent State, not united to the remainder of Britain. Let us assume, that when the Germans withdrew, the British in Surrey invited the British Army to enter their country. Would the British Army have been guilty of "unilateral aggression", if it had entered Surrey at the request of its British inhabitants?

Yet this exactly was what the Arab Legion had done on May 15th, 1948. For two months before the end of the mandate, King Abdulla and the Trans-Jordan government had received a stream of letters, petitions, telegrams, deputations and telephone messages, begging them to come to Arab Palestine as soon as the mandate ended. Nobody who witnessed the wild enthusiasm of the reception accorded to the Arab Legion could doubt for a minute that the people had invited them to come.

When the UNO protest was presented to King Abdulla on May 16th, 1948, the Arab Legion had entered the part of Palestine allotted by UNO to the Arabs, at the request of the latter. It had not anywhere even approached the boundary of the Jewish area, as defined in the partition scheme. The Jews, on the other hand, were already in occupation of considerable areas allotted to the Arabs and had begun (as will be seen later) to conquer Arab Jerusalem. But no United Nations protest was addressed to the Jews.

The Jews of course justified their presence in the Arab area by the need for keeping up communications with the Jews in Jerusalem, which the Arab irregulars had been attempting to close. The whole country was already in chaos. To say the least of it, the problem was extremely involved. The unhesitating condemnation of Jordan within a few hours was difficult to justify, whatever the other Arab States may have said or done. For Jordan was an independent State, and had indeed opposed the idea of an invasion by the other Arab States.

*　　*　　*　　*　　*

The question of who was the aggressor in Palestine as a whole may have been open to argument, but there can be no genuine doubt as to who were the aggressors in Jerusalem. A month before the end of the mandate, after heavy fighting between Jews and Arabs in the streets of Jerusalem, the British High Commissioner, General Sir Alan Cunningham, had succeeded in arranging a truce, which was on the whole well observed by both sides. The day before the last British were due to leave, on May 14th, the Consuls-General of the United States, France and Belgium formed themselves into a truce committee, with the object of securing the prolongation of the truce in the Holy City after the end of the mandate. The Jordan government made every effort to prevent fighting in the city, both to avoid the destruction of the Holy Places and also for military reasons. The area which the Arab Legion was expected to defend after the 15th May was approximately equal to the combined areas of the English counties of Kent, Surrey and Sussex. Four battalions would obviously be lost in trying to hold a front 160 miles long against the Israeli army, which would undoubtedly be many times more numerous.

It was therefore most undesirable that the Arab Legion be compelled simultaneously to fight in Jerusalem. The Jews were expert in street fighting and in house-to-house encounters. The Arab Legion would lose much of the advantage of its higher standard of tactical training and mobility. Even if two thousand men (or nearly half the Arab Legion) were put into the city, they would be greatly outnumbered by the Jews. With our slender man-power and no reserves, we could not afford a slogging match.

On May 13th, the last remaining units of the Arab Legion withdrew to the east of the Jordan with the exception of a few men who were cut off in Hebron, the Jews having closed their only escape road, which passed through Jerusalem.

The British High Commissioner left Jerusalem on the morning of May 14th, and with him the last British troops. He had not been gone half an hour before fighting broke out in the streets. The British Army had held a series of massive buildings in the centre of the city, which dominated the remainder. The Hagana slipped into these buildings as the last British soldiers were preparing to leave. The plan had obviously been carefully prepared. Within an hour, the whole city was engaged in heavy fighting. Officers of the

Hagana in specially prepared vans fitted with loudspeakers, drove through the streets calling out in Arabic: "The Jericho road is still open. Fly from Jerusalem before you are all killed!" [1]

The Arab Legion was miles away behind the Jordan. In Jerusalem were only Arab irregulars, with no organization and no leader. Early on May 15th, the Hagana advanced in three columns to clear the Arab part of the city. In the south, they occupied the railway station, the German colony and Allenby Barracks. On the north, they cleared the Shaikh Jarrah quarter and established contact with the Jewish garrison of the Hadassa Hospital and the Hebrew University on Mount Scopus. The remaining Arab irregulars took refuge in the Old City and closed the gates. The Hagana loudspeakers continued to blare out in Arabic: "Take pity on your wives and children and get out of this blood bath." "Surrender to us with your arms. No harm will come to you." [1]

* * * * *

The four regiments of the Arab Legion which were to cross to Palestine on May 15th had been camped in the desert just north of Zerqa. They were to move on May 14th from Zerqa to Amman and thence down the long twisting road to the Jordan valley, four thousand feet below. They were to bivouac on the east bank of the Jordan and cross the Allenby Bridge at dawn on May 15th. The mandate was to end officially at midnight, May 14th–15th, though the British in practice evacuated Jerusalem on the morning of May 14th.

It was a sultry May day, with a haze of dust hanging over the roads. In the city of Amman and in every village along the road, the people were gathered, cheering and clapping wildly as each unit drove past. The flat roofs and the windows were crowded with women and children, whose shrill cries and wavering trebles could be heard above the roar and rattle of the vehicles, and the cheering of the crowds of men beside the road.

The troops themselves were in jubilation. In some trucks, the soldiers were clapping and cheering. In others, they were laughing and waving to the crowds as they passed. Many of the vehicles had been decorated with green branches or bunches of pink oleander flowers, which grew beside the road. The procession seemed more like a carnival than an army going to war.

I joined the column as it passed through Amman and drove with the troops to the Jordan. As I overtook and passed the various units, many soldiers saluted with broad grins. Others called out: "Long live the father of Faris!"

It was evening before the last unit debouched from the moun-

[1] Levin, *Jerusalem Embattled.*

tains into the plain of the Jordan valley, and swung off the road to
its bivouac area. Already thin columns of blue smoke were rising
into the air from scattered bivouacs spread over the plain. Away to
the south, imprisoned between the rocky walls of the mountains of
Judaea and Moab, the Dead Sea lay like a silver mirror. The sun
sank in a golden glory behind the mountains of Judaea, the tiny
spires on the summit of the Mount of Olives showing, far away and
above us, like thin black hairs against the golden sky. Jericho, at the
foot of the Judaean mountains to the west of us, on the other side of
the plain of the Jordan, was already in purple shadow. To the east
of us, the steep wall of the Trans-Jordan mountains was lit up by a
rose-pink glow from the setting sun. Then the grey shadow climbed
swiftly up the mountain face from the valley below. For a few
minutes, the rocky crests were pink in the sun and then suddenly
they also were grey.

Up and down the wide valley of the Jordan, little groups of
camp-fires twinkled in the growing darkness. The country was
dotted with high thorn bushes, which loomed up as black masses on
the dim grey plain. A whitewashed cottage showed up in the
gathering dusk amid the tall bushes. Above this darkening twilight
scene shone an almost apocalyptic glory. Overhead the sky was still
pale blue, fading away in the distance to a light primrose, beyond
the silver surface of the Dead Sea. The whole of the vast expanse of
sky, from the blue overhead to the gold away on the horizon, was
streaked and flecked by strips and fragments of fleecy clouds, dyed
a flaming scarlet by the last rays of the setting sun. The splendour of
scarlets, blues and golds, the grey plain and dark mountains below,
provided a breath-taking picture. Gazing silently at so glorious a
vision, I almost felt as if the Angel Host might, at any moment,
come pouring down from Heaven, in a tumble of white wings, from
out of those scarlet clouds. I could almost catch the first distant
strains of their music, praising God and saying . . . —and suddenly I
remembered that Bethlehem itself lay only a few miles away in
that dark line of Judaean hills.

The air was still and silent. A gentle breeze, fragrant of grass and
moisture, came up from the River Jordan. A boy passed, leading
home a flock of black goats, whose little feet made a chorus of pitter-
patters on the gravelly soil. They passed and all was silent again.
The sky had turned grey, and night was closing down. I got back
into my car and drove up the now deserted twisting mountain road
to Amman.

In Amman, I found that, by some miracle, the telephone line to
Jerusalem was still intact. The King and the government were
receiving heart-rending appeals. The telephone rang every few
minutes. "The Jews are advancing everywhere. The city is in con-

fusion! Everywhere the noise of shooting is deafening! All Arabs will be massacred! For God's sake, come and save us! Come! Come! Quickly!"

The King and the Prime Minister were deeply moved. I begged them to communicate with the Consular truce committee.

"If we move into Jerusalem," I kept repeating, "we shall use up half our army. Then we cannot hold the rest of the country. If the Jews occupy the rest of the country, Jerusalem itself would be out-flanked and fall. So in the end Jerusalem also would fall." The King telephoned the Belgian Consul-General. The truce committee was in touch with both sides, he said. Fighting was admittedly in progress, but the Consuls still hoped to make some progress the next day. The King agreed to wait and hope.

I went back to my house, full of anxious forebodings. I knew the extent of Jewish preparations. I knew that the Arabs had no plan and that there was no co-operation between them. We still had received no ammunition. The people expected us in two or three days to take Tel Aviv. How was I to act amid so much folly?

I fell upon my knees. "O God," I said, "I am not equal to these events. I entreat Thee to grant me Thy help. I beg Thee to direct everything to a good ending—if it be Thy will."

VI

The Battle For Jerusalem

Jerusalem . . . succeeded as it were to the inalienable inheritance of
perpetual siege, oppression and ruin. Jerusalem might almost seem
to be a place under a peculiar curse: it has probably witnessed a far
greater portion of human misery than any other spot upon earth.

MILMAN, *History of the Jews*

VI

THE BATTLE FOR JERUSALEM

THE military situation on the morning of May 15th, when the Arab Legion crossed the Allenby Bridge, was confused. We were aware that the Egyptian army proposed to enter Palestine through Gaza, and that the Syrian and Lebanese armies would intervene from the north. We were in ignorance of the strengths or intentions of these other forces. The Iraqi army, we knew, proposed to cross the Jordan opposite Beisan, with one armoured car regiment and one battalion. The "Salvation Army"—Liberation Army —was engaged in looting all and sundry somewhere north of Nablus.

Part of our 12th Garrison Company was cut off in Hebron. Of our two brigades the 1st, consisting of the 1st and 3rd Regiments, had been allotted the Nablus area, while the 3rd Brigade, consisting of the 2nd and 4th Regiments, was to concentrate at Ramallah. We had deliberately called our 2nd Brigade the 3rd, for purposes of deception. We also had a dummy 4th Brigade headquarters in Ramallah. Each brigade had one battery of four twenty-five-pounders. The Arab Legion had no engineers.

In the north, the 1st Regiment deployed to cover the approaches to Nablus from the west and north. The 3rd Regiment remained in reserve behind Nablus.

The narrow lane leading from Jericho to Nablus was used by both brigades. Empty vehicles returned down the earth track from Ramallah to Jericho. All the deployment went smoothly with no traffic blocks, breakdowns or road accidents. All along the route of the advance, the scenes of the day before were repeated. The inhabitants of every village were in the streets, cheering, clapping and waving. There could be no doubt of the sincerity of the welcome which the Palestinians extended to us.

Meanwhile, throughout May 15th, the truce committee in Jerusalem laboured in vain to prolong the truce for the Holy City. They telephoned desperately first to one side, then to the other. The Arabs would agree to stop if the Jews did this, the Jews would not agree unless the Arabs did that, and the arguing and prevarication went on without result.

The British Army's insistence that every man of the Arab Legion must be out of Palestine by May 14th was diplomatically correct, but, in the light of what was to follow, it may well be argued that it

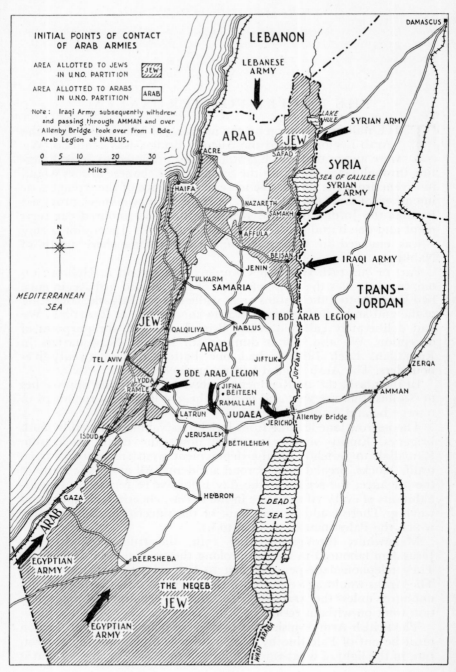

INITIAL POINTS OF CONTACT
OF ARAB ARMIES

AREA ALLOTTED TO JEWS
IN U.N.O. PARTITION [JEW]

AREA ALLOTTED TO ARABS
IN U.N.O. PARTITION [ARAB]

Note: Iraqi Army subsequently withdrew
and passing through AMMAN and over
Allenby Bridge took over from 1 Bde.
Arab Legion at NABLUS.

0 5 10   20   30
Miles

was responsible for the ruin of a large part of Jerusalem. For the truce committee complained that it was unable to find any responsible Arab leader with whom to negotiate, or who could make his orders obeyed. Moreover, the absence of any Arab military force in Jerusalem when the mandate ended, offered to the Jews the irresistible temptation to seize the whole defenceless city and incorporate it into the new Israel. If the British could have handed over the Arab quarters of Jerusalem to the Arab Legion, the truce committee would at least have found a responsible commander to deal with, who could enforce his orders. In addition, the sight of such an Arab force in front of them might have caused the Jews to pause. The truce might have been renewed. Jerusalem would have remained divided as it is today, but the Holy City would have escaped the partial destruction which it suffered, and many Jewish and Arab lives would have been saved.

Such conjectures are of little value. Several weeks before the end of the mandate, a staff officer of the Hagana had said to a senior Arab Legion officer, "We know what you are going to do. We do not mind your occupying the Arab areas of Palestine, on condition you do not interfere in Jerusalem." "And what will happen if we do?" our officer had enquired. "You will only enter Jerusalem over our dead bodies," the Jewish officer had replied. Perhaps the Jews had long beforehand determined to seize the whole of Jerusalem.

The three areas of Palestine which the Arab Legion was charged to defend formed the three districts of Samaria, Judaea and Hebron. They extended from north to south down the length of the Palestine mountains. The Jews were in the flat coastal plain, between the mountains and the sea. The western face of the mountains was steep and rugged, and offered excellent defensive positions. It had frequently happened before in history that the people holding the mountains had successfully resisted invasion from the plains. In the Third Crusade, for example, Richard Cœur de Lion had occupied the coastal plain, but the Muslims held the mountains and Richard was unable to fight his way up. If we had been in Saladin's position, we might have held all the Israeli forces at bay at the foot of the mountains for a long time.

In our case, however, there were already 100,000 Jews in the city of Jerusalem, on the ridge of the mountains. The Holy City was therefore not only of immense moral and religious value. It was the key to the military situation. It was on the very crest of the mountain range. If the Jews captured the whole of Jerusalem, they could drive down the main road to Jericho, and the whole position in Palestine would be turned. If the Jews could seize Allenby Bridge, the Arab Legion in Palestine would be cut off from its base, and would suffer a military disaster. Either, therefore, we must arrange a truce in Jerusalem, or else we must concentrate on holding the city, in which case the remoter rural districts might be lost.

The Jordan government, and particularly the King, appreciated my views and did all that lay in their power to secure a truce. In the last two days of the mandate, confusion was worse confounded by the arrival of the Arab League in Amman, and the claim of the League Secretary, Abdul Rahman Pasha Azzam, to speak in the name of all the Arabs.

Throughout May 15th and 16th, the truce committee struggled on with gradually diminishing hopes of success. Every now and again there was a glimmer of hope. The Jews had agreed to cease fire and observe the truce—but in every case the report was again contradicted. Once we were told that the Jewish Agency had refused responsibility for renewed Jewish attacks, which, they alleged, were being carried out by dissident terrorist groups.

And all the time those anguishing telephone calls had continued—"Save us! Help us! They are up to the Jaffa Gate! They have occupied the Shaikh Jarrah! They are scaling the walls of the Old City! Save us! Help us!"

Throughout the Palestine troubles, Western Europe and America showed an annoying propensity for reading lectures to the Arabs, constantly warning them that the West regarded Jerusalem as the Holy City. Nobody seemed to realize that Jerusalem was as precious to the Arabs—Muslims and Christians alike—as it was to the West.

While our two brigades were deploying in the Nablus and Ramallah areas, two of our independent infantry garrison companies (the 1st and the 8th) moved up the direct road which led from Jericho to Jerusalem. On May 16th they reached the Good Samaritan Inn, half-way up. On May 17th they occupied the Mount of Olives, which overlooks the city from the east.

Meanwhile the battle was increasing in intensity inside the Holy City. On May 15th the line of division between Jews and Arabs had run approximately north and south. North of the Old City, the line coincided with the boundary between the Jewish and Arab quarters. Mea Sherim was a Jewish quarter, Shaikh Jarrah and the Musrara were Arab. In the centre, the Arabs defended the walls of the Old City. But behind this general line, there were two islands of Jews (see the maps on pages 112 and 122). The first and most formidable enclave was built on Mount Scopus, the ridge which ran north-east of Jerusalem, to the Mount of Olives. On it stood the massive stone buildings of the Hadassa Hospital and the Hebrew University, which dominated all that part of Jerusalem which remained in the hands of Arabs. The second Jewish enclave was within the walls of the Old City.

The ancient walled city of Jerusalem almost coincides in area with that captured by Titus. Inside the walls, the old houses are built one on top of the other and the narrow streets are in many places only wide enough for three people to walk abreast. The Old City is built on a ledge of hillside sloping down from west to east and the majority of the streets climb up and down in steps beneath the tall overhanging buildings. The inhabited portions of the Old City were divided into four quarters. Of these, the largest were those on the north occupied by the Muslims and Christians respectively. The southwest corner of the city contained the Armenian quarter, while between it and the Temple area was the Jewish quarter.

Harrat al Yahood, or the Jewish quarter, had long been inhabited by religious Jews, quiet peaceable folk, content to spend their gentle lives within the hallowed walls of David's City, the low hill of Mount Zion above them on the west, the sacred precincts of the Temple a few hundred yards below them to the east.

These two Jewish enclaves presented, in more peaceful times, two contrasting aspects of Jewry. On Mount Scopus the massive blocks of the Hadassa Hospital were fitted with all the latest installations of modern medical science. Two hundred yards beyond the hospital, crowds of bare-headed Jewish students trooped into the University buildings. Meanwhile, in the Jewish quarter of the Old City, rabbis, with long white beards and bent with age, clung faithfully to the law and traditions of Moses. Pale young men, their hair hanging in corkscrew ringlets beside their hollow cheeks, hastened timidly along the narrow streets.

The truce committee appealed to both sides to cease fire on the evening of May 15th. The Arabs agreed, but in the evening firing did not cease. Again the truce committee struggled with the telephone. Firing would cease on the morning of the 16th. But instead of ceasing, the noise became louder. On the 15th the shooting seemed to be limited to rifles and machine guns, but early on May 16th Jewish mortars came into action and the rattle of machine-gun fire was interrupted by the loud crumps of mortar bombs bursting in the Arab quarters.

Meanwhile, Amman also was tense. The King looked tired and hollow-cheeked. The Prime Minister was suffering under the strain. Every hour or two, the telephone would ring. The Jews were attacking the Old City. They had scaled the walls on Mount Zion. They were up to the New Gate. The Jerusalem police were holding the Citadel. An Irish Roman Catholic priest, Father Eugene, was manning the walls. Thus hour after hour the news came through, always followed by the same appeals. "Save us! Our ammunition is finished! We can hold on no longer! Where is the Arab Legion? *Min shan Allah*! For God's sake! Save us!"

On May 17th, I drove across the Jordan valley soon after dawn, and up the newly opened earth track from Jericho to Beiteen. Divisional headquarters was in a shallow valley behind the village, their vehicles scattered here and there in the fields and along terraced vineyards. We had cleared the Jewish colony of Kolundia north of Jerusalem. The people of Nebi Yaqoub had themselves withdrawn to the city. As I stood, truckloads of Arab villagers went by. The men were singing loudly, clapping their hands and firing off rifles into the air. The trucks were laden with furniture, windows, boxes and every kind of plunder. They had obviously been looting the captured colonies of Nebi Yaqoub and Kolundia.

"Why don't they keep their bullets for the enemy?" growled a passing soldier, as the trucks bumped on down the lane to the accompaniment of a new fusillade of rifle shots.

The situation in Jerusalem was still obscure. Perhaps the truce committee might yet succeed. Meanwhile, however, the road from Tel Aviv to Jerusalem was open. Weapons, reinforcements and convoys could reach Jewish Jerusalem from the coastal plain. Whatever might happen in Jerusalem, it did not appear advisable to allow yet more Jewish troops and weapons to reach the city. If they cleared the city, they could drive on down to the Jordan and cut off the whole of Palestine. We accordingly sent our newly raised 4th Regiment to Latrun, to prevent the Jews from using the main road to Jerusalem.

At half-past eleven in the morning, while with divisional headquarters, I received the following signal from Amman: "His Majesty the King orders an advance towards Jerusalem from the direction of Ramallah. He intends by this action to threaten the Jews, in order that they may accept a truce in Jerusalem."

Half an hour later, at noon on May 17th, a further and longer telegram arrived. It read as follows:

"From the Minister of Defence to Glubb Pasha. His Majesty the King is extremely anxious and indeed insists that a force from Ramallah with artillery be sent to attack the Jewish quarters of Jerusalem. The Jews are attacking the gates of the Old City in order to break into it. An attack on the Jews would ease the pressure on the Arabs and would incline the Jews to accept the truce for Jerusalem. The Belgian Consul has been here and His Majesty has gathered from him that such action on our part might frighten the Jews and make them less obstinate. His Majesty is awaiting swift action. Report quickly that the operation has commenced."

The situation was one requiring a decision. Was there still any hope of a truce for Jerusalem, which alone would give us some chance of defending the rest of the country? If we intervened in the city, would the chances of a truce be increased or decreased? Could the Jerusalem Arabs hold on for another twenty-four hours? We moved our outposts a little nearer Jerusalem in the north. A troop of two twenty-five-pounders took up a position from which they could support an advance if ordered. The 1st and 8th Infantry Companies were still on the Mount of Olives east of Jerusalem.

Next morning, May 18th, I was back at divisional headquarters once more. The atmosphere there was less tense and emotional than in Amman, with that telephone constantly ringing. The King was haggard with anxiety lest the Jews enter the Old City and the Temple area, with the Great Mosques. His father, the late King Husain of the Hejaz, was buried in the precincts, a fact which added a note of personal anguish to the King's religious and political hopes and fears.

The Arab defenders of the Old City seemed to be failing. The Jews were reported to have broken into the Old City by the Zion Gate and to have made contact with the Jewish quarter inside the walls. This operation had been carried out by the Palmach, the spearhead of the Israeli army. The Jews were now everywhere using mortars and armoured cars as well as small arms. A major battle had developed in Jerusalem. There seemed to be little hope now of saving the Jerusalem truce.

The whole responsibility seemed to rest on me alone. I had opposed both the King and the government for forty-eight hours, in the hope of obtaining a truce. If, by any chance, the Old City should suddenly fall, all would be lost. Something must be done at least to prevent that. It was still early morning. I decided to use one of the infantry companies then on the Mount of Olives.

The morning was still bright and cool when the 1st Infantry Company filed down the lanes from the top of the Mount of Olives and past Gethsemane, the same gardens through which Our Lord was led away by the soldiers to His Passion. They crossed the little valley of Kidron, past the tomb of the Virgin Mary, then up the slope where Saint Stephen was stoned outside the walls. Passing through the gate, they entered the walled city. An hour later they were manning the walls from whose site, nearly nineteen hundred years ago, the Jews themselves had cast their darts at the advancing legions of Titus.[1]

The arrival of the one hundred men of the Arab Legion on the walls of the city revived for a moment the courage of its Arab defenders. I calculated that their presence would suffice to check the Jewish attack on the walls for a few hours. The Palmach were driven out. They had entered by blowing in the Zion Gate; now the

---

[1] The walls from which the Arab Legion fought were not strictly speaking the same walls, in the sense of being the same stones. However, through a great part of their length, they were more or less on the same site as those from which the Jews resisted the Roman attack.

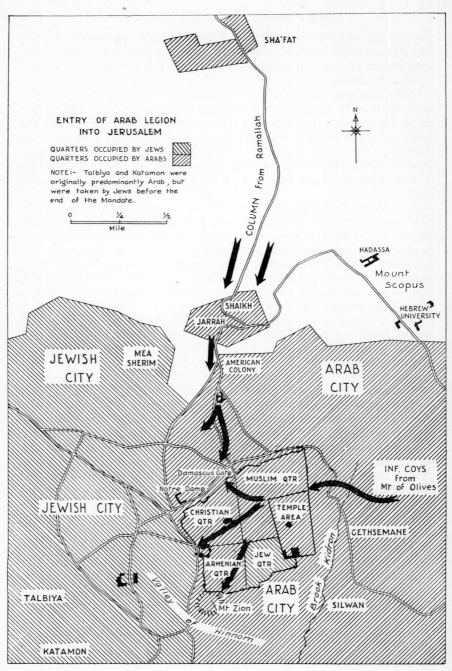

ENTRY OF ARAB LEGION
INTO JERUSALEM

QUARTERS OCCUPIED BY JEWS
QUARTERS OCCUPIED BY ARABS

NOTE:- Talbiya and Katamon were
originally predominantly Arab, but
were taken by Jews before the
end of the Mandate.

0   ¼   ½
Mile

SHA'FAT

COLUMN from Ramallah

HADASSA
Mount
Scopus

HEBREW
UNIVERSITY

SHAIKH
JARRAH

JEWISH
CITY

MEA
SHERIM

AMERICAN
COLONY

ARAB
CITY

Damascus Gate

Notre Dame

MUSLIM QTR

JEWISH CITY

CHRISTIAN
QTR

TEMPLE
AREA

INF. COYS
from
Mt of Olives

GETHSEMANE

ARMENIAN
QTR

JEW
QTR

Valley of

Mt Zion

ARAB
CITY

Brook Kidron

SILWAN

TALBIYA

Hinnom

KATAMON

gate was blocked once more with heaps of rubble and coils of wire. But one hundred men of the Arab Legion could not control the situation in a city which contained 100,000 Jews. Moreover, the Old City was an island in the centre of Greater Jerusalem. The Jews were in occupation of Shaikh Jarrah—soon they would attack the Mount of Olives, and then the Old City would be cut off from the east and surrounded. There seemed to be no alternative but to break into Jerusalem from the north, clear the Shaikh Jarrah and establish contact with the Old City. Then a continuous line of defence could be built up across the city and the Jewish offensive halted.

On the other hand, to commit one or more of our four operational regiments to street fighting in Jerusalem would make it impossible to hold the partition plan boundary elsewhere. The 4th Regiment was already engaged with the enemy at Latrun. The 1st and 3rd Regiments were required to hold Samaria. The 1st Regiment was already engaging a Jewish force at Qalqiliya. In addition to this, our men would be at a disadvantage in street fighting. They were all bedouins or peasants—some had never been in a large city. They became confused in a maze of streets, but for them the fields and mountains, by day or night, held no terrors. The Jews, on the other hand, were almost entirely city dwellers, and they were also fighting in a city with every stone of which they were familiar. Thus to throw our troops into the city would certainly mean heavy casualties, which could not be replaced, and would involve abandoning Samaria. I had asked divisional headquarters to consider a plan for intervening in Jerusalem with a brigade of infantry, but after working on the plan, they reported that it was not feasible. Two battalions would be lost in so large a city.

In the evening I left divisional headquarters and drove down the soft earth track which we had opened from Beiteen to Jericho. At every curve of the track, the heavy following cloud of chalky dust curled over the car in a choking white fog. The sun was already setting behind me, and the sky in front of me to the east was a pale yellow over the rocky mountains, beyond the Jordan. All of a sudden I made up my mind. There was no use any longer hoping for a truce in Jerusalem.

As soon as I reached home, I went to my room and wrote out the signal myself. "I have decided to intervene in force in Jerusalem." Divisional headquarters were ordered to attack Shaikh Jarrah at dawn on the 19th and break through, so as to establish contact with the Old City. The 8th Infantry Company on the Mount of Olives was to move forward across the Kidron and join in the defence of the Old City. The die was cast.

*   *   *   *   *

The operation which I ordered was one which, I suspect, no regular soldier would have undertaken. The four battalions of troops which we possessed were already scattered over an area of two thousand square miles. To collect a force in any way commensurate with the task would have meant abandoning all the rest of Palestine, and would in any case have taken two or three days, by which time the Jews would have captured all Jerusalem.

It was already dark when my signal was sent off from Amman and I had ordered the attack for the next morning. Isolated detachments would have to be collected during the night and commanders would have no time to reconnoitre, to arrange a fire plan or to co-ordinate with the artillery, which was represented by four twenty-five-pounders.

In spite of these difficulties, the Arab Legion attacked the Shaikh Jarrah at 3.45 a.m. on the morning of May 19th. The force which advanced into the city of Jerusalem consisted of one company of infantry and one squadron of armoured cars, four six-pounder anti-tank guns and four three-inch mortars. The artillery in support consisted of four twenty-five-pounders which, however, were only allowed to fire a few rounds at intervals, owing to shortage of ammunition. The total force which moved forward into Jerusalem consisted of about 300 men. Before them lay a great city which contained 100,000 Jewish inhabitants. Thus was eventually carried out that operation, which had been reported impracticable for an infantry brigade.

Four years later, I stood on the rising ground overlooking Shaikh Jarrah with a distinguished British general, and described to him what happened on that cloudless May morning in 1948. "Well I'm blessed!" he exclaimed. "Why, the whole thing was lunacy! That isn't soldiering!" "Anyhow, it worked," I said. "I advise you not to try a show like that a second time," he replied.

The Jews had for weeks been erecting concrete defences in their quarters of the city. Streets had been closed by concrete walls and road-blocks, and concrete pill-boxes and machine-gun emplacements, trenches and barbed wire covered every approach. On the Arab side, of course, nothing had been done—there were no leaders, no plan and no organization.

Our armoured car squadron led the advance but was held up by a concrete road-block in a cutting before reaching the first houses. It was half-past seven in the morning before the attacking force completed the occupation of the Shaikh Jarrah suburb and cleared it of the enemy.

A further massive concrete road-block was encountered round an S-bend in the road leading out of the Shaikh Jarrah quarter into the city. Major Slade, who was commanding the attacking column, dismounted from an armoured car under heavy Jewish mortar fire to examine this obstacle and was immediately wounded. Eventually, a six-pounder was dragged up under heavy fire and blew the road-block away.

The task of the Arab Legion column was to advance down the axis of the Ramallah–Jerusalem road, fight its way through the Arab residential quarter of Musrara to the Old City, and establish contact with its defenders.

Immediately on the right of the road, and about 300 yards from it, lay the Jewish quarter of Mea Sherim. The column advancing from Shaikh Jarrah to the Old City, therefore, was doing a lateral advance across the front of a built-up area of houses, entirely manned by Jews. The Shaikh Jarrah quarter was separated from Musrara by an open space 250 yards wide, which was commanded by fire from Mea Sherim at a range of 300 yards. The column had to cross this space under heavy fire, after which it became involved in the build-ings in the Musrara quarter.

By 2 p.m. the armoured car squadron at the head of the column had reached the Damascus Gate and had established contact with the Old City. Armoured cars are of no use in the dark in narrow streets, and they were withdrawn from the Musrara at nightfall. However, after a day of battle, the main column was firmly estab-lished in Shaikh Jarrah.

It had already been necessary to start borrowing troops from Samaria, and a company from the 1st Regiment reached Shaikh Jarrah during the morning. Another company arrived during the day. The total force holding Shaikh Jarrah was therefore now about five hundred men. Two garrison companies, giving a total of two hundred men, were holding the Old City. The withdrawal from the Musrara had broken communication between Shaikh Jarrah and the Old City.

A Jewish writer, who was in Jerusalem at the time, described the Arab Legion attack as follows:

"The Legion launched the attack with four batteries of heavy guns, smaller artillery units, two infantry regiments, and large units of tanks and armoured cars. After the artillery barrage, they advanced in massed strength, tanks in the lead. . . ."[1]

*   *   *   *   *

Our intervention in Jerusalem had been carried out at only a few hours' notice, with the result that divisional headquarters had been obliged to use several sub-units which happened to be at hand. The operation had been sufficient to halt the Jewish offensive and to clear Shaikh Jarrah. With heavy fighting still going on, it was

[1] Levin, *Jerusalem Embattled.*

essential to withdraw these odd companies, collected in haste from here and there, and to hand over the defence of Jerusalem to a single tactical unit. The 3rd Regiment from the Nablus area was the only unit available. Its use in Jerusalem meant the virtual abandonment of Samaria, an area of more than one thousand square miles, which would have to be defended by the 1st Regiment alone, with no artillery. It had been precisely to avoid such a necessity that we had made so many efforts to secure a truce in Jerusalem.

From May 15th to 21st, the 3rd Regiment had been held in reserve in an olive grove behind the town of Nablus. For six days, with the radio reporting battles all over Palestine, the soldiers had fretted and cursed in inaction. I had visited them myself two days earlier, and had been greeted with eager questions—"When can we fight?" The adjutant had taken me aside and begged me to allow the regiment to move up into battle.

At half-past four on the evening of May 21st, the brigade commander arrived in their olive grove and told the regimental commander that they were to move to Jerusalem. The C.O. called the officers to a conference and in a few minutes the glad tidings had spread through the regiment. Men lying listlessly beneath the olive trees, or sitting in circles on the ground round the inevitable coffee-pots, suddenly leaped to their feet.

"What? What was that? Jerusalem? *Al hamdu l'Illah!*—Praise be to God! What did you say? O Hamed! O Qasim! O Abdullah! Jerusalem! We are going to Jerusalem! We are going to Jerusalem!" Broad smiles, cries of joy, men ran hither and thither—the bivouac beneath the trees was suddenly in a hum of joyous voices.

On Friday, May 21st, the regiment moved southwards from Nablus, along the road to Jerusalem, and halted to cook a meal at Jifna. (A Seleucid army had once bivouacked here before attacking Jerusalem, in the days of the Maccabees.) The officers assembled at 6.30 p.m. for final orders. The first wild enthusiasm had by then somewhat subsided, at least among the officers, who realized something of the problem of breaking into a city of 170,000 inhabitants (100,000 of them hostile) with a weak battalion and no first-line reinforcements to replace casualties. At ten o'clock at night, the regiment climbed back into their vehicles and the column moved forward towards Jerusalem once more.

An improvised hospital had been established in the boys' school in Ramallah and was already full of wounded from the Jerusalem fighting, most of them from the 2nd Regiment. The classrooms were hot and airless, even though all the windows were open. Outside, the green crops were standing knee-high in the fields. Muffled thuds were borne on the still air from the south, where the battle raged in Jerusalem. There were no beds and the wounded lay on stretchers or on the bare floor, some in wide-eyed silence, others tossing and turning uneasily. Somehow the news reached these hot dark classrooms on that May evening—"The 3rd Regiment are going through to fight in Jerusalem." A rumble of vehicles became audible down in the little town. Silent figures slipped out from beneath their blankets and tiptoed from the rooms. As the trucks passed through the town in the darkness, shadowy figures called to them. "I am Muhamad Hareithan, 2nd Regiment. Take me with you, brothers!" When the medical officers came on their rounds the next morning, half of their patients had vanished. They were battling once more through the streets of Jerusalem.

The 3rd Regiment halted and got out of their vehicles just before the village of Sha'fat. They scattered in the fields beside the road and quickly lay down and fell asleep in the green corn. Their trucks turned round and drove back to park at Kolundia. It was a still, warm May night and the moon shed its white light over the hills and fields and the still figures of the sleeping soldiers. The silence was broken only at intervals by distant crumps, and the faint rattle of machine-gun fire in Jerusalem. Every now and again a little breath of wind sighed across the fields of standing corn.

There were only two hours of sleep; at 2.30 a.m. the regiment was moving again. This time the infantry were on foot, plodding slowly forward beneath their equipment, weapons and ammunition. At 3.50 a.m. the 3rd Regiment crossed the start line. It was already growing light and as they moved over the open ground towards Shaikh Jarrah, they came under fire from both flanks, on the east from Hadassa and on the west from the Jewish quarters of Jerusalem.

The infantry passed through the Shaikh Jarrah quarter, already held by our troops, and re-emerged into the open space which divided that suburb from the city. The noise increased to an inferno. The Jews opened up with all their weapons. The mortar platoon of the 3rd Regiment came into action, adding to the deafening noise of the Jewish mortars and machine guns.

عزيزي غلوب باشا

ان موقع القدس عند العرب والمسلمين ونصارى العرب معلوم وان وقوع اي كارثة بها لاهل البلاد من اهلها كان بقتلوا او جلوا امر عظيم الثمر علينا ولا يزال الوقت ليس بالمايوس منه وانى امر بلزوم الاحتفاظ بما هو تحت ايدينا اليوم البلدة القديمة وطريق اريحا اما بواسطة القوة التي في نواحي رام الله او بارسال قوة من الاحتياط العام هناك ان ارجو ان تنفذوا هذه الاوامر بكل سرعة يا عزيزي

توقيع عبد الله

My dear Glubb Pasha,

The importance of Jerusalem in the eyes of the Arabs and the Muslims and the Arab Christians is well known. Any disaster suffered by the people of the city at the hands of the Jews—whether they were killed or driven from their homes—would have the most far-reaching results for us. The situation does not yet give cause for despair. I accordingly order that everything we hold today must be preserved—the old City and the road to Jericho. This can be done either by using the reserves which are now in the vicinity of Ramallah or by sending there a force from the general reserves. I ask you to execute this order as quickly as possible, my dear.

(*signed*)   ABDULLA.

A personal letter from King Abdulla to the author illustrating His Majesty's intense anxiety over the fate of Jerusalem. (See page 110 for his telegrams on the same subject.)

VII

Not English But Angels

O be favourable and gracious unto Sion: build thou the walls of Jerusalem.
Psalm li. 18

Speak ye comfortably to Jerusalem, and cry unto her, that her warfare is accomplished.
Isaiah xl. 2

VII

NOT ENGLISH BUT ANGELS

THE 3rd Regiment was enlisted from the nomadic tribesmen of the desert—men of unquestioning faith and simple and straightforward outlook. Speaking of the hermits of the desert, Origen, the early Christian historian, wrote: "They dwelt in the desert where the air was more pure, the Heaven more open and God more familiar." As I looked at the 3rd Regiment, I involuntarily thought of these lines.

The issues at stake in this battle seemed to them simple and obvious. The Holy Places of Jerusalem were being attacked. They would save them—a duty imposed alike by their belief in God and their devotion to the army.

The portion of Jerusalem immediately north of the walls of the Old City is called the Musrara quarter. It was largely dominated by a block of massive buildings which constituted the Monastery of Notre Dame de France. This vast fortress had been held by a party of Arab irregulars since the end of the mandate but was captured from them by the Jews before the Arab Legion entered the city. To recapture it was the 3rd Regiment's final objective. Unfortunately the leading company of these bedouin soldiers, inexperienced in street fighting, went down the wrong street, and the anti-tank guns had disappeared in an unknown direction and could not be found. The regiment seemed to have vanished completely into the smoke and dust of the city.

For several hours, the regimental commander crouched in a house in Shaikh Jarrah, amidst a frequently deafening roar of mortar bombs, endeavouring to obtain news of his regiment. At last, at about noon, a message was received to say that 4 Company had reached the walls of the Old City at the Damascus Gate. 2 and 3 Companies were still not located. The city between him and the Damascus Gate was covered by a haze of dust and smoke. The C.O. decided to look for his regiment in person, and regimental headquarters, accompanied by a troop of armoured cars, moved forward into the streets of the city.

In this remarkable operation, the regimental headquarters in their vehicles drove up a long street which ran southward between houses to the Old City. The right-hand side of the street seemed to be occupied by Jews, to which the whole column thus presented its flank. At length this running the gauntlet came to an end and regi-

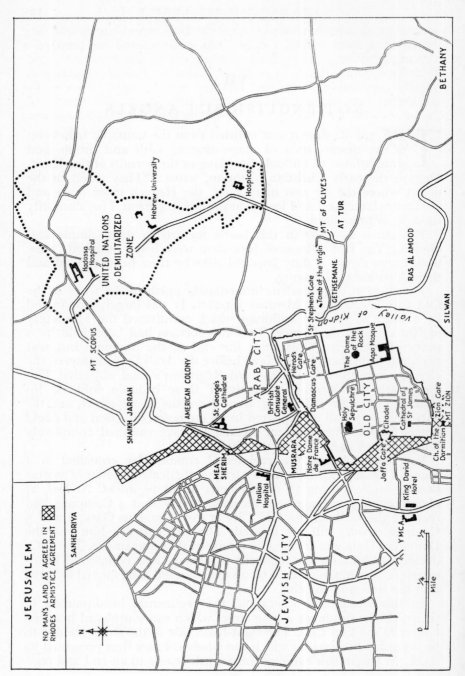

JERUSALEM

NO MAN'S LAND AS AGREED IN
RHODES ARMISTICE AGREEMENT

SANHEDRIYA

N

MT SCOPUS

SHAIKH JARRAH

UNITED NATIONS
DEMILITARIZED
ZONE

Hadassa
Hospital

Hebrew University

Hospice

AMERICAN COLONY

St. George's
Cathedral

British
Consulate
General

ARAB CITY

MEA
SHEARIM

MUSRARA

Italian
Hospital

Notre Dome
de France

Damascus
Gate

Herod's
Gate

St Stephen's Gate

Tomb of the Virgin

GETHSEMANE

MT of OLIVES

AT TUR

RAS AL AMOOD

Valley of Kidron

SILWAN

The Dome
of the Rock

Aqsa Mosque

OLD CITY

Holy
Sepulchre

Citadel

Cathedral of
St James

Zion Gate

MT ZION

Ch. of the
Dormition

Jaffa Gate

King David
Hotel

JEWISH CITY

YMCA

0   ¼   ½
Mile

BETHANY

mental headquarters arrived outside the Damascus Gate, where they broke into some empty houses and endeavoured to prepare a defensive position. They found themselves in the front line, confronting the massive walls of Notre Dame de France, which completely overlooked them. No infantry was in sight. Two of the armoured cars, the martial ardour of their crews still unsatisfied, had driven out into the square outside the Damascus Gate, and were engaging the frowning walls of Notre Dame with their two-pounders and machine guns, thereby adding to the already deafening battle noises in regimental headquarters.

The British Consulate-General was at the time situated outside the Damascus Gate, and immediately behind the houses in which the 3rd Regiment had established themselves. Jewish fire from Notre Dame which missed the 3rd Regiment passed over or into the British Consulate. The Consul-General was not a little distressed at this situation and addressed a note to regimental headquarters requiring them to move elsewhere—an order not easily complied with in the heat of battle.

And heat it was. Not only from shot and shell, but from the blazing sun in the parched city, crumbling into dust beneath the shells and bullets. Somehow, tea was produced and mugs passed from hand to hand, while dusty smoke-grimed faces grinned and nodded in appreciation.

At last, at 2 p.m., the rifle companies were located. Guides were sent to lead them to the defensive positions which they were to occupy in the narrow streets beneath the high walls of Notre Dame from which the Jews dominated the whole area. The troops, including the afternoon and evening approach march, had been on the move nearly continuously for twenty-four hours and had been fighting in the city beneath a scorching sun for nearly twelve. They had suffered casualties which, in the absence of trained reserves, we could ill afford. This day also was killed the commander of the 3rd Rifle Company, Lieutenant Aid Idailim. Fifteen years before, he had come to me in the desert—a boy, in his early teens—to enlist as a trooper in the Desert Patrol. We had served together for a great part of these fifteen years—or had frequently met—while he developed into what his commander had described as a most charming and gallant officer. Now he lay still beneath a blanket in the shelter of a half-wrecked building in the dusty streets of Jerusalem. Only stretcher cases were with difficulty evacuated. Those wounded who could still stand up refused to go. "It was the same story all the way through," wrote a British officer. "Those with minor wounds concealing the fact and carrying on with a song in their hearts."

But though the men were still cheerful, they were terribly tired, and the commanding officer wondered whether it would be possible to wake them if the enemy attacked during the night. But this day of battle had probably exhausted the Jews likewise, for the night passed quietly.

Sunday morning, May 23rd, dawned without further incident beyond spasmodic shelling and bursts of machine-gun fire. Meanwhile, although a loose defensive line had been established across the streets from the Old City to Shaikh Jarrah, the Jews still held Notre Dame. It was time to complete the task which had been left unfinished the day before.

The attack began at 12 noon, supported by two six-pounder anti-tank guns and four three-inch mortars. The noise was soon deafening once more, but a pea-shooter would have been as effective as a six-pounder against the walls of Notre Dame. The Holy Catholic Church seemed to have built for eternity.

The infantry made slow progress through the narrow streets and houses, towards the towering walls of the monastery. Brick walls, little back gardens, and a rabbit warren of streets and buildings were surroundings to which the bedouins were unaccustomed. Some of the houses were occupied and had to be cleared of the enemy room by room. Five men claiming to be Russian Christians were found crouching in one house and were captured and sent back. This incident indeed speaks highly for the self-control of the soldiers, for the Russians were found in the house from the windows of which Aid Idailim had been shot the day before.

As they drew nearer to the walls of Notre Dame, the infantry came under enfilade fire from the Italian Hospital, another large block of buildings about 300 yards to the north. Fire was also being directed on them not only from Notre Dame, but from the roof of the French Hospital behind it. Our own infantry were already too close beneath the walls of the monastery to allow of any shelling by mortars or artillery to support them. The action continued indecisively throughout the afternoon and night. At seven o'clock on the morning on May 24th, a report was received that 4 Company were in Notre Dame. They had indeed entered the grounds of the monastery, but immediately came under heavy fire from the windows of other wings of this great block of buildings. At the same time, a party of Arab irregulars, who were occupying a house to the right rear of the regiment, saw figures moving in the garden of the monastery and opened a heavy fire on our leading infantry.

In spite of this double fire, however, the infantry clung to the garden, and at nine o'clock, ten men actually got into the buildings, found themselves cut off and nearly surrounded and were obliged to fight their way back to their comrades in the garden. By five o'clock on the afternoon of May 24th, the casualty situation was serious. Of the 200 infantry who had set out to attack Notre Dame at noon on May 23rd, nearly half were either killed or were stretcher cases—the walking wounded as usual remained in the line. 4 Company had lost all its officers and N.C.O.s except one. At five o'clock on the afternoon of May 24th, the attack was abandoned.

Throughout three days of battle, the officers and men of the 3rd Regiment had fought with unflagging bravery and smiling cheerfulness. Always thirsty, dirty, and even hungry, they fought on with unwearying energy and determination. "No troops would have done better and most not as well," wrote their commanding officer, Bill Newman—and he was an Australian and knew something about fighting-men. The Jews referred to May 24th as a "bloody day of slaughter".

Two days later, I visited the 3rd Regiment headquarters at the Damascus Gate. We stopped beneath the eastern walls of the Old City outside St. Stephen's Gate. It was on this spot that the saint was alleged to have been put to death by the Jews nearly two thousand years ago. I climbed into an armoured car, and a soldier slammed the door, calling out cheerfully, "In God's safe keeping." The armoured car chugged up the hill to the north-east corner of the Old City walls, by the Stork's Tower. We rounded the corner of the walls and turned west, three hundred yards to Herod's Gate. The driver closed the vizor in front of him, leaving only the narrow slit to see through. There was another three hundred yards to cross from Herod's Gate to the Damascus Gate—this time in full view of Notre Dame at a range of about four hundred yards.

"We place our confidence in God," shouted the driver as we topped the rise beyond Herod's Gate. The Jews had apparently been on the alert for this very thing. Within a matter of seconds, a deafening staccato of machine-gun fire broke out all around us. Where it all came from or where it was going it was impossible to tell from inside the armoured car, peering as best we could through the narrow slits. The armoured car rattled and lurched over the road—once a smooth tarred surface, now strewn with stones and debris. Then the car swung sharply to the right and I bumped my head against the steel side of the armour beside me. We rattled into a side street, and a row of houses shut out the view of Notre Dame. Suddenly the deafening rattle of machine-gun fire ceased and complete silence ensued. The armoured car pulled up. The heavy door swung back and a smiling soldier called out, "Praise God for your safety."

I clambered out of the armoured car into a narrow street. Several vehicles were parked on the pavement close beneath the houses. Tired and dirty soldiers saluted. A notice above an open door announced that it was the Ferial Hotel.

I walked up a narrow staircase to a landing on the first floor. The building was strewn with dust, fragments of broken stone and glass. The windows towards Notre Dame had been blocked up with sand-bags, so that the rooms seemed half dark when one came into them from the bright sunlight. "This way, sir," said a voice, and I found myself in a small room, destitute of furniture except for two packing-cases upside-down and an iron bedstead, possibly a relic of the hotel.

Bill Newman, a little drawn and unshaven, was sitting on a packing-case. Others came in. Mugs of tea appeared. The rattle of machine guns began again. Ghazi al Harbi, a veteran of thirty years of war up and down Arabia, entered and shook hands. The tears ran down his wrinkled and weather-beaten face as he begged for per-mission for one more try to take Notre Dame. "We'll do it this time, O father of Faris," he assured me. But I vetoed any more attempts. The 3rd Regiment was now only five hundred strong, spread out over a thousand yards of streets and houses. Behind them there was not a single soldier from Jerusalem to Amman. Without a man in reserve and with ammunition which would scarcely be enough for another fortnight's fighting, we could not afford to embark on adventures, particularly in street fighting. The Old City had been relieved, the Holy Places saved, and a thin defensive line established across the city. The Jewish drive to seize the whole of Jerusalem had been stopped short. With this we must be content. Outside Jerusalem, thousands of square miles of country allotted to the Arabs under the partition scheme must also be defended, almost without troops, ammunition or money. How was it to be done? How long might the fighting last? We could not at this stage afford to lose precious trained soldiers merely to capture one block of buildings. "We will take it later on," I said. "If God wills," replied Ghazi quietly.

While this fighting was going on in Jerusalem, the infantry com-pany cut off in Hebron had joined a number of Arabs from neigh-bouring villages and had captured the suburb of Ramat Rahel, south of Jerusalem. The Arabs then dispersed to loot, with the result that the Jews reoccupied the suburb while the Hebronites had gone home with their plunder.

Meanwhile, inside the Old City, the two Arab Legion companies were fighting a double battle. On the one hand, they lined the city walls on the west, from the Zion Gate, through the Citadel (built on the site of Herod the Great's towers) and round opposite Notre Dame to the Damascus Gate. From the Zion Gate to the Citadel the walls were built on the top of a glacis, overlooking the valley of Hinnom. To assault this sector of the wall was therefore extremely difficult. Throughout the rest of the front, however, buildings came right up to the walls on the outside. In the north-west corner of the Old City particularly, the walls were completely overlooked by higher buildings on the outside, particularly Barclays Bank and the Convent of Notre Dame. But although these buildings enabled the Jews to overlook the walls and snipe the men holding them, the actual masonry face of the walls in most places still presented an obstacle to a Jewish infantry attack.

There was something strangely moving to me in seeing my own soldiers on these historic walls, their rifles thrust through mediaeval loopholes, shaped long ago to the measurement of cross-bows.

Whatever the Press might say in Europe or America, no doubts assailed the troops who peered between the crenellations of those ramparts. By turning their heads, they could see the Dome of the Rock and the Aqsa Mosque from which the Prophet Muhamad had ascended to Heaven. If the soldier were a Christian, the dome of the Holy Sepulchre lay only a few hundred yards behind him, while over the city roofs he could see the gardens on the Mount of Olives, where his Lord had suffered in anguish before His Passion.

These men had no doubts. They were fighting and dying—*fi sabeel Illah*—in the path of God.

One morning during this early fighting in Jerusalem, I was summoned to the palace. The King had that hollow sunken expression which he wore in times of anxiety.

"I conjure you by God to tell me the truth," he said. "Can we hold Jerusalem, or will the Jews take it?"

"If God wills, they will never take it, sir!" I answered.

"I want you to promise me," the King went on, "that if you ever think the Jews will take Jerusalem, you will tell me. I will not live to see them in the Holy Places. I will go there myself and die on the walls of the city."

"If God wills, that will not happen," I said.

*   *   *   *   *

Before the entry of the Arab Legion, the Palmach on Mount Zion had broken into the Old City and made contact with the Jews inside it. They brought eighty men as reinforcements, and renewed supplies of rations and ammunition. When the Arab Legion arrived in the Old City a few hours later, the Jewish forces were obliged to withdraw and the Zion Gate was blocked up again. The Jews remained on Mount Zion outside the city walls.

On the top of Mount Zion stood the massive Church of the Dormition, the tall belfry of which overlooked a great part of the Old City from the south, just as Notre Dame overlooked it from the north. High in the belfry of the Dormition, Jewish snipers looked down on the lanes and open spaces within the walls, and took a heavy toll of civilians who were careless enough to come into view.

At the time of Christ, Zion had been within the city walls. Tradition places here the house of Caiaphas, where Our Saviour was brought after His arrest. Here also is shown the place where St. Peter heard the cock crow and went out and wept bitterly. Nearby is the reputed site of the Upper Room, where Our Lord partook of the Last Supper. The whole of the Old City was built in mediaeval style, houses crowding on top of one another, and cellars and courtyards sinking down into the earth. The only thoroughfares were narrow streets, often paved in steps. In many places the narrow bazaars were roofed over, while the cobbled alley-ways were spanned by bridges of flying buttresses connecting houses on opposite sides of the street. Sometimes these bridges carried whole buildings, so that the narrow lanes passed through tunnels under blocks of houses. Old Jerusalem, moreover, is built on several small hills divided by little valleys, with the result that the narrow paved streets often enough climb up and down in steps, or in steep irregular slopes between overhanging houses.

Of all the narrow, tortuous and overcrowded quarters of Old Jerusalem, the Jewish quarter was perhaps the most crowded and ramshackle. A pedestrian threading his way through the narrow alleys caught glimpses through half-open doors of tiny inner courtyards, crowded with women and children, with staircases going up to rooms above, and steps going down to subterranean dwellings below. The whole of this teeming rabbit-warren lay on top of the spoil and rubble of centuries—perhaps rather millennia—of poor human dwellings. Throughout most of Palestine, the Jews were not Jews only—they were also (some predominantly) Germans, Russians, Poles or Americans. The ugly blocks of concrete flats, the cheap, slightly flashy and rather jerry-built modernism, testified to the cosmopolitan origin of the inhabitants. But the Jewish quarter of the Old City was essentially Jewish and nothing else—the ancient Judaism of the Law and the Prophets, the Middle Ages and the Ghetto.

So gentle, poor and old-world a community was but ill-fitted for fighting. Indeed, if its members had been left to themselves, the destruction of the Jewish quarter might have been avoided. But before the end of the mandate, a force of Hagana had been slipped into the city, and a fight became inevitable.

While the Arab Legion were defending the ancient walls of the city against repeated Jewish attacks from the outside, they were themselves besieging the inhabitants of the Jewish quarter within the walls. The total strength of the Arab Legion inside the walled city was about four hundred all ranks, of whom the greater part were manning the walls and repulsing Jewish attacks from without.

PLATE 2

Villagers of Sha'fat with the armoured car captured from the Jews

PLATE 3

In the Citadel of Jerusalem, a platoon of the Arab Legion falls in, preparatory
to manning the walls of the Old City. Herod the Great and Godfrey de Bouillon
both held castles on the site of the Citadel

PLATE 4

Morning inspection in the Citadel of Jerusalem

PLATE 5

A platoon of the Arab Legion manning the ancient walls of Jerusalem,
"their rifles thrust through mediaeval loopholes, shaped long ago to the
measurement of cross-bows"

Only about a hundred men could normally be spared to fight in the Jewish quarter, though they were assisted by a small number of irregulars and civilian police.

It was sometimes possible to use a three-inch mortar, but most of the time the fighting consisted of slow progress from house to house. A hole was knocked in the wall, a hand-grenade thrown in, and then the troops crawled through into the room, weapons at the ready. Then, slowly and carefully, they opened the door into the next room, and followed from room to room, down dark passages, up and down tiny steps and staircases, out into courtyards and down into cellars. Sometimes explosive charges were laid against a dividing wall and detonated. The Arab Legion in those days was still armed with Piats (an abbreviation for Projectors, Infantry, Anti-Tank). The original role of this weapon was to incapacitate a tank at short range, but it was equally effective against masonry, and for breaching walls from one room or house into another.

The lanes in the centre of the Jewish quarter were dominated by the domes of two synagogues, which overlooked all the streets and houses in the vicinity. From these domes, Jewish snipers fired constantly at the surrounding quarters, whenever an Arab showed himself. The Arab Legion commander attempted at first to spare the synagogues, and when fire was opened from them, he warned the Jews that he would be obliged to fire. After the passage of forty-eight hours without a reply, fire was opened on the synagogues also.

The Jews in the Old City resisted the Arab Legion for ten days, withdrawing gradually from house to house in the mediaeval rabbit-warren of the Jewish quarter. On May 28th, white flags appeared on the roofs of the little group of houses into which the Jews had withdrawn. Two old rabbis, their backs bent with age, came forward down a narrow lane carrying a white flag.

There were about 1,500 Jewish prisoners captured in the Old City, including women and children. About three hundred of these were Palmach or Hagana soldiers, not residents of the Jewish quarter. They had been sent in to fight, some before the end of the mandate, and some after May 15th, but before the arrival of the Arab Legion, when the Jewish forces had scaled the walls of the city and for a few hours had re-established contact with the Jews within.

I visited the Old City shortly after the surrender. The prisoners had been moved to a large modern building, just beyond the limits of the Jewish quarter. On the first floor of this building, many large rooms were occupied by them, while others sat or lay in the wide stone corridors. Men and women lay side by side, most of them looking pale and tired. A few had limbs bandaged owing to minor wounds. Arab orderlies and soldiers of the Arab Legion moved here and there through the crowd of Jews, speaking a word, giving a drink of water or talking among themselves.

As I came up the passage, the soldiers smilingly came to attention with a clatter of weapons. Two or three Jews came forward and shook hands. None of them had any complaints to make. A few attempted to produce documents testifying to their good characters in the days of the British mandate.

Two days later, the Hagana prisoners and young Jews of military age were transferred to a prisoner-of-war camp east of the Jordan. The old men, women and children were sent across the lines to the Jewish side, under the supervision of the Red Cross. As the sad little caravan straggled through the narrow alley-ways of Old Jerusalem, Arab Legion soldiers were seen to be helping along the sick and the old women, and carrying their little bundles of possessions.

"Well, that is what I call chivalry," exclaimed a European Press correspondent, as he watched the convoy hobble past.

It was our answer to Deir Yaseen (see Chapter IV, page 81).

The Iraqi army, as has been already mentioned, had decided to carry out an independent crossing of the River Jordan east of Beisan with a force of one armoured car regiment and one infantry battalion. They had met with considerable opposition and were unable to cross.

In view of the fact that the Arab Legion had been compelled to fight in Jerusalem and that Samaria was consequently denuded of troops, I proposed to the government that the Iraqi army take over Samaria. The proposal was agreed to and the first Iraqi elements began to arrive in Nablus on May 22nd. The 1st Regiment, Arab Legion, less one company which had been borrowed for Jerusalem, had hitherto been the sole garrison of Samaria. On May 22nd, it handed over to the Iraqis and moved south to the Ramallah area.

On that day, the Arab Legion had been heavily engaged in Jerusalem, while the 4th Regiment was in action against the enemy at Latrun, blocking the road from Tel Aviv. These two battles were sixteen miles apart. The intervening country was fortunately mountainous, but one metalled road crossed it from the Jewish side. This road ran from Abu Ghosh, on the main Jerusalem–Tel Aviv road to the village of Biddu and thence to Ramallah. (See the map on page 169 for sites of Biddu and Radar, which is mentioned below.) If a Jewish column had advanced up this road, our positions would have been penetrated. A company of 2nd Regiment had been posted to close this possible enemy line of approach.

The key to this sector was a single, very high hill north-east of Abu Ghosh, where the British forces had erected a radar station during the Second World War, and which had consequently always since been called "Radar". The Israeli army held this hill, with seventy or eighty men. It had been enclosed in thick barbed-wire entanglements by the British. The only approach from our side was by a narrow track which ran along a knife-edge ridge of hill, and had been blocked by a concrete road-block and mine craters. A group of large Jewish settlements lay about two miles to the west of Radar hill.

One company of the 1st Regiment was detailed to take this hill, supported by the battalion three-inch mortars. The company was equipped with hand wire-cutters, as no other means of cutting the wire were available. Two twenty-five-pounders were borrowed for the occasion but were able to fire for only nine minutes during the advance of the infantry, owing to lack of ammunition.

The operation began at 3.45 a.m. on May 26th. The infantry advanced with great gallantry in face of considerable automatic and rifle fire. The first man up to the wire cut his way through, a few yards from the Jews. Just as he jumped the last strands and ran forward, he was shot dead, but another and another were behind him. The 1st Regiment broke into the enemy's position at 4.30 a.m. The enemy left thirteen dead. Others were shot as they escaped towards the Jewish colony to the west. The garrison was about equal to the attacking force. The 1st Regiment suffered three killed and sixteen wounded, most of them in a sharp hand-to-hand engagement in the enemy's position. Both the company commander and his second in command were wounded. The company commander reached the enemy's position on all fours, dragging a broken leg behind him. He refused to be evacuated until the position was captured and consolidated. The wire was found to have consisted of a double apron fence, with four coils of Dannert wire between them. The ground outside the wire was liberally sprinkled with anti-tank and anti-personnel mines.

Israeli forces in the days following made repeated attempts to retake Radar, and suffered heavy casualties, but never succeeded.

* * * * *

The Jewish advance in Jerusalem having been halted, the centre of gravity of the fighting was now moved to Latrun, where the 4th Regiment was holding the end of a mountain spur, just where it ran down into the coastal plain. This spur, which was crowned with the ruins of a castle believed to date from the Crusades, overlooked the main road to Jerusalem. All the efforts of the Israeli forces were henceforth devoted to attacking Latrun and opening the road to Jerusalem.

From May 25th onwards, the intensity of the attacks was increased.

At 3.30 a.m. on May 25th, the Israelis attacked with a brigade of infantry, supported by a heavy three-inch mortar bombardment and high-velocity guns of about seventeen-pounder calibre. The engagement lasted for several hours before the enemy withdrew. The 4th Regiment counted six hundred dead Jews in front of our positions. Many weapons and much equipment was abandoned by the Israelis in their withdrawal, including 200 rifles, and a quantity of Bren guns, Vickers and three-inch mortars.

In further enemy attacks, 300 Israelis were killed, and then again 300. On another occasion, 200 enemy dead were counted. The Israelis employed great numbers of mortars at Latrun, and each attack was preceded by a considerable bombardment. The mortars and bombs were manufactured in Israel. They made a deafening noise on detonation, but it gradually became apparent that they inflicted few casualties. The fragmentation of the bombs was not good. Instead of breaking up into large numbers of fragments, the case only broke up into a few large pieces. These repeated heavy attacks continued until the end of the fighting on June 11th.

Throughout all the fighting, the Arab Legion proved itself the master of the battlefield. Never on any occasion did it lose a position. Never was it obliged to retire. In attack, the only failure was that of the attempt to seize the Convent of Notre Dame in Jerusalem. I myself forbade further efforts, in order to avoid casualties.

But if the Arab Legion was undefeated in the field, in the air it did not exist. We did not possess a single aircraft. It is true that Israel at that time had neither bombers nor fighters, but several aircraft were over our positions every day on reconnaissance. To be able to examine and photograph the enemy's positions from the air completely unmolested is a great help to generalship!

While these engagements had been in progress, the other Arab League armies had also been in action. The Egyptian army had advanced almost unopposed to Isdud, and here had halted. The Iraqi army had taken over the Samaria district from us.

On June 3rd, the Israelis staged a major operation to capture the town of Jenin. They were repulsed with heavy casualties by the Iraqis.

On the sector from Qalqiliya to Tulkarm, the Iraqis were only twelve to fifteen miles from the sea, and in some places only six miles from the main north-to-south road from Haifa to Tel Aviv. The Israelis would obviously have been extremely sensitive to any Iraqi advance in the coastal plain, but the Iraqi commander in every case found himself unable to attack.

The Syrians had begun on May 16th by capturing the town of Samakh, on the Syrian border at the southern end of the Dead Sea, but they then halted and no further operations resulted. The

Lebanese captured the village of Malikiya, on the border of Lebanon, but advanced no farther.

After June 1st the Arab advance seemed to be petering out. The Arab Legion was holding a front of seventy miles with four battalions which had already suffered nearly twenty per cent casualties. Ammunition, excepting ·303, was running very low. Frequent attempts had been made to co-operate with the Egyptian army, but without success.

On May 22nd an Egyptian army column reached Bethlehem from Beersheba and Hebron, and demanded to take over the sector. It will be recollected that a weak company of about a hundred men of the Arab Legion has been cut off in Hebron on May 14th. This company had been holding the Bethlehem sector as best it could for a week, assisted by the local villagers. We had no desire to become involved in a quarrel with the Egyptians, and therefore secured the consent of the government to withdraw our company across the hills east of Bethlehem, and leave this sector to the Egyptian army.

Politically the Egyptians showed no desire to co-operate in the Hebron area. On the contrary, they seemed to wish to penalize any of the inhabitants who showed any regard for Jordan, and to desire to organize pro-Egyptian political parties in the district.

On May 30th orders were received from the British government that all British Army seconded officers were immediately to leave their commands and withdraw from battle. The reason for this order was that the Security Council, at a meeting on May 29th, had adopted a British resolution calling for a four weeks' truce in Palestine. The resolution called upon all governments to refrain from sending war material to either side. There was no mention in the resolution of the recall of nationals of other countries who might be fighting. The British government, however, presumably bowed to pressure in New York to withdraw its regular officers from the Arab Legion. We were surprised to hear after this incident that a colonel in the United States army, David Marcus, was commanding the Israeli forces which were attacking Latrun.

We were not a little aggrieved at the action of the British government. As has already been related, Mr. Bevin had agreed to the proposal for the Arab Legion to occupy on May 15th the areas of Palestine allotted to the Arabs. It is true that it was not then anticipated that there would be a war, but Trans-Jordan had done everything in its power to avoid war. Circumstances beyond the control of the Trans-Jordan government had involved us in war, namely the decision of the other Arab governments to invade, and the attempt made by the Israelis to seize all Jerusalem.

A military treaty of alliance existed between Britain and Jordan. Certainly this treaty contained a clause to the effect that nothing in it should prevent either government from carrying out its obligations to the United Nations. But as the Jordanians said—"What is the use of a treaty if either side can abandon its ally in a crisis, on the grounds that UNO wishes her to do so?"

The withdrawal of the British officers was a shattering blow. They included all operational staff officers, both the brigade commanders, and the commanding officers of three out of the four infantry regiments, and all the trained artillery officers. The artillery having only been raised three months before, none of the Jordanian officers were yet really competent to direct the fire of the guns.

The Arab Legion was in a peculiar position. From 1926 to 1939, it had been employed as a gendarmerie. It was only expanded into a military force in 1940. The most senior Jordanian officer in the army, therefore, had only eight years' service. The few senior officers in the Arab Legion had spent most of their lives on police duties and were untrained for war. The British regular officers were therefore the keystone to the whole edifice in 1948. The simultaneous departure of them all might well have caused a complete collapse. The Arab Legion, which was still everywhere engaged in desperate battles, was saved from disaster by the spirit and enthusiasm of the troops.

Personally I was not affected by the order, not being a regular officer. Shortly afterwards, however, I received a communication from the British Legation. This document referred to a British law, known, I understand, as the Foreign Enlistments Act. It appeared that under this Act, I might be exposed to a charge of having taken service, "without His Majesty's cognizance", with a foreign Power engaged in war. I replied that if His Majesty had no cognizance of my presence in Jordan, His Majesty must be suffering from loss of memory. I have no doubt that the British Legation tore up my reply and put it in the waste-paper basket. Perhaps it was just as well.

*   *   *   *   *

The village of Bethany, the home of Lazarus, Martha and Mary, still nestles in a tiny valley under a spur of the Mount of Olives. This spur, still planted with olive trees, shuts out Bethany from a view of the Holy City. Over this spur ran the path by which Our Lord every day came and went to Jerusalem, when He stayed with His friends in Bethany. Where the path tops the spur after climbing up from Bethany, the Holy City suddenly comes into view, a mile away across the valley of Kidron. It was when Our Lord topped this rise and suddenly came into view of the Temple and the City, that He pronounced His lamentation over Jerusalem:

"O Jerusalem, Jerusalem, thou that killest the prophets, and stonest them which are sent unto thee, how often would I have gathered thy children together, even as a hen gathereth her chickens under her wings, and ye would not!"

The motor road from Bethany now follows the contours round the spur instead of climbing straight up and over it, as did the track two thousand years ago. The modern tourist, however, still comes suddenly into view of the city as he rounds the spur, just as the little group of Galilean peasants did when they topped the rise so long ago. At the bend of the road round the spur, there is now a group of houses which the Arabs call Ras al Amood, or Head of the Column. From here, an uninterrupted view of the Old City lies before the observer.

It was at this place that I met Lash one day at the end of May, to discuss the situation in Jerusalem. We stood on the crest of the spur between the walls and houses. Above us, on our right, the hillside was covered with graves, stretching up to a group of monasteries on the crest of the Mount of Olives. Beneath our feet lay the deep gorge of the Kidron, with the village of Silwan (the old Siloam) climbing down the side of the gorge below us.

Straight opposite, at our own level across the narrow gorge, were the walls of the Old City, the Temple area, the Dome of the Rock and the Aqsa Mosque, on the site of the Temple of Solomon. Over all this scene, so venerable with ancient history, shone the glorious Mediterranean sun in a cloudless blue sky.

We sat beside the road and talked. We had carefully left our vehicles farther down the road, as Head of the Column was in view of the enemy from Talpioth, just south of the city. Suddenly there was a deafening crash behind us in the cemetery. Fragments of gravestones flew into the air, and hummed over our heads, hitting the walls of the houses with a whack. We took no notice—it is undignified for commanders to run away. A few minutes later, another followed suit—crash—whirr! We tried to talk on, in even, uninterested voices. I heard an orderly nearby whisper to another soldier: "*Ma yahimhum!*—They don't care!"

A third followed—then fortunately an interval. We took advantage of it.

"Perhaps we could talk better in that house opposite," I said in a casual voice. "It would be rather undignified to be hit on the head by a tombstone."

We sauntered across the road, trying to appear unconcerned. The house opposite was a coffee-shop. The owner was still doing business in spite of the Jewish mortars. He came forward obsequiously.

"Welcome! What are your orders?" he said.

"Have you a room with a table?" we asked.

"Certainly, sir! Certainly." He bustled along in front and showed us upstairs. The first floor had been let as a flat, but the family had not such calm nerves as the coffee-shop man. They had obviously decamped in a hurry. There were tables and chairs in the sitting-room.

"This is better," we said. "We can spread out our maps on the table."

"I'll bring you coffee," said the proprietor briskly, running downstairs.

We resumed our talk, leaning over the map on the table. Suddenly there were two more crashes in quick succession, one on the road a few yards from where we had been sitting. We continued to talk, but it was difficult to concentrate—one was tempted to listen for the next one coming. The coffee-man reappeared with cups on a tray.

"God destroy their houses!" he remarked with a grin. "They must have seen you. They watch this bend in the road."

"Sorry," we said. "We seem to have got you into trouble."

"It does not matter," he answered cheerfully, pouring out the coffee. "God curse their fathers!"

There was another crash, followed by screams and lamentations from the street below. We jumped up and looked out of the window. An old woman driving a donkey had been hit. The soldiers ran out and picked her up. Blood was flowing from the calf of one of her legs. The troops comforted her—just as British troops would do in similar circumstances.

"It's all right, Auntie! It's only in your leg! Try to stand up. There you are! A flesh wound only. Don't be frightened!"

The old lady continued to scream.

"Come along, Auntie! We'll tie it up for you. Khalaf, where's your field dressing?"

"Come in here, Auntie. Sit down and we'll bandage it for you!"

Two stalwart young men took her by the arms and carried her into the coffee-shop.

We drank our coffee and finished our talk.

"I suggest we meet somewhere else next time," I said.

"Not a bad idea," said Lash.

I jumped into my car and drove back towards Bethany. My escort followed me in a Land Rover. As we rounded the spur, I heard the distant rat-tat-tat of a machine gun, and overhead a faint *whit— whit—whit*. We were round the spur into Bethany and out of sight. Looking back, I saw that the Land Rover had stopped. I ran back to see what the matter was. A young soldier was sitting up, with a dark stain on his battle-dress blouse under the armpit.

"Badi has been hit, sir," said the sergeant. "It sounded like a Vickers gun. It must be a very long-range shot."

NOT ENGLISH BUT ANGELS

In the middle of the little village of Bethany is the Convent of the Resurrection. It is a convent of the Russian Orthodox Church, belonging to White Russian nuns and monks. Unexpectedly, the convent is directed by two Englishwomen, Mother Mary and Mother Martha—assumed names, Bethany names, of course. They are women with sweet patient faces who devote themselves to the care of the poor, and the upbringing of orphans and destitute children.

"We will go into the convent," I said.

We rang the bell. An old Russian woman opened the door.

"Mother Martha?" I said enquiringly. She motioned us to come in. Then, seeing the soldier soaked in blood:

"*Meskeen! Meskeen!*"[1] she said compassionately, hobbling off.

Soon Mother Martha arrived, capable and businesslike. The blood-soaked sleeve was ripped off, to show a flesh-wound in the arm.

"*Al hamdu l'Illah!*" said the sergeant, "God be praised! It's in the flesh! You'll be all right!"

We all echoed "Praise be to God." Mother Martha bustled around. An Arab girl brought the inevitable coffee. A Russian monk with a long white beard hobbled in—he had been a general in the Czarist army once, whispered Mother Martha.

"Thank you so much, Mother Martha," I said. "I'm sorry we gave you so much trouble."

"We'd do anything for your men," said Mother Mary. "Before the British left, they advised us to escape from Bethany. When they had gone, and the Jews began to bombard, the poor people in the village were so frightened. When your men came, we were safe again. They are always so polite, so courteous and so grateful."

"In 1915, I nursed the soldiers in Russia," said Mother Barbara, who was a White Russian. "They were like your men, so simple, so brave and so polite."

"Since they have come," concluded Mother Mary, "it is as though we had been surrounded by hosts of angels."

"*Non Angli sed angeli!*" I said, laughing.

*　　*　　*　　*　　*

Across the road from the Convent of the Resurrection, there was a little Greek convent and church with a surprisingly bright little dome painted royal blue. The first-line transport of the companies fighting in Jerusalem had been parked behind the convent. Father Theodosius was here in charge, a little Greek priest with a thick brown beard, and a gentle sweet smile. Greek Orthodox priests in Palestine are often criticized as having low standards of education. It is surprising, however, how often one finds them to possess these

[1] Miserable, unfortunate.

kind gentle faces. The foolish things of this world are so often more valuable than the wise.

Father Theodosius accepted every kind of refugee in his little church and convent—Muslims and Christians alike. They filled all the rooms and passages. Peasant women, sitting on the ground with the few little possessions they had saved, nursed their babies on the steps of the church. Swarms of children ran through the crowd and chased each other up and down the stairs. The good Father patted them on the head. "Poor people!" he said, in the few words of broken Arabic which he had mastered.

We must see his church, he insisted. Inside the door lay a large stone. It was the very stone, he explained, on which Our Saviour sat when He came to Bethany to raise Lazarus from the dead. He was sitting on this stone, resting at the entrance to the village, when Martha came out to meet Him.

Inside the church, Father Theodosius showed us a picture of the stoning of Stephen, to which he appeared greatly attached. He pointed out the walls of Jerusalem.

"Always Jews," he said. "Jews always make trouble." He shook his head sadly and sighed.

*   *   *   *   *

Curiously enough, a short time afterwards, I visited the village of Anata, north of Jerusalem. (Anata was the village of the Prophet Jeremiah, in the country of the tribe of Benjamin, a small area north of Jerusalem extending up to the modern Ramallah.) I sat in the village guest room and talked to the headman and the villagers. We spoke of the fighting, and of how the Arab Legion had saved Jerusalem when the Israelis were about to occupy it all. Others added praise of the discipline of the troops and how they never interfered with civilians, were always polite and never looked at women.

"By Allah!" said one, "if an Arab Legion soldier sees a woman, he looks away. They are more modest than the girls."

"*Rijalkum malaika!*" ("Your men are angels!") said the headman of the village solemnly, as though summing up the debate.

I was struck with the fact that this old Muslim peasant should use the identical words which I had heard from the English abbess of the Convent of the Resurrection.

He nodded his head slowly, repeating the phrase:

"Your men, sir, are angels."

VIII

The First Truce

For what can war but endless war still breed?   JOHN MILTON

VIII

THE FIRST TRUCE

WHILE these events had been going on in Palestine, the United Nations had been active at Lake Success. On May 28th, 1948, Count Folke Bernadotte, a member of the Swedish royal family, had arrived by air in Cairo in the capacity of United Nations mediator between Arabs and Jews. On May 29th, the Security Council passed a resolution calling on all the combatants to agree to a four weeks' truce.

On June 1st, Count Bernadotte arrived in Amman, and I saw him for the first time. I was immediately impressed by him. He was a man on whom I knew at once that I could rely. He would never betray a trust, I was convinced. I have not met many men like that. (Another was Field-Marshal Lord Gort—an honest and brave man, who, one felt, would always stand by a subordinate.)

Bernadotte was tall, slender, pleasant and earnest, with a quiet wit of his own. The United Nations colours are blue and white, which happened to be the same as those of Israel. When Bernadotte first landed at Jerusalem airport, he was wearing a blue-and-white United Nations arm-band. Lash was there to meet him.

"I am sorry to see, sir," Lash remarked facetiously, "that you are wearing an arm-band in the Israeli colours."

"Ah," said Bernadotte, "but I do not wear my heart on my sleeve. My heart is of a strictly neutral tint."

From June 1st to June 11th, Bernadotte worked untiringly for a truce. The principle of the truce was that neither side should gain any military advantage thereby. In other words, if fighting were to recommence after the truce, the relative strengths of the two sides would be identical with that before the truce. This condition made it essential that neither side be allowed to bring in either personnel or material during the truce. The Israeli government insisted that immigration must continue. The Syrians and Egyptians objected. The problem which affected us most was that of Jerusalem. There was a shortage of food and water (and possibly ammunition) in Jerusalem. Bernadotte explained that, during the truce, sufficient food and water must enter Jerusalem to enable the inhabitants to live on it for four weeks. Thus at the end of the truce, the stocks in Jerusalem should be the same as they were at the beginning. The Red Cross was to supervise the convoys entering Jerusalem from the coastal plain. The Arabs suspected, perhaps with some justice, that the Jews would import into Jerusalem much more food than they would eat in the four weeks. It was certainly noticeable that, whereas before the truce all the efforts of the Israeli forces were concentrated with frenzy on trying to open the road to Jerusalem, when fighting recommenced after the truce, they seemed much less concerned with the plight of the city.

On June 7th, we were officially notified that the truce would begin on June 11th, 1948, at six o'clock in the morning, Greenwich mean time.

The fighting in Palestine presented an entirely new military problem, and one which, to the best of my knowledge, has no precedent in the history of war. Military operations are usually carried out on the assumption that the war will continue until one side or the other is defeated. Hence the object of the operations is not to occupy this province or that, but to destroy the enemy's army. This done, the victor can dictate such peace terms as appear good to him. But in the case of the operations in Palestine, this was not the case. There was a third party, the United Nations, constantly intervening. In the present instance, we had four days more of fighting, after which there was to be a truce. There was no question of destroying the enemy's forces in four days. The problem was how to employ the four days in such a manner as to be in the best possible military position when the truce began.

From the very beginning of hostilities, I had told both the King and the government that we could not hold Lydda and Ramle. These two towns had been given to the Arabs in the UNO partition plan. They were situated on the flat coastal plain only fifteen miles from Tel Aviv, and were almost entirely surrounded by Jewish colonies (see the map on page 144). We had proposed to capture the Jewish colony of Ben Shemen, which lay across the only road connecting Lydda to the Arab area, but the mayor of Lydda had begged us not to do so. He alleged that he was on good terms with the Jews and proposed to defend his town by diplomacy. If the Arab Legion came round attacking Jewish colonies, the Jews, he said, would turn on Lydda.

The small numbers of the Arab Legion in comparison with the Israeli forces made it essential for us to fight in defiles at the foot of the mountains. Here, a single battalion could hold up the Israeli army, as indeed it had done at Latrun. But if a single battalion were to venture out into the open plain, it would be overwhelmed. Or, if it were to repulse every attack on itself, its line of communications across the plain would be cut off.

During the first month of hostilities, we had held our own against all comers, by holding the defile at Latrun. If we had ventured farther afield to Lydda and Ramle, the enemy would have broken through at Latrun and driven up the road to Ramallah in the centre of the Arab area.

I was interested to read many years later, in a Jewish work, that this point was fully realized on the Israeli side. It was agreed amongst them that an attack on Lydda and Ramle would compel the Arab Legion to weaken the garrison at Latrun, in order to send to the help of Lydda and Ramle. This would enable the Israeli forces to break through at Latrun.

I had explained this situation to the King and the Prime Minister before the end of the mandate and had secured their consent to the principle that Lydda and Ramle would not be defended.

As soon as the Arab Legion crossed the Jordan on May 15th, the Jordan government had appointed military governors to Hebron, Jerusalem, Ramallah and Nablus, in order to continue the civil administration. I discussed the appointments with the Prime Minister. When I asked about the arrangements for Lydda and Ramle, Taufiq Pasha replied:

"We have decided that we cannot hold Lydda and Ramle. If we appoint a military governor, and then the Jews take them, it will look worse." So Lydda and Ramle had no governor. During the month's fighting, there had been no government in these two towns. The civil police had disbanded themselves.

I accordingly suggested to the Prime Minister that we should send a token force to Ramle twenty-four hours before the truce began. Once the truce had begun, military movements might be prohibited. If this force went to Ramle before the truce, we could reconstitute the police and administration as soon as fighting ceased. The Prime Ministry agreed, but still did not send a governor. The 5th Independent Infantry Company, a garrison company of just over a hundred men, moved across country and into Ramle on June 9th.

At six o'clock Greenwich time on the morning of June 11th, all firing ceased on the Arab Legion front. A sudden silence prevailed. There was spasmodic shooting and mortaring by the Israeli forces on June 11th, but on a very small scale. The Arab Legion did not reply.

The control exercised by the Red Cross on convoys to Jerusalem seemed to be anything but efficient. On June 12th, for example, it was reported that Jewish transport was passing up the road to Jerusalem night and day. Protests to the truce commissioner and Count Bernadotte only produced promises to investigate, but meanwhile the convoys continued.

As soon as the truce seemed to be established, I went to see the Prime Minister. I explained the precarious nature of our position, the heavy casualties and the absence of reserves. I asked if he would

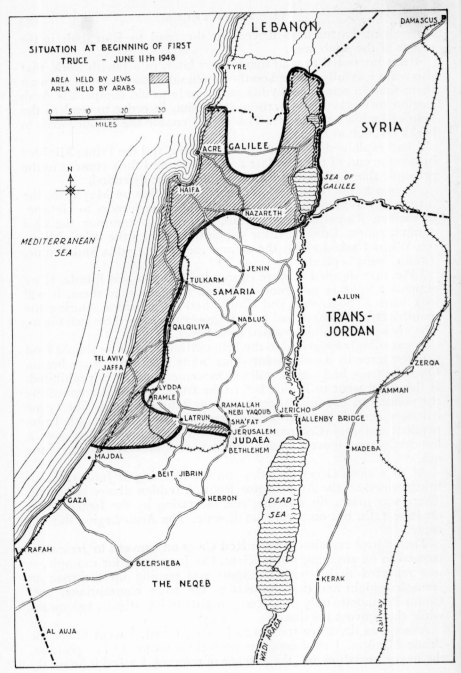

SITUATION AT BEGINNING OF FIRST
TRUCE — JUNE 11th 1948

AREA HELD BY JEWS
AREA HELD BY ARABS

0   5 10   20   30
MILES

N

LEBANON

DAMASCUS

TYRE

ACRE GALILEE

SYRIA

HAIFA

SEA OF
GALILEE

NAZARETH

MEDITERRANEAN
SEA

JENIN

TULKARM   SAMARIA

AJLUN

QALQILIYA   NABLUS

TRANS-
JORDAN

TEL AVIV
JAFFA

ZERQA

LYDDA
RAMLE

AMMAN

RAMALLAH
NEBI YAQOUB
SHA'FAT
JERUSALEM
JUDAEA
BETHLEHEM

LATRUN

JERICHO

ALLENBY BRIDGE

MAJDAL

MADEBA

BEIT JIBRIN

GAZA

HEBRON

DEAD
SEA

RAFAH

BEERSHEBA

KERAK

THE NEQEB

AL AUJA

WADI ARABA

Railway

PLATE 6

From the Arab Legion trenches at Latrun. Crossing the picture in the middle distance is the main road from Jaffa to Jerusalem, which was closed by the Arab Legion. On the left the road passes between three or four houses and enters the wooded gorge of Bab al Wad. Note the nature of the rocky Palestine hills in the background

PLATE 7

Count Folke Bernadotte—"tall, slender, pleasant and earnest, with a
quiet wit of his own"

sanction further enlistments, so that we should be better placed if there were any more fighting.

"There won't be any more fighting," he said to me, shaking the first finger of his right hand to the right and left, in a gesture of prohibition. "No more fighting! I and Nokrashy Pasha[1] are agreed on that, and if we two are agreed, we can sway the rest. No! No more fighting!"

I tried to point out that it might not rest solely with us. What would happen if the Jews started fighting again? But Taufiq Pasha was adamant.

"No more fighting," he said, "and no more money for soldiers."

As a result, this priceless month's respite was almost entirely wasted. We used it, however, to group the independent garrison companies. The three companies which were in the Old City we called the 6th Regiment, and we collected three other garrison companies and called them the 5th Regiment. This meant no increase in strength—it merely made these odd companies easier to handle.

As soon as it became clear that the truce was functioning in a satisfactory manner, Count Bernadotte set himself to produce a revised plan for a final solution. His draft proposals were issued on June 28th, 1948. The salient points in his plan were:

(a) That the Arab areas of Palestine be united to Jordan, and that Jordan, so constituted, should form a union with Israel.

(b) The union should handle economic affairs, foreign policy and defence for both Israel and Jordan.

(c) Subject to the instrument of union, Jordan and Israel would each control its own internal affairs.

Attached to the proposals was an annex dealing with territorial matters. In it, Count Bernadotte suggested that all or part of the Neqeb be included in Jordan, in return for which all or part of western Galilee should be Jewish. He further proposed that Jerusalem should be Arab, that Haifa be a free port and Lydda a free airport.

The proposals were considered to be favourable to Jordan, and were thus opposed by Egypt, Syria and Saudi Arabia, who were jealous of any increase in the power of King Abdulla. The Jews rejected the proposal, chiefly on the grounds that they would never agree to Jerusalem becoming Arab. Jordan might have accepted the plan, but it was useless to attempt to do so when both Jews and Arabs rejected it. How a union between Israel and Jordan would have worked is extremely problematical, but the plan is now only of academic interest.

One agreement was, however, concluded which was to result in a considerable problem for Jordan. The massive Jewish buildings on

[1] The Egyptian Premier.

Mount Scopus have already been mentioned. They consisted of the Hadassa Hospital and the Hebrew University, both great mountains of stone, situated on high ground dominating the Arab side of the city and cut off from the Jewish city by the suburb of Shaikh Jarrah. As soon as the Arab Legion had intervened in Jerusalem, Mount Scopus had been isolated. The Jews, however, had left a military garrison in the Hadassa and the University, which continued to fire into the backs of the Arab Legion who were defending Jerusalem. When we retaliated with mortars or, on one occasion, with the twenty-five-pounders, there was an outcry about Arabs shelling hospitals. The Jordan government was informed that both the Hospital and the University had been built with funds voluntarily subscribed in the United States. Any attempt by us to destroy or capture these buildings would, we were told, produce intense indignation in America.

When, therefore, Count Bernadotte suggested that the buildings be demilitarized and handed over to the United Nations, the solution seemed to be a reasonable one. The Israeli government agreed to the proposal, but requested permission to leave some Jewish civil police in the buildings to prevent pilfering of the valuable medical equipment and the literary treasures in the University. Count Bernadotte was very explicit in his statement that Mount Scopus would henceforward be solely under the control of the United Nations. He said that it was his intention little by little to replace the Jewish by United Nations police. How this agreement was ultimately carried out after the death of the Count will appear later on in this narrative.

* * * * *

When the fighting began in May 1948, we in Trans-Jordan had scarcely heard the word publicity. We had no idea of how to deal with the Press. Many reporters came to us while the fighting was in progress and we gave them leave to go wherever they wished. But their efforts seemed to make little impression on the Press of the outside world. I have already described how the Arab Legion came to intervene in Jerusalem, and how anxious the Trans-Jordan government had been to prolong the truce in the Holy City. Moreover, when the Arab Legion did intervene, it did not attack the Jewish city, but limited itself to recovering those Arab quarters which the Jews had captured in the preceding five days. Even so, it did not succeed in reoccupying all that the Jews had seized after May 15th.

The greater part of the Press in Europe and America, however, depicted the Arab Legion as having made a brutal, unprovoked, sacrilegious attack on the peaceful and holy city.

I remember particularly one American correspondent whose

cables to his New York newspaper were especially clear and objective. Six days after the fighting began, he received a cable from
his newspaper which said:

"Do not send reports on Arab troops. Require only descriptions
heroism Jewish soldiers."

We never asked for or expected propaganda in our favour, but
we were admittedly disappointed to hear that a leading American
newspaper would not even publish true accounts of our actions,
while making strenuous efforts to obtain accounts of the heroic deeds
of the other side. Heroic as the Jewish soldiers might be, this newspaper's approach seemed to be insufficiently objective.

But no amount of propaganda could conceal the fact that the
Arab Legion had done more fighting and had won more glory than
any other Arab army. The kings of Egypt and Saudi Arabia were
by no means gratified by this, for both were jealous of King Abdulla.
Nevertheless, the fact remained that the latter had gained immensely in prestige, owing to the successes won by his army. His
rivals doubtless thought that it would be well to pretend to conciliate him. He was accordingly invited to pay official visits to Cairo
and to Saudi Arabia, and in both places was given a triumphal
reception.

*   *   *   *   *

The four weeks' truce was due to end on July 9th. After July
1st Count Bernadotte applied himself to the task of renewing it.

The geographical position of the Arab armies when the truce
came into force on June 11th was on the whole satisfactory. The
coastal plain and the plain of Esdraelon were still held by the Jews,
but these areas were in reality preponderantly Jewish. They were
thickly studded with Jewish colonies, and most of the land there had
been bought by Jews. The only major exception was the Arab city
of Jaffa and the Arab orange groves on the east of it. Meanwhile,
nearly all the Arabs in these preponderantly Jewish areas had fled
to the neighbouring Arab countries.

The greatest injustice in the UNO partition plan had been the
award of the Neqeb as far down as the Gulf of Aqaba to the Jews.
In this area, the population was still preponderantly Arab; the
Neqeb had always been Arab in history. If the Arab States had
demanded the rectification of the border in the debate on the partition plan in the United Nations in October and November 1947,
they might well have secured the modification of the dividing line
in this area. But the Arab idea of rejecting everything left the field
clear to the Jews, and no criticism of the details of the plan was
voiced at Lake Success. At the end of the first month's fighting, however, the Neqeb was in occupation by the Egyptian army.

The Jewish claim to the Neqeb was what today we may fairly call "imperialism". It was not a Jewish area and there were very few Jews in it. But it had strategic advantages. Firstly, it cut off Asia from Africa, leaving no land-bridge between Egypt and the Arabs. And secondly, it gave Israel a port on the Red Sea, which at some date in the future would enable her to trade alike with Europe and with Asia, without using the Suez Canal. These were imperialist objectives; the seizure of territory belonging to someone else, in order to strengthen her military and economic position.

It is true that David carried his conquests as far as Aqaba, one thousand years before Christ, and that his ships sailed from that port. But this predominance was lost soon afterwards. In any case, Israel could scarcely claim territory by the right of conquest three thousand years ago, for since that date the district had been successively conquered by Egypt, Persia, Greece, Rome, the Arabs and the Turks, each of whom had been in control for centuries.

Although the Arabs were favourably placed at the end of the first month of fighting, we knew that they had in reality shot their bolt. If on May 15th they had rapidly brought their full forces to bear, and had then advanced energetically, they might have succeeded in overrunning the new Jewish State. But they were far from doing this. Most of them completely underestimated the task, despatched quite inadequate forces, and came to a halt as soon as they met resolute opposition. Trans-Jordan alone had thrown all her available forces into the struggle on the first day.

In addition to this half-heartedness, all the Arab armies were now complaining of lack of ammunition, except possibly the Egyptians (who had seized our ammunition ship). Inexperienced in war, the Arab governments had omitted to lay in stocks of ammunition in peace-time. Such expenditure is indeed unpopular in peace, for ammunition is expensive and its purchase gives no great satisfaction to the public.

In spite of all these difficulties, the Arabs were in a comparatively advantageous position when the first truce was declared. If they had agreed to prolong that truce and to take the final solution once more to the United Nations, a substantial modification of the 1947 partition plan might well have been secured by them.

I took every opportunity to press these views on King Abdulla and the Jordan government. I pointed out that the Arab armies had lost the momentum of their advance. None of them appeared very aggressive, and most of them were complaining of lack of ammunition and equipment. Meanwhile, the Jews, who had been nearly swept off their feet in the first rush, had had time to organize their plans.

Moreover, in spite of the Security Council resolution calling upon all members to abstain from supplying weapons or ammunition to combatants, Israel had reached an agreement with Czecho-Slovakia to supply warlike stores. Aircraft and weapons were continually arriving in Israel by air. The Arabs had no contacts behind the Iron Curtain. The Western Powers had previously supplied them with arms, but they were now respecting the Security Council resolution and refused to smuggle weapons, even to their friends. Israel was also able to manufacture certain weapons—notably mortars and mortar bombs—whereas the Arabs had no such factory. It was obvious therefore that, as time went on, the Arabs would grow weaker while the Jews would grow stronger and stronger. To come to these obvious conclusions required no great stroke of genius.

Bernadotte had assessed the situation. In his book, *To Jerusalem*, he has the following paragraph referring to July, before the truce ended:

"Information reaching us at about this time from various sources strengthened my impression that the Arabs, from the military point of view, were in a difficult position. If they continued the war, and if they did not then get material help from England or some other quarter, they would probably have no prospect whatever of winning."

As the time approached for the truce to come to an end, the Arab League Political Committee was summoned to Cairo. Before his departure, I begged Taufiq Pasha, the Prime Minister, to insist on the renewal of the truce, impressing on him that the Arab armies would henceforth grow weaker and weaker, and that nothing could be gained by renewing hostilities. The King was no less emphatic. Taufiq Pasha was confident that, in accordance with his agreement with the Egyptian Premier, Nokrashy Pasha, he would secure the renewal of the truce. The deputy Chief of Staff of the Arab Legion, Major-General Abdul Qadir Pasha al Jundi, accompanied Taufiq Pasha as his military adviser.

We received no further news of the deliberations of the Arab League Political Committee until one day a telegram arrived giving the time and date of the Prime Minister's return. I met the party at Amman airport. While the Cabinet ministers were greeting Taufiq Pasha, I took Abdul Qadir aside.

"Well," I said, "what happened?"

"They have decided not to renew the truce, but to start fighting again."

My heart sank.

"Why?" I exclaimed. "What madness! What resources have they got? What do they think they can do?"

"I don't know," replied Abdul Qadir Pasha. "Nokrashy Pasha insisted on a renewal of the fighting."

In the evening, I was summoned to the palace, where I found

the King and Taufiq Pasha in consultation. I felt gloomy. The decision seemed to me fatal from a military and diplomatic point of view. The Jews had agreed to prolong the truce, the Arabs had refused; the United Nations and the Great Powers would all be alienated by such action. I said something of the kind. I also reminded Taufiq Pasha that we had not much ammunition left. He was a little annoyed at what he took to be an implied criticism of himself.

"I was in a minority of one," he said. "All the others wanted to renew the fighting. If I had voted alone against it, we should only have been denounced as traitors, and the truce would still not have been renewed. Jordan cannot refuse to fight if the other Arabs insist on fighting. Our own people here would not stand for that."

"But how can we fight without ammunition?" I asked.

"Don't shoot unless the Jews shoot first," he said.

Such were my instructions at the commencement of this second period of fighting.

The King was as distressed as myself at this fatal decision. Count Bernadotte, who came to Amman on July 9th, records in his diary— "King Abdulla expressed his extreme uneasiness at the prospect of the war breaking out afresh."

I saw Count Bernadotte for a few minutes. He was leaving for New York to report to the Security Council. It was obvious to me that the longer the fighting went on, the more the Arabs would lose.

"The only thing now," I said to the Count, "is for the Security Council to take really strong action. They must insist on an immediate cessation of the fighting."

"I'll do my best," he replied, as he shook hands to say good-bye.

I never saw any report on the secret proceedings of the Arab League Political Committee. From what I could gather verbally, however, from those who were present, it appeared true that Nokrashy Pasha had pressed for a renewal of hostilities. Taufiq Pasha, who had previously believed that Nokrashy Pasha had pledged himself to renew the truce, was thereby completely nonplussed.

During the first period of fighting, the Egyptian Press had daily announced the dazzling victories of the Egyptian army. The public were expecting an early end to the war, the occupation of Tel Aviv by the Egyptian army, and the surrender of Israel. Instead of that, they were told that a month's truce had been agreed to. The Egyptian people were incensed—they had been given to understand that complete victory was in their grasp.

During the period of the truce, criticism of the government increased in Egypt. To silence this criticism, the Egyptian Prime Minister decided to start hostilities once more. The future of the Arabs of Palestine was sacrificed to Egyptian politics.

According to the information which reached us in Amman, all the chiefs of staff of the Arab armies were in favour of prolonging the truce. All stated that they had reached the limit of their power to advance, that they were short of ammunition and equipment and were not in a position to continue hostilities—but the politicians insisted. This at least is the version which was promulgated in Amman. Finally, a fantastic decision was taken. It was resolved that the truce would be terminated and hostilities renewed, thereby presumably restoring the popularity of the politicians. In view, however, of the unfavourable state of the Arab armies, no attack was to be made. The Arab armies were to be instructed to assume a passive defensive.

It might have been supposed that the Arabs would only renew hostilities if they stood to gain something thereby. But in order to gain something, it was necessary to attack and destroy the enemy, or at least to drive him back and occupy better positions. The decision to adopt the passive defensive made it impossible to hope that anything would be gained. Thus the Arabs decided to fight, hoping that nothing would be lost thereby, but under no illusion that anything could be gained. The only advantage of not renewing the truce was that the Egyptian ministers in office might, for a few days, renew their popularity. I can recollect no precedent in history for such irresponsible action on the part of those in power. Presumably the politicians hoped that they would regain their reputations for patriotism by refusing to renew the truce, and that the Security Council would then insist more forcibly. They could then bow to the inevitable, and explain to their constituents that they had done their best to destroy Israel, but that the Western Powers had compelled them to stop fighting.

On the other hand, the Western Arabs—the Egyptians, Palestinians and Syrians—have that logical mentality which deals only in purely intellectual conceptions. Such people are incapable of compromise. To them, it was unjust that the Jews should forcibly invade and conquer their country—and that was the end of it.

Count Bernadotte encountered this factor on at least two occasions in his negotiations with the Arabs—in Nokrashy Pasha and Abdul Rahman Pasha Azzam, Secretary-General of the Arab League. When he pointed out that if the truce were not renewed, the Arabs might be defeated, they replied to the effect that this might be true, but that it was better to lose all than consent to a wrong.

When the Political Committee of the Arab League met in Amman, immediately before the end of the mandate, I happened to be summoned to see King Abdulla. I was shown into his study immediately after the members of the Committee had left.

As I entered, he looked at me and shook his head.

"If I were to drive into the desert and accost the first goatherd I saw, and consult him whether to make war on my enemies or not, he would say to me, 'How many have you got and how many have they?' Yet here are these learned politicians, all of them with university degrees, and when I say to them, 'The Jews are too strong—it is a mistake to make war,' they cannot understand the point. They make long speeches about rights."

King Abdulla never could see eye to eye with the Egyptians. Perhaps their differences were not solely due to a clash of interests, but also to some organic difference in their mental make-up. For King Abdulla was a practical man, always ready to make a bargain or consider a compromise.

I myself encountered the same attitude in Taufiq Pasha, who, although Prime Minister of Jordan, was originally a native of Acre on the Mediterranean coast. I was one day explaining to him what would happen if the Jews broke through at a certain point, and how we should then have to withdraw from a neighbouring position.

"You cannot withdraw," he said.

"But if we do not withdraw, a large part of the army will be cut off and destroyed," I said.

"Better to have the army destroyed than to give up part of the country to an enemy who has no right to it," retorted the Prime Minister.

"But if the army is destroyed, the enemy will take the whole country, not only the small area from which we would otherwise have withdrawn. That surely would be much worse," I argued.

"It would be better for history," he replied.

There is no doubt therefore that this peculiarity existed in the mentality of the Levantine Arabs; a kind of "justice though the heavens fall".

"Better for us all to be exterminated than for us to agree to give up a yard of our country," a Palestinian said to me.

There may be something admirable in this resolution to demand that which is right, regardless of the cost. But the effect on the fate of the Palestine Arabs was utterly disastrous. Many opportunities for compromise were offered them and might, if accepted, have saved them. But they were utterly intransigent, and, as a result, they were destroyed.

But perhaps, on the other hand, this was yet another example of the maxim applicable in so many spheres of life—that that which is hidden from the wise and prudent is revealed to babes. It is an error to which our age is peculiarly liable, because we so frequently mistake knowledge for wisdom. In the Arab countries, where knowledge is still a novelty, it commands even more reverence than in Europe.

A man who has passed difficult academic examinations is often thought, by that fact alone, to be qualified for high office. It is a tragic error. Examinations are passed by remembering facts learned —a process which has nothing to do with wisdom. To live wisely, we need common sense, a quality not necessarily acquired at universities, but which may distinguish shepherds no less than scholars. Indeed, in the Arab countries, shepherds may more likely possess it than university graduates. For knowledge is still rare in the Middle East, and its possession therefore liable to give rise to intellectual pride, whereas, in the pursuit of wisdom, no quality is more necessary than humility.

IX

Lydda, Ramle and Latrun

I will lift up mine eyes unto the hills, from whence cometh my help.

Psalm cxxi. 1

LYDDA, RAMLE AND LATRUN

I DO not know whether the Israelis received information of the Arab decision to renew hostilities, but at the same time to remain on the passive defensive. They probably did so, for the Jewish intelligence services were good and the Arabs very addicted to talking. The result of this decision was, of course, to surrender the initiative to the Israeli forces, encouraging them to attack wherever they liked, undisturbed by any fear of an Arab offensive.

During the truce the Israeli forces had been regrouped; time had been available for planning, and, above all, a regular flow of weapons and ammunition had been obtained from Communist Czecho-Slovakia. A considerable number of aircraft were also flown in to Israel, bought surreptitiously in various countries and smuggled out with fictitious destinations. By the end of the truce, an Israeli air force was already in being. As far as is known, no arms or ammunition were received by the Arabs during the truce. They had no contacts in Communist countries, nor did they have the facilities for secret purchase and smuggling which were available to Israel, owing to the presence of Jews in every country in the world.

The Arabs had nearly shot their bolt by June 11th, when the first truce began. But it would have been far better to continue fighting then, than to give the Israelis a month to reorganize and obtain weapons and aircraft, and then begin again. Still, as before, there was no co-operation, and no exchange of information between the Arabs, except between the Arab Legion and the Iraqi army.

The position of the Arab Legion when fighting recommenced was a difficult one. The so-called 3rd Brigade of the Arab Legion consisted of the 2nd and 4th Regiments, and was in the Latrun area.

The Iraqi army was holding the front line in the Samaria district, its southern flank reaching to Majdal Yaba. There was thus a gap of fifteen miles between the Arab Legion at Latrun and the Iraqi army at Majdal Yaba. This gap was filled by the two Arab towns of Lydda and Ramle, still held by their inhabitants and by various Arab irregulars. Ramle and Lydda, however, were in the flat coastal plain. The first foothills began some five miles east of the two towns. The first outcrops of the main range of mountains petered out into the plains along the line Latrun–Beit Sira–Qibya–Rantis.

As long as the two Arab towns of Lydda and Ramle held out,

the right flank of the Arab Legion at Latrun was covered, as also was the gap between it and the Iraqi army. We had an inkling that the Israeli forces would this time attack Lydda and Ramle. If we sent one of our two Latrun battalions forward to the two towns, it would immediately be cut off from us and surrounded, especially as the Jewish colony of Ben Shemen lay astride of the road. The Israeli forces would then be able to surround and contain Lydda and Ramle, and concentrate against our battalion remaining at Latrun. It will be noticed that Latrun commanded two roads—one the main road up to Jerusalem, and the other a branch road leading from Latrun to Ramallah. If, therefore, the Israelis had overrun the single battalion at Latrun, they would not only have opened the Jerusalem road—they could also have driven straight up to Ramallah, and thence turned southwards to outflank Jerusalem or northwards to Nablus behind the Iraqi army. A major disaster to both the Arab Legion and the Iraqi army would have resulted, and the whole of Palestine would have been lost. Latrun was therefore the key of the whole front. To weaken its garrison would have been madness.

We endeavoured to strengthen Lydda and Ramle as best we could. Several hundred tribesmen from Trans-Jordan were sent there, equipped with old rifles by the Arab Legion. They were good men, but of course absolutely devoid of military training. Besides, in Lydda and Ramle there was no leader. We sent all the spare weapons we could collect to help the people of the two towns. We were aware, however, that if these places were seriously attacked they would fall. In that event, we should somehow have to close the gap between ourselves and the Iraqis. No troops whatever were available for this purpose. Every soldier in the Arab Legion was already in the front line with not a single unit in reserve—a most unfortunate position for a commander.

As I have already mentioned, the Prime Minister of Jordan had refused to consent to an increase of strength during the truce, on the grounds that there would be no more fighting. We were also already over our authorized budget strength, because we had kept on some of the infantry garrison companies, financial provision for which had ceased on April 1st. I retained these units on my own initiative, and I have no hesitation in saying that, if this had not been done, the greater part or all of Palestine would have been lost. However, we did the best we could. An intensive drive was made in Trans-Jordan. The office orderlies in the Arab Legion headquarters were sent. The greater part of the Desert Patrol—nearly a hundred men—were turned into soldiers. They had no tactical training; their duties were patrolling the desert to prevent animal thefts and to settle disputes, but they were good men and true.

The Israelis had decided again to put in their principal effort against the Arab Legion. The whole of the Palmach was allotted to the task. This "spearhead" of the Israeli forces now consisted of about 6,500 men, organized, roughly speaking, into a division of three brigades. Priority had been given to it in the issue of equipment and it had been well supplied with vehicles, particularly jeeps, armoured half-tracks, armoured cars and field artillery. Air support had also been provided for this Israeli *corps d'élite*. The duty allotted to it was to take Latrun from the Arab Legion.

During the first month of fighting, the Israeli forces had thrown themselves night after night against the Arab Legion position at Latrun without success. After every attack, they had recoiled, leaving hundreds of dead on the ground. This time they had a new plan—they would outflank and surround this strongpoint, which they could not capture by a direct attack. They decided first to take Lydda and Ramle and then to cut off Latrun by advancing to Beit Nuba and Beit Sira.

Against the Palmach, the Arab Legion had about 1,200 men in the Latrun area—a ratio of more than five to one.

The Israeli offensive began on July 9th, one brigade advancing from the north-west from the direction of Tel Aviv and the other from the south. Both brigades moved into the area east of Lydda and Ramle, so as to cut them off from any assistance which might come from the Arab Legion (see the map on page 160).

On July 10th, at 1 o'clock in the morning, the Palmach entered Innaba village from the south. From the north, the other brigade captured Wilhelmina, and then Lydda airport. The southern column then captured Jimzu, the northern brigade taking Abbasiya and Yahudiya.[1]

As soon as it was obvious that the Jews had launched a major attack in the Lydda and Ramle area, it became necessary to produce more troops either to assist Lydda and Ramle, if that were possible, or to fill the gap between Latrun and the Iraqis at Majdal Yaba, if Ramle and Lydda were to fall. The 1st Regiment had been holding the Nebi Samwil and Radar sector. They were hastily replaced by the three garrison companies that now formed the 5th Regiment. The 1st Regiment moved north-west to Beit Nabala, which it reached at 3 p.m. on July 10th.

It will be remembered that the 5th Independent Infantry Company had been sent to Ramle the day before the truce began, in order to enable Trans-Jordan to claim Lydda and Ramle for the Arabs if negotiations followed the first truce, as the Prime Minister stated would be the case. They had also been instructed to reconstitute the civil police, and for this purpose had occupied the Lydda

[1] O'Ballance, *The Arab-Israeli War*.

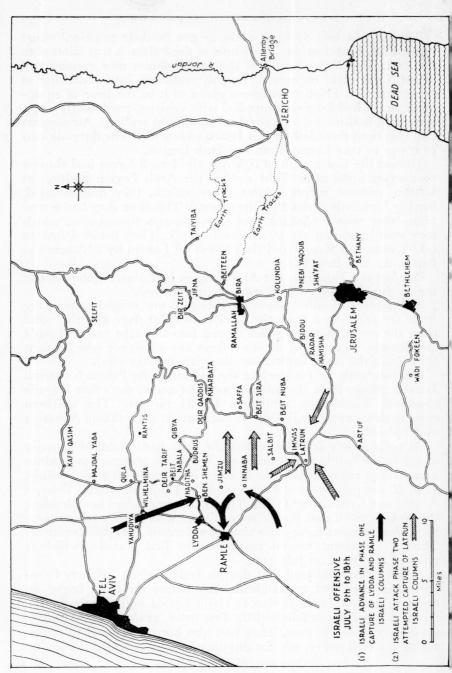

ISRAELI OFFENSIVE
JULY 9th to 18th

(1) ISRAELI ADVANCE IN PHASE ONE
   CAPTURE OF LYDDA AND RAMLE
   ISRAELI COLUMNS

(2) ISRAELI ATTACK PHASE TWO
   ATTEMPTED CAPTURE OF LATRUN
   ISRAELI COLUMNS

0   5   10
Miles

PLATE 8

Arab refugee women and children from Lydda and Ramle, resting after their arrival in the Arab area

PLATE 9

Notre Dame de France. It will be seen that Notre Dame completely overlooked the walls of the Old City, seen in the foreground. Beyond the group of figures on the roof can be seen the white houses and trees of the Shaikh Jarrah quarter. Ramallah is on the police building. On the 9th, when the truce ended, they were still there, and when the Palmach broke into the town with a force of two brigades advancing from the east, the 5th Company—little more than a hundred men—engaged them from the police building and forced them to withdraw. The 5th Company also claimed to have destroyed four Israeli armoured cars. Meanwhile the 1st Regiment occupied Deir Tarif.

Again, during these two days of Lydda and Ramle, we suffered that stream of heart-rending appeals which had poured in upon us during the days of the Jewish attack on Jerusalem from the 15th to the 20th of May. The telephone was cut from Lydda and Ramle, but there was a wireless set in the police station. There was nothing for it but to steel one's heart. I am no Napoleon—but I do not believe that any commander in his senses, in our situation, would have sent a unit forward to Lydda and Ramle. Only disaster to the whole country could have resulted.

We were indeed not the first soldiers to have found ourselves in an unenviable position. We had advised the government not to fight, and had informed them that our resources were not sufficient and that we should inevitably be the losers. The government had not made any attempt to supply more money, and had refused to sanction any increase of strength. Not only so, but the government was fully aware that we could not hold Lydda and Ramle, and had agreed to the fact before the end of the mandate on May 15th. The full blame for the fall of the two towns was, however, to be directed against the army alone.

My principal anxiety was still the Beit Nuba–Beit Sira area. I ordered the division to build up a defensive position on the line Imwas–Salbit–Jimzu–Haditha, but the commander of the 3rd Brigade replied that he had no troops. On July 11th, he sent a patrol to Jimzu, which found an Israeli force in occupation, but drove it out, killing ten of the enemy. When our patrol withdrew, the Israelis reoccupied Jimzu.

Meanwhile the 1st Regiment were engaged with the enemy at Deir Tarif. A troop of armoured cars was sent by the regiment to endeavour to ascertain the situation in Lydda. Under the command of Lieutenant Hamed Abdulla, a most determined officer, this troop drove past the Jewish colony at Ben Shemen and engaged strong enemy concentrations on the outskirts of Lydda. This patrol behaved in a most gallant manner, engaging and scattering several Israeli units. For a short time, friends and enemy alike thought that they were the advanced guard of a column coming to relieve Lydda. But soon it became apparent that the armoured cars were unsupported. Hamed could see the enemy attempting to cut his road back to Deir Tarif. He was obliged to withdraw. His reconnaissance had, however, established that the Israelis were present in strength. In actual fact, with three armoured cars he had challenged two infantry brigades.

Concerned as I was with the build-up of this defensive line, I decided to withdraw the 5th Infantry Company, which was surrounded in Lydda police headquarters. Orders were signalled accordingly, and the company slipped out as if by a miracle during the night of July 11th to 12th, arriving at Beit Sira in good order with all their weapons. After forty-eight hours of battle, this night withdrawal through the enemy's lines, without losing a man or a rifle, was a remarkable example of good order and discipline.

On July 12th, a patrol from Beit Sira to Jimzu found the village strongly held and was unable to make much impression. A second armoured car patrol from Deir Tarif towards Lydda was unable to get through. On the morning of July 12th, the Israelis completed the occupation of Lydda and Ramle.

No sooner were the enemy in the towns than they set about an intensive house-to-house search, all men of military age being arrested and removed to concentration camps. Then Israeli vans fitted with loudspeakers drove through the streets, ordering all the remaining inhabitants to leave within half an hour. The mutual exchange of accusations of atrocities during or after a war serves no useful purpose. Suffice it to say that houses were broken into and women sufficiently roughly handled to give point to the warning to be clear of the town in that time.

Perhaps thirty thousand people or more, almost entirely women and children, snatched up what they could and fled from their homes across the open fields. The Israeli forces not only arrested men of military age, they also commandeered all means of transport. It was a blazing day in July in the coastal plains—the temperature about a hundred degrees in the shade. It was ten miles across open hilly country, much of it ploughed, part of it stony fallow covered with thorn bushes, to the nearest Arab village at Beit Sira. Nobody will ever know how many children died.

I do not think that the Arab Legion had been guilty of such ruthlessness. The Liberation Army, it is true, had shelled Jewish Jerusalem, with no apparent military object. The Israelis had also complained that the Arab Legion shelled Jerusalem, but on our part such shelling was never indiscriminate. Every shell was directed against a military target, but it was not possible to ensure that every shot was a hit. In any case, the Israelis were shelling the civilian quarters of Arab Jerusalem before the Arab Legion arrived.

It is true of course that the persecuted Jews of Europe suffered far worse tortures, but these were not inflicted upon them by the Arabs of Palestine. One would have hoped that people who had

suffered as much anguish as have the Jews would have sworn never
to inflict on others the tortures which they themselves had endured.
The Arab Legion endeavoured to fight the Israeli army but not to
injure civilians. Perhaps nowadays such standards are obsolete.

*   *   *   *   *

Fighting continued on the 12th July, at Deir Tarif, where the
1st Regiment captured an enemy armoured half-track, four German
machine guns, and a seventeen-pounder gun, and destroyed three
armoured cars.

Throughout these operations, constant fighting had been in
progress in the Old City, which was packed with civilians. On July
12th, I walked round the Old City, visiting all the posts on the walls.
As I was passing along the narrow lane leading from the New Gate
to the Jaffa Gate (it used to be called the Street of Saint Francis),
a series of loud bursts occurred somewhere in front of us in the
crowded city.

"That's the Jewish heavy mortar they use to shell the town,"
said one of the troops.

Suddenly round a corner of the narrow cobbled lane appeared
four stretcher bearers, in white coats. They ran silently in their
rubber shoes on the cobbles. Between them on the stretcher, face
downwards, lay a young woman, motionless, her bright cotton
frock soaked with blood at the shoulders. In a few seconds, the little
group had run silently past us and down another turn in the narrow
streets, when a second similar party rounded the corner in front of
us. The four men ran with hard, set faces. On their stretcher, also
face downwards, lay a little girl of perhaps eight years old. She too
was motionless. She was clean and neatly dressed, with a bright
blue bow of ribbon in her shining hair.

O God! Why do such things have to happen?

*   *   *   *   *

When I was visiting the Old City, I did not know of the Lydda
and Ramle refugees, who at that very moment were fleeing in their
thousands over the dusty foothills.

It was only late that night, when I was already asleep, that the
telephone rang by my bedside. It was Lash. He confirmed that the
Israelis were in occupation of Lydda and Ramle, and gave me some
first account of the tragedy of these tens of thousands of fugitives.
The effect in Ramallah he said was catastrophic. Officers and men
of the Arab Legion had been stoned in the streets, and had been
hissed and cursed, with cries of:

"Traitors! Traitors! Worse than Jews!"

Many of the fugitives, he said, had nothing to eat. There was not enough bread in Ramallah. I rang the supply depot at Ramallah and ordered the troops' ration bread to be distributed to the fugitives. I arranged for truckloads of bread to be loaded in Amman and to leave at once for Ramallah.

Then I lay tossing on my bed. Admittedly I had never foreseen that the operations in Lydda and Ramle would have led to a human catastrophe on this scale. But even if I had known, what else could I have done? To have rushed troops impulsively forward to Lydda would have allowed the enemy to break through to Ramallah, and then these scenes would have been enacted—not only in Lydda and Ramle, but twenty times magnified over the whole of Palestine. I could not see that I could have taken any other course.

In any case, it was heart-breaking that the officers and men of the Arab Legion should be stoned, abused and spat upon by the people of Palestine and hissed at as traitors. Against heavy odds, they had saved Jerusalem. They were at this very moment in battle from Latrun to Deir Tarif against five times their numbers. Already nearly one man in four of those who crossed the Allenby Bridge on May 15th was killed or wounded. I knew that they would go on to the last man—to save that country whose people were now calling them traitors.

Soon the tragic stream of destitute humanity poured into Amman, and part of it flowed on to Zerqa. An exhausted family were found sheltering in a cave in the hill on which our house was built. Kind people went out to them with food and blankets. They had a sick child, but no doctor could be found in the confusion. In the morning, the charitable neighbours returned to offer help. The refugee woman was sitting on a stone gazing straight before her with a stony face.

"How are you this morning? How is the little boy?" the visitors asked. But the mother seemed no longer conscious of the world. She stared in front of her, silent, without moving a muscle. A little girl pulled one of the visitors by the sleeve, and pointed to a tiny figure, covered with a blanket. "He's dead," she said.

In another cave, a baby six months old was found crawling over the dead bodies of his father and mother. How the parents died, no one knew. There was no time for an inquiry.

*   *   *   *   *

It was unfortunate for us that, immediately after the end of the truce, the British Foreign Secretary, Mr. Ernest Bevin, had issued an appeal to both sides to cease fighting. Then came the occupation of Lydda and Ramle by Israel. The Palestinian Arabs are extremely intelligent. But their subtlety makes them unwilling to accept the obvious. They tend instinctively to seek a complicated and involved explanation for every event. The fall of Lydda and Ramle soon after Mr. Bevin's appeal gave them a clue. Of course that was the explanation! Mr. Bevin wanted the war to stop. The Jews had agreed to renew the truce, the Arabs had refused. Therefore, in order to persuade the Arabs to stop fighting, Mr. Bevin had ordered me to allow Israel to capture Lydda and Ramle. The Arab Legion could easily have defended these places—but I had prevented them from doing so, in accordance with Mr. Bevin's secret orders. The plot was obvious, and I had sacrificed tens of thousands of Arabs in order to further Britain's wicked intrigues.

Meanwhile, Count Bernadotte was active at Lake Success. The United States member of the Security Council, Mr. Jessup, had submitted a draft resolution, in which the Security Council "ordered" the governments concerned to cease fire. The resultant truce was not to be for any definite period, but until a peaceful adjustment of the Palestine situation was reached. The resolution was debated on July 13th, 14th and 15th.

The Arabs had been unsuccessful on all the fronts. The Egyptians had suffered a number of checks and showed no signs of advancing. In Galilee, the "Salvation Army" was defeated by the Israelis—it had indeed spent more time in looting than in fighting. The Syrians were pinned on the frontier. Fearing that the Arabs would again reject a truce and that, as a result, the Egyptian army would meet with serious reverses, I wrote a manuscript letter to Taufiq Pasha, the Prime Minister, urging upon him the advisability of agreeing to a new truce. The Arab Legion, I said to him, was not in a critical situation. We had never planned to hold Lydda and Ramle, as he himself knew. Otherwise we could hold the Israeli attacks on our front. But, according to the information I had received, I said, I feared that other Arab armies would meet with a disaster if the fighting were prolonged.

Two hours after sending this personal letter to the Prime Minister, I was summoned by telephone to the palace. When I entered the King's office, I found the whole Cabinet in session there. Taufiq Pasha, holding my letter in his hand, was sitting beside the King. I was motioned to a chair amid a tense silence. Then Taufiq Pasha asked His Majesty for permission to read my letter. He began in a voice which seemed to be almost choking with rage. Slowly he read it out. I had begun my letter by saying that I was sorry to trouble his Excellency at such a moment. Taufiq Pasha stopped, after reading this phrase, and remarked sarcastically, "Very kind of him to be so considerate." He then continued until he had read the whole of it.

The King was looking grim. For the first and only time in the long years during which I served him, he also doubted me. He turned and looked at me gloweringly.

"If you don't want to serve us loyally, there is no need for you to stay," he said.

Then the ministers took up the attack.

"Very remarkable that we never heard anything about a shortage of ammunition until Mr. Bevin wanted the fighting to stop," said one.

"They say the stores are full of ammunition," said another.

A tense silence followed. I made no defence. What was the good of arguing? I knew what they thought and in their state of mind at the time I could not have convinced them to the contrary. The Prime Minister had of course known about the shortage of ammunition for weeks, and about our ammunition ship seized by the Egyptians. He was then Minister of Defence, as well as Prime Minister, and it was my duty to tell him. Perhaps he had not told his colleagues. When they accused me now, he did not tell them that he had known about it all along.

I did not feel annoyed. I only felt tired. What was the good of it all? The troops were fighting against desperate odds. In Ramallah they were being hissed at as traitors. The King and the Cabinet were calling me a traitor, and suggesting that I was concealing the ammunition and allowing my own soldiers to be killed, for some remote political reason. In London, a member had asked in the House of Commons how it was that a brutal British general was allowed to commit outrages against the Jews.

We sat in tense silence for several minutes. Then I turned towards the King:

"May I go now, sir?" I asked.

"All right," he replied.

I walked across the room, turned at the door and saluted, and went out. There was nothing else to be done.

*   *   *   *   *

Now that the Palmach were in triumphant occupation of Lydda and Ramle, the Israeli forces proposed to outflank Latrun from the north by capturing Beit Nuba and Beit Sira, and thereby cutting off Latrun from Ramallah. If they could capture Beit Sira, they would both have cut the road to Latrun and also opened for themselves the road to Ramallah and the heart of our whole position and that of the Iraqi army. The Palmach accordingly pulled themselves together after the fighting, and prepared to undertake this second and more decisive phase of their offensive. Lydda and Ramle had been a disaster for the civil inhabitants, but it had not vitally affected the main objects of the campaign.

To meet any further advance by the Palmach, the commander

of the 3rd Brigade had withdrawn two companies of the 2nd Regiment from Latrun and had also taken over the 5th Independent Infantry Company, which had slipped out of Lydda on the night of July 11th/12th. This force was grouped around Beit Sira, under the brigade commander's personal command. The 2nd Regiment had been deeply stirred by the sight of the fugitives from Lydda and Ramle. They surrounded the brigade commander and demanded insistently to be allowed to attack, and to avenge the unfortunate victims.

On July 15th, the Palmach resumed their advance in force from Lydda by way of Jimzu (see the map on page 169). On the morning of the 16th, they attacked Al Burj and Bir Ma'in. I had several times told divisional headquarters that these places should be strongly held as defended localities. This did not seem to have been done. In the afternoon of the 16th, the 2nd Regiment carried out a counter-attack and recaptured Al Burj.

A British officer in this attack (himself the wearer of a D.S.O. and a Military Cross) submitted a written report, from which the following is an extract:

"I have seldom seen a more cool, steady and determined advance from the start line to the objective (which was 1,200 yards) by the troops of any nation, under a fire which was as heavy and accurate as in a European attack—than the advance on Al Burj which was made by 2 and 3 companies, 2nd Regiment of the Arab Legion."

The attack was preceded by a troop of armoured cars commanded by Hamdan al Biluwi.[1] Eighteen years before, Hamdan had been one of my first ten recruits to the Desert Patrol—an ugly, undersized little bedouin boy. But appearances are deceptive, for he had a lion-heart.

A reconnaissance role until contact was made with the enemy was, however, by no means to his liking. Hamdan's armoured car was more often than not required to be a tank. The attack on Al Burj was no exception. The armoured car troop, forgetting to report back any information they obtained, drove straight at Al Burj in front of the infantry. Amid the wild crashes and turmoil of the battle, the driver suddenly called out:

"I'm hit! I can't see! I've lost my eye!"

It was true. A splinter had torn across one of his eyes, and blood was pouring down his face.

"You don't have to see," said Hamdan. "Keep straight ahead and put your foot hard down on the throttle."

It says much both for Hamdan's leadership and the driver's own spirit that he obeyed without a complaint. With a large piece of his face shot away, he kept the armoured car heading straight for

---

[1] See *The Story of the Arab Legion.*

the village of Al Burj. I have no doubt that Hamdan would have taken the village single-handed, or died in the attempt, if an Israeli soldier, unseen in a slit trench, had not fired a Piat and hit the vehicle. The armoured car was a hopeless wreck. But someone dragged Hamdan from the damaged vehicle. In hospital, the surgeon removed more than a hundred pieces of metal from his body—and he lived.

Although the 2nd Regiment got into Al Burj, the brigade commander decided that he had not enough men to hold it, so it was abandoned again in the evening. The troops withdrew to the Beit Sira crossroads.

During the heavy fighting in these villages, in which the Arab Legion were greatly outnumbered, the 1st Regiment had unfortunately inclined away to the north. It is true that they had been told to contact the Iraqi army, who were at Majdal Yaba, but such contact could have been established by a patrol. It was obvious to us (but not, of course, at unit level) that the main battle was for the possession of the Beit Sira crossroads, in order to outflank Latrun and break through to Ramallah. Only two companies of 2nd Regiment and the 5th Independent Company barred the way to the Palmach. But the 1st Regiment on July 16th, like Grouchy before Waterloo, was pursuing an enemy away from the main field of battle. The regiment engaged an Israeli force at Qula and, driving it from its position, was indulging in an enjoyable pursuit in a north-westerly direction.

While this heavy fighting was going on in Al Burj and Bir Ma'in, the 1st Brigade had opened an offensive battle in Jerusalem. The attack was carried out in the New City, from Musrara into the Jewish quarter of Mea Sherim. The attack opened at 8 o'clock on the morning of July 16th and lasted until 12 noon. The Jews were unable to stand up to the 3rd Regiment, who captured several blocks of buildings, in which they consolidated, inflicting heavy losses. The 3rd Regiment were very aggressive and their morale was sky-high.

From the strategic point of view, it did not seem to me that this advance could exercise much influence on the whole picture. Clearing buildings in a city is an expensive operation and the capture of a few blocks of houses did not seem of vital importance. Later, however, it was reported that the Jews themselves had been planning an offensive, but that the 3rd Regiment advance had disorganized them and caused a good deal of alarm. As a result, no Israeli attack in Jerusalem materialized.

In the Beit Sira area, there was a lull on July 17th, while both sides reorganized after the heavy fighting of the 16th. Meanwhile orders were received that all parties had agreed to comply with the

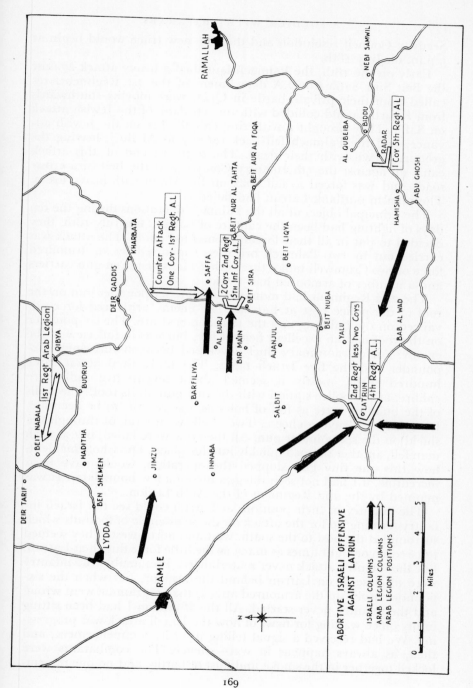

RAMALLAH

NEBI SAMWIL

AL QUBEIBA   BIDDU

1 Coy 5th Regt AL

RADAR

ABU GHOSH

BEIT AUR AL FOQA

HAMISHA

AL FOQA

BEIT AUR AL TAHTA

Counter Attack
One Coy - 1st Regt A.L.

KHARBATA

SAFFA

2 Coys 2nd Regt
5th Inf Coy AL

BEIT AUR AL TAHTA

DEIR QADDIS

AL BURJ

BEIT SIRA

BEIT LIQYA

BEIT NUBA

1st Regt Arab Legion

QIBYA

BUDRUS

BIR MAIN

AJANJUL

YALU

2nd Regt less two Coys

LATRUN   4th Regt A.L.

BAB AL WAD

BEIT NABALA

BARFILIYA

HADITHA

INNABA

SALBIT

DEIR TARIF

BEN SHEMEN

JIMZU

LYDDA

RAMLE

N

ABORTIVE ISRAELI OFFENSIVE
AGAINST LATRUN

ISRAELI COLUMNS
ARAB LEGION COLUMNS
ARAB LEGION POSITIONS

0   1   2   3   4   5
Miles

Security Council resolution and that the new truce would begin at
5 p.m. on July 18th.

Early on the 18th, the Palmach launched a heavy attack against
the Beit Sira–Saffa front. A detachment of the 1st Regiment, re-
called from their private battle in Qula, were moving southwards
from Kharbata and collided with the left flank of the Jewish attack
on Saffa. They brought a withering enfilade fire on the Jewish advance, and the Palmach fell back rapidly to Al Burj, leaving the
ground strewn with their dead. The southern end of this attack
came up against the 5th Infantry Company at the Beit Sira crossroads and was forced to fall back on Bir Ma'in with heavy losses.
The plan to outflank Latrun had failed.

The principal object of all the Palmach operations during the ten
days of fighting had been the capture of Latrun. On July 18th, they
decided to put in all their forces in one final effort. The attack was
carried out by two Palmach brigades, supported by an armoured
force of two Cromwell tanks, three other tanks, ten Bren-gun carriers
and a number of armoured half-tracks.

The 2nd Regiment had mounted a single six-pounder gun on the
roof of the police post at Latrun. The enemy armoured force advanced on the building and the tanks opened fire. The six-pounder
on the roof had an excellent field of fire, but was in full view of the
enemy. An extraordinary duel developed between this single six-
pounder and the five Israeli tanks. The tanks fired about three
hundred shells, mostly it seemed about seventy-five millimetre
calibre, at the police station with the tiny gun on its roof. The walls
of the building were as full of holes as a sieve—or, to be accurate,
let us say a Gruyère cheese. Two shells went straight through the
shield on the six-pounder gun. All the crew were killed, but as each
man fell, another stepped quickly into his place. The whole incident,
how this one tiny gun stopped the operation, would have been
incredible, if I had not seen the gun myself a few hours later. It was
manned by the 2nd Regiment of the Arab Legion.

The infantry in their positions at Latrun could see the Israeli infantry forming up for the attack on the semi-circle of foothills which
surrounded the post to the south, west and north-west. They seemed
to be seven or eight times as many as the little force dug in at Latrun.
But the infantry attack never materialized. Presumably the infantry
were to close in on Latrun behind the armour, but when the six-
pounder broke up the armoured attack, the programme went wrong
and the infantry never started. All the afternoon I had been sitting
in my office waiting for news of how the Israeli attack was progressing. We had received a signal telling us of its commencement, and
then, as always happens in war—silence. The combatants were
locked together in the smoke and dust of battle, and no-one remem-

bered the haggard commander pacing anxiously up and down his office, far behind the front line, while he watched the minutes tick by.

"Any signals through from div. headquarters?"

"No, sir. Nothing yet."

There was nothing I could do, in any case. There were no reserves which could be thrown in to sway the battle. Only the troops could fight it out—and the truce was to begin at 5 p.m.

At half-past three, I gave it up and went home for a cup of tea. Either the Jews were now swarming over our positions—or they would have pulled back, as so often before, leaving the ground strewn with their dead.

* * * * *

Whatever worries I encountered in the world, there was always the love and solace of home.

"To be happy at home," said Dr. Johnson, "is the ultimate result of all ambition, the end to which every enterprise and labour tends, and of which every desire prompts the prosecution."

I went round to my house. My wife had laid tea under the vine pergola in our tiny garden. I sat down, looking at the outline of the trees against the deep-blue sky, as I had so often before. What was happening under that pall of smoke at Latrun?

The telephone bell rang in the house. I ran as fast as I could across the little garden, in by the garden door, and picked up the receiver.

"Glubb Pasha here," I said. In my heart, I added, "O God! Let it be good news!"

"This is Lash here, sir," said a voice.

"Well, what's the news?" I asked, trying to make my voice impassive.

"This Jewish attack has been repulsed," came the calm reply. "Our six-pounder knocked out all their tanks. We've just sent two infantry sections out with Piats, to see if they can finish off the tanks. I'm afraid the ground's too open and they won't be able to get near enough. Akkash has gone with them."

"But what about the infantry attack?" I asked.

"Their infantry haven't attacked at all. They don't seem to like the look of us. Fire is slackening off now. Looks as if the show's over!"

"Well done, old man!" I answered. "That's grand! Give all the troops my love."

I ran out of the house, shouting: "Hurrah! hurrah!" and did a Scottish reel on the garden path.

My wife looked up from her tea in surprise.

"My dear!" she said. "What on earth is the matter?"

"We've done it!" I shouted. "Five tanks knocked out by one six-pounder! Can you beat it? Infantry never came over at all! The whole thing was a fiasco!"

"How wonderful!" she said. "But meanwhile I've poured out your tea and it's getting cold. And I made these potted meat sandwiches all specially. I don't believe you've had anything to eat all day."

X

Knight Without Fear

O Jerusalem, Jerusalem, thou that killest the prophets, and stonest
them which are sent unto thee.   *Matthew* xxiii. 37

X

KNIGHT WITHOUT FEAR

BERNADOTTE had summoned a meeting in Jerusalem to discuss some way of making the July 18th truce effective. We met in an upper room in the Raudha, a massive building one side of which overlooked the Temple area and the Dome of the Rock, and which had, until May 15th, been used as a school. The governor of Jerusalem was there, the head of the police, the commander of the Arab Legion 1st Brigade, and several United Nations observers. It was a hot July afternoon. The room was full of flies, which settled on our hands and faces, and buzzed on the window-panes. Every now and then, there was the "crack" of a rifle from an Israeli sniper, or a burst of machine-gun fire crackled overhead. This was the "shooting truce".

I felt sleepy in the hot stuffy air of the room. Bernadotte was giving a talk on the role of the UNO observers. I looked idly out of the window by which I was sitting. Across a narrow lane—perhaps no more than twelve feet wide—was the wall of a convent. My eye was caught by a marble plaque in the wall:

"Locus in quo Pilatus Jesum apprehendit et flagellavit et milites plectentes coronam de spinis imposuerunt in capito ejus."[1]

Nearly two thousand years ago in that very place! He was flogged and put to death to illustrate His own precept—"I say unto you, that ye resist not evil." Yet here we were, after nearly two thousand years, still resisting evil.

*   *   *   *   *

In spite of everything we could do, frequent shooting continued after the commencement of the second truce. We could not avoid a suspicion that the Israeli army had been annoyed at the conclusion of the truce when operations had been going well for them, and that they hoped, by frequent shooting, to create an incident which would provide an excuse for a resumption of hostilities. But they were also acutely conscious of world opinion, and their local military aggressiveness was accompanied, in the international field, by constant complaints of Arab attacks.

Captain Slattery[2] was an officer in the United States Air Force

[1] "The place in which Pilate arrested Jesus and flogged Him, and the soldiers plaited a crown of thorns and placed it upon His head."
[2] This is not the officer's real name, as I have not been able to obtain his permission to use it, but the incident and conversation are exact.

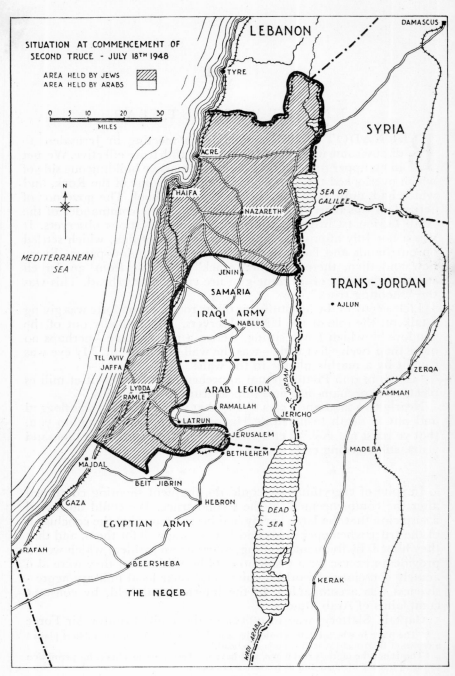

SITUATION AT COMMENCEMENT OF
SECOND TRUCE - JULY 18TH 1948

AREA HELD BY JEWS
AREA HELD BY ARABS

0   5   10   20   30
MILES

N

LEBANON

DAMASCUS

TYRE

SYRIA

ACRE

HAIFA

SEA OF
GALILEE

NAZARETH

MEDITERRANEAN
SEA

JENIN

SAMARIA

TRANS-JORDAN

IRAQI ARMY

• AJLUN

NABLUS

TEL AVIV
JAFFA

ZERQA

LYDDA
RAMLE

ARAB LEGION

AMMAN

RAMALLAH

LATRUN

JERICHO

R. JORDAN

JERUSALEM

MAJDAL

BETHLEHEM

MADEBA

BEIT JIBRIN

GAZA

HEBRON

DEAD
SEA

EGYPTIAN ARMY

RAFAH

BEERSHEBA

KERAK

THE NEQEB

WADI ARABA

PLATE 10

Infantry of the Arab Legion repelling an Israeli attack on the Old City of Jerusalem

PLATE 11

The six-pounder at Latrun after the battle. Note the torn and battered gun shield. The gun is on the roof of the police post, which was held by one platoon. The main Latrun position is on the distant hill on the right and a UNO observer in Jerusalem. His name and attitude to life suggested that he was Irish, but his drawl showed that he came to us from the southern states of the Union. One day he came to one of our battalions in Jerusalem, in response to a complaint of Israeli firing on civilian vehicles. The Arab Legion battalion commander complained to him that the Israelis were constantly shooting, but that the Press in Europe and America always blamed the Arabs.

"The Jews are better at paper work," said the captain. "They write five protests to every one that you put in. Anyone who read only the protests would think the Arabs were always in the wrong."

"But you don't think that, do you?" enquired a young Arab officer earnestly.

"Wa-al," said Slattery slowly, "all UNO observers, you know, are neutral." He paused and lit a cigarette, and then added, "But I guess some of them are a darned sight more neutral than others."

"About seven or eight o'clock in the morning," said our battalion commander, "and from half-past three onwards in the afternoon, a machine gun shoots from near the Italian hospital. It chooses only civilian vehicles—usually a passenger bus or a truck with a crowd of Arabs riding in it. Yesterday two old Arab women were killed in a bus. If we send one of our armoured cars out on the road, the firing stops."

"I'll go and sit out on the road and see what happens," said Slattery.

"Perhaps you ought to have an armoured car with you," said the battalion commander. "What will you do if the Jews start shooting?"

"I'll get out my little pencil and paper and write a report," said the captain. "Then I'll send one copy of the report to the UNO observer on the Jewish side and another copy to Haifa. Then old Slat's work is done!"

"Do you think that UNO will stop them?" enquired the battalion commander innocently. "They haven't hit anyone in the Arab Legion—only civilians, chiefly women."

Slattery surveyed him kindly but pityingly.

"UNO won't sta'ap them," he drawled, "but I guess they'll make it illegal."

*   *   *   *   *

I walked out of the gate of my front garden one hot bright August morning to get into my car and drive to the office. A ragged bedouin boy was standing beside the road. When he saw me he called out:

"I want your help, O Basha![1] I am your guest."

[1] The letter P does not exist in the Arabic alphabet and many Arabs cannot pronounce it.   Pasha is originally a Turkish word.

He had one of those frank, open faces which can sometimes be seen amongst the tribes. He gave me a dirty piece of paper, inscribed in pencil in a shaky hand. It was from Aid ibn Rubaiyan, the shaikh of a section of the Dahamshah, themselves a branch of the great bedouin tribe of Aneiza. The letter was to introduce the boy, who wished to be a soldier. Then Aid added these lines:

"We long for you to return to us. The *effendis* [1] only want money. But we who want glory want you back."

The letter had come five hundred miles across the waterless desert, from the water-holes of Shabicha. For a moment I could see that glaring dusty hollow, the rows of ragged black tents, the flies and the dust, the herds of great camels, the desert horizon with its range after range of pale blue hills. In the middle stood Aid's big tent, the coffee pots, the threadbare carpets, and Aid himself leaning over the shoulder of the only man in the camp who could write and saying: "Tell him we want him back because we love honour, not money."

* * * * *

I have related how the Prime Minister had told me, before the fighting began, that the Arab Legion must fight the Jews on its peace-time budget, and how subsequently Abdul Rahman Pasha Azzam, Secretary-General of the Arab League, had promised us funds up to £3,000,000 and had paid us £250,000 in cash. After the conclusion of the second truce, I asked our finance department for a statement on expenditure. I was a little taken aback to discover that the £250,000 had already been over-expended. I requested the Trans-Jordan government to ask Azzam Pasha for another credit. After all, we had spent only a quarter of a million out of the promised three millions, and we had done nearly all the fighting. I was therefore not a little surprised, a few days later, to hear from the government that Azzam Pasha refused to pay any more. The Trans-Jordan minister in Cairo had reported that the Secretary-General had cancelled all promises of help to the Arab Legion, on the grounds that the Trans-Jordan government was not giving full support to the policy of Egypt. It seemed difficult to justify such action, because the money belonged to the Arab League and had been subscribed by all its members. Azzam Pasha was, in theory at least, Secretary-General of the Arab League, not an official of the Egyptian government.

This refusal placed us in an awkward situation, because we had already overspent the £250,000. A quarter of a million does not go far in a war. I consulted the Minister of Defence. He suggested that we both report to the Prime Minister.

[1] *Effendi* is the word used for Mister. In this instance the reference is to civilian government officials.

When we entered Taufiq Pasha's office, the Minister of Defence explained the situation. The Prime Minister was very angry.

"Did I not tell you that we had no money?" he demanded. "I warned you not to exceed your budget heads. Don't you know Finance Regulations? Where am I to get the money from to pay for what you have overspent?"

Taufiq Pasha was worn out. Essentially a man of peace, hating everything military, he had been living on his nerves for three months. He looked drawn and ill. Indeed, we were all tired. While, however, trying to allow for the Prime Minister's exhaustion, my own position seemed to me ridiculous. I could not stop a battle to ask the Minister of Finance how much money there was left in the budget under items "ammunition" or "petrol". When the Prime Minister repeated his rhetorical question, "Where am I to get the money from?" I also lost my temper.

"I suggest you deduct it from my pay," I said sarcastically.

Taufiq Pasha was furious. The Minister of Defence was horrified, and hustled me hastily from the office. "I never knew you had a temper like that," he said as we drove away together in his car.

"I am sorry," I answered. "It was very wrong of me. But after all, we have been fighting a war."

Taufiq Pasha rang the bell violently, called for his car, and drove straight up to the palace to complain to the King. His Majesty poured oil on the troubled waters. It was decided that I should be given a month's leave in Europe for a rest.

In 1948, there was no direct air service from Amman to Europe. We flew to Cairo to take an airliner for London. The only aircraft with available accommodation was T.W.A. to Paris. We booked by that.

On arrival at Cairo airport, we were surrounded by Egyptian journalists.

"Why did you betray the Arab cause?" "Have you been dismissed?" "Why did you give Lydda and Ramle to the Jews?" "Is it true that you alone were responsible for the Arab defeats?"

The manager of the American airline rescued us and gave us his car. He had booked a private room at Shepheard's Hotel for the afternoon. We blessed his name for his kindness and forethought.

We landed in Paris at two o'clock in the morning. I woke the children, who were fast asleep, and stumbled in the semi-darkness to the door. Suddenly, as we emerged on the gangway, we were blinded by a torrent of flashlights. Hundreds of cameras pointed at us. Then the journalists fought all round us.

"Are you dismissed?" "Do you expect to go back?" "Is King Abdulla dissatisfied with your conduct of the operations?" "Would you say that all Lawrence's work with the Arabs had been undone?"

The manager in Cairo had cabled the office of the company in Paris to help us. The local manager appeared and rescued us. He put us in his car and told the chauffeur to drive off at once.

"Keep driving round and round the square," he told him. "Drive fast and don't stop, whatever happens."

We tore round and round a Paris square for twenty minutes, almost literally on two wheels. Fortunately there was not much traffic at 2.30 a.m. Eventually our friend the manager arrived, having collected our luggage, and we at last reached an hotel.

In London we thought we should be at home. It was therefore a disappointment when a detective took me on one side at the airport, and asked me to register at a London hotel in the name of Mr. Smith.

"We have reports that there are Jewish terrorists looking for you," he said. "They seem to think that you alone saved the Arabs from a complete disaster."

"I wonder if you could ask them to ring up Cairo and compare their intelligence reports," I said. "One side or the other must have got their facts wrong."

But Mr. Smith did not long survive at the hotel. The Press were waiting for me again when I came down for breakfast next morning. No wonder, perhaps, that one London daily noted that "Glubb Pasha was looking tired and ill, with deep bloodshot eyes."

* * * * *

Before I left Amman, I had an audience with King Abdulla, who gave me a letter to be delivered personally to Mr. Ernest Bevin.

"What instructions do you wish to give me, sir, in case Mr. Bevin asks me any questions?" I enquired.

The King replied with an Arab proverb. "*Irsil ameen wa la tuwassi.*" "Send a faithful messenger without instructions."

I called on Mr. Bevin at his official residence in Carlton House Terrace. He received me in a small office and opened the conversation with bitter complaints against the Arabs, whom he had done his best to help, but who had in reply only loaded him with complaints and abuse.

I did not attempt to interrupt this outbreak. In fact, most of what he said was quite true. When he seemed to have finished, I intervened.

"What you say may be quite true," I said, "but it does not apply to Trans-Jordan or King Abdulla."

He answered more quietly:

"Yes, you are right. Trans-Jordan is different."

* * * * *

At last we escaped for a few days into the country. It was pleasant to have time once again—time to write letters, to have a bath, to look out of the window at the quiet fields and trees—time to try to think what it was all about.

There is so rarely time to think nowadays. Day and night we are feverishly hastening in one direction or another, but whether it is the right or the wrong direction, we do not know. Whether what we are doing will ultimately be for good or evil, we can't think. There is no time.

*　　*　　*　　*　　*

We returned to Jordan by air on Friday, September 17th, 1948. We were to change at Paris into the T.W.A. airliner for Cairo. As we were waiting at Orly at eleven o'clock at night, I walked up and down in front of the airport buildings. It was a dark night, except where the glow of the city lit the horizon with a pale diffused light. A man walked up to me.

"May I have your comments on to-day's tragic event?" he asked. He pulled out a reporter's notebook and pencil.

"What tragic event?" I asked.

"Haven't you heard?" he replied. "Count Bernadotte was assassinated today in Jerusalem. May I have your comments?"

"I am sorry," I said. "I have no comments."

I walked into the airport waiting-room. I was tired and felt that I must sit down. It seemed to have turned chilly. I shivered and pulled my coat round me.

*　　*　　*　　*　　*

On the morning of Friday, September 17th, Bernadotte had taken off from Damascus airfield and landed at Kolundia, north of Jerusalem. He drove up to Ramallah to see Lash. In the course of the conversation, reference had been made to the increased sniping in Jerusalem. Lash had said that he hoped that the Count would accept an Arab Legion armoured car escort. One of the United Nations observers suggested that the visit to Jerusalem should be postponed.

"No!" said Bernadotte. "We cannot allow ourselves to be frightened out of doing our work."

An Arab Legion armoured car accompanied the Count from Ramallah into Jerusalem, where he crossed to the Jewish area. Just as he drove over the line, an American journalist, standing by, called out:

"Good luck to you."

"Thank you," replied the Count with his usual broad smile. "I shall need it!"

The party lunched at the Y.M.C.A. in Jerusalem with a number of the United Nations observers. After lunch, with a convoy of three cars, the Count drove out to Government House, the former official residence of the British High Commissioner for Palestine. After inspecting the house and garden (where it was proposed that UNO headquarters be established), and viewing the city from the roof, the party returned to Jerusalem. As they drove through the Katamon quarter, they came suddenly on a jeep, which was standing in the middle of the road. As the convoy approached, the driver appeared to be trying to turn. He fumbled with the gears, went backwards and forwards, and finally stopped in the middle of the road again. There were four men in the jeep, in the uniforms of the Israeli army. The Count's convoy consisted of three cars, containing United Nations personnel and an Israeli liaison officer. There was no Israeli escort. No one in the convoy was armed.

Three of the occupants of the jeep jumped out and walked towards the UNO convoy, which had been obliged to halt because the Jewish jeep was blocking the road. Count Bernadotte was in the third or rear car. One of the Israelis walked down one side of the cars and two walked down the other. They went straight to the third car. The driver remained seated in the jeep.

The single man went up to the window of Count Bernadotte's car. The passengers thought that he was a Jewish soldier about to ask for their passes, and began to pull them from their pockets. Suddenly the man thrust the mouth of an automatic pistol through the window and fired a burst of shots at point-blank range at the Count and at the French Colonel Serot, who was sitting beside him. At the same instant, the other two Israelis pulled out automatic pistols and fired at the wheels and radiators of the cars—presumably to prevent pursuit. The men then jumped into the jeep, which disappeared at full speed. A truck, full of Israeli soldiers, was seen to be halted some forty yards away. It subsequently transpired that the murderers in their jeep had been waiting on the road for at least an hour before the convoy arrived. Count Bernadotte had received six bullet wounds, one of which, through the heart, must have caused death instantaneously. Colonel Serot had received seventeen bullets

Next day, the murderers, who belonged to the Stern Gang Jewish terrorists, sent the following letter to the Press:

"Although in our opinion all United Nations observers are members of foreign occupation forces, which have no right to be on our territory, the murder of the French Colonel Serot was due to a fatal mistake: our men thought that the officer sitting beside Count Bernadotte was the British agent and anti-Semite, General Lundström."

General Lundström was Count Bernadotte's chief of staff and an officer in the Swedish army.

The Count's body was taken by road to Haifa on September 18th. The convoy passed our positions at Latrun, where an Arab Legion guard of honour was drawn up to pay the last homage to the dead.

Meanwhile I had arrived back in Amman. We waited in tense anxiety to know what would happen next. Count Bernadotte was the representative of the United Nations, a close relative of the King of Sweden, and a man who had devoted his life to charitable and humanitarian causes. Surely the United Nations would vent signal punishment on those who had so brutally assassinated their emissary. As the days passed, and nothing happened, we began slowly to realize how utterly ineffectual and impotent UNO was. As far as we could discover, no retribution was inflicted—indeed there was scarcely criticism. The lesson was not lost on anyone in Palestine, whether United Nations officers, Arabs or Jews. More than once, in the ensuing years, did I express to a United Nations observer the hope that he would put in a strong report on some outrage. More than once, I received the same reply: "No, I am not going to put in a strong report. I am not anxious to be another Bernadotte." The average United Nations officer in Palestine was of high quality, but it is difficult to expect a man to court death in the service of so indifferent a master as UNO. Moreover, Jews and Arabs alike were beginning to realize that it was safe to do anything to UNO—no dangerous reactions were likely to ensue.

Count Bernadotte had been an officer in the Swedish Cavalry. He was a devout Christian—a man who seemed to have passed his life in philanthropy—a Christian idealist.

> [1] And from the tyme that he first began
> To ryden out, he loved chivalrye,
> Trouth and honour, freedom and courtesie.
> And evermore he hadde a sovereign price.
> And though that he was worthy he was wyse,
> And of his port as meke as is a mayde.
> He never yet no vilonye had sayde
> In al his lyf, unto no manner of wight.
> He was a verray parfit gentil knight."

[1] Chaucer, Prologue to *The Canterbury Tales*.

Note. The account of the murder has been taken from the epilogue of Count Bernadotte's book, *To Jerusalem*.

XI

The Shooting Truce

'Tis true that we are in great danger;
The greater therefore should our courage be.

. . . .

Out of this nettle, danger, we pluck
this flower, safety.

SHAKESPEARE

The only worth-while security is courage.

R. BABSON

XI

THE SHOOTING TRUCE

THE day after my return to Amman I was obliged to devote to formal calls. I paid my respects to the King. Taufiq Pasha, restored to equanimity, hoped I had enjoyed a well-earned rest. In the office, everyone was smiling.

The next day I was up early. In Amman we always set our alarm clock for 5 a.m., or, in slack times, for 5.30. (It was a trial, on waking up in London at five o'clock, to find that we could not have tea till 7.30 and breakfast till 9 a.m.) The sun was just up as I drove down the hill and through the town. People were already going to work— a shopkeeper on the pavement, busy opening his shutters, stopped and looked round. He waved his hand, and called:

"Good morning, O father of Faris!"

"Good morning," I called back. "How are you?" It was good to be back.

We took off from Amman airport in the golden morning light. I was to fly to Jerusalem, visit the troops in the city and then drive on down to Latrun. I wanted to have a quick look round, to hear the opinions of the men in the line, and to bring myself up to date with recent developments.

We skimmed the crests of the hills which lined the eastern escarpment of the Jordan valley and saw the ground drop away beneath us in steep slopes and crags, divided here and there by deep gorges cutting through the mountains to the Jordan plain. Now, four thousand feet below us, the River Jordan meandered in endless serpentine twists. On our left, and far below, confined between the parallel rocky ranges of mountains on the Palestine and Trans-Jordan sides, lay the gorgeous blue of the Dead Sea. Nearly two thousand years ago, the Roman-Jewish historian Josephus had recorded his astonishment at that marvellous blueness.

From the airstrip at Kolundia, I drove to the city. Constant sniping and periodical mortaring had continued ever since the second truce began. Indeed, the situation was not unlike that on a quiet sector in France in 1916 or 1917. On neither side did the troops come out of their positions to attack, but both sides fired periodically.

At the entrance to the city, I was put into an armoured car. A soldier closed the door. The driver, who obviously took his soldiering seriously, shut down the vizors firmly. The vehicle drove off, clanging and rattling as armoured vehicles will. I could just see the sunny outside world through a narrow slit at the level of my eyes. We swung round a corner into a street of pleasant villas, each with a small garden. Some of the houses had obviously been abandoned, and stood half derelict with shell-holes through their roofs, window-panes broken and doors wrenched from their hinges. Their gardens were strewn with rubbish, paper and old tins. But in other houses there were signs of habitation: curtains at some of the windows, a stout woman hanging washing on a line in the yard.

A nurse in her white cap came out of a house and walked down the road. Other women were on the footpath. I put my hand on the driver's arm. "Stop," I said. He changed gear and the lumbering armoured car slowed down.

I opened the door and looked out.

"Don't open the door, sir!" said the driver sternly.

"Why not?" I said. "I want to get out."

"No, sir! You ought not to do that! A stray bullet or a Jewish sniper might get you."

He looked at me anxiously. He was very young. A new moustache was just beginning to pencil his upper lip.

"I take refuge with God," I replied. "I really cannot rattle through Jerusalem in a huge armoured car with the vizors closed, while the streets are full of women wandering about unconcerned."

The young soldier surveyed with distaste two remarkably pretty girls in brightly coloured summer frocks, and with high heels, who walked past arm in arm.

"It does not matter much if the Jews kill a few girls," he remarked, "but an army is no good without its general."

In the Musrara quarter of the New City, our men held a line of posts in semi-ruined houses. I crawled into a trench which began in the back garden of a house and led, through a hole in the wall, into the former kitchen. Through a narrow slit, almost bent on all fours, we emerged into a small space about ten feet long and three broad which had been dug out of the foundations. A narrow loophole looked out at ground level. In it sat a soldier, a pair of field glasses in his hand, his rifle beside him on a ledge.

He looked round as I crawled in and, seeing me, broke into a grin.

"Praise God for your safety," he said—a common greeting to people returned from a journey. I could not help smiling.

"Praise God for yours!" I said. "I have been safely in England, while the Jews have been shooting at you in Jerusalem."

He laughed and edged out of the way to let me look through his loophole.

"The Jews have got a platoon in the third house down the street—the one with the vine climbing up the balcony," he said. "Their sentry is in that window—the one closed up with new sandbags. You can see him move sometimes—There! Did you see him?"

I crawled back and up a step into a large basement room, where six or seven soldiers were sitting drinking mugs of tea. They might have been any soldiers in any war.

"Welcome, boys!" I said. "How are you all?"

"Welcome! Welcome!" came a chorus of voices. Several came up to shake hands. "Praise God for your safety," they said politely.

Several crowded round and asked eager questions:

"When can we start fighting again?" they said.

From Jerusalem, I drove by car through Ramallah and down past the steep crags and ravines of the west face of the Palestine mountains, to Latrun on the edge of the coastal plain. Only a few miles ahead could be seen the blue Mediterranean, and the sand dunes near Tel Aviv. The narrow strip of plain between was Israel.

Everywhere the troops were smiling—everywhere they said: "Praise God for your safety"—everywhere they asked when they could begin fighting again.

What a joy to be back once more among soldiers.

*　　*　　*　　*　　*

An extraordinary incident had taken place at Latrun. One of the men had remarked several times that he felt there should be more active fighting. He told a comrade that he was going to kill some Jews. He then slung his rifle across his shoulder, climbed out of his trench and walked quite openly towards the enemy. The two front lines were here about four hundred yards apart. He walked about two hundred and fifty yards, then carefully chose a suitable place, and lay down facing the Jews. During all this time, no one had fired at him; presumably they thought he was a deserter coming over to them.

When he had lain down, he deliberately loaded, took aim and fired at the Israeli front-line posts, and continued shooting steadily until he had emptied his pouches. Then he stood up and walked carefully back, amid a hurricane of shots. He was just able to collapse into our trenches, with six bullets in his body. Four months later he was back on duty!

*　　*　　*　　*　　*

It was already sunset when I landed once more at Amman airport and drove back through the town and up to my house. As I walked up the garden path, I could hear the piano and fresh young voices were singing:

> "He promised he'd bring me a bunch of blue ribbons
> To tie up my bonnie brown hair."

I stopped and listened, and then tiptoed up the steps, and opened the front door.

"Oh, dear! what can the matter be?
Dear, dear! what can the matter be? . . ."

As I walked in, the piano stopped. The drawing-room door was suddenly flung open and two small figures shot out and wrapped themselves round my knees.

"Oh, Deedee! Do you know what has happened? We'll give you three guesses! You'll never guess! What do you think?"

I gave it up. They looked at one another in triumph.

"Tibby's had her kittens in your cupboard! On top of your shirts! Two are tabby and one is yellow! Come and see!"

I was seized by both hands and dragged into our bedroom.

*   *   *   *   *

Shortly before his death, Bernadotte had presented a further report. The burden of his recommendations was his insistence on the necessity for prompt and firm action by the United Nations. He recommended the modification of the UNO partition scheme in such a way as to give the Neqeb to the Arabs, and in return, Galilee and Jaffa (given by UNO to the Arabs) to the Jews. His intention was to give each side a solid and homogeneous block of territory, instead of the cross-overs, pockets and corridors in the United Nations plan. Lydda and Ramle were to return to the Arabs, Jerusalem was to be placed under UNO control. Both Jews and Arabs promptly rejected his solution.

Meanwhile, however, the Egyptian government had not forgiven Trans-Jordan the successes won by the Arab Legion. Both Egypt and Syria were determined that, whatever happened to Palestine, King Abdulla should not profit. Accordingly the Arab League, led by Egypt and Syria, suddenly announced on September 22nd the formation of an "Arab Government of All Palestine". The members of the "Cabinet" proved to be nearly all supporters of the ex-Mufti. It was proclaimed that a "Constituent Assembly" would meet at Gaza on September 30th, to pass a vote of confidence in this new government, which existed only on paper, with no country, no budget, no army and no officials. This extraordinary manœuvre was generally interpreted as an Egyptian attempt to secure control over all Arab Palestine through a puppet government, while at the same time depriving Trans-Jordan and King Abdulla of any authority in the country.

While the Arab governments were engaged in these activities against one another, the Jews had been steadily building up their armed forces. An aerial ferry was working constantly between

Czecho-Slovakia and Israel, bringing in more arms from behind the
Iron Curtain. Although the United Nations observers were by
way of having the right of inspection of the armed forces on both
sides, the Israeli government suddenly prevented them from visiting
their aerodromes. It became increasingly obvious that Israel was
flying in new aircraft, and was building up a powerful air force.

On November 13th, 1948, the London *Daily Telegraph* reported
from Hof, Bavaria, as follows:

"Czecho-Slovakia has supplied the Israeli Air Force with at least
100 Messerschmitt fighter planes, a Jewish informant declared
here today. He asked that his identity be withheld for fear of
reprisals.

"Airfields at Zatec, Chomutor, Rekycany and Pisek were used to
despatch the planes, he said. Pilots flying supplies to Palestine
included former United States Air Force officers and Hungarians.
As many as four transports a day had left Zatec."

I felt that there was something to be said for the argument of a
Jordanian officer, who remarked to me that Britain was the worst
possible ally for the Arabs. When I asked him why, he replied:

"Because she does not cheat the United Nations. Russia and the
Communist countries belong to the United Nations in just the same
way. They, however, support a United Nations resolution in Lake
Success, but then secretly go against it."

But while Russia and her satellites were thus actively assisting the
Jews, they did not neglect the Arabs either.

Communist pamphlets began to appear in the hands of the
public, signed "National Freedom Front". The burden of their case
was that the disasters suffered by the Arab armies were due to the
reactionary governments which held power in the Arab countries.
These "reactionary elements" were the tools of Anglo-American
imperialism. The only way out was to destroy the influence of this
"imperialism". Thus Russia, while arming Israel and enabling her
to defeat the Arabs, was, at the same moment, telling the Arabs
that their lack of success was due solely to Britain and America. This
explanation was indeed almost universally believed, as the Western
Powers, who had hitherto alone supplied the Arabs with arms,
continued to observe the United Nations blockade, which the Communist governments were evading.

Meanwhile, Jewish aggressiveness continued to increase, particularly in Jerusalem, and incidents multiplied, especially after the
murder of Count Bernadotte. It was no longer possible to avoid the
suspicion that the Israeli forces were rapidly building up their
strength in order to recommence open war, and that they were intensifying armed clashes in order to prepare a suitable pretext for
the resumption of hostilities.

The appearance of the Arab Government of All Palestine had revived the courage of the Mufti's armed retainers in Jerusalem. This organization had dubbed itself "Al Jihad al Muqqaddas", or the Holy War. In Jerusalem city itself, some of these men had fought side by side with the Arab Legion. But the greater part of it had collected in the country north of Jerusalem, where it had taken little or no part in the fighting, but was menacingly positioned across the Arab Legion communications. Writing on October 3rd, I made this entry in my diary:

"The position of Trans-Jordan is extremely awkward. We are still in action against the Jews, the Jerusalem truce is only partially effective, and we have daily casualties in killed and wounded. Yet behind our front line, the Mufti's emissaries are raising armed forces, which are drilling and training, but not taking part in holding the line. Now that the Arab League has declared a number of the Mufti's henchmen to be the sole legal Government of All Palestine, his retainers in the Jerusalem area have become distinctly hostile to us."

The Trans-Jordan government was in a dilemma. If it withdrew from Palestine and left it to the "government" appointed by the Arab League, the Israelis would have followed up and established their frontier on the Jordan. The Mufti's "army" could scarcely have stopped them for an hour. But if this had occurred, Trans-Jordan would again have been denounced as the traitor who had given the country to Israel. If, on the contrary, we held on, the Jews might launch a new offensive in Jerusalem, and the Arab Legion would find itself fighting Israel in front, with the Mufti's army behind it, astride its communications!

I noted in my diary: "Our situation is more like *Alice in Wonderland* —or perhaps Dante's *Inferno*—than real life."

The government of Trans-Jordan eventually decided to act. On October 3rd, 1948, I received a written order from the Minister of Defence, laying it down that all bodies of armed men in the area held by us in Palestine must either be under the orders of the Arab Legion or must be disbanded and disarmed forthwith. In view of the fact that the Mufti's "Holy War Army" were actively canvassing for the Government of All Palestine and refusing to co-operate with us, though they were present in our area, orders were issued to surround and disarm them. The operation was carried out and no opposition was encountered.

*   *   *   *   *

When the first truce came into force on June 11th, fire ceased almost immediately along the whole Arab Legion front. The second truce, however, was different. The Israeli forces continued to fire at irregular intervals, more especially in Jerusalem. The shooting in the city took the form of sniping, as much against civilians as against soldiers, and often of mortar bombardments. The Israelis manufactured their own ammunition, which was consequently always available in sufficient quantities. In the Arab Legion, however, three-inch mortar ammunition was still in very short supply. The UNO blockade was still in force, although Israel was receiving both weapons and ammunition from Czecho-Slovakia.

One night in Jerusalem city, the Israelis kept up a steady mortar bombardment of the civilian residential area. The UNTSO[1] staff were already installed, and we repeatedly rang them up and requested them to order the Israelis to cease fire, but without effect. At eleven o'clock at night, the mortars were still firing. Eventually the observers rang up our brigade headquarters.

"The best thing for you to do," said a voice, "is to fire a few rounds back into the Jewish city. Then the civilians over there will get scared and ask their troops to stop. They won't take any notice of us."

Orders were given accordingly. When the sixth Arab Legion bomb fell into the Jewish city, the Israeli troops ceased firing, and everyone went to bed.

A remarkably annoying incident made life more difficult at this stage. The end of the fighting in the Latrun sector has already been described. It left the enemy in possession of Bir Ma'in and Al Burj, and the Arab Legion in Beit Nuba and Beit Sira. Opposite Beit Nuba was a rocky hillock, overlooking the road from Beit Sira to Latrun. In theory, when the truce began, all troops were to stand fast in their final positions. The space between the lines was to be no man's land. But several days after the truce, the Israeli forces discovered that this rocky hillock called Ajanjul commanded the road to Latrun (see the map on page 169). They moved forward and occupied it. We complained to Count Bernadotte who arranged an investigation and found our complaint to be correct. He ordered the Israelis to withdraw. They took no notice. He ordered them again, with the same result. He knew that if he informed Lake Success, no action would be taken. Gradually we began to understand that the United Nations counted for very little. The Israelis continued to use Ajanjul to snipe traffic on the Latrun road.

*　　*　　*　　*　　*

Throughout the period from May 15th to July 18th, the Arab Legion had become famous all over the world. The many foreigners, pressmen, United Nations observers and diplomats who had witnessed the fighting, were fully aware of what the Arab Legion had

[1] United Nations Truce Supervision Organization.

done, against heavy numerical odds. Count Bernadotte had remarked to some of his United Nations officers that he himself was
by profession a soldier.

"There are plenty of people fighting in Palestine," he said, "but
only one army—and that is the Arab Legion."

Nevertheless, the outburst of violent vituperation which followed
the fall of Lydda and Ramle had by no means died away. Although
the Prime Minister had agreed they could not be held, in face of the
storm of resentment which burst around my head, he preferred now
to say nothing. Perhaps for generations to come, the history books
in most Arab countries will teach that Glubb Pasha betrayed the
Arabs and gave Lydda and Ramle to the Jews, in accordance with
orders received from Mr. Bevin in London.

The Jordan government itself was affected by these attacks on
me, which were especially bitter in Syria and Egypt. My chief in
the government was the Minister of Defence, but it had long been
the custom for the Prime Minister himself to take the portfolio of
defence. Now it was decided to appoint a full-time Minister of
Defence, and Fawzi Pasha al Mulqi was made my chief.

Many months afterwards, Fawzi Pasha told me that his brief
had been to find out what I was doing, and, if necessary, to supply
the evidence to secure my dismissal for treachery. Far from dis-
covering any malpractices, Fawzi Pasha was soon deeply impressed
and became, for the time being, our open champion. In the ensuing
eight years, I was to serve under many Ministers of Defence, and
I think that I may truly claim that every one of them left his post
with a deep respect for the Arab Legion and a personal friendship
for myself. I never had a single quarrel or difference with any one
of them.

From this time onwards, for the remaining eight years of my stay
in Jordan, I was the recipient of frequent threatening letters and
the victim of reported attempts at assassination. These rumours
were the more interesting because, whenever I visited the United
Kingdom, I was supplied with a guard of detectives, on the grounds
that the Jews were seeking to kill me. To be high on the list for
assassination by both sides was, I could not help thinking, a rather
exceptional distinction.

Meanwhile the Bernadotte report was before UNO Controversy
centred on the question whether the Neqeb (the Beersheba–Wadi
Araba area) was to be Israeli or Arab. The UNO partition plan
had awarded the whole area to the Jews, although there were very
few Jewish settlements there, and even historically it had never been
Jewish. The area was strategically important, because it divided
Asia from Africa. The Israelis also wanted a port on the Red Sea.
In other words, their claim could not be based on the humanitarian

need to settle refugees on the land, or on the right of purchase as in the case of so much land in the coastal plain, or on history. It was power politics.

In early October 1948, the *Spectator* of London published an article in which it was stated that the British and American viewpoints were moving farther apart. Britain, the paper continued, steadily supported the Bernadotte plan, but the United States was more concerned not to offend the Jews than anything else. The fact that the United States Presidential elections were to take place a month later may have influenced the policy of that country.

The question drifted on in the United Nations. Any decision seemed to be dependent on Anglo-American agreement. I find a rather bitter note in my diary: "All our troubles seem to be due to politicians—American as much as Arab—for the Presidential election seems to be spoiling all hope of a firm settlement by UNO."

The comparative strengths of the Israeli and Arab forces in the field on October 1st, 1948, was estimated at the time by a reliable source to be as follows:

Arabs

Egypt	15,000
Trans-Jordan	10,000
Iraq	15,000
Syria	8,000
Lebanon	2,000
Saudi Arabia	700
Irregulars	5,000
Total	55,700

Israelis

All categories	120,000

These figures are doubtless only approximate. They suffice, however, to show that the common impression that the heroic little Israeli army was fighting against tremendous odds (one army against seven armies was one of the expressions used) was not altogether correct. The Israeli forces were, generally speaking, twice as numerous as all the Arab armies put together. On the other hand, it is perfectly true to state that the Israeli forces were derived from a population, in October 1948, of between 900,000 and a million. The Arab forces were derived from a population of about forty millions.

It is difficult to avoid the impression that their successes in the July fighting gave the Israeli army confidence. They were, however, still lacking in weapons, artillery and aircraft, and accordingly decided to keep the truce lively by constant shooting, in order to be able easily to produce a pretext to recommence active operations when they so desired. As a result, the "shooting truce" was maintained for three months, while aircraft and weapons arrived in a steady stream in Israel from the Communist countries.

Meanwhile, the position on the Egyptian sector was extremely curious. The Egyptian army had built up a defensive front on the line Isdud–Iraq Suweidan–Falluja–Beit Jibrin–Bethlehem. They had constructed a number of strongpoints along this line. Two main roads led from the Egyptian front to their bases. One was the coastal road from Isdud to Majdal, Gaza and Rafah, the other ran from Bethlehem to Hebron, Beersheba and Al Auja. In between these roads lay several Jewish colonies, which the Egyptians had never mopped up. The Israeli forces in the north had maintained contact with these colonies, partly by air and partly by jeep and other vehicle patrols which crossed the Egyptian front line at night.

The theory of the truce, as laid down by Count Bernadotte, was that supplies should be maintained at the same level throughout the period. In other words, a "besieged" Jewish colony should receive as much food as it could eat day by day in order that—at the end of the truce—it would hold exactly the same stocks as it did when the truce began. Now this requirement made it necessary for Israeli ration convoys from the north to pass through the Egyptian lines under UNO arrangements, to take food to the besieged colonies from time to time. This process involved constant incidents, the Israelis complaining that the Egyptians had stopped their convoys and the Egyptians replying that the Israelis had opened fire.

For ten days prior to October 15th, the Israeli forces refused to allow United Nations observers to approach their front opposite the Egyptians, where they concentrated a force of some 15,000 men, including the Palmach division that had fought the Arab Legion at Latrun. When all was ready, the Israelis sent a convoy to cross the Egyptian lines and carry supplies to the besieged colonies in the Neqeb. The Egyptians fired on the convoy, as the Israelis doubtless expected that they would, thereby providing an excuse for the major operation which the Israeli forces had been preparing.

Various factors probably impelled the Israelis to make their attack at this moment. The Bernadotte plan was before the United Nations at Lake Success. The Neqeb had been allotted to Israel in the partition plan, but Bernadotte had proposed that it be given to the Arabs. Doubtless the Israeli government were of opinion that possession is nine points of the law. They decided to take the Neqeb before UNO could decide that they could not have it. It was also reasonably certain that the United States government would not

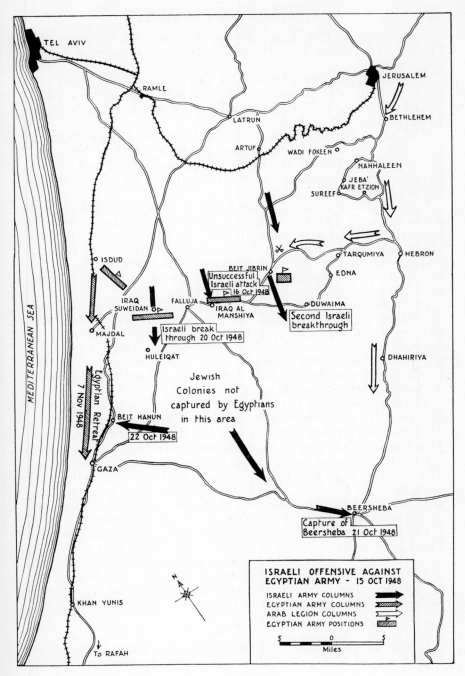

MEDITERRANEAN SEA

TEL AVIV

RAMLE

LATRUN

ARTUF

WADI FOKEEN

JERUSALEM

BETHLEHEM

NAHHALEEN

JEBA'
KAFR ETZION

SUREEF

TARQUMIYA

HEBRON

EDNA

ISDUD

IRAQ
SUWEIDAN

FALLUJA

BEIT JIBRIN

Unsuccessful
Israeli attack
16 Oct 1948

IRAQ AL
MANSHIYA

DUWAIMA

Second Israeli
breakthrough

MAJDAL

Israeli break
through 20 Oct 1948

HULEIQAT

DHAHIRIYA

Egyptian Retreat
7 Nov 1948

Jewish
Colonies not
captured by Egyptians
in this area

BEIT HANUN

22 Oct 1948

GAZA

BEERSHEBA

Capture of
Beersheba 21 Oct 1948

KHAN YUNIS

N

To RAFAH

ISRAELI OFFENSIVE AGAINST
EGYPTIAN ARMY - 15 OCT 1948

ISRAELI ARMY COLUMNS
EGYPTIAN ARMY COLUMNS
ARAB LEGION COLUMNS
EGYPTIAN ARMY POSITIONS

5   0   5
Miles

197

oppose anything that Israel did in the three weeks before the Presidential election, since the Jewish vote was thought to be all-important.

Accordingly, on the afternoon of October 15th, the Israeli air force, with its new aircraft recently smuggled in, opened a wide-spread offensive, by bombing the Egyptian bases and airfields at Majdal, Gaza and Al Arish.

The Israeli ground troops advanced during the night of October 15th/16th and simultaneously the garrisons of the "besieged" Jewish colonies behind the Egyptian lines sallied out and cut the Egyptian communications, sniped road traffic, and blew up the railway behind the Egyptian front.

Heavy fighting occurred in the Egyptian front-line positions, and it was not until October 20th that the Israeli column eventually broke through and took Huleiqat. The Israeli force went on in spite of the narrowness of the gap through which it had forced its way, and on the 21st it captured Beersheba. Thus the whole of the Egyptian army from Iraq Suweidan to the east was cut off from the remainder and from Egypt and its base.

From Beersheba, the Israeli forces turned west again and endeavoured to break through to the coast at Beit Hanun. On October 22nd, they captured Beit Hanun, thereby cutting both the road and the railway, but they were held before they reached the sea. As a result of this attempt to cut their communications, the Egyptian army withdrew from Isdud and Majdal, passing along the seashore west of Beit Hanun.

The Egyptian defeat in the Neqeb was chiefly due to bad generalship on their part. They suffered from a Maginot line mentality. Their troops were deployed in a long line from Isdud to Beit Jibrin. This line was defended by trenches and other fixed defences. The units in this line were static, and there were, apparently, no reserves. The attacking force used by the Israelis was about equal to the total strength of the Egyptian army in the field. But the Egyptian forces were scattered over a wide area and were immobile. Thus the Israeli commander was able to concentrate an overwhelming force at the point in the Egyptian line where he chose to break through. The Egyptian forces being immobile, their commander could not move them to the point of danger when the Israeli attack developed.

Apart from the errors of command, some of the troops fought well in defence, this being particularly the case where there were Sudanese soldiers, as opposed to Egyptians proper.

*   *   *   *   *

It will be recollected that an infantry company of the Arab Legion was in Hebron on May 15th, when the mandate ended.

When, however, the Egyptians arrived, in the second half of May, they demanded the withdrawal of this company, claiming that Hebron and Bethlehem were in the Egyptian sector. As we had no surplus of man-power, I secured the approval of the Trans-Jordan government to our withdrawal of this company, and the area was left to the Egyptians.

As soon as the extent of the Egyptian defeat on October 20th to 22nd became apparent, we were faced with an entirely new situation. One course open to us was to attack somewhere on our front—Jerusalem or Latrun or elsewhere—in order to draw Israeli forces on ourselves and thus relieve the pressure on the Egyptian army. It was, however, doubtful if this would be of much help, as we did not know of the Egyptian defeat until after it had occurred; the Egyptian army never informed us of its operations. There was little prospect of regaining much lost territory by attacking at Latrun or Jerusalem, and it was becoming increasingly obvious that this war was not covered by the rules of strategy. It is an axiom of war that the object of all military operations is to destroy the enemy's forces. Once this task has been accomplished, the victor can dictate such terms as he wishes. The seizure or evacuation of territory is irrelevant, except in so far as it assists or hampers the main objective—namely, destruction of the enemy's forces. Russia, for example, both in 1812 and in the Second World War, surrendered vast tracts of territory, in order to lure her enemies to their doom and destroy them.

But the war in Palestine was different, because there was no chance of its being fought to a finish. It was not a straight military war, but a combination of politics and war. Standing, as it were, on the touch-line were the Great Powers, all immensely stronger than the combatants. They were almost certain to intervene and stop the fighting in a few days. Moreover, the United Nations showed a lamentable tendency to acquiesce in every *fait accompli*. The only thing that really interested them was to stop the fighting, and in order to do so, they were prepared to acquiesce in everything that had happened. This was indeed a comfortable creed for petty conquerors. The art obviously was to seize whatever territory you coveted, and then, when the Security Council ordered you to cease fighting, to obey with protestations of devotion. It was fairly safe to assume that you would be able to keep what you had snatched.

On this occasion, the Israelis had defeated the Egyptians and appeared to be in a position to occupy the whole of Palestine south of a line drawn east and west through Jerusalem. The Egyptian army was cut in half by the Israeli advance to Beersheba. The western half in Gaza was still in touch with Egypt and might continue operations. The eastern half in Hebron was cut off from its base, and was therefore unlikely to resist the Israeli army for long.

It was obvious that the Israelis could occupy Hebron and Bethlehem whenever they so desired.

Two courses therefore were open to the Arab Legion:

(1) To carry out diversionary attacks in the Jerusalem or Latrun areas, to draw Israeli forces away from the south. No considerable territorial gains could be expected from such action.

(2) To send a force round the east side of Jerusalem and down to Bethlehem and Hebron, and save this district for its Arab inhabitants.

Of these, we chose the latter.

On October 22nd, the day the Israeli army took Beit Hanun, the Arab Legion collected an improvised column north of Jerusalem. It consisted of two companies of infantry and a squadron of armoured cars, a total of about 350 all ranks. No artillery could be spared. This force carried out a detour to the east of Jerusalem, and along rough earth tracks from Bethany to Bethlehem. In view of the fact that both the Israelis and the Egyptians were using about 15,000 men each in the battle, a reinforcement of 350 Arab Legion seemed somewhat inadequate, but we were unable to risk our main front by sending more.

Meanwhile, however, the Security Council issued its usual appeal for a cease-fire, which was to take effect from three o'clock in the afternoon on October 22nd. Both sides agreed.

On October 23rd, the heads of all the Arab governments, or their representatives, met in Amman to discuss how to help the Egyptians. Nokrashy Pasha, the Prime Minister of Egypt, and Jameel Mardam, Prime Minister of Syria, were the chief speakers. Jameel Mardam voiced the opinion that it was disgraceful that the other Arab armies had not come to the assistance of Egypt. All agreed that they would come to her assistance next time, but that there did not appear to be any need to do so now, as the cease-fire had been accepted. The Prime Minister of Syria waved his hand across the map, and explained how, if this kind of thing happened again, the Syrian army would break through between Hule and the Sea of Galilee, and would capture Nazareth and Safad. He hoped in that case that the Iraqi army would capture Affula. (See the map on page 106 for places mentioned.) General Saleh as Saib, Chief of the General Staff of the Iraqi army, looked at the Syrian Premier somewhat sardonically. Finally, he remarked that, if the Syrian army did all the Prime Minister proposed, the Iraqi army would co-operate.

The Arab Legion attempted to bring the discussions out of these airy clouds and down to earth.

The cease-fire had left the Egyptian army split into three groups:

(1) The Gaza group, on which the Isdud–Majdal garrison was withdrawing.

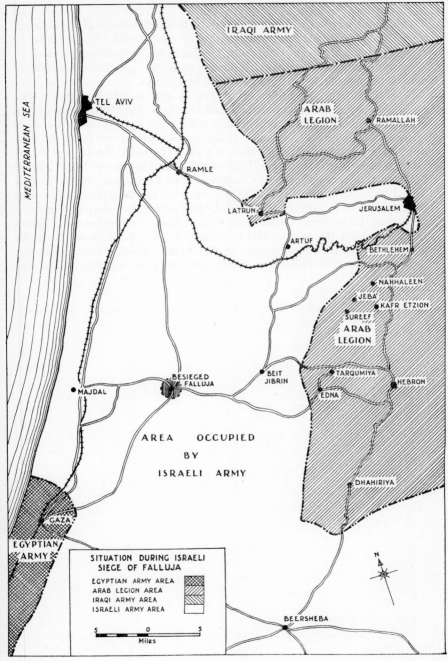

MEDITERRANEAN SEA

IRAQI ARMY

TEL AVIV

ARAB
LEGION

RAMALLAH

RAMLE

LATRUN

JERUSALEM

ARTUF

BETHLEHEM

NAHHALEEN

JEBA

KAFR ETZION

SUREEF

ARAB
LEGION

BESIEGED
FALLUJA

BEIT
JIBRIN

TARQUMIYA

HEBRON

MAJDAL

EDNA

AREA   OCCUPIED

BY

ISRAELI   ARMY

DHAHIRIYA

GAZA

EGYPTIAN
ARMY

SITUATION DURING ISRAELI
SIEGE OF FALLUJA

EGYPTIAN ARMY AREA
ARAB LEGION AREA
IRAQI ARMY AREA
ISRAELI ARMY AREA

5   0   5
Miles

N

BEERSHEBA

201

(2) The troops cut off on the east in the Bethlehem–Hebron area.

(3) The garrisons of Egyptian front-line posts on the sector between the two Israeli "breaks through", which had taken place at Iraq Suweidan and Beit Jibrin. These garrisons, which amounted to some 2,500 men, were now besieged at Falluja.

The most urgent problem was how to rescue this besieged garrison. The Arab Legion column had reached the Hebron area, but was too weak to undertake any offensive operations. We consequently suggested that the Iraqi army extend its front to take over Latrun from us, and that we then transfer the troops in the Latrun sector to Hebron. This would enable us to build up in Hebron a force sufficient to extricate the Egyptians from Falluja. The Iraqis, however, replied that they were not in a position to take over Latrun. As a result, the Arab Legion was left to do everything— to defend its original front from Beit Nabala to south-east of Jerusalem, to hold the whole Hebron district and in addition to rescue what it could from the *débâcle* in the south. Neither the Iraqis, the Syrians, nor the Lebanese, were prepared to change their dispositions.

XII

We Stand Alone

In war, moral considerations make up three-quarters; the balance
of actual forces accounts only for the remaining quarter.
NAPOLEON BONAPARTE, *Observations sur les affaires d'Espagne*

XII

WE STAND ALONE

WHY Israel accepted the cease-fire on October 22nd is not known. Presumably political considerations were involved. In a purely military direction, the cease-fire seemed likely to deprive the Israeli army of some of the fruits of victory. It must, however, be remembered that Israel had defiantly flouted the United Nations. Not only had she built up her army and air force during the truce, in spite of the United Nations observers, but the acting mediator's report to the Security Council left little doubt that Israel had deliberately broken the truce by a carefully planned large-scale attack against the Egyptians. The Israeli government therefore probably agreed to the truce, not desiring to drive UNO too far. The Israeli army, however, interpreted the cease-fire in a somewhat elastic manner.

A new Israeli column had meanwhile started southwards from Artuf, with a view to clearing the Arab villages from there to Beit Jibrin and then capturing Hebron (see the map on page 197). On October 24th, the Israeli radio announced that their forces would shortly occupy Kafr Etzion, the former Jewish colony between Bethlehem and Hebron. Unknown to one another, the Arab Legion column was moving down from Bethlehem to Hebron, and the Israeli column was travelling parallel to it from Artuf to Beit Jibrin. The Israeli force visited all the Arab villages on their route, driving out the civilian inhabitants, who poured into Bethlehem as fugitives. The eviction of all Arab civilians had now become a recognized feature of Israeli military operations.

The Arab Legion left small forces to hold the Bethlehem area, and itself went on to Hebron. On the evening of October 26th, it swung out of Hebron and down the narrow winding road between pine-clad mountain slopes to Tarqumiya, where it harboured for the night.

October 27th was spent resting and maintaining vehicles in Tarqumiya. It was decided that a reconnaissance force of seven armoured cars under Major Lockett would reconnoitre Beit Jibrin on October 28th. The following account was written by an officer who took part in this operation:

"The grey light of dawn was just beginning to creep over the Hebron hills as the crews of the armoured cars quietly checked their vehicles drawn up in harbour in Tarqumiya village and made them ready for action. Not much was said, but there was an air of quiet expectation abroad and a certain amount of hand-shaking and well-wishing went on between the men taking part in the patrol.

"Just before six o'clock, the sun appeared over the hilltops, sending one bar of vivid orange light leaping into the sky, where it stood suspended for perhaps half a minute before it was merged into the general splendour of the approaching day. As though they had been waiting for this signal, seven engines barked into action, seven hands were raised in a 'ready to move' signal, and on a signal from the leading vehicle, the cars moved slowly off down the valley.

"The road to Beit Jibrin is a winding white strip writhing down the narrow valley as though trying vainly to escape the hills which threaten to block it at every turn. The road itself was inches deep in fine, white, penetrating dust, and as the armoured cars rolled along, each half-concealed in a pillar of dust, with flags fluttering from their aerial masts and the now rapidly rising sun gilding the stubby outlines of their armour, they were strangely reminiscent of a line of battleships moving majestically through a heavy sea.

"Just outside Beit Jibrin village the road rises slightly and runs through a small copse before it twists and turns through the white buildings of the village. It was inside this copse that the first car in the column halted while the sergeant commanding the vehicle jumped out, cocked sub-machine gun in hand, and crept forward to see what lay immediately over the rise; during this period the other armoured cars slipped up behind and stopped in line on the road, engines were switched off, and the dust settled while no sound disturbed the stillness of the morning except harsh metallic scrapings as the silent crews of the armoured cars slipped belts of ammunition into their Browning guns, and the breech-blocks of two-pounder cannons were opened in readiness.

"All eyes were now fixed on the sergeant, who was perhaps one hundred yards forward of the leading armoured car, his khaki-clad body, topped by scarlet headdress, the only thing moving in the landscape. He was crawling with irritating deliberation to the top of the small tree-crowned rise, where his body stiffened on the ground as his eyes rose above the level of the hill and he looked down into the valley and on to the village itself. There was no movement from him for perhaps a minute, and just for that moment there was no sound at all, everything still, and the cars stood waiting.

"Suddenly he leaped to his feet and came running back to the column of vehicles, shouting excitedly, almost dancing across the ground and waving his gun in the air. As he clambered on to his vehicle, panting with exertion, his face split with an excited grin, he shouted: 'There are about thirty Jewish armoured cars coming along!' He had hardly said these words before a vague humming and sound of vehicle engines, many and moving fast, could be heard from the direction of the village, steadily increasing in volume and sounding rather ominous and strangely disturbing with each second that passed.

"There was hardly any sound from the armoured cars as they fanned out left and right on either side of the road and stood there in an inverted 'V' with the point towards Beit Jibrin, the muzzles of their guns moving smoothly round in the direction of the oncoming vehicles like the snouts of a band of some queer monsters scenting their enemy.

"The leading armoured car moved a little forward in order to catch first sight of the oncoming vehicles, and it was from this car that the first shot of the engagement came. It was debated with a certain amount of seriousness afterwards if the sergeant in charge of the vehicle had any knowledge of billiards and knew the meaning of 'in off', or if he had perhaps been influenced by war-time reports of 'skip bombing', but the fact remains that the first shot from his car sailed deliberately across the valley, over the village and striking the ground about thirty yards short of a Jewish half-track vehicle, ricocheted off the ground and flipped into the vehicle, which spun round in a half-circle, smoke pouring from its engine and stood still there, flaming. The Jewish crew of the vehicle jumped out, but were met with a burst of machine-gun fire which left their bodies twitching on the road beside their burning vehicle.

"The first shot was the signal for all the guns to crash into life, and for the next thirty minutes the situation was almost too confused to recall. Jewish armoured cars were racing in every direction all over the landscape, vainly trying to escape the fire of the Arab guns, but spread out in the valley the cars were an easy target, and as one after the other slewed round flaming, the excited Arab Legionaries were almost screaming with delight. Scattered burning vehicles dotted the landscape, and the Arab Legion troops found themselves under very heavy machine-gun and light-automatic fire which indicated that they were in the midst of quite a strong position. So, deliberately, the fire of the Arab armoured cars was turned on to these machine-gun nests, and one after the other they were silenced. As their green-clad soldiers fled for the shelter of houses, they dropped on to the ground under the intense fire from the armoured cars, sometimes to rise again and stagger forward a few yards only to meet a hail of tracer bullets which left them motionless on the ground whilst the Arab troops in their armoured cars slapped each other on the back, yelling with laughter, and now and then popped their heads out of their cars to scream out: 'Al Jeish al Arabi— the Arab Legion—is here!' There was one gunner who, every time his guns found their target, be it man or vehicle, pressed his trigger, wiped the back of his hand quickly across his mouth and shouted: 'Al Jeish al Arabi, made in England!' By this time, the Arab armoured cars had worked their way forward into the village of Beit Jibrin. The undamaged armoured cars had all fled from the scene and the machine-gun nests having been silenced, there was a lull in the battle whilst the Arab Legion armoured cars moved slowly forward with the houses of Beit Jibrin village on their left and a deep wadi on their right.

"In the centre of the village there was a small furry donkey, quietly cropping the grass, evidently not at all disturbed by the noise that had been going on around him and not caring to give the passing vehicles more than a sleepy passing glance before turning his attention again to his food.

"It was about this time that Major Lockett decided that the purpose of the recce had been fulfilled and he began giving orders for the vehicles to withdraw from the village. The enemy must have been waiting for just this chance, for no sooner had the cars started turning round than a hail of large calibre mortar bombs began to fall in the narrow area of the road and wadi. It is estimated that in ten minutes more than eighty bombs fell around the cars. The whole area was thick with the dust of the wadi as the crashing bombs churned it into the air, and the air itself was full of flying pieces of metal, chunks of masonry and slivers of wood torn from nearby trees by the exploding bombs.

"One armoured car received a direct hit when a bomb exploded inside it, killing the crew of three, and another was so damaged by a bomb bursting close to it that, despite many attempts, it was found impossible to tow it away, and so the noise was increased as these cars were destroyed by our own guns. As they burst into flames, the ammunition and shells inside them exploded, sending streams of tracer bullets into the air, and pillars of smoke from the armoured cars climbed slowly upwards.

"As this work was completed and the mortar bombs were still falling, the five remaining armoured cars withdrew to Tarqumiya village, leaving behind them at least six burning Jewish armoured cars and one truck destroyed, whilst the ground in the whole area was dotted with the corpses of at least forty Jewish soldiers whose spread-eagled bodies paid adequate tribute to the power and accuracy of Arab Legion fire. The Israeli force had been about five times as strong as the Arab Legion party.

"During the heavy mortar fire in the defile, special tribute should be paid to two sergeants of the Arab Legion. One of them, with astounding coolness, attempted to fix the tow rope to the damaged armoured car under very heavy fire directed immediately at his

PLATE 12

From the Arab Legion trenches at Latrun, looking out across the flat coastal plain

PLATE 13

War Office Official Photograph

"The King still maintained his usual spirits." King Abdulla enjoying a joke with the author vehicle. The other assisted him in this work and carried on, refusing to leave, even though seriously injured by a bullet through his thigh; with a blood-soaked trouser leg he hopped on one leg to his armoured car, took command, led it out of battle and then collapsed through loss of blood.

"Under an olive tree in Tarqumiya village, there are three mounds of earth that hide all that is left of three very gallant soldiers from Trans-Jordan who will never see their country again, but the manner of whose death was an inspiration to the whole Arab Legion."

It seemed to be almost certain that the Israeli force was a column advancing to capture Hebron. This gallant little action saved the city. The Arab Legion then placed a force astride the Beersheba–Hebron road south of Dhahiriya, and proceeded to establish defensive positions to cover the area. An area of some six hundred square miles had been saved for the Arabs by a tiny force of 350 all ranks of the Arab Legion. In the face of an army of 15,000 Israelis, such a feat could not have been performed had it not been for the fact that the area was mountainous. The "spinal cord" of Palestine is the range of mountains which extends from Galilee to Hebron. West of Nablus and Jerusalem, the mountains are only divided from the sea by a flat coastal plain averaging ten to fifteen miles wide. West of Hebron, however, the coastal plain is twenty-five miles wide. The battle between the Israelis and the Egyptians had taken place in this wide plain. The Palmach had meanwhile been developed into an improvised armoured division, consisting of a few tanks, but mostly armoured cars, Bren carriers, armoured half-tracks and great numbers of jeeps. In this light, dry soil, wheels could drive across country almost as freely as tracks. The Palmach division thus formed a spearhead which broke through the static Egyptian front and drove on far behind the Egyptian lines, cutting their communications and capturing their bases. It was a Blitzkrieg exactly on the lines of the Battle of France in May 1940. If the 350 men of the Arab Legion had been out in that open plain, they could have done little against the Israeli "armoured division". But they saved six hundred square miles of the Hebron mountains, because the "armoured division" could not operate there with the same ease as in the plains.

It is interesting to remember how frequently this contest between armour and infantry had halted a battle line at the foot of these same Palestine mountains. Not everybody realizes that the present government of Israel holds very little indeed of the country held by the Children of Israel at the time of David and Solomon. For the Kingdom of David coincided very nearly with the present Kingdom of Jordan, the coastal plain (now Israel) being then the land of the

Philistines. There are many references in Joshua and Judges to the fact that the Philistines and the Canaanites dwelt in the plains and had chariots of iron, and thus the Children of Israel could not conquer them in the plains. The Philistines were industrially more advanced than the Israelites, just as the Jews of Israel today have more industries than the Jordanians. When the psalmist exclaimed, "I will lift up mine eyes unto the hills, from whence cometh my strength," he was not merely writing poetry. He was expressing the tactical policy of the army of David in its wars against the Philistines. The same words could well have served as the motto of the Arab Legion in 1948.

The Arab Legion could not have held the Lydda and Ramle area —though it was only fifty square miles—because it lay in a flat open plain. It saved six hundred square miles of the Hebron district because it was mountainous. But even with these explanations, the feat was remarkable. In any case, the correct use of ground is one of the secrets of the military art.

*　　*　　*　　*　　*

The United Nations resolution ordering a cease-fire on October 22nd also ordered both sides to withdraw to the positions they held prior to the breach of the truce on October 15th. The Israeli government replied, refusing to withdraw. On October 29th, the Security Council, then in session in Paris, was to have voted on an Anglo-Chinese motion proposing the consideration of the imposition of sanctions on Egypt or Israel, if they did not comply with the order to withdraw. On October 30th, the voting was unexpectedly postponed, owing to an overnight change on the part of the United States delegation. It was generally believed that the American *volte-face* was due to the personal intervention of President Truman. The Presidential election was due to take place four days later, and there was still that Jewish vote. Israel was thus able successfully to defy the Security Council's orders.

Meanwhile, in the extreme north, the remnants of the "Liberation Army" still held a few Palestinian villages, immediately south of the Lebanese border. On October 28th, an Israeli force attacked and, in three days, drove the motley Liberation Army across the border into Lebanon. The Israelis followed them over the line, occupying a strip of Lebanese territory.

Thus on November 1st, 1948, the Arab Legion found itself in a somewhat uncomfortable situation. The Egyptian, Lebanese and Syrian armies were *hors de combat*. Only the Iraqi army and the Arab Legion remained in the field. The occupation of the Hebron district had doubled our front. We were holding a length of about one hundred miles with about 10,000 men. Financial discretion had been thrown to the winds and we had been recruiting so fast that we had nearly doubled our strength in six months. Naturally this rapid increase had led to an equivalent drop in efficiency. Indeed, men were being sent to units in the line with virtually no training. An average of fifteen days elapsed between the enlistment of a recruit and his arrival in the front line. The only other occasion I know of when soldiers were turned out so quickly was with Hodson's Horse at the siege of Delhi.

The Arab Legion with 10,000 men was therefore facing the Israeli army with about 120,000. The Iraqi army had 19,000 all ranks. In addition to this numerical disparity, the Arab Legion had finished (or very nearly) all its stocks of twenty-five pounder ammunition, four-point-two-inch mortar, three-inch mortar, Piat, six-pounder anti-tank guns, and No. 36 (or Mills) hand grenades.

At about this time, I was visited by the correspondent of a leading New York daily paper, who told me that the Arab Legion had run out of artillery ammunition. When I asked him what made him think so, he told me that he had heard it at Lake Success! If our situation was so well known in Lake Success, it could scarcely be unknown to the Israeli army.

Meanwhile, however, although the fact that Israel was receiving arms and ammunition from Czecho-Slovakia was well-known, the UNO blockade was still in force, and the British government refused to supply us. In spite of this, both Russia and Israel "denounced" Britain for having supplied arms and ammunition to the Arab Legion during the truce! It was natural enough that they should make this charge, in order to cover up the fact that they themselves had been cheating. It was perhaps more annoying that our Arab allies likewise refused to believe that we were not receiving supplies. The Arab Legion, they claimed, was commanded by British officers. King Abdulla was Britain's devoted ally. It was ridiculous to suppose that Britain would leave her ally exposed to attack without ammunition. Hence, they concluded, if we claimed to be short of ammunition, we were obviously lying. No doubt we made such statements because we did not want to fight. The only possibility in which nobody believed was that it was out of loyalty to UNO that Britain did not give us ammunition.

Meanwhile the refugees continued to pour in. The Israelis were now deliberately driving out all Arabs, a process assisted now and again by the usual "calculated massacre". On October 31st, United Nations observers reported that the Israelis had killed thirty women and children at Dawaima, west of Hebron. It would be an exaggeration to claim that great numbers were massacred. But just enough were killed, or roughly handled, to make sure that all the civilian population took flight, thereby leaving more and more land vacant for future Jewish settlement. These particular villages west of Hebron were to remain vacant and their lands uncultivated for eight years. When I left Jordan in 1956, plans for Jewish settlements in the area were, for the first time, beginning to take shape.

On October 26th, the Israeli broadcasting station indulged in a rather unusual sally. Commenting on the Neqeb battles and the Israeli attacks on Latrun in May, June and July, the speaker remarked that an Arab Legion soldier was the equal of an Israeli soldier, but that one Israeli was equivalent to three Iraqis or to six Egyptians. As for the Syrians, they said, the number of them required to equal one Israeli ran into astronomical figures. The Arabs say that there are three forms of drunkenness—drunkenness of wine, drunkenness of love and drunkenness of victory. The Israeli radio was a good deal intoxicated with victory. Another broadcast talk referred to Israel's "historical boundaries from the Euphrates to the Nile".

The Israeli radio also announced that Aqaba must be captured. Now Aqaba was within the old borders of Trans-Jordan, and consequently was covered by the Anglo-Jordan treaty. It was also Trans-Jordan's only remaining outlet to the sea. As a result, the Trans-Jordan government asked the British government to assume responsibility for the defence of Aqaba. Soon afterwards British troops landed in the village, and a naval frigate anchored offshore.

On November 3rd, King Abdulla received a personal message from the Egyptian Minister of Defence begging him to suggest to King Farouq that it was time to make peace. The fact was that no politician was willing to risk his reputation for patriotism by making such a suggestion. King Abdulla was probably thought to be simple and honest enough to be a useful cat's-paw. If he were to suggest it, peace could be made—and it would always be possible to put the blame on King Abdulla, on the grounds that it was his idea.

On November 2nd, there were again street demonstrations in Amman. All the Arab governments were denounced by the crowd for their failure to defeat Israel. I personally, however, came in for the largest share of denunciation. A crowd, chiefly school-children, gathered outside Arab Legion headquarters, shouting, "Down with Glubb Pasha! Liar and traitor!"

Meanwhile it was gratifying to know that on November 4th, Mr. Ernest Bevin, answering a question in the House of Commons, stated that I was not liable to five years' imprisonment for enlisting in a foreign army without His Majesty's cognizance.

On November 6th, the Israeli Prime Minister, Mr. Ben Gurion, sent a message to Mr. Stalin, assuring him that the Israeli nation would never forget the help and support given to it by Russia in 1948.

* * * * *

A considerable portion of the Egyptian forces was still in the Hebron–Bethlehem sector, cut off from its base and the rest of the Egyptian army. We were obliged to take them on our ration strength. They were too demoralized to fight, and drifted about the streets of Bethlehem with nothing to do.

Meanwhile I continued to enlist men as fast as possible. On November 14th, for example, I wrote to Lash saying:

"I am collecting a new force in Amman, which I hope will consist of 300 men. It is partly recruits and partly old soldiers, whom we have succeeded in bringing back from civil life. I should like to train them for a fortnight, if no crisis arises meanwhile."

The British refused to give us ammunition, but they agreed to send barbed wire. We worked day and night. If the Israelis were to attack us they would not have a walk-over.

* * * * *

While the Israelis on the one hand were assuming an increasingly arrogant attitude, they simultaneously showed signs of desiring to conciliate Trans-Jordan. On November 17th, for example, Mr. Shertok, the Israeli Foreign Minister, made a violent speech before the Political Committee of the United Nations in Paris. At the same time, in Jerusalem, the Israeli authorities, through certain consuls, suggested a "real cease-fire" between themselves and the Arab Legion in the city. Meanwhile, in one night, they fired sixty rounds of twenty-five pounder into our position in Jerusalem. We made no reply. It was annoying to think that the Jews had captured these twenty-five-pounder guns and ammunition from the Egyptians, who had themselves seized our ammunition ship with our twenty-five-pounder ammunition in May. Perhaps these sixty shells were really our own.

When I saw King Abdulla on November 21st, I asked him his opinion on the Jewish advances for a "real cease-fire" in Jerusalem. He looked at me with a twinkle.

"I'll tell you a Turkish proverb," said His Majesty. "They say— 'If you meet a bear when crossing a rotten bridge, call her—dear Auntie!' "

The King, while fully realizing now that the Arab Legion was virtually alone, still maintained his usual spirits. He was constantly on the move, and was especially fond of visiting Jerusalem. I was with him one night when he slept in Ramallah. A deputation of Muslim religious leaders called to pay their respects—seven or eight venerable old men with white turbans on their heads and long white beards. The King, though himself an extremely conscientious Muslim, was in a playful mood and could not resist the temptation to tease such venerable visitors. The conversation turned to Ramadhan, the Muslim month of fasting, during which no Muslim is supposed to eat or drink from the first dawn to sunset. The King engaged the Mufti of Jerusalem in the following exchange:

THE KING: "Why does smoking a cigarette break your fast, O Mufti?"

MUFTI: "Because the smoke enters your body, Your Majesty."

THE KING: "Then what happens if the cook breathes in some smoke when he is cooking the dinner?"

MUFTI: "That does not break his fast, because such smoke is not delicious."

THE KING: (A band is playing outside) "Does music break your fast?"

MUFTI: "No, sir."

THE KING: "Why not? It is much more delicious than cigarette smoke. In any case, why should a hypodermic injection break your fast? You cannot say that to be punctured with a needle is delicious!"

"Is it wrong to look at a pretty woman?" next enquired His Majesty with assumed innocence.

The learned shaikhs pulled long faces, and replied solemnly: "A sin, Your Majesty, a sin."

The King gave me a sidelong glance with a wicked twinkle.

"I don't see how you get that," said His Majesty. "The Holy Quran says—'If you see a woman, avert your gaze!' Now, obviously you cannot avert your gaze unless you have already been looking!"

The good shaikhs were somewhat taken aback by these views. The Mufti, however, who was not to be so easily defeated, remarked that we must insist that all women be veiled, and then no problem of looking at them would arise, because they would be completely invisible.

"That's all very well," answered His Majesty, winking at the company, "but nowadays, far from veiling, they go and bathe in the sea. What are we going to do about that, O Mufti?"

But even the Mufti was a man. "Is that so?" he replied, also winking at the company. "What a pity I am no longer a young man!"

*   *   *   *   *

Although the Israelis had accepted the Security Council cease-fire order, they continued their military operations wherever it suited them. Particularly were they anxious to secure the surrender of the Egyptian troops besieged in Falluja. How to rescue this force became the problem of the hour.

A British officer of the Arab Legion volunteered to walk through the Jewish lines into Falluja, and find out their real situation. Geoffrey was not a regular officer, but he had achieved a reputation for bravery during the war. When conditions were peaceful, he appeared to be a nervous wreck, but in a desperate situation he became perfectly calm. He was one of those rather tragic products of war, a man to whom the risks of battle had become a necessary tonic. He could not live without a war, and he wandered the world from war to war, seeking ever more desperate situations.

Geoffrey was as good as his word. He passed through the Jewish lines on foot, accompanied by an Arab corporal, spent two days with the Egyptians in Falluja, and then walked back through the Israeli army again. He reported that the Israelis were shelling and mortaring the garrison of Falluja day and night. The troops were chiefly Sudanese and seemed to be in good heart. The Israelis, however, refused to allow any convoy to enter Falluja.

It will be remembered that the Israeli excuse for starting the Neqeb battle was that the Egyptians would not allow convoys to go to the besieged Jewish colonies in the Neqeb. Now, however, that the boot was on the other leg, and the Israelis were besieging a force of Egyptians, they themselves refused to allow an Egyptian convoy to go through. What was sauce for the goose was obviously not sauce for the gander!

How to rescue the Falluja garrison became the chief preoccupation of the Arab League. A plan was eventually produced by the politicians, according to which Trans-Jordan, Iraq and Syria would each contribute a battalion. The resulting force of three battalions would relieve Falluja!

Who but a politician could think of such an idea? Three different battalions from three different armies would carry out a joint operation in mountainous country at night—apparently without even a single commander. We continued to press for the Iraqi army to take over Latrun, and promised that, if this were done, we would relieve Falluja. The Iraqis regretted their inability to do this, but sent one battalion to Bethlehem as their contribution to the joint operation.

It was obvious that nothing would come of all these consultations. I accordingly sent Geoffrey once more to walk through the Jewish lines to Falluja and offer them a plan. Our proposal was that, on a night agreed upon, the Egyptians should walk out of Falluja to the east. We should advance to meet them and engage from the rear any Jewish forces attempting to bar their way. The distance between us was about twelve miles. The Egyptian garrison was a weak brigade group, about 2,500 strong. They would have had to abandon or destroy their heavy stores, but I still believe that eighty per cent of the personnel would have reached our lines in safety. Geoffrey passed successfully through the Israeli lines, but the Egyptian commander rejected the proposal. This was the end of our attempts to relieve Falluja. The garrison actually held out until they were relieved by an armistice, when they marched out with the honours of war. Their dogged resistance was a fine performance.

*   *   *   *   *

On November 28th, a meeting occurred in Jerusalem between Lieut.-Colonel Abdulla al Tell of the Arab Legion and Colonel Moshe Dayan, who was commanding the Israeli troops in Jerusalem. The object of the meeting, which took place in the presence of UNO representatives, was to secure a "real cease-fire" in the city. This meeting was to a great extent successful. Firing almost ceased in the city, with effect from November 29th, and later on, the real cease-fire was extended also to Latrun.

Meanwhile, however, an increasing Israeli concentration was being built up south of the Dead Sea. On November 30th, the Israeli and Arab Legion commanders in Jeruslem met again. The Arab Legion commander was instructed to inform Colonel Moshe Dayan that Trans-Jordan did not want a cease-fire in Jerusalem if Israel was going to start a new campaign south of the Dead Sea. Colonel Dayan promised to try to stop the troop movements south of the Dead Sea. The Israeli radio announced that these moves had been purely defensive "to meet Arab aggression". Considering that Jordan had no troops south of Amman, such an excuse was scarcely credible.

*   *   *   *   *

On December 1st, 1948, a conference of the principal leaders of Arab Palestine assembled in Jericho, and drew up a resolution in favour of the unification of Trans-Jordan and what was left of Arab Palestine. On December 13th, the resolution was considered by the Trans-Jordan Parliament and the necessary modification of the Trans-Jordan constitution was passed into law.

This development aroused a fury of resentment from the other Arab States. Egypt, which had just lost all the territory she had occupied in Palestine, was the most resentful, but Syria was scarcely less so. Ibn Saud, hereditary enemy of the Hashemite royal family, was alarmed at any increase in the power of King Abdulla. The remaining Arab League States agreed not to recognize the unification of Trans-Jordan and Arab Palestine.

A statesman has been defined as a man who thinks of the next generation, whereas a politician is a man who thinks of the next election. King Abdulla was a statesman. He was a good political strategist, his mind was broad enough to consider the whole world

as his stage, and he looked fifty years ahead in time. But he was a
poor political tactician—he was never thinking of the next election!

In reality, the unification of Arab Palestine with Trans-Jordan
was not a subtle plot by King Abdulla. It was the spontaneous
and genuine desire of the Palestinian people. Without a government
or an army of their own, they had no alternative but to join another
existing government, the army of which was already defending their
country. In spite of the opposition of all the other Arab countries,
the Arabs of Palestine have never shown the least inclination to
reverse their decision of December 1st, 1948.

The Egyptian-sponsored Government of All Palestine, previously
established in Gaza, had meanwhile withdrawn to Cairo. On
December 8th, it adopted a resolution rejecting Abdulla as ruler of
Palestine.

*   *   *   *   *

The struggle round besieged Falluja continued, the Israeli
forces tightening the siege and at the same time shelling and
attacking the garrison. On November 19th, the Egyptian army,
presumably in the hope of easing the pressure on Falluja by creating a diversion, had advanced to the east from their positions between Khan Yunis and Gaza. They continued to advance short
distances until December 10th, when they began to shell the Jewish
colony of Nirim. The Israelis thereupon decided to renew large-
scale operations.

On December 22nd, 1948, the Israelis launched a new offensive
against the Egyptian army in Gaza. Fighting lasted until January
7th, 1949, when a fresh cease-fire was agreed to.

A meeting was arranged at Rhodes, under the auspices of the
United Nations, between Egypt and Israel, and an armistice was
signed on February 24th. Lebanon signed an armistice with Israel
on March 23rd. On March 30th, Colonel Husni az Zaim carried out
a *coup d'état* in Damascus, and seized supreme power. The Jordan
government, at the same time, was informed that the Iraqi army
was about to withdraw from Palestine.

We were left alone to fend for ourselves.

XIII

Twelve to One

No great improvements in the lot of mankind are possible until a great change takes place in the fundamental constitution of their modes of thought. JOHN STUART MILL

XIII

TWELVE TO ONE

EARLY in May 1948, I had given a talk to a number of Trans-Jordan officers of the Arab Legion in Amman, on the situation at that time before the fighting began. Amongst other things, I had said that the Trans-Jordan government thought it inadvisable to engage in hostilities with the Jews, but that some of the other Arab governments insisted on doing so. I was afraid, I had said, that the time would come when those who were today so anxious to fight would drop out of the struggle, and that we, the Arab Legion, would be left to face the Jews alone. Some of the officers had thought my forebodings too pessimistic. On this issue, they believed that the Arabs were united, and that they would stand and fall together.

Less than a year later, my unhappy prophecy was fulfilled. Egypt and Lebanon had signed an armistice and Syria was *hors de combat* owing to an internal crisis. Iraq refused to negotiate an armistice, but expressed her intention to withdraw, which would leave eleven thousand men of the Arab Legion confronting ten or twelve times as many Israelis.

*   *   *   *   *

Meanwhile, in January 1949, a debate took place in the House of Commons which was to foreshadow the disastrous lack of appreciation of the realities of British interests—lack of clear thought which was to produce tragic results in the ensuing years.

The Labour government agreed to a full-dress debate on Palestine. Mr. Ernest Bevin opened with a speech in defence of his policy. If British interests were to be the basis of British policy, Mr. Bevin's ideas were undoubtedly right. The only criticism which could perhaps be made against him was that Britain should not have evacuated Palestine on May 15th, 1948, and left the country to ruin. If partition were the solution, she should have stayed on and enforced it. She should not have abandoned the country until the Jewish and Arab governments were established, and any necessary exchanges of population had taken place. But the storm of criticisms directed against Mr. Bevin were not based on these considerations—it was a storm of confused emotion. This extraordinary problem, on that evening, divided the British against one another—divided them into partisans—pro-Arabs and pro-Jews. The British Commonwealth was forgotten.

Mr. Bevin suffered the same fate as everyone else who has been rash enough to try to solve this intensely emotional problem. He was accused of partiality by both sides. In this Parliamentary debate, he was charged with having urged the Arabs to fight the Jews. It is ironical to remember that Mr. Bevin was believed by the Arabs to be responsible for giving me secret orders not to defend Lydda and Ramle against Israel, for hampering their war effort and trying to prevent them fighting!

Perhaps it was unfortunate that, in his speech, he did not limit himself to the cold facts of British interests, but himself indulged in emotional references to half a million Arab refugees.

Let us, however, forget the passionate partisanship of those who, forgetting their own country, espoused the cause of one side or the other. What were the British interests involved, to which so little reference was made in this debate?

Britain has been profoundly interested in the Middle East, ever since she acquired interests in India, let us say, two hundred years ago. She protected these interests for more than one hundred and fifty years by always remaining friendly with the government of the area, in those days the government of Turkey. It is significant that, if Britain realized the importance of the Middle East to herself, her enemies have always reached the same conclusion. European conquerors engaged in a mortal struggle with Britain always believed the Middle East to be vital to her. Napoleon landed in Egypt and marched up to Palestine—not out of enmity to Turkey, but as a means of destroying Britain. Having failed in Egypt, he later camped his army at Boulogne in order to invade England. The Kaiser's Germany, at the beginning of the First World War, attacked the Suez Canal from Palestine, while simultaneously the German army was battling for the Channel ports. Twenty-five years later, Hitler's Germany prepared to invade England, and at the same time crossed the Western Desert to attack Egypt.

Whether we agree with them or not, Britain's enemies have always believed the two chinks in her armour to be the Middle East and the English Channel.

The Middle East originally was important to her as being the half-way house from Britain to India, the Far East and Australia—and such it still is both for shipping and aircraft. Today, of course, it is also of immense interest owing to its oil. But it is also the only land-bridge to Africa—Egypt, indeed, is the gateway to Africa. Arab nationalism has given Egypt a vital connection with the Arabs proper in Arabia, and with the arabicized people of North Africa. But in addition, Egypt has affinities with the Sudan and with Africa —at least as far south as the influence of Islam stretches.

If we look at the map, we see the vast extent of territory from

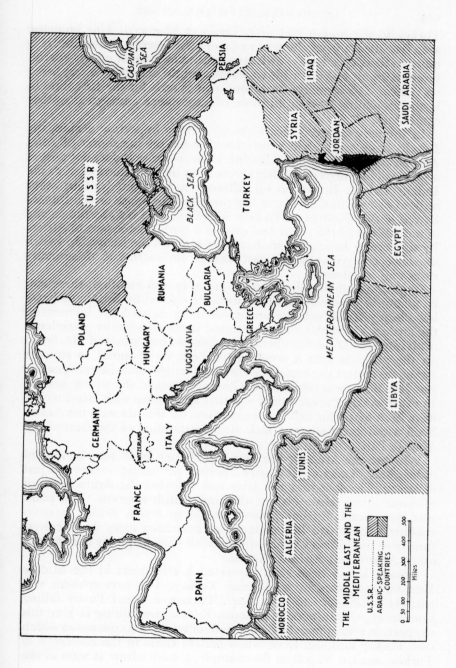

THE MIDDLE EAST AND THE MEDITERRANEAN

U.S.S.R. ....

ARABIC-SPEAKING
COUNTRIES ....

0 50 100   200   300   400   500
Miles

CASPIAN SEA

PERSIA

IRAQ

SAUDI ARABIA

SYRIA

JORDAN

USSR

BLACK SEA

TURKEY

EGYPT

RUMANIA

BULGARIA

GREECE

MEDITERRANEAN SEA

POLAND

HUNGARY

YUGOSLAVIA

LIBYA

GERMANY

SWITZERLAND

ITALY

FRANCE

TUNIS

ALGERIA

SPAIN

MOROCCO

223

Turkey to the Sudan and from Persia to Morocco. This immense area has always been thought to be of vital interest to Britain. It is more so than ever today, owing to the importance of oil, its central position for air travel (or air warfare), and the influence it can bring on Africa. The formerly dark continent is now for the first time in history assuming its rightful place of importance amongst the other continents.

In the very centre of this wide and vitally important region, the Israelis have established a tiny beach-head on the shores of Asia. As a means of transit, Israel is of no value, because it does not possess a wide enough area stretching across from the Mediterranean to the Indian Ocean. It has no oil. Moreover, far from leading other nations of Asia and Africa, it has provoked the more or less intense hatred of the whole area. To be a friend of Israel is to be the enemy of most of the Middle East and even of a considerable part of Africa. By supporting Israel, Britain has lost nearly all the friendship which she once enjoyed over this vast tract of the earth and these many races and countries.

Neglecting all considerations of morality and emotion, there can be no doubt whatever that the assistance offered by Britain to Israel has destroyed the prestige and profoundly injured the interests of the former. Of course, there are moral issues which take precedence of all interests. If the members of Parliament had attacked Mr. Bevin on the grounds that it would have been more moral to support Israel, no matter the cost, then their case might have been arguable. But Mr. Bevin was criticized for having "backed the wrong horse". In other words, the argument was that an alliance with Israel would have been better for British interests than an alliance with the Arabs. Such a statement shows a lack of understanding of the facts of the Middle East.

Whether the Arabs or the Jews are "better men" may be argued indefinitely. Races are not often "better" or "worse"—they are just different. The fact that the Jews had defeated the Arabs was not relevant to the basic factors affecting British interests. The point was that Israel did not possess the things which British interests required: the broad belt of territory stretching from the Mediterranean to the Indian Ocean—the oilfields—or the power to influence other Asiatic and African nations.

Britain, it has been said, protected her interests in the Middle East for 150 years by supporting Turkey. This arrangement was entirely satisfactory to both sides. Turkey, a Great Power falling into decay, was in need of support. Britain was willing to give this support, in return merely for the right of transit—a concession which cost Turkey nothing. Even when Britain came to the assistance of Turkey, against Napoleon for example, she withdrew as soon as the

PLATE 14

The Jewish quarter of the Old City, looking north-east from near the Zion Gate. The roofless large white building is the ruined synagogue. On its left, the Dome of the Rock. On its right, the long roof with a small dome at the right-hand end is the Aqsa Mosque. In the background, the Mount of Olives

Soldiers representing different Arab Legion units marching from barracks to take part in a ceremonial parade

PLATE 15

French were driven out. She therefore gave no pretext for Turkish resentment—at any rate until she occupied Egypt.

The agreement concluded in 1915 with the Sherif Husain and the support accorded by Britain for the formation of the Arab League after the Second World War were both attempts to restore the system which had worked successfully for 150 years with Turkey, namely, a local government which, with our support, would be strong enough to resist encroachment by any other Great Power.

In so far as Israel was concerned, to save the persecuted Jews of Europe was doubtless a noble task. But the proposition which I venture to submit is that the Jews should not have been settled in Palestine by the use of military force, and against the will of the people already living in that country. That was indeed the heart of the matter. To give help to persecuted Jews, both moral and material, would have been a generous policy. Britain and America could have mediated between them and the Arabs, but the fatal error was to use violence—and to leave a tradition of violence, which Jews and Arabs alike only too readily absorbed. Neither side considers any solution to their present deadlock, except violence.

The Jews, of course, reply that they do not want to be a minority in an Arab area, as they have for centuries been minorities in so many other countries. They want a country where all the people will be Jews—or, if not all, then any minorities will be negligible in proportion to the Jews. They have, they claim, secured their aim in the foundation of Israel, and they could not have secured it by any other means than violence. But have they secured it and for how long? The Crusaders conquered a greater area of territory and held it for a hundred years—but there are no Crusaders now. Selfish violence sooner or later brings retribution, though it may be long coming.

* * * * *

I have diverged too far in considering the interests of Britain. Our theme was the British parliamentary debate and the criticism of Mr. Bevin's policy of "backing the Arabs". The Labour government had a large majority and won the debate. The Conservatives had opposed Mr. Bevin's policy, perhaps only because they were in opposition. But a large number of Labour members had abstained or absented themselves. The government won a technical victory, but in practice it was badly shaken. The Israeli victories over the Egyptians had deeply impressed the world. The government shifted its policy. The retention of Arab friendship was essential; all British interests in the Middle East were in their hands by the facts of geography. The British government decided to continue to be friends of the Arabs, but also to be helpful to the Jews, in view of the political support which it was apparent that they could muster.

This, ever since 1949, has been the policy of successive British governments, Conservative and Labour alike. The result has been that we have been denounced as hypocrites by both sides.

*   *   *   *   *

On May 11th, 1949, Israel was admitted as a member of UNO. Jordan was debarred from membership because she was an ally of Britain and consequently Russia vetoed her admission whenever it was proposed.

In subsequent Press interviews, the members of the first Israeli delegation to UNO admitted that they had gone to Lake Success with some trepidation. To their surprise and delight, they were greeted with felicitations rather than criticism. I find an entry in my diary which reads:

"The Israeli victories in UNO were more surprising than those in the Neqeb. They had killed Count Bernadotte, UNO's special envoy. The acting mediator, Dr. Bunche, had reported that the Israeli army had made a deliberate attack on the Egyptian army, which could not be explained by the excuse that the Egyptians had fired on a convoy. UNO had then ordered the Israeli government to withdraw its forces to the positions held before the October 15th offensive, but they had refused. On December 22nd, the Israeli army had renewed their offensive against the Egyptian army in Gaza, again in spite of a UNO truce. The pretext for the Israeli offensive had been that the Egyptians would not allow convoys to pass through their lines to the besieged Jewish colonies in the Neqeb. Yet when, as the result of the October 15th attack, the Jewish colonies were relieved and the Egyptians in their turn were besieged, the Israelis refused to allow Egyptian convoys to pass through to Falluja. All these actions had been carried out in defiance of UNO, and yet many of the delegations at the United Nations had greeted Israel with enthusiasm as their latest fellow-member."

It is true that the political and military action taken by Israel from October 1st to December 31st, 1948, exhibits a rare degree of skill and boldness. The Israeli performance could not fail to arouse admiration in both politicians and soldiers. But the United Nations was an organization designed to preserve peace. It could only do this by enforcing its authority, or at least by maintaining its prestige. By welcoming a government which had repeatedly defied its authority, UNO destroyed its own influence in the Middle East. Both Arabs and Jews learnt this lesson. From 1949 onwards, both sides treated the United Nations and the Truce Supervision staff in Palestine with scant respect, rarely, if ever, complying with their instructions.

*   *   *   *   *

At the beginning of this chapter, we left the Arab Legion in Palestine about to face the Israeli army alone. The Egyptian, Syrian and Lebanese armies had abandoned the field. The Iraqi army was still in position holding the district of Samaria, but the Iraqi government had stated that it proposed to withdraw its troops as soon as possible. The Israeli forces had driven almost all the Arab inhabitants from the area allotted to Israel by the United Nations, and also from the territory conquered by them even though not given to them in the partition plan. Upper Galilee formed the only exception. These refugees were flooding into all the surrounding Arab countries, but more than half of them were in Jordan. It was obvious now that the Israeli government had adopted as its settled policy the expulsion of all Arabs from territories it conquered, and if any more territory were seized by Israel, further waves of Arab refugees would be driven into the surrounding countries.

In January 1949, the strength of the Arab Legion in Palestine had risen to 11,143 officers and men. We were never officially informed of the strength of the Iraqi forces in Palestine, but they were probably in the region of 19,000. This would give a total of 30,000 all ranks for the two armies. As against this, Israel may have had 120,000 to 150,000 all ranks—let us say four times as many.

In these circumstances, the Jordan government received, in the middle of February, an invitation from Dr. Bunche to send a delegation to Rhodes, to negotiate an armistice with Israel under United Nations auspices. The invitation was accepted, and the Jordan delegation proceeded to Rhodes by air on February 28th. The Egyptians and Lebanese had already signed, Syria was in the throes of revolution, and on Jordan fell the onus of concluding an armistice for the Iraqi front.

Dr. Bunche was conducting the Rhodes negotiations. His plan was that both sides should immediately sign cease-fire agreements for their whole fronts, in order to ease the tension. The armistice agreement could then be negotiated in a less strained atmosphere. The cease-fire draft agreement provided that: "no elements of the ground or air forces of either party would advance beyond or pass over the line now held." The Jordan government expressed its readiness to sign such an agreement. It requested that the undertaking be made to cover both the Iraqi and Jordan fronts, in view of the fact that the Iraqis were about to withdraw from Palestine. The Israelis demurred, whereupon the Jordan government offered to sign forthwith for the Arab Legion only, but with a clause automatically extending its provisions to the Iraqi front, when that army withdrew. While this argument was in progress, the departure of the Iraqi army was agreed on between the Jordan and Iraqi governments. It was to commence on March 13th, 1949. The

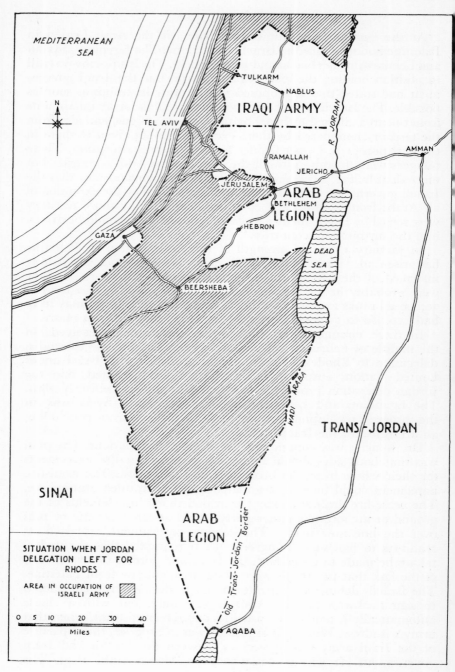

MEDITERRANEAN
SEA

N

IRAQI ARMY

TULKARM
NABLUS

TEL AVIV

R. JORDAN

AMMAN

RAMALLAH
JERICHO

JERUSALEM
BETHLEHEM
ARAB
LEGION

HEBRON

GAZA

DEAD
SEA

BEERSHEBA

WADI ARABA

TRANS-JORDAN

SINAI

ARAB
LEGION

Old Trans-Jordan Border

SITUATION WHEN JORDAN
DELEGATION LEFT FOR
RHODES

AREA IN OCCUPATION OF
ISRAELI ARMY

0   5   10   20   30   40
Miles

AQABA

argument on the application of the preliminary cease-fire to the Iraqi front was still in progress on March 8th. We could not but suspect that the Israelis would postpone signing the cease-fire until the Iraqis withdrew on March 13th, and then seize the opportunity to follow up the retreating Iraqis and occupy some more territory before the Arab Legion could take over. As the days passed, the tension and anxiety increased. The Israelis were intoxicated at their successes in the field, their cordial reception in the United Nations, the enthusiastic support of the U.S.A., and the swing of opinion to their side in Britain, as evidenced in the parliamentary debate on the Middle East. The whole world was on their side.

Then it suddenly appeared that they had another project in hand.

*　　*　　*　　*　　*

Until the October 15th Jewish attack on the Egyptians, the Egyptian army had held the whole of southern Palestine as far east as the Wadi Araba. With the collapse of Egypt, the Arab Legion had occupied the Hebron area, as described above. It had also occupied a wedge-shaped area of southern Palestine, connecting Sinai to Trans-Jordan between the Dead Sea and the Gulf of Aqaba. On February 25th, the Jordan government had protested to Dr. Bunche against Israeli troop movements north of this area. Although Dr. Bunche was in Rhodes, General Riley, an officer of the U.S. Marines, was in Palestine representing the United Nations. Dr. Bunche cabled General Riley, who replied that he had investigated the complaint, and no such Israeli troop movements had occurred.

After the arrival of the Jordan delegation in Rhodes, we signalled them to the effect that further Israeli forces were concentrating north of our positions in the area. We gave the location of the front line held by us, and we instructed our delegation to inform Dr. Bunche forthwith of the Israeli troop movements and of our own front line. A reply was received to the effect that the Israelis denied any military movements in the area. On March 2nd, the United Nations observers in Jordan informed us that they were aware of the Israeli troop movements in the south, and had reported them to their immediate superiors, the UNO observers in Haifa. Meanwhile the Jordan and Israeli delegations in Rhodes had met and shaken hands, and had been sitting together for several days engaged in negotiations.

On March 7th, the Jordan government despatched the following wireless signal to the delegation in Rhodes:

"Inform Dr. Bunche as follows. Considerable force of Jewish jeeps and armoured cars supported by aircraft crossed our lines

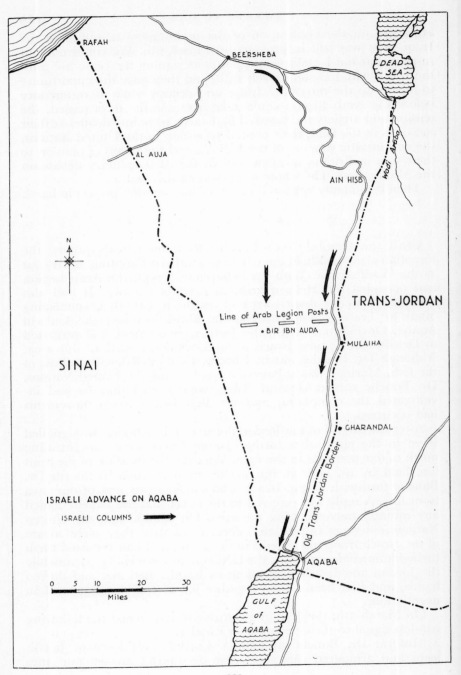

RAFAH

BEERSHEBA

DEAD SEA

AL AUJA

Wadi Araba

AIN HISB

N

TRANS-JORDAN

Line of Arab Legion Posts

• BIR IBN AUDA

• MULAIHA

SINAI

• GHARANDAL

ISRAELI ADVANCE ON AQABA

ISRAELI COLUMNS

Old Trans-Jordan Border

• AQABA

0   5   10   20   30
Miles

GULF
of
AQABA

morning seventh March one kilo west of Bir ibn Auda. Situation will
be extremely delicate unless Israel stops active military operations
during negotiations."

We had been watching the Israeli military concentration in the
south for more than a fortnight, but both the United Nations and
the Israeli delegation had categorically denied its existence. On
March 7th, this force launched an attack on our positions. On
March 8th, the Jordan government again signalled the delegation
as follows:

"Jewish forces are advancing on the Gulf of Aqaba in two columns.
One column at Bir Melhan. Main column moving down Wadi
Araba reached Mulaiha. Enemy forces estimated strong battalion
group or brigade. Jewish aircraft active over whole area. Inform
Dr. Bunche Trans-Jordan government deeply disturbed by these
operations while both delegations are actually negotiating at
Rhodes."

A reply was received from Dr. Bunche on March 9th, asking for
further details. Meanwhile, on the same date, the Jordan government again signalled the delegation:

"Military operations against Arab Legion in Wadi Araba
continue. Israeli forces attacking Arab Legion positions. You will
make strong protest forthwith to Dr. Bunche and ask him to stop
Israeli attacks while negotiations are in progress."

On March 10th, after so long denying any military movement
in the south, and after five days of prevarication in Rhodes, during
which they constantly postponed signing the cease-fire agreement,
the Israeli delegation came out in the open. They informed the
Jordan delegation that the area extending southwards to the Gulf
of Aqaba had been allotted to them by the 1947 partition plan and
that they proposed to occupy it. This was in direct contradiction of
the assurances they had been giving us for the previous fortnight.

It will be seen that, in this respect, the Israeli policy was one of
"heads I win and tails you lose". Where an area allotted to them in
the partition plan was still occupied by Arab forces, they claimed
that they were legitimately entitled to drive those forces out. The
partition plan was here the touchstone. But where Israeli forces
were in occupation of an area allotted to the Arabs by the United
Nations, they were entitled to remain. In these circumstances,
military occupation established a sufficient right.

In actual fact, of course, Israel was victorious. She had not
defeated the Arab Legion, but she had defeated other Arab armies
and was left facing the Arab Legion with a ten-to-one superiority
in numbers. UNO had failed to cause her to withdraw from the
Neqeb. It was certain that UNO would fail again if it tried to
interfere.

The force with which the Arab Legion had occupied the southern wedge amounted to a weak infantry company—perhaps a hundred men. This small force had held a line of pickets running approximately east and west, at a distance of fifty-five miles north of Aqaba. It withdrew before the advancing Jewish forces, the aircraft of which also joined in the operations. The Arab Legion had no aircraft. Eventually the Arab Legion force took up a company position on an east and west line, about forty miles north of Aqaba. Here it was attacked on the afternoon of March 9th, but the attack was repulsed. The Israelis were aware that British troops had landed in Aqaba and seem to have suspected that the force in front of them might be British.

On the evening of March 9th, I received an account of the attack and its repulse. A second signal from the commander, addressed to me personally, asked whether he should withdraw and allow the Israeli forces to pass, or whether I ordered him and his men to die in their present position. It was impossible for me to appreciate so far away what were the chances of resistance. It was not possible to reinforce him. The Israelis had interior lines, and could reinforce their Wadi Araba column from Beersheba quickly. There were no Arab Legion forces in Trans-Jordan. Any reinforcements sent would have had to be withdrawn from the Jerusalem area through Amman. There were no metalled roads south of Amman, and the reinforcements would have been obliged to cover two hundred and sixty miles along earth tracks to reach our company in the Wadi Araba. The process could not have taken less than three days. With exposed flanks, the company could not have held up for three days in the open desert so large an enemy force, with air support. In any case, in the north, the Iraqis were about to withdraw, leaving the Arab Legion to hold the entire front. I signalled back that I left full discretion to the local commander.

That night, the Amman English Amateur Dramatic Society was giving a representation of "The Importance of Being Earnest". While the audience laughed at Wilde's witticisms, I sat in miserable anxiety thinking of that handful of Arab Legion, lying out beneath the stars in the Wadi Araba.

Next morning the Jews bombed and shelled our positions, almost till noon. Then they put in a full attack. The position was empty. The Arab Legion had slipped away. On the evening of March 10th, the Israelis reached the sea. British forces watched them arrive from the Trans-Jordan side of the bay.

The next day, March 11th, the Israeli delegation signed the cease-fire agreement in so far as the Arab Legion was concerned. It was obvious that they had been procrastinating, in order first to complete their advance to the Gulf of Aqaba.

We had not yet, however, finished with Israel's dynamic diplomacy or, perhaps I should say, they had not finished with us.

*   *   *   *   *

On March 11th, as I have said, the preliminary cease-fire was signed, but it was signed for the Arab Legion front alone. The Israelis refused to include any mention of taking over from the Iraqis. Mr. Shertok, the Israeli Foreign Minister, meanwhile made a statement admitting that Israeli troops had reached the Gulf of Aqaba. He added that if the Iraqi forces withdrew, nothing would prevent Israeli forces from occupying their positions, in order to keep order in that territory. The proposal to occupy another country "to keep order" was somewhat reminiscent of Hitler. Obviously we were in for another war of nerves.

On March 13th, however, in spite of the cease-fire agreement, an Israeli military force embarked in launches from the south end of the Dead Sea, and landed at Ain Jeddi on the western shore. The Trans-Jordan government again protested to Dr. Bunche, stating that it was difficult to negotiate with Israel while her military forces were still constantly seizing new territory.

Meanwhile the Jordan government had persuaded the Iraqi government not to withdraw its forces on March 13th. Dr. Bunche informed the Jordan delegation that he would press the Israelis to sign a cease-fire agreement for the Iraqi front also, but it seemed likely that these negotiations might take several days. The Jordan government was apprehensive that the Iraqi army would withdraw and the Israeli army attempt to conquer the territory thus exposed while the new cease-fire agreement was under discussion. The Jordan government believed itself to be justified in entertaining these suspicions, because it was precisely during the negotiations for the Arab Legion cease-fire that the Israeli forces had commenced their advance to the Gulf of Aqaba.

United Nations observers in Bethlehem reported that the Israeli forces were advancing at a number of places in the Hebron area. The Arab Legion forces in the area were so small that they could not hold a continuous line. The Israelis, while avoiding a clash with the Arab Legion, were pushing forward between Arab Legion posts, trying to occupy more villages. We were faced with a wild grab for territory, even while the negotiators were sitting round the table in Rhodes. Although UNO had laid down a no-man's-land on the Hebron sector, the Israelis now occupied it entirely, without reference to the United Nations observers. In the north, the Iraqis reported that the enemy appeared to be concentrating fresh forces on their front preparatory to an attack. On March 13th, the Israeli government cabled Dr. Bunche to the effect that it would consider the taking over of the Iraqi front by the Arab Legion to be a violation of the existing truce, and that the Israeli government reserved all its rights. The pressure was becoming intense.

It is simple enough to read of these movements, sitting comfortably in our homes many years later. It is impossible to reproduce the tension and anxiety of those days, the constant reports of fresh Israeli advances, the constant procrastination in Rhodes, the Iraqis gradually slipping out, and 11,000 Arab Legion (still without ammunition) facing ten times their numbers.

Unfortunately, at this stage King Abdulla's anxiety became too deep to resist. Through a private emissary, he contacted the Israelis direct. The object of the recent manœuvres then became obvious. The Israeli government would consent to the replacement of the Iraqi army by the Arab Legion if the latter agreed to withdraw a certain distance, all along the Iraqi front. The withdrawal asked for amounted to a belt of an average width of two to three kilometres on a front 180 kilometres long.

In general, the fighting line ran along the foothills of the mountains, occasionally projecting into the coastal plain. A number of Arab villages situated actually in the coastal plain had resisted every Israeli attack for ten months, although defended only by the villagers themselves. The narrowness of the coastal plain—Israel's wasp waist—had undoubtedly caused much uneasiness to the Israeli army staff. Their present demands were principally intended slightly to widen the coastal plain, and to obtain for Israel certain hilltops which would prevent their being entirely overlooked by the Arab Legion, which held the mountains above them.

It can probably be assumed that the object of the Israeli demand was strategic, rather than economic. Nevertheless, the coastal plain strip to be surrendered included some of the richest land still in possession of the Arabs, the mountain country being far less fertile. The total area demanded was perhaps some 400 square kilometres, whereas the whole area defended by the Arab Legion and the Iraqi army amounted to some 6,000 square kilometres. The area to be given up therefore represented some 6·6 per cent of the whole. In return for the surrender of this territory, the Israeli government promised immediately to agree to a full armistice and the take-over by the Arab Legion from the Iraqis. If we refused, the Israelis explained verbally, they were ready to reopen hostilities. This message was sent direct to King Abdulla, not through the Rhodes arbitrators. The King passed it to the Prime Minister, who addressed me a letter. After stating the Jewish demands, he asked for my written answer to two questions.

(a) If we refused this offer, and the Israelis renewed hostilities, could we hold their attack everywhere on the present line?

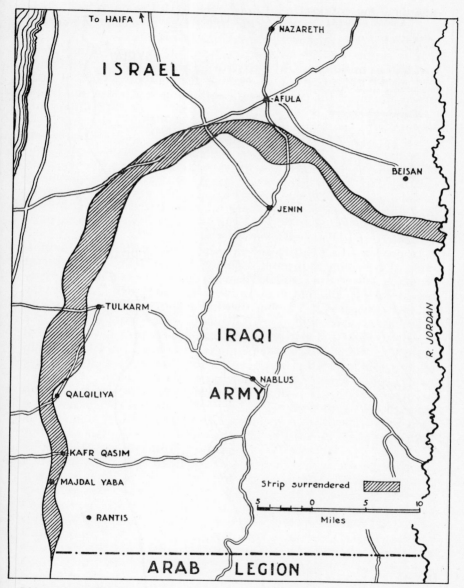

To HAIFA ↑

ISRAEL

NAZARETH

AFULA

BEISAN

JENIN

TULKARM

IRAQI

NABLUS

ARMY

QALQILIYA

KAFR QASIM

MAJDAL YABA

Strip surrendered

RANTIS

5   0   5   10
Miles

R. JORDAN

ARAB LEGION

Map to show strip of territory surrendered to Israel at Rhodes, to secure Israeli agreement to an armistice on the Iraqi front.

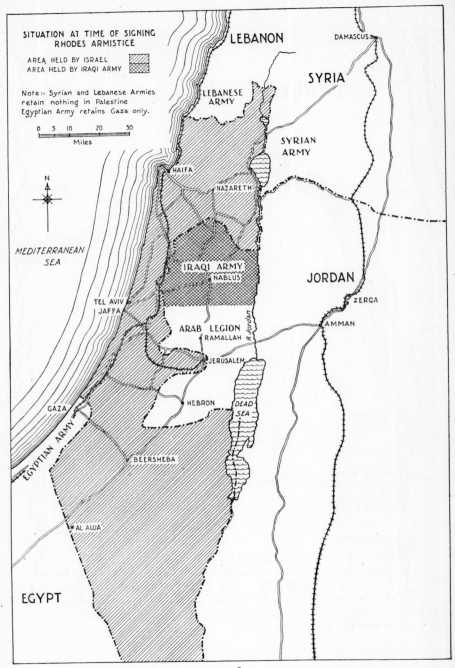

SITUATION AT TIME OF SIGNING
RHODES ARMISTICE

AREA HELD BY ISRAEL
AREA HELD BY IRAQI ARMY

Note:- Syrian and Lebanese Armies
retain nothing in Palestine
Egyptian Army retains Gaza only.

0   5   10   20   30
Miles

N

LEBANON

DAMASCUS

SYRIA

LEBANESE
ARMY

SYRIAN
ARMY

HAIFA

NAZARETH

MEDITERRANEAN
SEA

IRAQI ARMY

NABLUS

JORDAN

TEL AVIV
JAFFA

ARAB LEGION

RAMALLAH

R. Jordan

ZERQA

AMMAN

JERUSALEM

HEBRON

DEAD
SEA

GAZA

EGYPTIAN ARMY

BEERSHEBA

AL AUJA

EGYPT

(*b*) If we could not hold them on the present line, and hostilities were resumed, against the Arab Legion alone, was it possible that the Israeli forces might seize a greater area than that now demanded?

I replied in writing that, if hostilities were renewed against the Arab Legion alone, we could not hold the present line after the Iraqis had gone. Moreover, if war recommenced, the Israelis might seize more territory than they were now asking for.

On thinking over this problem, only one course seemed to me to be still open. It was a direct appeal to the U.S.A. and Britain. It must be remembered that both Israel and Jordan were still bound by the Security Council truce of July 18th, 1948. For Israel to resume hostilities with Jordan, merely on the grounds that she was greedy of more territory, would therefore be an even more flagrant defiance of the United Nations than any yet perpetrated. UNO itself, having no forces, would be unable to act, but Britain and America together could undoubtedly call Israel to order. I drove down to see the King at Shuna. The Prime Minister had gone to Beirut. The King liked my suggestion and telegrams were accordingly sent off to London and Washington.

Meanwhile the pressure was too much for the Jordan government. Further Israeli troop movements were reported. The Jordan government agreed to initial an agreement covering the surrender of territory, in order to gain time. They inserted a clause to the effect that the agreement would not be valid unless it was countersigned by the Jordan Prime Minister, who was away in Beirut. This would provide a way out if the British and Americans agreed to intervene.

Soon afterwards, the reply came from the United States government. It was to the effect that Washington had been informed that a preliminary agreement had already been initialled. In view of this fact, the United States government was unwilling to intervene.

The agreement was signed, and following it, on April 3rd, 1949, the Israeli–Jordan armistice. The Arab Legion completed its takeover from the Iraqi army on April 12th. We sent 2,000 men to take over from some 19,000 Iraqis.

With the formation of the new Hashemite Kingdom of Jordan, the names Palestine and Trans-Jordan, used in the past, were no longer entirely suitable. As a result Arab Palestine was officially designated as West Jordan, or more colloquially West Bank, while the former Trans-Jordan was know henceforward as East Jordan or East Bank.

XIV

A Sea of Troubles

Envy never makes holiday.
                          FRANCIS BACON

The danger chiefly lies in acting well:
No crime's so great as daring to excel.
                          CHARLES CHURCHILL (1760)

XIV

A SEA OF TROUBLES

THE publication of the text of the Jordan–Israeli armistice agreement was greeted by a storm of vituperation from Egypt and Syria, and from many of the people of Palestine. The point which particularly roused their anger was that a strip of territory had been surrendered without fighting. If the Arab Legion had been defeated in battle, it was said, they would have been excused. But to give up territory without a fight obviously proved treachery. From here, it was only a step to the statement that I was secretly helping Israel, or that King Abdulla had received a bribe.

We had no propaganda machine with which to answer this onslaught. It seemed obvious to us that, if we had renewed hostilities, we might have lost far more. Of course it was possible that the Israelis were bluffing and would not have renewed hostilities, but in any case, with no other enemy in the field, they could certainly have taken the remaining Arab villages in the coastal plain.

It did not seem to occur to anybody that the Arab Legion had been compelled to sign the armistice because the other Arab armies had either already concluded armistices, or had withdrawn from the field, and that thereby we had been left alone. Statements regarding our shortage of ammunition were put down as a trick, although it was the Egyptians themselves who had seized our ammunition ship.

As the armistice was in theory a military armistice, not a political peace, the Rhodes delegation had consisted of officers. They had, however, been forbidden to agree to anything without reference to Amman, and every word had been submitted to the Prime Minister by cypher cable, or by officers flying backwards and forwards. Thus in reality every phrase had been approved or even dictated by Taufiq Pasha. As soon, however, as he saw the storm burst, he withdrew himself as much as possible, allowing all the criticisms to descend upon the Arab Legion.

When the Rhodes delegation returned by air to Amman, they were received on the airport by a messenger telling them to go quietly and separately to their homes. It was explained to them that many people wished to kill them, and that if they entered the town together, they might be recognized and a riot might result.

Soon afterwards, a riot did occur in Nablus, the capital of the Samaria district, to which the surrendered area belonged. Crowds demonstrated in the streets, shouting:

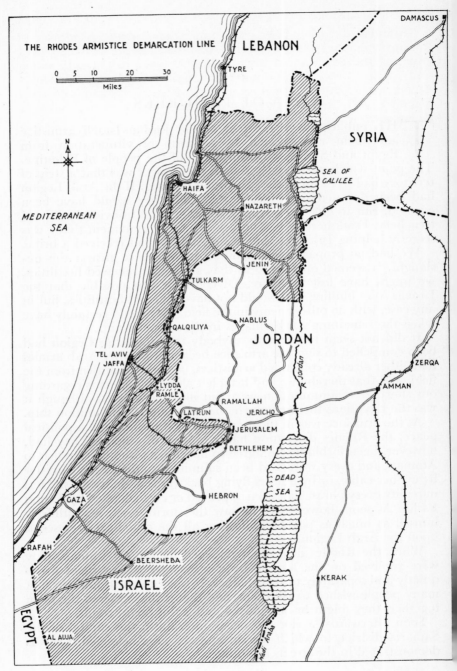

THE RHODES ARMISTICE DEMARCATION LINE

LEBANON

DAMASCUS

0 5 10 20 30
Miles

N

SYRIA

MEDITERRANEAN
SEA

TYRE

SEA OF
GALILEE

HAIFA

NAZARETH

JENIN

TULKARM

NABLUS

QALQILIYA

JORDAN

TEL AVIV
JAFFA

ZERQA

AMMAN

LYDDA
RAMLE

LATRUN

RAMALLAH

JERICHO

R. Jordan

JERUSALEM

BETHLEHEM

DEAD
SEA

HEBRON

GAZA

RAFAH

BEERSHEBA

KERAK

ISRAEL

EGYPT

AL AUJA

Wadi Araba

"Abdulla the cad! Sold our country for cash!" A section of armoured cars was sent to form a road-block to prevent the crowd reaching the government buildings. They were pelted with stones and called: "Liars!" "Traitors!" "Jews!" The troops had strict orders not to fire or use their weapons. Eventually they took off their webbing belts, and swinging the brass buckles above their heads, a dozen soldiers dispersed the crowd.

The Arab Legion had won world-wide recognition for its stubborn fighting, always against heavy odds. The enemy themselves had paid them tribute. In Trans-Jordan, they were the beloved army of the people. All of Palestine that had been saved had been preserved by the Arab Legion and the Iraqi army, although the latter, by its final precipitate withdrawal, had compelled the surrender of that strip of country. The other Arab armies had saved nothing from the wreck. Yet by a curious irony, the first resentment of the Arabs of Palestine was directed against the Arab Legion, which alone was accused of deliberate treachery. In the course of the ensuing few years, skilful propaganda turned the whole question upside-down. Eventually, to the Arab world at large, the Egyptian and Syrian armies became the heroes and the Arab Legion the villains of the drama. This was not entirely so in Palestine. A great number of the people of that country gradually recovered from the mental paralysis which had been caused by their disasters. As they came to know the officers and men of the Arab Legion, they realized that charges of treachery and cowardice against such men were ridiculous. But in other countries, where we were not personally known, the campaign of vilification bore full fruit.

The real fact was that the Egyptian government had led the Arab League to war in May 1948 against the advice of Jordan. Egyptian leadership had ended in a fiasco, whereas the Arab Legion had gained in prestige and had actually saved a considerable part of Palestine. It was necessary for Egypt to find an excuse for her failure. She was also intensely jealous of Arab Legion successes, contrasted with her defeats. These two factors were further accentuated by King Farouq's jealousy of King Abdulla, and by the general anti-British trend of Egyptian policy. For the army which had outshone that of Egypt was the army of King Abdulla, and it had been trained and led by British officers. All these facts were intolerable to the dignity of Egypt.

Meanwhile, in Amman, an anonymous defender had come to our assistance. The Egyptian broadcasting station had made some contemptuous reference to Trans-Jordan as having a population of only one per cent of the Arab world—half a million out of fifty millions.

Shortly afterwards, pamphlets were distributed in Amman, of which the following is a summary:

"Trans-Jordan need not be ashamed if she constitutes only one per cent of the Arabs, for she did more for Palestine than the remaining ninety-nine per cent. Her army is still defending the Holy Land, while the other armies have disappeared.

"When Jerusalem, the Holy City, was in danger, it was the Arab Legion alone which rescued it.

"When the Egyptian army withdrew after its defeat, the Arab Legion alone saved the Hebron district, for which the Arab League had made the Egyptian army responsible.

"All the engagements in which the Arab Legion fought were bitterly contested against heavy odds. The battle for Latrun and Bab al Wad lasted three months and that for Jerusalem for nine months, firing continuing regardless of the truces.

"The Arab Legion inflicted more casualties on the Jews than any other Arab army. It also captured more prisoners than any other Arab army.

"The Arab Legion captured seven hundred Jewish prisoners of war and lost only four, all of them seriously wounded.

"The Arab Legion is still defending the Holy Land from Jewish attack. In doing so, it constitutes the first wall of defence for all the other Arab countries. Syria is secure as long as the Arab Legion is in Palestine.

"If Trans-Jordan were rich and great like Egypt, Iraq or Syria, she would have done far more. The Egyptian announcer said that she is only one per cent of the Arabs—and she did all this! Pray tell us what the ninety-nine per cent did!"

*   *   *   *   *

The Rhodes agreement had established a so-called Mixed Armistice Commission in Jerusalem, to superintend the execution of the armistice. It was to consist of five members—a chairman representing the United Nations, two Israelis and two Jordanians. Decisions were to be made by majority vote. In practice, the two Israelis always voted on one side and the two Jordanians on the other. Actually, therefore, decisions were taken by the chairman alone; whichever side he voted with had thereby a majority.

The Rhodes armistice agreement was not, as had been hoped, the first step to peace. Long years of shooting, uncertainty, death and disorder still lay before us. When the fighting ended, as so often happens in wars, the soldiers of the Arab Legion and the Israeli army felt a certain respect for one another. It was the public and the politicians who whipped up the hatred on both sides—politicians often themselves not constitutionally violent, but anxious to conciliate their own extremists by professing hatred. As time went on, hundreds of complaints accumulated, and the Mixed Armistice

Commission was unable to keep pace. A complaint submitted (say) in April, came up for consideration in June or July. Eventually a system was produced by which an incident involving loss of life was declared an emergency case, and was dealt with quickly. Cases not described as emergency cases dragged on for months.

Even when, in an emergency case, one side or the other was condemned for a breach of the armistice, nothing more ensued. The case was filed and soon forgotten. Like all other international institutions today, the United Nations Truce Supervision Organization in Palestine was ineffective because it had no forces at its command. In the end, the Mixed Armistice Commission, not unlike Lake Success, tended to be merely a platform for political speeches. The Israeli and Jordanian teams came to hate one another. There was little or no attempt to settle anything, or even find out the truth. One got the impression that the speakers were often addressing the public in their own countries, rather than trying to solve a dispute.

*   *   *   *   *

Ever since 1920, there had been constant riots and rebellions in Palestine. After each period of disorder, the situation had eventually returned to normal, and the people had gone back to their usual avocations. When the armistice was signed, some of the refugees innocently thought that they could now go home again. Others had fled so hurriedly that they had left behind everything they possessed. Others had lost relatives in the confusion of their flight, and now set out to look for them. For one reason or another, a number of refugees walked back into what was now to be Israel, as soon as the armistice was signed.

It will be recollected that the 1947 partition scheme left within the proposed Jewish State as many Arabs as Jews. People wondered how the Jewish State would be able to exist. As matters turned out, the Jews had succeeded in driving out nearly all the Arabs, except for a small number, chiefly in Galilee. One thing on which the Jews were determined was that they were not going to let those Arabs back.

At the beginning, many refugees went back innocently and unarmed. None, I believe, in those days crossed the armistice line in order to fight or injure the Jews. The majority went to try to rescue some of their belongings, or to look for missing relatives. The Israelis were ruthless. Many of these unfortunate people were shot on sight by Israeli posts or patrols, without even the formality of arrest or questioning. Cases occurred of farmers going out to plough their land, and being shot dead by Israeli patrols as they drove their ploughs across their own fields. The farmers had not realized that, owing to a line drawn on a map somewhere, half of their fields were no longer their own.

The ruthless manner in which the Israelis dealt with any Arabs they found soon disposed of the innocent returning refugees. The great majority of them gave it up, and made no further attempt to return home. But a small number of the more desperate decided to go. This time they armed themselves and went by stealth at night. They were still, however, principally intent on seeking the property which they had left behind. Probably at this stage, none had any aggressive intentions, but if they met an Israeli patrol, they fired.

By their drive to the Gulf of Aqaba, the Israelis had cut the only land-bridge between Asia and Africa, and had physically divided the Arabic-speaking world in two. There had always been a frequent coming and going across Sinai, between Arabia and Egypt. There was now no longer any legal way of going. In addition, during the Israeli offensive against the Egyptian army in October 1948, some of the Arab inhabitants had fled to Gaza, others to Hebron. Friends and relatives had lost one another, and now Israeli territory lay between them. There being no longer any legitimate way to reach Egypt from Arabia or vice versa, those who had any reason for doing so crossed the intervening Israeli territory by night. These also were at times intercepted by Israeli patrols. From these comparatively harmless beginnings, new hatreds were built up.

It was not always the Arabs who crossed the demarcation line first. Economic conditions in Israel were severe, and the rations of the army were not all they might have been. Meat was especially scarce. In these circumstances, Israeli patrols along the armistice line could see flocks of sheep and cows grazing on the Arab side. The temptation to fire a few shots at the herdsman and bring in a lavish supply of fresh meat was sometimes difficult to resist. Sometimes indeed the sheep were actually grazing on the Israel side. Soon armed Arabs began deliberately to cross the border to steal. They killed only incidentally, if they were likely to be caught. The Israelis could not retaliate by stealing, so they did so with their army. The Arab Legion never crossed the line.

Gradually incidents began to increase in scale. On March 20th, 1950, for example, six armoured Israeli vehicles crossed the line into Jordan. It was reported by United Nations observers that they had killed a woman, two girls, two men and a number of animals.

On the same day, two Jews were found murdered west of Jerusalem, although there was no proof that the murderers were Arabs.

Here is another official report, chosen at random:

"On May 21st, 1950, an Arab named Ahmed Abdul Hai was living in the village of Kafr Qasim, on the Israel side of the armistice line. He asked the permission of the Israeli military governor to emigrate across the line and go and live in Jordan. The permission of the military governor was granted and Ahmed Abdul Hai set out on the morning of 21/5/1950. He was walking on foot with his family and the Israeli military governor provided him with an escort as far as the demarcation line.

"On crossing the line, his family, who were carrying all their worldly possessions, were exhausted. He accordingly told them to sit down and rest on the Jordan side of the line, while he went to the nearest Arab village to obtain some transport. The Jewish escort left them and returned to Kafr Qasim.

"While Ahmed was away, an Israeli patrol came down the line. They saw the family sitting in a group on the ground, just inside Jordan. The family consisted of three women—Ahmed's mother, wife and sister, and his infant son. The Jewish patrol opened machine-gun fire on the little group at short range. Ahmed's little boy and his mother were killed, and his sister was dangerously wounded. His wife took cover and escaped unhurt."

Thus the size of incidents kept increasing. Hate and violence built up more and more.

On Wednesday, May 31st, at dawn, two trucks each carrying about fifty Arab detainees set out from Qatra prison near Rehoveth in Israel territory. At 9 p.m. the same day, they arrived at the demarcation line in the Wadi Araba, south of the Dead Sea. During the journey of approximately sixteen hours, the prisoners received no food or water, nor were they allowed to descend from their trucks for any reason whatever. Their eyes had been blindfolded all day. At 9 p.m., in the dark, they were ordered to get out of the trucks. They were then taken forward three or four at a time, were told that they were now facing Jordan, and bursts of Bren-gun fire were directed above their heads to make them run. They wandered in nearly waterless desert for periods of from thirty-six to forty-eight hours, when they were either picked up by Arab Legion patrols or by local bedouins. About twenty died on the way or were lost and were never heard of again.

The survivors stated that they had been in prison in Israel for periods varying from six weeks to four months, in different prisons. All complained of violent ill-treatment and many bore on their bodies the marks of beating. One had had his finger-nails torn out—a form of torture said to have been used by the Nazis in Germany. Several had teeth broken and claimed that this injury had been inflicted by blows from the rifle butts of Israeli soldiers or police. A British officer of the Arab Legion, a medical representative from UNRWA,[1] a United Nations observer and a photographer were

[1] United Nations Relief and Works Agency for Palestine Refugees in the Near East, established on December 8th, 1949.

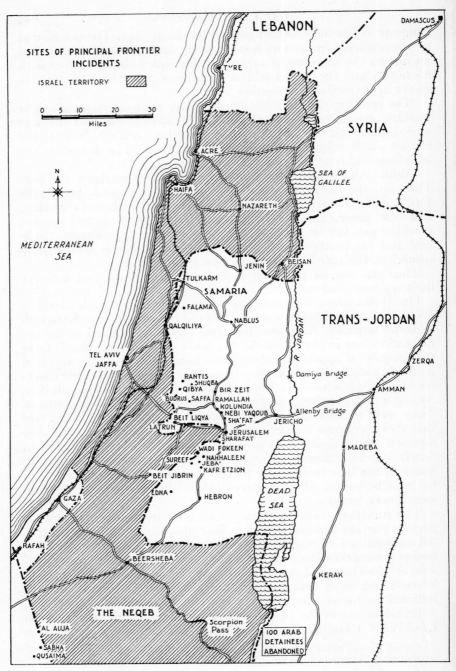

SITES OF PRINCIPAL FRONTIER
INCIDENTS

ISRAEL TERRITORY

0 5 10   20   30
Miles

N

LEBANON

DAMASCUS

TYRE

SYRIA

ACRE

SEA OF
GALILEE

HAIFA

NAZARETH

MEDITERRANEAN
SEA

JENIN

BEISAN

TULKARM

SAMARIA

FALAMA

NABLUS

QALQILIYA

TRANS-JORDAN

R JORDAN

TEL AVIV
JAFFA

ZERQA

Damiya Bridge

AMMAN

RANTIS
SHUQBA
QIBYA

BIR ZEIT

BUDRUS SAFFA

RAMALLAH
KOLUNDIA
NEBI YAQOUB
SHA'FAT

BEIT LIQYA

LATRUN

Allenby Bridge

JERICHO

JERUSALEM
SHARAFAT
WADI FOKEEN
NAHHALEEN
JEBA'
KAFR ETZION

MADEBA

SUREEF

BEIT JIBRIN

EDNA

HEBRON

DEAD
SEA

GAZA

RAFAH

KERAK

BEERSHEBA

THE NEQEB

Scorpion
Pass

AL AUJA

SABHA
QUSAIMA

100 ARAB
DETAINEES
ABANDONED

248

sent to investigate. The physical marks of beatings, broken teeth, torn-out finger-nails and other wounds on their bodies were photographed. Every man's statement was taken. Here are a few at random:

(1) I live near Hebron. Thirty days ago I went harvesting with others near the Israel border. While we were working, a force of Jews came and took us prisoners.

(2) I am a refugee from Gaza. As I was poor, I slipped across the line and back to my old village. I had hidden some money there, and hoped to dig it up and live on it. I was arrested by the Jews and taken to the camp at Qatra, where I was beaten and tortured.

(3) I am a refugee from Gaza. There was no work there and I am poor. I tried to walk across to Hebron in order to go to Jerusalem to find work. I was arrested by the Jews and put in prison in Qatra and tortured.

Nearly all the statements were of the same kind—either people trying to cross between Hebron and Gaza, or people who had gone back to try to recover something from their homes. A few, however, claimed that they were not refugees but residents in Israel, and that they had been arrested in their homes.

This problem of the eviction of resident Arabs was to constitute an irritant for years. The Israeli government passed a nationality law to the effect that every Jew all over the world was automatically an Israeli citizen, but that an Arab must prove his claim to Israeli nationality. Thus an Arab might be the descendant of ancestors who had lived for untold centuries in that part of Palestine now called Israel. Suddenly he could be challenged by the Israeli government. The onus of proof was on the Arab—it was for him to prove that he was an Israeli, not for the government to prove that he was not. If any of his papers were declared to be not in order, he was arrested and expelled into Jordan. This process was to continue for years to come.

The Rhodes armistice agreement included a clause to the effect that civilians were not to cross the demarcation line. Thus whenever an "infiltrator" did so, the Israeli government claimed that Jordan had committed a breach of the armistice. Such a claim would only have been valid, morally at least, if the Jordan government had encouraged the individual to go or at least had winked at his going. In practice, however, the Jordan government never ceased to make every effort to prevent their going. To claim that all or many Israelis were aware of the maltreatment of Arab infiltrators would be unwarranted. Probably the great majority would have been horrified. The fact remains that such things were done, and produced a disastrous psychological reaction among the Arabs, greatly intensifying their hatred.

Jordan felt herself helpless in the face of such actions. Jews all over the world exercised an immense influence, particularly in the field of the Press and publishing. We decided to enter the contest for publicity. We found a member of the British Parliament who asked a question in the House of Commons. We compiled a file on the incident of the expulsion of the hundred Arabs, complete with photographs, and circulated a few copies. This move was remarkably successful. Although, as opposed to the Arabs, Jews almost monopolized world publicity, they were extremely sensitive to any publicity unfavourable to them. After taking this action, we received no further complaints of torture.

But although the Jordan government was anxious to prevent refugees from crossing the line, other agencies were at work to encourage them to do so. As early as March 1950, I find in my notes a record of an Israeli complaint of two Jews found murdered. I had noted on the report the significant question: "Could this be the Mufti's work, in the hopes of embroiling Jordan with Israel?" In later years, the Egyptian government was to admit—even to boast of— the fact that it was assisting refugees to raid Israel from Jordan. In 1950, we believed the Mufti to be organizing these incidents, together with certain extremist organizations in Egypt and Syria. Ibn Saud produced funds to encourage infiltrators at various times.

The Jordan government did not discourage infiltration out of friendship for Israel, but for more practical reasons. Jordan's relations with Egypt, Syria and Saudi Arabia were strained. If Israel were to attack Jordan, the other Arab governments would be unlikely to be either able, or anxious, to give effective aid. Jordan with her settled population of about one million, had half a million refugees, who thereby constituted thirty-three per cent of the population. At the same time, the country had very little revenue. Egypt, with a population of twenty millions, had 250,000 refugees, or 1·1 per cent. Moreover, these 250,000 refugees for whom Egypt was responsible were all concentrated in the Gaza strip, and were not allowed into Egypt, except by special permit. Iraq and Saudi Arabia had large oil revenues and virtually no refugees. Thus Jordan, the poorest of the Arab League member States and the least in population, was bearing nearly all the burden of the disaster. She was in no position at this stage to throw down the gauntlet to Israel. But Egypt and Syria and certain private societies and individuals were desirous only to destroy Jordan, even if Israel were to be the instrument for her destruction. Israel was aware of these facts, but she also wanted to destroy Jordan. For if Jordan were to collapse, Israel could hope to advance her frontier to the Jordan river or beyond. Consequently the Israeli government did not concern itself with the debate as to whether the Jordan government was organizing or preventing infiltration. If the infiltrations came from Jordan soil, then the reprisals would be directed against Jordan.

*   *   *   *   *

It must not be forgotten that the whole problem of embittered refugees was the result of the ruthless expulsion of all Arabs by the Israelis in 1948. The story which Jewish publicity at first persuaded the world to accept, that the Arab refugees left voluntarily, is not true. Voluntary emigrants do not leave their homes with only the clothes they stand up in. People who have decided to move house do not do so in such a hurry that they lose other members of their family—husband losing sight of his wife, or parents of their children. The fact is that the majority left in panic flight, to escape massacre (at least, so they thought). They were in fact helped on their way by the occasional massacre—not of very many at a time, but just enough to keep them running. Others were encouraged to move by blows or by indecent acts.

Human beings have an infinite capacity for forgetting unpleasant facts. The public in Israel had forgotten that they drove out these refugees with savage harshness, and were now genuinely indignant and aggrieved that the refugees should want to infiltrate back to their homes. The Israeli government, full of outraged indignation, determined to inaugurate direct reprisals.

At first small parties of Israeli soldiers were used—a section of seven or eight men. If numerous cases of infiltration had occurred, an Israeli section crossed the line one evening, entered an Arab village, shot the first two or three Arabs they met, and then withdrew. Sometimes they threw a bomb into a lighted window, where a village family was sitting.

In the face of these incidents, the Arab Legion issued ten rifles to every village within three miles of the demarcation line. Arab Legion N.C.O.s were posted in the villages to train the people to shoot, to teach them to mount sentries and to patrol round their villages. As a result, a number of Israeli "reprisal" raids were repulsed. The Israelis consequently increased the strength of their raids. They began to use platoons of twenty or twenty-five men, and to employ military tactics and covering fire. The ten rifles per village were no longer enough. Twenty rifles per village were issued.

On June 7th, 1950, a meeting was held in Arab Legion divisional headquarters to consider how to prevent infiltration into Israel. Recommendations were subsequently made to the government to ask the United Nations to order the withdrawal of both armies to a distance of five kilometres from the border, and to move back all refugee camps to a distance of twenty kilometres. It was requested that all village headmen, and governors of districts and sub-districts, be made responsible for all incidents of infiltration. A complicated system of police and army patrols at night was organized. The government was also asked to give power to administrative officers to try and sentence infiltrators, as law courts were unable to try offenders for an offence technically committed in Israel.

While, however, we were clear that incidents were not in the interest of Jordan, the issue was not so plain to the public, and even less so to the refugees. Organizations in other Arab countries, and embittered extremists in Jordan, represented infiltrators as noble patriots, heroically carrying on the struggle against those who had driven them from their country. King Abdulla, the Jordan government and the Arab Legion were, in contrast, described as traitors, co-operating with Jews and British imperialists to prevent the Arabs from recovering their rights.

As time went on, the infiltrator returning to collect his possessions became rarer, but cases increased of purely technical crossing of the line. In many cases, the line crossed a ploughed field belonging to a farmer, of which he was henceforward only entitled to plough two-thirds (let us say), the remaining third being in Israel. It had been his field and his father's and his grandfather's before him, but if he ploughed it all now, he might be shot by a passing Israeli patrol. Similarly, the demarcation line might pass between a man's house and his garden. If he went out to pick his own apples and olives, he might pay for it with his life.

XV

Building an Army

Active valour may often be the present of nature; but patient diligence can be the fruit only of habit and discipline. So sensible were the Romans of the imperfection of valour without skill and practice, that the name of an army was borrowed from the word which signified exercise. Military exercises were the important and unremitted object of their discipline. The recruits and young soldiers were constantly trained; nor was age or knowledge allowed to excuse the veterans from the daily repetition of what they had completely learnt.

GIBBON, *Decline and Fall of the Roman Empire*

XV

BUILDING AN ARMY

I HAVE already told how the infantry garrison companies had been raised during the Second World War to help the allies by guarding vital points in the Middle East. The companies should have been abolished before April 1st, 1948, but I had retained some of them, without financial provision. Three of these companies had been moved into the Old City of Jerusalem in May 1948, and had defended the walls, at the same time capturing the old Jewish quarter within the walls. One of these companies was commanded by a young major called Abdulla al Tell. This young man had enlisted early in the Second World War and, being well educated, he became an orderly room clerk, and later obtained a commission. He was promoted major in March 1948.

The King was profoundly devoted to Jerusalem, and insisted on going there to pray, even while the fighting was still in progress. On one such occasion, during the first month of fighting, His Majesty noticed Abdulla. Although Jewish mortar bombs were falling around, he gave His Majesty a lucid description of the situation. The King was attracted by this young man. He looked at his shoulder and saw a crown.

"I make you a lieutenant-colonel," said King Abdulla, in a sudden moment of emotion.

Abdulla al Tell was not the man to let His Majesty forget. A fortnight or so later, the King looked at me coyly one day when I was with him and said:

"Pasha, I made Abdulla al Tell a colonel."

"That is difficult, sir," I said. "He is not the senior major, he has no tactical experience and he has only been a major for two months."

"For my sake, you must do it this time," the King replied. "I gave him my word before a number of people."

I could not help thinking that, nearly two thousand years ago, another king of a kingdom almost the same as Jordan today, had done much the same. "And the king was exceeding sorry; yet for his oath's sake, and for their sakes which sat with him. . . ." The result was John the Baptist's head on a charger. Little did we know that King Abdulla himself was this time to be the victim. The promotion was gazetted.

During the first truce, the three infantry companies in the Old City were combined to form an improvised battalion and Abdulla took command. Most of the limelight was directed upon the Old City during the fighting. Reporters thronged to interview "Colonel Tell", whom they described as commander of the Arab forces in Jerusalem. In reality he was now commanding one battalion. Another battalion and other units were outside the walls.

To be made a hero and daily reported in the Press is heady wine for a young man. It has destroyed better men than Abdulla al Tell. When the second truce put an end to the fighting, he began to discuss the political situation with prominent people in Jerusalem, allowing it to be understood that he thought little of the Jordan government; if he had been in charge, the hostilities would have ended differently.

I spoke of these affairs to the government, and informed them that the battalion commanded by Abdulla al Tell was due for transfer to another sector. The King still trusted and liked him and wanted him in Jerusalem. It was agreed that he should give up his battalion and become governor of Jerusalem. Meanwhile, King Abdulla looked upon the armistice as the first step to peace. All the Arab governments concerned were meeting the Israelis on the various armistice commissions. King Abdulla decided to explore the possibilities of peace. He wrote to certain Jews whom he knew. The letters were sent through Abdulla al Tell.

During the summer of 1949, Abdulla al Tell became even more outspoken in his criticisms. He was now under the civil authorities, not under the Arab Legion. The government became concerned. One day Abdulla came to see me. He told me that I was his father and he had come to me for advice. Should he resign from government service? He added that he would be willing to stay on, if he were given the rank of brigadier. I replied that it would not be feasible to make him a brigadier. Only eighteen months before, he had been a captain. As regards resigning, I said that, if he did so, he would become purely negative—one more bitter idle man, constantly criticizing and intriguing. The country was bankrupt and half in ruins. It needed positive men to build up its strength.

He thanked me cordially and withdrew. A few days later he resigned from government service and retired to his native town of Irbid, near the Syrian frontier. The Egyptian government was still conducting a violent propaganda campaign against Jordan and King Abdulla. Hearing that Abdulla al Tell had resigned, it offered him a salary if he would come and live in Egypt. The offer was accepted. He arrived in Egypt at the end of January 1950.

No sooner did he reach Egypt than he threw all shame to the winds. It must be recollected that he had been the recipient of extraordinary favour and promotion from King Abdulla, who had raised him in under two years from a company commander to governor of Jerusalem, and who had trusted him to carry his secret correspondence. It appeared that Tell had opened the King's letters confided to his safe keeping and had taken photostatic copies, a fact that proved he was contemplating treachery even when he was high in the King's favour. The photostats of these letters Abdulla al Tell now presented to the Egyptian Press. He also gave interviews in which he stated that the British officers in the Arab Legion had prevented their units from fighting, in order to help the Jews, and that King Abdulla was a traitor to the Arab cause. He went so far as to say that King Abdulla was alone responsible for the loss of Palestine. The fact that the Arab Legion had saved all that was saved of Palestine seemed to have escaped the notice of the public. It was agreed that the Arab Legion alone had been responsible for what was lost!

The Press in Egypt was now in full cry and outdid even Abdulla al Tell. One Egyptian newspaper claimed to have discovered secret documents proving that King Abdulla and I had sold the plans of the Arab armies to the Israelis. My photograph was published beside that of Moshe Dayan, commander of the Jewish forces in Jerusalem, to whom I was alleged to have passed the plan of campaign of the Arab armies. A Syrian paper published a statement to the effect that a "secret military organization" in Syria had sworn to murder King Abdulla.

Abdulla al Tell demanded that the Arab League send a court of inquiry to Amman to investigate the treachery of the Jordan government and of the Arab Legion.

*　　*　　*　　*　　*

King Abdulla was completely indifferent to this furore. He was in favour of peace with Israel, and said so perfectly frankly. In every previous crisis in Palestine, he had proved to be right and everybody else had proved to be wrong. He had advocated acceptance of the UNO 1947 partition in principle, but the others had insisted on fighting. When the fighting was over, the Arab League itself had demanded the enforcement of the 1947 partition—when it was already too late.

The King was of the opinion that better terms would be obtained by negotiating now than by waiting longer. His country alone was ruined. His army was extended along a front of nearly four hundred miles in daily contact with the enemy. The economic life of Jordan had been killed, because Haifa was her natural port. It was impossible to export anything through Beirut, which meant an additional land haul of 120 miles, or by Aqaba, which meant paying Suez Canal dues on the passage to Europe. No other Arab countries had lost much owing to the creation of Israel. Their trade was unaffected. The number of refugees in their countries was negligible.

They had been injured only in their dignity. They thought that a refusal to treat was the most dignified attitude for them to maintain. They made no allowance for their little ally, who was in desperate physical need. Perhaps the mere fact that King Abdulla admitted his desire for peace was enough to cause the Arab League to declare that talk of peace was treason to the Arab cause. To the politicians and the lawyers, to negotiate with the Jews was to recognize the legality of their presence, which would be tantamount to signing away their right to their country and their homes.

King Abdulla's approach was more practical. "Israel is stronger than Jordan, therefore we cannot fight them. Israel wants peace. Why not see what they have to say? Perhaps we shall get better terms that way."

The King's attempted negotiations with Israel failed, for two reasons. The first was the intense agitation raised by the other members of the Arab League, which frightened the government, though not the King. The second reason was that the Israelis, though apparently desirous of peace, wanted it only on their own terms. They were not prepared to make adequate concessions. King Abdulla realized that, if he were to make peace, he would have to be able to show substantial advantages therefrom. With Israel unprepared to make concessions, there was little inducement to defy the other Arab countries.

*   *   *   *   *

All these bitter and furious political storms went far to poison life and work in Jordan. But there were other aspects which were sheer joy. The principal of these was, of course, the build-up of the Arab Legion itself. I have already stated that the British subsidy sanctioned for 1948/9 was £2,500,000. In practice, nearly the whole year was spent in war—or at least "shooting truces" and war alternately. At the end of the financial year, we had spent a little more than £6,000,000. We had, in May 1948, received £250,000 from the Arab League. Later the Jordan government itself contributed some £300,000. The balance was eventually paid by Britain. Indeed, there was nothing else to be done, unless Jordan were to cease to exist. The other Arab armies had all retired from the field, and, if Britain had refused her help, the Arab Legion would perforce have dissolved, Israel would have advanced to the Jordan, and a further half-million Arab refugees would have been thrown on the world. With this debt cleared, we were faced with the problem of the future.

The Arab Legion had grown up spontaneously during the Second World War, new units being added here and there, as the circumstances of the moment seemed to necessitate. It finished the war with a brigade of three infantry battalions, operationally trained but without supporting arms, and about 3,500 infantry, in the form of independent companies with no battalion organization. The only operational staff was that of the brigade—Arab Legion H.Q. being a static "War Office". Our problem now was how to shape these miscellaneous units into a balanced army capable of operations. By the time that the Rhodes armistice was signed, we had nine infantry battalions. These required brigade H.Q. staffs and a divisional staff. Then the supporting arms and services had to be raised: artillery, engineers, signals, supply and transport, workshops, medical, works, pay and all the network of organization of an army. Many of these arms and services were highly technical. The number of officers in the army had, for a start, to be doubled, but only the best material must be sifted and accepted. This necessitated machinery for selection of cadets from civil life and of N.C.O.s suitable for commissions; then a cadet training school for potential officers, followed by a whole system of officers' courses and officers' promotion examinations, so as to maintain the necessary level of efficiency in every rank. To create all this officer machinery itself required officers—to select, to train and to examine—and thus increased the shortage of officers at the moment. Many officers already in the service were lacking in education, in view of the more complicated technical standards now required. An education corps had to be created.

All the same difficulties applied to the N.C.O.s and men—selection, training, education, advanced technical training. Great quantities of equipment were required, including technical equipment, workshop equipment, engineer stores, wireless and signals. The British Army had to be persuaded that these things were necessary. Indents had to be prepared in quintuplicate in English, although all the clerks worked only in Arabic.

Then, of course, there were no barracks. The army had been built up from 6,000 to 12,000 during the fighting in 1948. When the hostilities ended, these troops needed camps—they had passed a year in trenches.

Budgets are the nightmare of all armies, but our budget had to be prepared in English and in Arabic, and to be accepted by both the British and the Jordan governments.

The Israelis published no details of their defence expenditure, and indeed the total amount of the budget for their army was so concealed under item headings that it could not be ascertained. The British government, however, published the amount of the subsidy. Not only so, but Jordan members of Parliament demanded the publication of all the items. Their idea may well have been a laudable (or otherwise) ambition to retain parliamentary control, but it made secrecy impossible.

It was frequently stated in the British Press that the subsidy was paid to me, and that the Jordan government had no control of Arab Legion expenditure. This was quite incorrect. My financial powers were limited to £200 only. Any expenditure above that sum had to be sanctioned by both the Ministers of Defence and of Finance. For some extraordinary reason, I had no powers of "write-off". If (let us say) a tent caught fire and two greatcoats, a blanket and a pair of boots were burnt, the Prime Minister in person had to sanction the write-off, even if a court of inquiry had already investigated and reported. No army was ever more tied up with financial regulations.

All this immense activity was required with no trained or experienced officers. The number of officers available was not enough for the combatant units in the field. There was not one Jordanian officer trained in staff-work. Fortunately the British Army came to our rescue and we secured the services of a number of British officers of very high quality. Lash was succeeded on his retirement in 1951 by Brigadier (later Major-General) "Sam" Cooke. He was a magnificent organizer and trainer. A great measure of the very high standard of efficiency reached by the Arab Legion from 1949 to 1956 was due to his patient and devoted labours. Many other British officers laboured incessantly. It was all joy to serve in the Arab Legion, because both officers and men were so keen, so enthusiastic and so desirous to learn. After serving in conscript armies, British officers found it intensely gratifying to work in an army where every man's only ambition was to be a fine soldier. Not only was there a waiting list for enlistment, but once a man entered the army, it was almost impossible to get him out.

An immense pride, enthusiasm and *esprit de corps* inspired all ranks. The British officers were as proud of the Arab Legion as were the Jordanians. We set ourselves the same standards of technical efficiency as the British Army, although we had no industrialism in the country on which to rely for trained tradesmen. Nearly all recruits were agricultural workers or herdsmen. About one-third could not read and write. Yet from such material we built an entirely mechanized army, the technical level of which almost, if not quite, equalled that of the British Army, and in some directions surpassed it. Our signallers, for example, were on the whole above British Army standards. In discipline, drill, tactics and weapon training, we aimed at the same standard as the Brigade of Guards.

Once a year, the Arab Legion staged a ceremonial review in honour of the King—although half the army was still in trenches facing an active enemy on a 400-mile front. I do not believe that any army in the world could have staged a better review. A British Commander-in-Chief who saw it sent me a letter of appreciation.

"It is perhaps the last great military spectacle of its kind which can still be seen in the world," he wrote.

It may be wondered how we had time to produce such a ceremonial parade, while simultaneously fighting a semi-war, and while building up an army to the highest technical levels. The answer is simple: morale, keenness, pride, *esprit de corps*—call it what you will. No officer or man in the Arab Legion was content with less than perfection.

People who have never been soldiers sometimes imagine the military profession to be brutal. They think that the chief pre-occupation of soldiers is killing people. In reality, the enemy occupies very little of the soldier's thoughts. Soldiering is not a profession which breeds hatred. On the contrary, on the rare occasions on which "enemy" soldiers meet one another, they usually fraternize. The soldier recognizes in the enemy soldier a poor devil suffering the same afflictions as himself. His inclination (unless some particular atrocities have bred resentment) is to offer a cigarette and ask what the rations are like on the other side. But meetings with an enemy are rare. Otherwise the soldier's life is, above all things, a life of comradeship. Fears, discomforts, sufferings, dangers, borne together—borne in real and heartfelt companionship—these are the things which breed a love and a pride between man and man, and which make the soldier's life a joy. The courage, the endurance, the grousing, the humour, the pathos—the very intensity of the soldier's emotions shared with his mates—transform a good unit into a brotherhood which the old soldier, perforce discharged at last and alone as an individual, cannot remember without a heartache.

As I write, I sit in the window of my house, looking out over my garden and the green peaceful English countryside beyond. I have no complaints. It is true that, in the end of my career, I was dismissed, but in any case I should have had to leave, sooner or later. We all grow old. My only regret is that I have been arbitrarily cut off from my comrades in arms.

In the Arab Legion, we tolerated no racial, religious or class distinctions. The British officers were not a class apart. On any given occasion, the senior officer present commanded irrespective of race. British officers saluted Arab officers senior to them in rank. The division between British and Arab was not the only potential source of dissension in the army. In Jordan itself, there were Arabs and Circassians, Christians and Muslims, townsmen, countrymen and tribesmen, and different tribes unfriendly to one another. Latterly, there were East and West Jordanians—or, as we used to say, Palestinians and Trans-Jordanians. Every one of these distinctions was capable of giving rise to intrigue and dissension. But we took a strong stand—no member of the Arab Legion could be allowed to intrigue against a comrade or say anything which would wound or offend him. As soldiers, we were all comrades and shared a common glory.

One of the most tragic illusions which has obtained currency in some countries in the last fifty years is the idea that deliberately inculcated hate makes soldiers fight better. We cannot blame this fault on Jews or Arabs, because, to the best of my knowledge, it originated with the Germans in the First World War. Perhaps it was rightly attributed to Nietzsche.

Man is said to be a moral animal. He will make greater efforts for noble than for ignoble causes. Liberty, peace, protection of a man's country and home, will excite soldiers to greater efforts than will hate or the desire to injure. Hate will give rise to destructive activities, to looting, murder, torture and atrocities. It will not make soldiers steadier in battle.

I never felt any hate for Germans or for Jews. But I would have died as readily for Jordan in Palestine as for Britain in Europe.

*   *   *   *   *

It was tragic that the British officers, without whom this amazing build-up would have been impossible, worked day and night, in return only for abuse, libel and sneers, not from their comrades, but from the other Arab countries, and from certain politicians and lawyers in Jordan—principally from the West Bank. To them, Britain was the Power responsible for the destruction of their country. In the British officers of the Arab Legion, they could see only the enemies (as they imagined) of the people of Palestine.

The ordinary British officer was probably largely unaware of all this detraction and vilification. It was I who was the chief sufferer, because I lived principally in an Arab world and knew what was being said and written.

One Sunday evening, I was reading the lessons in the Anglican Church in Amman, and came to II Corinthians, Chapter 6. With only a few emendations, it struck me how applicable it was to that little band of British officers, which devoted itself so whole-heartedly to the Arab Legion:

"Giving no offence in any thing, that the service be not blamed.

But in all things approving ourselves, in much patience, in afflictions, in necessities, in distresses, in tumults, in labours, in watchings;

By knowledge, by patience, by kindness . . . by love unfeigned;

. . . by honour and dishonour, by evil report and good report;

as deceivers, and yet true; as unknown, and yet well known; as dying, and, behold, we live; . . . as sorrowful, yet alway rejoicing."

* * * * *

Ever since I had been commander of the desert area before 1939, I had taken an interest in teaching boys. Now with an army the numbers of which were rapidly growing, I had a problem on a larger scale. For soldiers had families—and half the army was always deployed in forward positions on the demarcation line. These could not have their children with them, but they still wanted them educated. Others were in permanent camps in East Jordan (formerly Trans-Jordan) and required schools within reach of their camps.

The Jordan government regretted its inability to help. Within a few years, we built up an Army Education Branch, which eventually provided for several thousand children. We derived a double advantage from this system. Not only were facilities available for the education of soldiers' children. In addition, all the boys joined the Arab Legion on discharge from school—not compulsorily but voluntarily. By 1955, all workshop apprentices, signals pupils and other technical branches were being recruited from Arab Legion schools. All officer cadets in 1955 came from Arab Legion schools likewise.

The need for the production of officer cadets, apprentice tradesmen and future N.C.O.s from Arab Legion schools was to become more pressing as time went on. The government schools were saturated with politics, and many school-teachers were Communists. In Arab Legion schools, every effort was made to teach the boys a straightforward open creed—service to king and country, duty, sacrifice and religion.

* * * * *

In addition to schooling, both officers and other ranks wanted houses. As a result, we evolved a system of loans for the purpose of building houses. Each request had to be checked to make sure that the petitioner really proposed to build a house. Soon there was a long waiting list. Building advances were repaid by deductions from pay, carried out through the Finance Department. As many of the applicants were busy all day—and so was I—it became customary to deal with building loans in my house at night.

The public health facilities in Jordan were very inadequate, as the government was too poor to meet the demand. Surgeons were especially scarce. I did not like any officer or man to be worried about the health of his family. I accordingly arranged with a number of private hospitals to operate on members of soldiers' families, on a note signed by me. The bill was subsequently passed to the Finance Department, who recovered the cost from the officer or man in easy instalments.

On days in which I worked in the office, I usually left the house at 7 a.m. and returned about 4 p.m. It was then that the real day's work began, for the morning was occupied with conferences, visits to the King or ministers, reception of callers and suchlike duties. I scarcely put pen to paper in the office. When I returned home, I took three or four boxes of papers with me.

The two more or less official schemes I have just mentioned were handled nightly from my house. The applicants forgathered behind the house in a small compound reserved for my escort. Soon other soldiers with personal troubles came too. Nothing official was dealt with. Complaints regarding service, pay, leave, promotion, or any other official matters, were rigidly confined to official channels. But a great variety of private matters were brought up. One soldier's brother was involved in a blood feud; the father of another had a lawsuit about land; a third wanted a letter to the Lands Department for a permit to plough up a piece of waste government land; a fourth wanted to marry a girl whose father wished to give her to a more wealthy suitor.

These evening sessions soon expanded beyond the Arab Legion. Refugees, tribesmen, orphans, hard-luck stories—they rolled up in their dozens. Some we could help, some we could not. At about nine or half-past nine, my wife would call plaintively from the drawing-room:

"My dear, the dinner will be ruined if you don't come soon."

Then I would hastily sign a few more forms and cheques and, giddy with the long day's work, would cry:

"That's enough! Finished! Anyone not dealt with can come tomorrow."

The men of the escort would take up the cry:

"*Ta'alu bukra, ya nas! Ta'alu bukra!*" ("Come tomorrow, O people! Come tomorrow!")

This procedure may sound chaotic to Europeans. Perhaps it was. But it was much more congenial to Arabs than the cold regulations of government departments. In any case, government offices in the East tend to close their doors on the poor. Arabs (in spite of paper democratic constitutions) still prefer to deal with a person than a department. In the old days, before the offices of democratic governments shut their doors on the poor, Arab Amirs used to sit at open meetings in the market squares of towns, and all and sundry could stand up and complain. The Amir, if he thought that the complaint was justified, would call up a slave or a retainer, and tell him what action to take. The slave would leave, accompanied by the petitioner, to right the latter's wrongs. Rough-and-ready justice, but at least it was quickly settled; there were no lawyers to spin it out and impoverish plaintiff and defendant alike.

One day, when I was sitting in a village on the West Bank talking to the village headman, the conversation turned to the British mandatory government.

"They brought the Jews and ruined our country," said the old man.

Then he shook his head sadly and added:

"But the British were generous, and they always helped the poor."

Direct British rule is disappearing. History will record that we sailed the seas, that we conquered, that we ruled. But will she remember also that we loved—and especially that we loved the poor?

* * * * *

King Abdulla's memoirs were published. A special edition was made available to officers and men, and for it a "military preface" was written for the benefit of the troops. I think it is worth reproducing.

"In these days, we see men who have invented bombs and machines and electricity and other things and who are so pleased with their own cleverness that they say there is no God. They hope that their inventions will save mankind, but we see these inventions turning only to the destruction of mankind. These men are clever but they are not wise—the fear of God is the beginning of Wisdom.

"Soldiers are nearer to death than other men, and it is essential for us to understand who we are. It is necessary for us to realize that God, not men, created the Universe, and only God, not men, can control it. We must not fall into the same errors as the Unbelievers and count up our guns, our bombs, our tanks and our aeroplanes, and pray to them for deliverance. This is a new idolatry, like those men who once worshipped stones and trees.

"Men have always lived and died, Nations have risen and fallen, wars have come and gone. God alone is eternal, and rules life and death, victory and defeat.

"All that we soldiers have to do is to do our duty to God, the King and the nation.

"Let us remember, for the rest, that God created the world and He rules it alone."

Such was the spirit which inspired the Arab Legion—and which has now become only a memory.

* * * * *

Ever since the Jordan government asked Britain to occupy Aqaba in the winter of 1948–49, the British Navy had left a ship there.

One day we heard that the next ship to take a turn at this duty would be the destroyer, H.M.S. *Chequers*, and that the Duke of Edinburgh was serving on board as a lieutenant. King Abdulla invited the royal guest to visit Amman, and, on January 24th, 1950, the Amir Tellal was sent to call on the Duke on board the ship at Aqaba.

There were no Arab Legion units in Aqaba at the time, with the exception of administrative staff in the port. An infantry battalion and a band were accordingly sent there, to provide a guard of honour. I flew to Aqaba in advance of His Highness the Amir, in order to receive him on the airport. We lunched on board as guests of the Duke, and in the afternoon I accompanied the Amir Tellal on a cruise down the Gulf. The Amir formed a genuine attachment to the Duke, and they seemed to feel at home with one another.

In the evening, the Arab Legion entertained the Amir.

Aqaba provides a complete contrast in scenery to the remainder of Jordan. The greater part of the country consists of limestone mountains (the desert itself being mostly a limestone plateau) and averages over 1,500 feet above sea-level. The climate, the trees and the vegetation are Mediterranean. But Aqaba is on the Red Sea. The little houses of the village are made of whitewashed mud plaster. Clumps of palm-trees lean over the shingly beach, like a scene in Hawaii or the South Pacific. Across the sparkling blue waters of the Gulf, the rusty red cliffs of Sinai lie scorched beneath a burning sun.

After dinner, we sat out near the shore with the Amir. The evening breeze, cool after the heat of the day, whispered in the tall slender palms. Overhead a full moon shed a pale radiance on the mountains and the little white village, and made a silvery path across the waters of the Gulf. The troops had lit a fire in the open, on which they were brewing the inevitable round after round of tea and coffee. Every now and then, somebody would throw an armful of brushwood on to the fire, the flames would leap and throw, for a minute or two, a flickering light on the crowd of soldiers and villagers, mingled in a circle round the fire.

Then the troops began to dance. In the *debka*, the dancers (who of course are all men) stand in a circle, joining hands. In the centre, a man plays a little limpid tune on a reed pipe, his cheeks blown out with a reserve of air, for the Arabian piper has no bag such as Scottish pipers use. Then the dancers would spring to life, going round and round in a circle, hopping, jumping, thumping, sometimes joining hands, sometimes clapping in time with the rhythm. Visitors from as far afield as Greece, Turkey and Pakistan, have told me that the peasants in their countries dance in much the same manner.

After the villagers came the bedouins. Their performance was of a different nature. Whereas the villagers' dance is quick, energetic and active, to cheerful little tunes on the pipe, the bedouins move with a slow and dignified grace. Two lines of men formed up, holding hands and facing one another, and began a kind of slow chant. One line recited a verse, the other answered it. Their bodies swayed slowly and rhythmically. Occasionally they advanced a few steps towards one another, and then retired again. Between the two lines, the leader swayed and turned, slowly and gracefully, a drawn sword above his head. He improvised the words of the chant, which the other dancers took up from him, repeating the line backwards and forwards to one another.

> *"Ja al adu lil biladi.*
> *Qahharna fi Bab al Wadi."*

The moon shed its silver radiance over the swaying figures, the shrub-covered desert and the silent mountains.

> "The enemy came to the country.
> We drove him back from Bab al Wadi."

The monotonous chant was repeated backwards and forwards. The leader changed to a new verse:

> *"Ya Tellal, nejl al Ashrafi."*
> ("O Tellal, son of the Sherifs.")

The moon was low over the dark cliffs of Sinai across the bay when the Amir rose and said good night. The troops scattered in small groups, walking back to their tents. The coffee fire had sunk to a glow of red embers in the sand.

As I lay in bed before falling asleep, I could hear above me the whisper of the palms, and outside the window, the rhythmic plash of the Red Sea on the shingly beach.

XVI

The Father of his Country

And when he was come near, he beheld the city, and wept over it, saying, If thou hadst known, even thou, at least in this thy day, the things which belong unto thy peace! but now they are hid from thine eyes.
Luke xix. 41–2

The true gentleman is friendly but not familiar; the inferior man is familiar but not friendly. . . . The well-bred are dignified but not pompous; the ill-bred are pompous but not dignified.

CONFUCIUS

XVI

THE FATHER OF HIS COUNTRY

KING ABDULLA was anxious to meet and converse with all
his subjects. He was typical of the true aristocrat, so assured
of his own position that he was ready to mix and talk freely
with all. He was never haughty or defensive, in an attempt to preserve his rank or dignity. It had probably never entered his mind that
anyone could question either.

He strongly disliked being guarded, and would call out if any rash
but well-intentioned soldier or policeman should attempt to hold
back his subjects who wished to speak with him. Knowing as we did
the intense jealousy of and hostility to him which certain other
governments felt, the King's dislike of being guarded was a source
of anxiety to us. It was therefore with mixed feelings that we were
told one day that he wished to tour the front-line villages on the
West Bank.

The King flew from Amman to Kolundia (see the map on page 248),
the airport of Jerusalem, whither I had preceded him and where I
was waiting to receive him. A guard of honour was drawn up on the
airport, gleaming, faultless, rigid, with its regimental colours idly
waving in the fresh breeze of a cloudless mountain morning (Kolundia
is nearly three thousand feet above the sea). As I followed the King
inspecting the guard, my heart swelled to see those ranks of strong
young men, motionless, erect, looking straight to their front, so proud
of their profession and their army—the platoon sergeants, some of
them now veterans with rows of medals. I felt that our little army was
a living, palpitating being, all inspired with the same readiness for
sacrifice and the same noble ideals.

I drove in the King's car from Kolundia through those hills of
Judaea and Samaria which I was learning to love, and through
Ramallah, perched on the highest ridge of the mountains, the summer
resort of the country, a little town chiefly inhabited by Christians.
Here groups of girls walked through the streets, bare-headed and un-
veiled. Then through Bir Zeit, or the Well of Oil, surrounded by its
hills covered with the grey-green leaves of olive gardens. Then down
and down, along narrowing twisty roads, between deep ravines and
rock-strewn slopes, cut with infinite labour into terraces planted with
olives, fig-trees and vines. How often did the fig-tree and the vine
appear in the Bible story—these must always have been the staple
products of Judaea and Samaria. As we wound down the mountain

slopes, we could see below and in front of us the narrow coastal plain which was Israel, and beyond it the white outline of the coast and the misty blue Mediterranean.

In each village, the people had been lined up on either side of the street, with groups of women on the housetops. All cheered wildly, clapped, waved flags, and intoned: "Long live His Majesty the King." When we drove through Azzun, the enthusiasm rose to an even higher pitch. People ran along beside the car laughing and clapping. It was not possible to stop in every village, or we should never have been able to complete the programme, but in Azzun the King insisted on stopping for a minute or two. He descended from the car, and shook hands with the headmen of the village. A laughing, cheering crowd seethed around him. The village police pushed and struggled with the crowd good-humouredly. "That's enough! That's enough!" the policemen kept saying—but the crowd only laughed and jostled the more. Then he began to shake hands with them all. The escort tried to sort them into single file—"*Wahid wara wahid*" they kept shouting, "One behind one."

At last the King returned to his car, and we moved slowly forward again, amidst more cheering. By the time we drew clear of the crowd at the end of the village, I was deeply moved. One or two tears ran down my cheeks. We had fought for these people—and been cursed daily for it. Was it possible that they really knew and appreciated what we had done?

The King looked at me. He smiled and patted me kindly on the knee.

"You are too impressionable," he said. "They have affected you."

"They are good people, sir," I answered. "When a man sees them like that, it makes him want to fight for them."

On we went, through endless olive orchards, and then down and up a little valley and out of the trees on top of a low pass, by a shrine called Nebi Elias or the Prophet Elias. We were almost on the coastal plain now, only a few low foothills divided us from the narrow plain and the sea.

Qalqiliya had suffered particularly from the Rhodes armistice demarcation line. It was a little town in the coastal plain, immediately at the base of the last foothill. Three hundred yards west of the little town began the orange groves, which seemed to stretch as far as one could see across the plains to the sea. These orange groves had all been planted by the people of Qalqiliya, or their fathers before them, and had provided their only means of subsistence. Then had come the Rhodes armistice which had drawn the demarcation line between the houses of the little town and their orange groves. All the oranges had been taken over by the Jews, and the people of Qalqiliya were left sitting in their houses—destitute. In the autumn, they could

Arab Legion artillery—a twenty-five-pounder gun in action. "We set ourselves the same standards of technical efficiency as the British Army"

PLATE 16

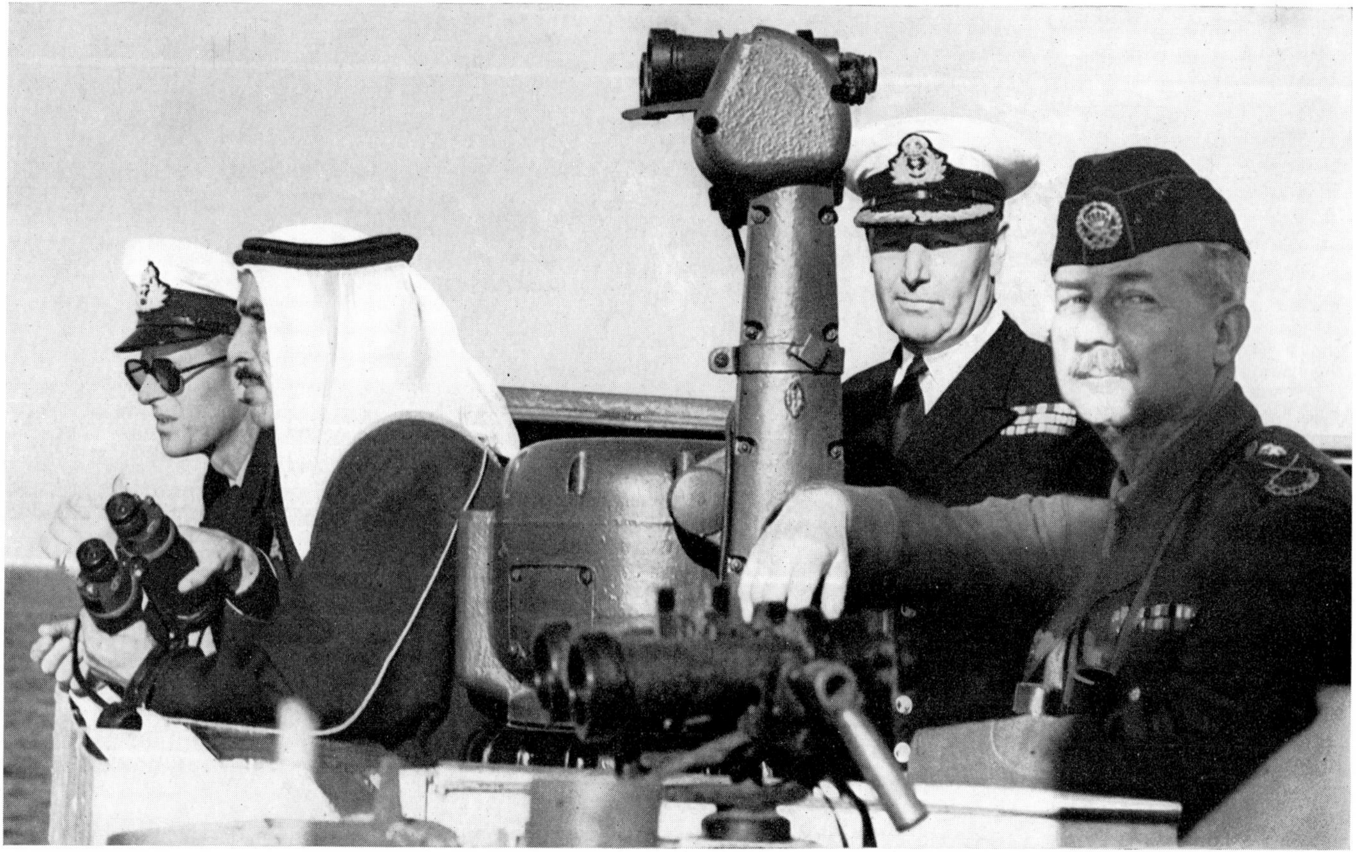

Crown Copyright Reserved

PLATE 17

On the bridge of H.M.S. *Chequers* at Aqaba. *Left to right:* Prince Philip, Duke of Edinburgh; the Amir Tellal; the captain of the see the Jews, only three hundred yards away, picking their oranges. All round the country north, south and west of Qalqiliya, on the coastal plain, and in gaps in the orange groves, new Jewish colonies were springing up like mushrooms, groups of little white houses— like the pre-fabs used in England after the Second World War—or like huge chicken farms with rows of little white hen-houses. The greater part of the Israeli army was only a few miles away across that plain; an Israeli aerodrome was only three or four miles distant; the aircraft could be seen taking off and coming in to land all day long. East of Qalqiliya lay the long range of the Palestine mountains, crossed only by occasional winding narrow roads, along which any Arab Legion reinforcements would have to come if the little town were attacked.

But the people of Qalqiliya were more virile than most. After a first period of despair, they had set to work. Behind the little town on the east lay the barren rocky hills; all their fertile land had gone to Israel. But they had already started to dig and level and terrace, to remake a living when all their old livelihood was lost. But there still remained the threat of those ever-increasing Jewish colonies so near to them.

If the people of Azzun had been enthusiastic, the people of Qalqiliya went mad. As soon as we drove into the edge of the little town, we were surrounded by a seething crowd. The Boy Scouts and school-boys had tried to line the streets, and were to cheer the King, but they also were swept away. We advanced into the main street at less than a walking pace. The escort cars in front and behind were cut off from the royal car by a surging sea of faces. Some crowded round, some climbed on the car, some stood on the running boards on either side and took advantage of the extra four inches of height to bellow to the others: "Long live the King! Long live His Majesty the King!"

The noise was deafening. I forced my way out of the car, pushing the door by main force to get rid of several men packed against it. I tried to struggle forward to clear some people who were dancing and shouting in front of the car and had thereby reduced it to a stand-still. "Open a road!" I roared. "*Iftahu tariq!*" Nobody took any notice. I thumped them on the back to make them listen, but they looked round at me with excited faces and bellowed, "Long live the King!" One or two of them grinned, and shouted: "Long live the father of Faris!" But they made no attempt to move. Suddenly I also felt a thump on the back. I looked round and saw the sergeant of my escort. "Get back into the car," he yelled in my ear. "You don't know who is in this crowd."

In a sudden lull, a voice called out: "O father of Tellal, protect us!" In an instant, the whole crowd took up the words in a thunderous chorus. "O father of Tellal, protect us!" "*Ya abu Tellal, hameena!*" Somehow the crowd got itself all facing one way, and we again moved slowly forward at about two miles an hour, the dense crowd moving with us, intoning, "*Ya abu Tellal, hameena! Ya abu Tellal, hameena!*"

After half an hour in this packed throng, we reached the little municipal building where the mayor waited to receive us, beneath chains of Jordanian flags.

When we eventually reached Nablus in the afternoon after this tour of frontier villages, I took the district governor on one side.

"What an amazing reception was given to the King everywhere," I said. "I cannot understand it. We are always being told that the people of Palestine hate him."

"Don't believe it," replied the governor. "The common people love him, but they have no means of expressing their feelings except on occasions like this. It is the lawyers, the politicians and the newspapers who do the propaganda against him, and who are usually the only voices heard. But you can't blame them—they have to earn their living."

*   *   *   *   *

It is curious in life how often we are deceived by over-simplifications. "Kings are reactionary and oppressive," "Democracy means freedom," "Representative government protects the rights of the people." It sounds so well—but how often the reverse proves in practice to be the case. King Abdulla was in many ways the greatest democrat in his country, far more so than his ministers. For he mingled with all classes, went everywhere and received everybody. He knew how the bedouin lived, and how the farmers worked, just as much as he knew the politicians and the merchants. I have heard him greet a Prime Minister in the morning by asking him how things were going. The Prime Minister replied with various comments on political matters.

"You only know about these cursed politics," replied the King. "I am distressed about this cold snap in the weather. It will kill many of the lambs. You must remember, Pasha, that men have to eat—that is more important than politics."

For King Abdulla was an all-round man, a man of culture. In November 1948, while the Israeli offensive against the Egyptians was in progress, I visited the King in his warm winter residence in the Jordan valley, a thousand feet below sea-level. I found him sitting in a chair in his drawing-room, looking out at the wide scrub-covered plain of the Jordan valley, falling away to the deep blue Dead Sea between its craggy precipitous mountains.

After greeting me, he said: "What do you think of this?" and he read out two verses of poetry. I could not catch the words.

"I am sorry, sir," I said, "I did not understand it."

He read it out again and once more I was obliged to make the same answer. The King smiled.

"Of course you didn't," he said. "It isn't Arabic, it's Persian. This is what it means in Arabic:

" 'Hafidh compared thy ringlets to daggers,
Hafidh was right!
And those daggers
Are plunged in my heart.' "

"Very pretty," I said.

The King sighed and put his book down on a little table beside his chair. "Well, Pasha," he said, "I suppose you don't want to talk about poetry. You want to tell me about wars and battles."

*   *   *   *   *

One day in July 1951, I had been visiting units on the West Bank. Just before sunset, I arrived at Kolundia, where an aircraft was waiting to fly me to Amman. The pilot accosted me anxiously.

"Have you heard what has happened, sir?" he asked.

"No!" I said cheerfully. "What is it now?"

"Riyadh as Sulh, the former Prime Minister of Lebanon, was in Amman this morning to see the King. When driving back to Amman airport he was murdered—it's only two hours ago."

In Amman! It was the first time a major political murder had occurred in Jordan. As the aircraft took off, I sat with a feeling of foreboding and anxiety. In Amman there was consternation. Riyadh as Sulh had been the King's guest. As he drove to the airport, preceded by a police car, another car had overtaken him. Several men armed with sub-machine guns had fired from the windows of the second car. All the murderers except one were either in custody or dead. There was one mitigating factor—the assailants were Lebanese, not Jordanians. They had followed their victim from Lebanon to Amman. Nevertheless, Amman was tense. The air seemed full of foreboding.

On Thursday, July 19th, the King was due to take a parade of the Arab Legion Air Force. He was desperately anxious to create a Jordan Air Force—Israel was believed to have two hundred aircraft. On this parade, four new Jordanian Air Force pilots who had qualified were to be presented by the King with their wings.

That morning the King received an anonymous letter, telling him that both he and I were to be murdered. I had been instructed to

report to the palace and accompany the King to the airfield. When
I arrived at the palace, he handed me this letter.

I drove to the airport in the King's car. Curiously enough, as we
drove past the camp of the Arab Legion Base M.T. Company, an
N.C.O. stepped out and pulled their flag down to half-mast. The
King pointed him out to me and laughed.

"He thinks he's in the Navy," he said. "They salute by hauling
down their flag!"

Twenty-four hours later when I passed there again, the flag was
at half-mast with reason.

* * * * *

The parade, though on a very small scale, was very well done.
The King was cheerful. We had lunch in a hangar, and then he took
off for Jerusalem where he was to sleep the night. He was devoted to
Jerusalem, and loved more and more to pray in the mosque there on
Fridays. On Friday morning, he drove to Nablus to pass the
time, as the service in the Great Mosque was not until noon. He
drank coffee with the mayor of Nablus, Suleiman Beg Togan, and
sat talking for an hour. Suleiman Beg looked at his watch.

"There is scarcely time to get back to Jerusalem for prayers, sir,"
he said. "Why do you not say your prayers here in our mosque in
Nablus today?"

But the King would not agree. "That which is written, must come
to pass," the Arabs say.

Ever since the murder of Riyadh as Sulh three days before, I
had felt tense and anxious. I had sent Colonel Habis Mejali with the
King, and had told him to be on the alert, especially at prayers in
the Great Mosque. I thought of telephoning to the commandant
of police in Jerusalem to urge him also to be particularly careful at
prayers in the Mosque, but I restrained myself. "They all know their
jobs," I thought. "I must not be fussy."

The King entered the vast courtyard of the Great Mosque of
Jerusalem a little before twelve. It was packed with untold thousands
of people, as was usual for the noon prayer on Friday. The people
opened a narrow lane down which the King walked, with the dense
crowd hedging him in on every side. He loved talking to his subjects,
and stopped several times to speak to people he recognized. Colonel
Habis and the escort surrounded him and tried to hold back the
crowd, but the King turned half irritably:

"*La tahabasni, ya Habis!*" he said. "Don't imprison me, O Habis!"[1]

As the party drew near to the door of the Great Mosque, Habis
and the escort again tried to surround the King, who repeated with
increased vehemence:

[1] This is a pun in Arabic.

"Don't imprison me, O Habis."

The King accordingly stepped across the threshold first, with all the escort behind him. The old shaikh of the Mosque, a venerable ecclesiastic with a long white beard, stepped forward to kiss his hand. At that instant, a man stepped out from behind the massive door of the Mosque and found himself beside the King and only a yard from him. He presented a pistol and fired at King Abdulla's head at a few inches' range. The bullet entered behind his ear and emerged from his eye. The King fell forward dead on the floor of the Mosque. His white turban rolled away across the marble pavement.

The murderer fired wildly right and left, as the escort dashed forward and shot him dead in his turn.

* * * * *

As it was Friday, I had dressed in plain clothes, and had gone down with my wife and the children to the bookshop in the town. Miss Halebi, the part-owner of the shop, greeted my wife. They began talking, and Miss Halebi said something about people dying. My wife suddenly felt an indescribable sensation of horror. It was twelve o'clock, and must have been almost exactly the moment of the murder. We wandered from the bookshop up a side street—Besman Street—to a favourite toyshop the children remembered. They were looking at toys when a policeman dashed in breathless.

"Sir," he said, "Muhamad Beg is looking for you!"

Suddenly I saw Muhamad Beg Suhaimat with a scared face, running along the footpath. "Where is the Pasha?" he called wildly. When he saw me, he came to me quickly.

"An attack has been made on our lord," he gasped. "The Prime Minister wants you at his house."

"What has happened?" I asked, as we ran to a car and jumped in. Muhamad Beg was still gasping for breath.

"I was listening to the broadcast of the prayers from the Mosque," he panted. "The reader was reading the Quran. Then suddenly I heard tac-tac-tac—a succession of shots. Somebody called out 'Our lord'—but I think perhaps nothing has happened, for the Quran reader went on reading. Then the telephone rang, and the operator told me that the Prime Minister wants Glubb Pasha at once."

The car was threading through the traffic and then raced up the hill on which the Prime Minister's house was situated. I jumped out at the gate and ran up the garden path and on to the veranda, praying again and again: "O God, let him be safe!"

The front door opened and somebody said: "Here is Glubb Pasha, sir!" In the entrance hall, several ministers were standing, all sobbing openly. The Prime Minister stepped forward towards me and began "Our lord ——" and then broke down in sobs once more. The room was full of men weeping unashamedly with tears streaming down their faces.

"Our lord is gone," sobbed Sameer Pasha.[1] "Call out the army and move troops into the town. There may be a revolution. . . ."

I was too stunned to weep.

"Very good, sir," I replied. "I will go and do so at once." I ran down the garden path to the street. Two or three officers and a group of men stood anxiously by the gate.

"What has happened? What has happened?" They pressed forward eagerly.

"Our lord is dead," I just succeeded in saying, with a choking lump in my throat. "Now it's up to us."

Muhamad gave a cry of despair. "*Allahu akbar! Allahu akbar!*" he repeated.

I jumped into my car and drove back to my house. I rang up brigade headquarters in Zerqa, twenty miles away.

"The King has just been assassinated," I said, trying to steady my voice. "There may be rioting and looting in Amman. Please send a battalion of infantry into the town immediately, and a second within two hours. How soon can the first battalion be here?"

Then we had to provide for Jerusalem. I spoke to Sam Cooke, the divisional commander.

"The King has been assassinated in Jerusalem," I said. "There may be looting or riots. You personally are responsible for law and order. Is that all right?"

"Yes, sir. I'll get on with that right away."

One thing about Cooke was that he was always calm. He spoke in the same voice as if I had said, "Come round and have a drink."

The telephone rang again. It was the Prime Minister.

"Where are the troops?" he cried anxiously. "They haven't come yet! The people will loot the town."

"They'll be in before long, sir," I said. "I have spoken to Zerqa."

Twenty minutes later the troops occupied the town. The government proclaimed a curfew. There were no disturbances. In Jerusalem, a few shops were looted before the troops took over.

That night I slept little and fitfully. In the morning, Arab Legion headquarters had sent an officer and a double escort to accompany me on my drive to the office. When I looked into our bedroom to say good-bye, my wife was kneeling by her bed. I knew what she was praying.

Later, the Prime Minister told me that the day before the King's

---

[1] Sameer Pasha Rifai had succeeded Taufiq Pasha as Prime Minister a few months previously.

death, he begged him to be cautious. "I believe in God. My life is in His hands," King Abdulla had replied.

* * * * *

It is one of the most remarkable proofs of T. E. Lawrence's influence on British policy after the First World War that an instinctive lack of sympathy between him and the Amir Abdulla was sufficient to cause the latter's statesmanship to be disregarded for twenty-five years. Both men felt this repulsion. "The general dislike of Lawrence's presence was clear," wrote the King in his memoirs, referring to the operations in the Hejaz in 1917.

King Abdulla had enjoyed a long experience of State affairs. He went to Constantinople in 1891 at the age of nine and was brought up there. He did not revisit Arabia until 1908, when he was already a young man of twenty-six years. In 1910, after only two years at home, he returned once more to Constantinople as member for Mecca in the Turkish Parliament. Before he reached the age of thirty, he was personally acquainted with the Sultan Abdul Hamid of Turkey, familiar with Cabinet ministers and entrusted with commissions of State. There was a certain fine largeness of mind and tolerance in the capitals of the old polyglot Empires, offering a deep contrast with the narrow and bitter fanaticisms which distinguish the little States into which the great Empires have been divided. There can be no doubt that King Abdulla's character was formed by his early upbringing amongst the ruling classes of the Ottoman Empire. It produced in him a wise and tolerant mind, more mature and mellow than those of the petty and fanatical modern politicians in the Middle East.

Yet this broad cosmopolitan outlook did not destroy his Arab loyalties. Describing the reception given to his father and family on their arrival in Arabia from Constantinople in 1908, he wrote in his memoirs:

"After the noon prayer, the Amir and his retinue set out on their ride to Bahra. The whole setting was an expression of national splendour and dignity. You could see nothing which was not Arab—riders, horses, fashions, customs, all were Arab and Hashemite. When we reached the plain of Jedda, the riders began to show off their horsemanship. . . ."

But it would be a mistake to canonize the memory of King Abdulla, and think of him as a saint, or even as a faultless hero. He was very human. He was frequently irritable with those in daily contact with him, though he was never so to me. He was not without spite for his enemies, and he never modified his actions or his words to appease them. He often talked too much about his plans and his emotions, even before unreliable, if not definitely unfriendly, people.

"A man whose enemy is his own tongue" was the description of him once given to me by the Amir Shakir ibn Zeid, the King's own cousin.

While sincerely religious, his religion was peculiarly limited. I remember one occasion when I was with him, and a young man came in to pay his respects. He was the son of some retainer of the royal family, and had been appointed as a schoolmaster in the rather remote little provincial town of Tafila.

"My lord, I am leaving for Tafila," said the young man. "Before starting, I came to ask Your Majesty's orders."

"May God give you success," said the King. "The most important advice I give you is to remember your religion."

"Whatever you order," replied the young man humbly.

"Religion consists in repeating the prayers five times a day, and in fasting the month of Ramadhan," continued King Abdulla. "Always remember that and God will give you success."

The potential schoolmaster kissed the royal hand and backed out of the room. It made a curious impression on me that so great a man should give so limited and formal a definition of his religion. There was nothing about intrigue, dishonesty or laziness—so often the shortcomings of minor officials in remote stations. Nothing, for that matter, about quality of life or character, let alone the difficulties of growing boys and how to influence them. The King of course was better in his own life than in this advice. He did have a sense of responsibility towards his people, even if he did not formulate it in words.

*   *   *   *   *

The King lay in state in the throne room of the palace in Amman. On the morning of the funeral, we filed in one by one and paid a last tribute to our beloved master. The funeral procession made a detour round the palace grounds to a grave dug on a ledge in the hills overlooking Amman. Two battalions of infantry lined the route presenting arms. As I walked in front of the gun carriage, I could see the tears running down the cheeks of the soldiers who stood with their rifles at the present. At the graveside, Sameer Pasha tried to make a speech, but his words were cut by sobs. As the coffin was lowered, I broke down myself and cried like a child. There were many distinguished people at the funeral. As we walked away, I heard one of them remark, "I could not have believed that a man could be so loved."

*   *   *   *   *

The murder proved to have been instigated by the relatives of the former Mufti of Jerusalem, Haj Ameen. The accused were tried by a special court, and four were condemned to death. The actual murderer had been killed by the King's escort. The Attorney-General also charged Abdulla al Tell as having been an accessory before the fact. He was, of course, in Egypt, working with the Mufti. I was called to give evidence as to the character and service of Abdulla. He was condemned to death *in absentia*.

When the sentence was published, Abdulla al Tell held a Press conference in Cairo, at which he accused me of "framing" the charge against him.

"If Glubb Pasha had been assassinated, I should have been the murderer," he told the Press. "But King Abdulla—no!"

The last time I had seen Abdulla al Tell, he had assured me that I was his father, and that he could take no decision without my paternal advice. It is remarkable what duplicity these young men can show.

* * * * *

After the King's murder, a Cairo newspaper published a list of Arab public men who had been assassinated in the five years from 1946 to 1951. It included two kings—King Abdulla of Jordan and the Imam Yahya of the Yemen; one president of a republic, Husni az Zaim of Syria; four prime ministers—Ahmed Maher Pasha and Nokrashy Pasha of Egypt, Muhsin al Brazi of Syria and Riyadh as Sulh of Lebanon; one commander-in-chief, Sami al Hennawi of Syria; the leader of the Muslim Brethren in Egypt, Shaikh Hasan al Benna; one cabinet minister, Amin Osman of Egypt, and several police chiefs and judges. Numerous unsuccessful attempts at assassination were made on other prime ministers, ministers and public men.

* * * * *

The King's eldest son, the Amir Tellal, was heir to the throne. In his lifetime, King Abdulla had been on bad terms with his son. As a result, he never allowed the Amir to exercise any public function, and he had spent twenty years sitting in his house with nothing to do. The politicians had seized upon what was a not unusual type of family father-and-son quarrel, and had endeavoured to make political capital out of it. In Syria and Egypt, and to some extent in Palestine, Amir Tellal was depicted as an Arab patriot who had quarrelled with his father because the latter was a British tool. This was pure fiction. The Amir's politics were the same as the King's: their lack of sympathy was domestic. A few weeks before King Abdulla was murdered, he said to me: "I have done my best. I have nothing of which my conscience accuses me. My only failure was that I was unsuccessful in the upbringing of my son."

For several years before the King's death, the Amir Tellal had suffered from occasional mental attacks. These had become increasingly frequent. When his father was killed, the Amir was in a mental hospital in Switzerland.

The disappearance of King Abdulla caused utter dismay and confusion in Jordan. His strong hand had been at the helm ever since Trans-Jordan had come into existence in 1921. He had fearlessly shouldered the responsibility for every decision. The politicians were scarcely more than yes-men. No political leaders or statesmen had grown up. The King had been all in all.

The Amir Tellal had, for many years, lived in a house only a hundred yards from my own. He had all the frankness and charm of his father. I had often called at his house, and can remember lunching with him, when his son, little Amir Husain, was allowed to come in after lunch to say "how d'you do." Amir Tellal was a devoted husband and father, and had found solace from the mortification he suffered in public life by taking refuge in family affection.

It was with immense enthusiasm that the people of Jordan heard that King Tellal would return from Switzerland on September 6th, 1951, and would mount the throne. The city was gaily decorated with flags and lined with troops. The people, orphaned for seven weeks without a King, were clad in their best. The new King arrived at the airport, and drove through the city with an escort of Arab Legion—the Royal Escort of Lancers, preceded by a squadron of the 1st Armoured Car Regiment. Twenty-one guns boomed from the citadel. The King took the oath, standing before the members of both Houses of Parliament. It was a day of relief from anxiety over the new King's health. Amman was full of smiling faces, even though many eyes glistened with tears as the new King drove by. For a moment we hoped that all would once more be well, and that past happy days were to be repeated.

These bright hopes were all too soon to prove vain.

XVII

Holding On

"O my God, my soul is cast down within me: therefore will I remember thee from the land of Jordan. . . . "   *Psalm* xlii. 6

> For loyalty is still the same
> whether it win or lose the game:
> True as the dial to the sun
> although it is not shone upon.
>
> SAMUEL BUTLER (1612–1680)

HIS EXCELLENCY THE CHIEF OF THE STAFF OF THE ARAB LEGION, GLUBB PASHA.

May God preserve him.

I send Your Excellency my compliments and respects and my sincere thanks for the excellent reception which took place on the day of my arrival, sincerely praying to the Lord that He may make this reign a reign of success and prosperity for all.

I am sending this letter to Your Excellency by hand of Sergeant Abdu Faraj abu al Sa'ad, who accompanied me from the time of my departure to my return and who was a good companion to me. I cannot forget his noble and generous conduct. I see myself unable adequately to reward him in view of his faithful comradeship. I ask your Excellency to help me in rewarding him for his services to me, in view of the fact that he is a member of our gallant army. I am confident that you will comply with my request by helping him with any matter concerning him in Arab Legion Headquarters which may have arisen during his absence with me.

I present Your Excellency with many thanks and my best compliments.

(signed) TELLAL.

September 1951.

NOTE. This personal letter to me illustrates the charm of King Tellal's character. The extremely courteous tone is noticeable, especially when addressed by a King to a subordinate, to whom he was entitled to give a direct order. The gratitude and consideration expressed for his servant are also typical.

الاستاذ مدير عام دائرة
الملوكية السنية الاردنية حفظه الله

اهدي لسعادتكم اطيب التحيات
والاحترامات وجزيل الشكر لحسن
الاستقبال الذي تم يوم وصولي
راجياً من المولى ان يجعل هذا
العهد عهد توفيق ونجاح للجميع

واني ارسل لسعادتكم هذا
الكتاب بيد الرقيب عبده فرج
ابو السعد الذي رافقني من
حين ذهابي وايابي وكان خير
رفيق لي لا انسى عمله النبيل
واني ارى نفسي عاجزاً عن
مكافأته لحسن رفاقته

التوقيع طلال

XVII

HOLDING ON

WHILE these tragic events were occurring in Jordan, the unending sub-war on the Jordan–Israel demarcation line not only continued unabated but even increased. Throughout this period, Israeli statesmen continued to state on the international stage, whether in Lake Success or elsewhere, that Israel was holding out the hand of friendship to the Arabs. The actual situation on the demarcation line, however, presented a different picture. Here the Israelis were constantly aggressive.

In the ten months from December 1949 to October 1950, 117 incidents of crossing the demarcation line (or of firing across it) were carried out by Israeli forces in uniform. During the same period, not one incident of the crossing of the line by men of the Arab Legion was reported.

During the same ten months, 76 cases of Israeli aircraft flying across Jordan territory were recorded. As Jordan had no aircraft, the Israeli air force ran no risk by flying over Jordan.

From the signature of the Rhodes armistice agreement to October 1950, 5,648 Arabs had been expelled from Israeli territory into Jordan. These were all persons resident in Israel when the armistice was signed. Infiltrators captured by the Israelis and returned to Jordan are not included.

At the same time, many Arabs, chiefly refugees, were still infiltrating across the border line—many of them to revenge themselves, by stealing, on the people responsible for their disasters. The basic difference between the two sides continued. From the Jordan side, the infiltrators were all civilians, in nearly every case destitutes. No cases of line-crossing were carried out by the Arab Legion. On the Israeli side, every incident was carried out by Israeli troops in uniform. In 1950 and 1951, the Israeli government was inclined to deny these incursions into Jordan territory by their troops, but in later years, it admitted the principle of reprisals.

We, on the Jordan side, never for a moment relaxed our efforts to prevent infiltration, but with half a million refugees, many of them vagabonding about the countryside, and a border nearly 400 miles long, it was not possible to guarantee that nobody would ever cross the line on a dark night. Nevertheless, the Jordan government had gone so far as to pass a special law making the mere crossing of the demarcation line an offence punishable by six months' imprisonment, even without any connected criminal offence.

The Jordan government did not limit itself to excuses. It put forward constructive proposals. The principal argument we used was that catching criminals was a police, not a military, operation. We accordingly suggested the closest co-operation between the police forces of the two countries. We suggested joint patrols, direct telephone communication across the demarcation line between Jordan and Israeli police officers, and frequent meetings between such officers. These proposals were embodied in a so-called "Local Commanders' Agreement".

For some reason, the Israelis never welcomed such intimate co-operation. When, under pressure from UNO, they accepted one or other of these measures, they denounced them again within two or three weeks. The Israelis complained so loudly and bitterly about refugee infiltration that we were at a loss to understand why they refused to co-operate. Jordan really wanted a quiet border, but could not guarantee to prevent all refugee incursions. Failing such complete prevention, Israel used her army in reprisal raids which usually fell on innocent people.

In Jenin (see the map on page 248 for the ensuing incidents), we happened to have a police officer who did make friends with his Israeli opposite number. The result was that, for months on end, no incidents occurred in that area. We pointed this out and suggested the extension of the system to other areas—but in vain. There were, of course, those on the Arab side who regarded every co-operation with the Jews as treachery. The Jordan government, however, took a more realistic view of the situation. If they could have attacked and defeated Israel, they would have done so. But they realized that daily shootings on the demarcation line did only harm. The whole problem of infiltration and reprisals was a deadlock. Both sides wanted a quiet border, but suspicion made their co-operation impossible.

On February 7th, 1951, at 3 a.m., three trucks emerged from Jewish Jerusalem. At a point two miles south-west of the city, they stopped and switched off their headlights. Some thirty Israelis dismounted, crossed the demarcation line and climbed the hill on the Jordan side of the line, to the little Arab hamlet of Sharafat. This tiny village was inhabited by only four or five Arab families. The Jews quietly surrounded the house of the headman, placed explosive charges beneath it and blew it up, with all the occupants still asleep. They then blew up the house next door, after firing indiscriminately on the inhabitants of the village or anyone attempting to escape. Two men, three women and five children were blown up in the headman's house. Three women and five other children in the village were wounded. The ages of the five children killed were thirteen years, ten, six, one and one. The wounded children were twelve, ten, eight, four and four years old respectively. As a pressman wrote at the time, "These were doubtless formidable enemies of the State of Israel." The reason for this outrage was never known. The hamlet of Sharafat contained no police, troops or armed Arabs of any kind.

Two nights later, a party of four or five Israelis knocked down the door of a house in Falama, a similar hamlet two kilometres inside Jordan. They threw in a hand grenade, killing a man, his son and daughter, who were asleep within.

Thus day by day the tale of murder and bloodshed continued.

In the Jordan Parliament, a number of Palestinian members claimed that the responsibility for all frontier incidents rested on the British officers of the Arab Legion alone. The British were, they alleged, in collusion with the Jews to kill Arabs.

In its number of March 2nd, 1951, *Truth* printed the following paragraph:

"Murders of Jordan Arabs

"When people perish in a Swiss or Austrian avalanche, or when they are killed by an earthquake in distant New Guinea, or when they meet death in any violent form, that fact is usually given bold headlines in British newspapers. There is one kind of violence which seems to be immune from Press publicity. It is the murdering of Jordan Arabs by Jews. News has reached *Truth* that, on February 7th, ten armed Jews entered Sharafat village, near Bethlehem. They surrounded the house of the *mukhtar*, laid explosives around it and blew it up with all its occupants, killing nine Arabs and seriously wounding four. The Press had no imposing headlines, or even a few lines, to spare for this cowardly murder, carried out on Jordan territory, 100 yards beyond the Israeli frontier.

"It was not the only incident of its kind. On January 29th, about sixteen Jewish soldiers approached Yalu village, near the Latrun salient, and fired and threw hand grenades at the villagers before being beaten off by the National Guard, but not before they had inflicted casualties. On February 3rd, a party of armed Jews attacked Saffa village, near Ramallah, killing two civilians and wounding another. The Jordan authorities are convinced that these 'frontier incidents' are part of a campaign of aggression designed to provoke retaliation and so 'justify' the rape of more Arab lands. Why does the British Press, which seeks out violence in the ends of the earth, draw the line at the Israeli-Jordan border?"

In the autumn of 1951, we in the Arab Legion were under simultaneous fire from almost every direction.

(1) The other Arab countries, Egypt, Syria and Saudi Arabia, assisted by the Mufti, and extremist organizations such as the Egyptian Muslim Brethren, never ceased to denounce our treachery, or the fact (as they claimed) that we were secretly helping the Jews.

(2) Israeli troops continued to raid across the demarcation line or to shoot across it, allegedly in retaliation for infiltration across the line by refugees from Jordan. The number of incidents in May 1951 was a record.

(3) Troops and police were in constant action, chiefly by innumerable night patrols, endeavouring to prevent this infiltration. The officers and men of the Arab Legion realized that infiltration did not seriously injure the Israelis, but that it gave the latter an excuse to deliver military reprisal attacks. Most of the men realized also that certain Arab governments were encouraging infiltration in order to injure Jordan. The other Arabs accused us of preventing infiltration because we were in secret league with the Jews.

(4) Jordanian members of Parliament from the West Bank claimed that the Jews were able to raid into Jordan and kill Arabs, because the British officers of the Arab Legion had ordered their men not to fire back. They had done so on secret orders from London, because Britain was still secretly the ally of Israel.

Constantly attacked and abused by Israelis and Arabs alike, our position may well be thought to have been a peculiarly unhappy one. But in practice this was only half the picture. Those who were nearest to us knew the real facts. All the public abuse was just politics. From both King Tellal and the Jordan government, I received full and generous support. The Arab Legion, officers and men of all ranks and units, were beyond praise. Whatever the politicians might say, we of the Arab Legion knew what we were doing. We realized that we were not defending only Jordan, but the whole Arab world. As long as we lay deployed only fifteen miles from Tel Aviv, the Israelis could not mount a major offensive against Lebanon, Syria or Egypt. These countries might denounce us as Jews or traitors, but in reality we were protecting them all, and were immensely proud of the fact. The morale of the Arab Legion was a revelation to a great number of foreign visitors. For these honest and simple men were convinced that they were giving all they had in a noble cause, and were filled with that exaltation which only voluntary self-sacrifice can produce.

Meanwhile the people of Palestine were also being gradually won over. In 1948 and 1949, many had been openly hostile. They were saturated with Mufti and Egyptian propaganda to the effect that the British and King Abdulla were secret allies of Israel; that we

PLATE 18

King Abdulla, dressed in white and saluting, leaving the Aqsa Mosque after Friday prayers. This picture was taken a few weeks before the King was murdered on a similar occasion. Behind the crowd can be seen the main doorway of the Aqsa Mosque, in which the King was murdered

PLATE 19

Visit of King Abdulla to the Arab Legion Air Force the day before his murder. His Majesty inspecting aircraft in the repair bay. *Left to right:* Sameer Pasha Rifai, the Prime Minister; His Majesty; and the author

PLATE 20

View of Jerusalem, looking west from the Mount of Olives, showing the Temple area, with the Dome of the Rock, and to the left of it, the Aqsa Mosque. On the left middle distance, Mount Zion. Tall houses in the background are the Jewish city beyond the walls could easily have captured Tel Aviv and Jerusalem in 1948, but that I prevented the Arab Legion from doing so, on secret orders from Mr. Bevin. As the years went by, however, the people of Palestine came to know the Arab Legion. They spoke to the troops, they mixed with the officers, they could not fail to see that these were splendid men, devoted to a cause. Some, it is true, persisted in stating that the British officers were secretly frustrating the patriotic efforts of their own troops, but the numbers of these doubters were decreasing, except indeed among the lawyers and politicians of Jerusalem, Ramallah and Nablus. The first to be convinced, and indeed to become our enthusiastic allies, were the people of the front-line villages, who could see the troops every day at work, living in trenches, watching, alert, on the move all night on patrol in streaming rain, or digging laborious defences, pouring with sweat, beneath an August sun. But that which really convinced the people of Palestine was the formation of the National Guard. We had built up this force for two reasons.

Firstly, it was obvious that we could neither rely on the other Arab governments if Israel should attack, nor could we long resist an enemy about seven times as strong as ourselves—at least in numbers and resources, if not in morale and determination. The annual budget of the Israeli army was some seven or eight times that of the Arab Legion. In civilian man-power, however, Jordan in 1951 was very nearly equal to Israel. We were holding a front of 400 miles. Obviously we must get more troops. The men were available, and anxious to enlist, but we had no money or equipment for them.

Secondly, the other Arab countries had never recognized the union of Palestine and Trans-Jordan. Some did not hesitate to foment dissension between West Bank and East Bank. One of the major points which they used to stir up resentment was that the Jordan government did not trust the Palestinians. The Arab Legion was depicted as a purely East Bank army. The Communists went farther. They labelled the Arab Legion—"The Anglo-Hashemite Army of Occupation in Palestine".

We obviously could not hold Palestine against the will of its inhabitants. Nor could we give it up. If Israel were to seize the remainder of the country, a further half-million Arab refugees would be created, and Trans-Jordan would be swept away under a flood of a million refugees which the country could never support. There was only one solution. We must take the Palestinians to our hearts. King Abdulla had already granted full Jordan citizenship to every Palestinian refugee—no other Arab country had accepted them as citizens. They could not be half-citizens. We must make them feel trusted, and the first sign of trust was to arm them.

The proposal was greeted with scepticism on both banks of the

Jordan. I remember a party in Ramallah at which all the notables of the district were present, and at which I propounded my idea of a National Guard without pay. The lawyers and intelligentsia of the town laughed pityingly.

"No-one from the villages will join," they said. "Fellaheen live for money. Good pay will get good soldiers. No money—no soldiers."

These highbrows (they are intellectually brilliant people) were mistaken, because they were cynical. It is difficult for cynics to be leaders. The common people, if you love and trust them, will support you; they will not follow those who suspect them. Trust brings out all that is best in men. The trusting are occasionally betrayed, but they win the hearts and the help of all that is best in the country.

We launched our plan for an unpaid army. I endeavoured to explain the facts as they were—both in lectures to officers and men of the Arab Legion who mingled constantly with the public, and in direct visits to villages on West Bank, particularly front-line villages. We had no money, I said, but we needed more soldiers. The Arab Legion could not be deployed on a front of four hundred miles. It was a *corps d'élite*, entirely on wheels. To put it into static defences would be to kill it. It must be the mobile reserve for the decisive battle. The People's Army must man the frontier. The little money we could raise would have to be spent on weapons, not on pay.

The extremists, of course, seized on these plans to explain that what had really happened was that the Arab Legion was going to retire from the front line, in order to allow the Israelis to capture more territory. But their jaundiced outlook had little effect on the frontier villages, though it produced an echoing reaction in certain other Arab countries.

The first beginnings of the National Guard consisted merely of a few men in the frontier villages, whom we armed and trained to resist Israeli reprisal raids. But we then were able to persuade the government to prepare a Bill making National Guard training compulsory for every male Jordanian of military age. Every man was liable to what amounted to a month's training a year. Many were the gloomy prognostications in which both friend and foe indulged. Some anticipated that, as soon as they were armed, the Arabs of Palestine would rise in rebellion. Others foresaw that they would all infiltrate into Israel and shoot Jews with their National Guard weapons. Neither of these things happened. The National Guard, realizing that they were trusted, lived up to the confidence we placed in them.

As the other Arab governments realized that the National Guard was becoming efficient, some of them (notably Egypt and Saudi Arabia) endeavoured to create dissension between it and the Arab

Legion. They praised it enthusiastically and offered to provide the much-needed funds for its maintenance. These tempting offers, however, stipulated the condition that the National Guard should be completely separated from the Arab Legion. Fortunately the Jordan government realized the impossibility (or the danger) of having two armies in one country. In practice, the National Guard would have become a rabble if separated from the Arab Legion. All the officers, all the instructors and the greater part of the N.C.O.s were regulars. The efforts of politicians to create friction between the National Guard and the regulars came to nothing.

* * * * *

One of the burning questions of the years from 1948 to 1951 was that of the internationalization of Jerusalem. The United Nations Trustee Commission spent months working out an exact constitution for the city. But, like so many other UNO projects, the plan was stillborn, because there were no international troops to enforce it. Israel agreed to internationalize the Holy Places, all of which were within the Old City and therefore in the hands of Jordan. In practice, the walled city was the strongpoint which had enabled the Arabs to hold on in Jerusalem. To disarm it, but not the Jewish city, would of course have been of considerable military advantage to Israel.

In the 1947 UNO partition plan, Jerusalem, it is true, was international, but it was then an island in Arab territory, with no physical connection with Israel. In this form, Jordan also would have welcomed its internationalization. But meanwhile, the Israelis had connected it by a broad corridor with the coastal plain. Any plan to internationalize Jerusalem, thus connected to Israel, would have been dangerous for Jordan.

Seen in cross-section, Jerusalem is on the summit of the ridge of the Palestine mountains (see diagram on page 22: section across Judaea). On the east, the country falls precipitously, 4,000 feet to the Jordan valley. On the west, however, this is not the case. There are other hills, as high as Jerusalem, west of the city boundary. If, therefore, both Israel and Jordan had withdrawn their armies from the city, the Israeli army would have been west of the city and on the same level, and could have driven into it any morning in a few minutes and seized it. The Jordan forces, on the other hand, would have been both farther away and two thousand feet below the city, down a steep slope. According to the 1947 UNO plan, the Israeli army would have been far away on the coastal plain.

But these purely military considerations were not all. According to the proposed UNO constitution, the city would have been governed by an elected council, with a UNO governor. The Jews already had a numerical majority of inhabitants and thus would dominate the city council. With the two races at bitter hostility, it is easy enough to understand that the Arab minority would have had a difficult time with the city council. While obstructing the Arab minority on the one hand, the Jewish majority would, with the other hand, have offered them a good price to sell out. Would not some Arabs at least, finding the conditions in Jerusalem so difficult, have disposed of their property in despair, and gone to live in Amman or Damascus?

Thus it seemed to us that, in a short time, the city would become more and more entirely dominated by the Jews. From the military point of view, this would have been well-nigh fatal. If once the Israeli army were fully established in Jerusalem, it had only to drive down to Jericho and the Jordan, and the Arab areas on the West Bank would have been cut off from Trans-Jordan. Not only so, but the Hebron area would have been cut off from the Nablus area.

It often seemed strange to us that Israel rejected internationalization. Presumably she did so on short-term emotional grounds. Israel had been set up, and its capital was in the City of David. But if the Jews had been willing temporarily to move the capital back to Tel Aviv, and give Jerusalem to UNO, they might have succeeded in forcing the Arab Legion out. This once done, the Israelis could have returned at their leisure. Fortunately, they did not think so.

The aspect of this problem which was most distressing was that all the other Arab countries demanded internationalization, right or wrong. Jordan, on this question, stood with Israel in rejecting internationalization, against the remainder of the Arab world. It was difficult to avoid the impression that the other Arab countries would accept any solution for Jerusalem, sooner than allow King Abdulla to have it.

I discussed this problem once with Taufiq Pasha, when he was Prime Minister, and I tried to explain to him the military dangers of internationalization. I urged him to explain them to the other Arab countries. But he refused to be drawn.

"The Jews will not agree to internationalization," he said, "and therefore it will not take place. So to discuss it is purely academic."

*   *   *   *   *

The happy early promise of King Tellal's reign was already clouding over. The illness from which the King was suffering was one which resulted in attacks of insanity, although between one attack and the next he was perfectly normal. He had always been a devoted husband and father. In 1943, he had served for a time as an officer in the Arab Legion, and it was noticeable then how anxious he was about his family. Whenever it was possible, he used to telephone to his house, in order to talk to his wife, the Amira Zein. He would enquire about every detail regarding his children, their health, their games, the funny things they had said, and all those little anecdotes which fond parents love to exchange.

It was, therefore, doubly tragic that his form of mental illness caused him, during an attack of insanity, to vent his anger, and even violence, on precisely those persons whom, when sane, he loved most. Add to this that, even when an attack was approaching, he could still retain enough self-control to carry through an audience with a distinguished visitor in a normal and indeed a very charming manner. This peculiarity (normal in this type of illness) resulted in many doubts as to his insanity on the part of strangers who had visited him and been accorded a charmingly courteous reception. For King Tellal had all the hereditary charm of his family. I have never in my life met with more kindness and consideration than I did from him.

By April and May 1952, however, anyone in Amman who had any connection with palace and government circles could not fail to be increasingly aware of the King's illness. I have already referred to the fact that, during the late King's lifetime, the Egyptians and Syrians, and the Palestine extremists, had built up the thesis that the Amir Tellal was a "noble patriot". It was alleged that he had been on bad terms with King Abdulla, because the latter was the "tool of British imperialism". King Tellal's insanity was joyfully seized on by the Press in these other Arab countries.

Reports were now widely published to the effect that King Tellal had been reported insane by a British doctor, on secret instructions from Whitehall, and that the British government wished to hand over the remainder of Palestine to the Jews, or had attempted to compel Jordan to make peace. King Tellal had objected. The British had accordingly arranged for a doctor to certify his insanity. Repeated reports were circulated that the King had assaulted me, had fired a pistol at me—and so it went on. The Israelis had no objection to adding to the confusion by publishing reports of actual or impending disorders in Jordan. As usual, we were under fire from all directions at once.

Soon after King Abdulla's death, an incident occurred which was trivial but had a significance we did not appreciate. A young officer of the Arab Legion was reported to be talking politics in an hotel in Amman. Investigation proved the report to be true. The officer in question was a young captain called Ali abu Nuwar. He had, it appeared, been stating that Jordan did not need British help, nor for that matter did it need a King. All the other Arab countries would stand by Jordan if she drove out the British. Ali, it appeared, had the idea of convincing King Tellal that he could afford to remove me, and reject British help. He made friends with the barber who cut King Tellal's hair, and asked him to intercede on his behalf with His Majesty to procure him a secret audience, at which he could convince the King of the soundness of his plans. Nothing, however, came of it. Either the barber did not tell the King or the latter was not interested.

I reported these incidents to Taufiq Pasha, who had replaced Sameer Pasha as Prime Minister. Never before had Arab Legion officers engaged in politics. It was obviously a development to be stopped before it could expand any further. In view of the uncertainty of the situation, resulting from the death of King Abdulla and the mental instability of King Tellal, it was decided to remove Ali abu Nuwar. He was appointed military attaché in Paris.

"When the political situation is more stable, he can be brought back," said the Prime Minister.

In May 1952, the King left once more for Europe with a view to receiving further medical treatment, but he went first to Paris, accompanied by Queen Zein and their children. Wherever the unfortunate royal family moved, they were pursued by the Press, by photographers, by politicians and intriguers. On June 6th, the King cabled from Paris, stating his intention to return and expressing (quite truly) his love and devotion to his country and people. If he had not been so sincere and so charming a man, his tragedy would have been less heart-rending. His mental condition deteriorated rapidly while he was in Paris, but he refused to receive medical treatment, and wandered to Lausanne.

Until a year before, observers obliged to admit the rocklike stability of Jordan in the midst of the storms and tides of the Arab world, usually added a note of warning. "Wait till King Abdulla dies," they said, "and Jordan will become like any other Arab country."

King Abdulla did not die—he was murdered. His successor was too ill to reign. The Israelis were being more difficult than ever on the demarcation line. Israel, and all the other Arab countries, were impatiently anticipating the collapse of Jordan, and preparing each to grab what it could. The Press of all these countries was reporting disturbances in Jordan, and accusing both the British and Jordan governments of inventing the King's illness in order to get rid of him. We felt that there was not much more that could happen to us—yet Jordan was as quiet and stable as ever. Indeed, two remarkable and encouraging facts emerged from the hostile foreign Press campaign against Jordan. The first of these was that the West Bank had no idea of secession, no matter what incitement to do so was offered to them. The second noticeable feature of the tragedy was the universal devotion to the throne. King Tellal was as popular—rather, as deeply loved—as ever. The Hashemite family still seemed to command the loyalty of the people of Jordan.

On July 4th, King Tellal returned to Amman. He had come to Beirut from Italy by sea, and had flown to Amman in an Arab Legion aircraft. It was the custom, when a King arrived by air, for me to meet him at the aircraft and accompany him to inspect the guard of honour, before he was greeted by the Prime Minister, the government and the other notables. This morning I was at my usual position at the foot of the gangway when King Tellal came out of the aircraft. But instead of merely returning my salute and passing on to inspect the guard of honour, he stopped, smiled and kissed me on both cheeks. He was given a truly royal welcome on his drive from the airport to the palace.

Throughout July, matters dragged on in uncertainty and unhappiness. The King was living in his palace, but was not exercising his sovereign rights, which were still in the hands of a council of regency. On August 11th, 1952, the Jordan Parliament was called into secret session and the King's medical documents were laid before it. After several hours' debate, it decreed the deposition of King Tellal and the succession of his eldest son, Amir Husain.

I was in England on leave on this tragic day. The deputy chief of the general staff of the Arab Legion, Major-General Ahmed Sudqi Pasha, was ordered by the Prime Minister to take the parliamentary resolution to the palace. The King received him with a sad dignity, which profoundly impressed all those who were present.

"I had expected this," he said. "Please thank the government and the Parliament on my behalf. I pray God to bless and keep my country and my people."

King Tellal went for a time to reside in Egypt. Later he moved to Turkey, where he lived sadly and almost alone in a villa near the Bosphorus.

So often in former years, Jordan had seemed to be threatened by imminent dangers. The Arab rebellion in Palestine in 1936 might well have dragged Trans-Jordan to disaster. In 1940, after the fall of France, German and Italian armistice commissions assumed control of Syria, a few miles away. In 1941, Iraq joined Germany and declared war on Britain, while the enemy pressed on against Egypt in the Western Desert. All Arabia seemed to be about to be lost. In 1949, Jordan stood alone facing Israel. In 1950 and 1951, the other Arab countries were attacking Jordan with unprecedentedly violent Press campaigns, until on July 20th, 1951, King Abdulla was murdered. Everyone, Arab, European and American alike, was convinced that Jordan would now collapse. But nothing of the kind occurred.

In reality, throughout the year from July 1951 to July 1952, Jordan seemed as stable as ever. The other Arab countries raged and stormed. The Israeli army raided and shot across the border. But inside Jordan, there was scarcely even a political meeting, a strike or a riot. A general election took place without so much as one arrest for disorder. Never was a single shot fired by the police or the army against a Jordan citizen. During the same period, there was a military revolution in Syria. Rioting had occurred in Baghdad. Martial law had been proclaimed in Teheran. Cairo had been nearly burnt down. There had been street riots in Beirut. The Israeli police had several times opened fire on rioting crowds. But Jordan still seemed to lead a charmed life.

The tragedy of King Tellal seemed to be rendered more poignant by the fact that, apart from his insanity, he appeared so ideally fitted to be King. He was in his early forties, the perfect age for a new King—old enough to be experienced, young enough to promise a long reign. He was of acute intelligence, outstanding personal charm, faultless private morals, and inspired by a deeply conscientious wish to serve his country and his people, with no selfish motives.

For thirty years, Jordan had ridden out every storm. Now, unknown to us, our luck was to turn.

XVIII

The Frontier of Hate

Our patience will achieve more than our force.

EDMUND BURKE

XVIII

THE FRONTIER OF HATE

THE Amir Husain was proclaimed King of Jordan on August 11th, 1952. I had ridden behind his father at his wedding procession in Amman eighteen years before. For that matter, I could remember meeting King Tellal when he was about to leave Jordan to be educated in England. I had been for more than thirty years in the service of the Hashemite family, in Iraq and in Jordan. I had known the old King Husain of the Hejaz, his sons, King Feisal I of Iraq, and King Abdulla of Jordan, then King Tellal—and now King Husain. I felt myself an old family retainer. I had seen them all grow up and grow old. Never from any one member of the family had I met with anything but the most perfect courtesy and kindness. In 1941, King Feisal II of Iraq and his uncle, Amir Abdulilla, the regent, had been driven from their country. The Arab Legion had played a principal part in their restoration. Such long and intimate association could not fail to result in devotion. I asked nothing more than to spend the remaining few years of my active life in the service of the young King—the fourth generation of Hashemites whom I had known.

I had often seen the Amir Husain in his childhood. I had seen the Amir Tellal playing ball with his little boys in the garden. The Amir Husain had shaken hands with me shyly when I came to lunch. He had been walking behind King Abdulla when the latter had been assassinated at the door of the Aqsa Mosque in Jerusalem. Then his father had become insane. What a tragic family story for a young boy!

When King Abdulla was alive, the Amir Husain had been sent to Victoria College, Alexandria, in Egypt, for his education. But when his grandfather was murdered in July 1951, his sudden elevation to heir apparent seemed to the government to necessitate a wider education. He was sent to Harrow. Soon afterwards I happened to be in England myself, and went out to Harrow to pay my respects. I was received by the Amir's housemaster, and I asked him how he was getting on.

"He's doing very well," said his housemaster. "The boys all like him. At the beginning of the term he went out to play rugger for the first time. He had never seen the game before, and was a bit lost to start with. But before the end of the game, he was tackling low like an old hand!"

I took the Amir out for the afternoon. We went to the Battersea Festival Gardens, but he was not amused. He did not want to go on the merry-go-rounds or the scenic railway. I must have misunderstood his age-group, or his early introduction to public affairs in such tragic circumstances had sobered him prematurely. On the return journey, we paid a visit to Fortnum & Mason. The Royal Chamberlain in Amman had been unaware that English public schoolboys had tuck-boxes. We repaired the omission.

After his father's abdication, King Husain left Harrow and returned to Amman on August 25th, 1952. He received an enthusiastic popular welcome. A king seventeen years of age, who had come to the throne in such tragic circumstances, could not fail to arouse the emotions of his subjects. But although he was king, he could not exercise his royal prerogatives until he came of age at eighteen years old. He returned to England for an abbreviated course at Sandhurst. A regency council acted for him in his absence.

*   *   *   *   *

Jordan had borne, and was still bearing, almost all the burden of the Palestine disaster. Yet in early 1953, nearly five years after the fighting in 1948, she was still the only stable Arab country, though there were already certain signs—little clouds no bigger than a man's hand—which seemed to me to foreshadow troubles ahead.

It had, of course, been the character of King Abdulla which had kept the country uniformly quiet and happy throughout the thirty years of his reign. But from 1939 to 1952, Trans-Jordan had been greatly fortunate in having, as British Minister, Sir Alec Kirkbride, a man who had served in the country since 1916. He, more even than I, had grown up and grown old with these people for thirty-five years. His influence was based on his own character and his long residence in the country, not on the accidental fact that he was British Minister. In the eighteenth and nineteenth centuries, British officials all over the world had become the fathers and mothers of innumerable races, merely because they had spent all their lives in one place. The British Empire was created by such men, who had spent lonely and devoted lives in far-away stations in the East. "Regularization" of the various services, the transfer of men from one place to another every three years, has destroyed the warm humanities which so often united these lonely "politicals" to the people amongst whom they worked. In so doing, regularization has also, for good or ill, destroyed the British Empire. The departure of Kirkbride to Libya put an end to a long and happy chapter in Anglo-Jordan relations.

Throughout the Second World War, Anglo-Trans-Jordan relations were extraordinarily cordial. This was not merely a question of policy—it was the common feeling of government and people alike, and was equally shared by the British people and army. But since 1948, these relations had almost imperceptibly cooled. And this not on the Jordanian side only—on the British also.

Undoubtedly much of the cooling of Britain's enthusiasm for Jordan was due to the Arab League and Arab policy in general. Although Jordan was still Britain's ally, relations between Britain and Egypt were strained. There were disturbances in the Suez Canal Zone, and British soldiers and Egyptian civilians were shot. Egypt claimed to be the leader of the "Arab race", including Jordan. On the other side, the Jewish viewpoint was well ventilated in the British Press, and the Jews also attacked "Arabs" as a whole, and sometimes Jordan in particular. But while Jordan was attacked by Israel and lost popularity in Britain, as being one of those troublesome Arab States, she was the victim of constant hostility on the part of those same Arab States, as being an ally of Britain.

The Anglo-Jordan treaty was a remarkable document as treaties go, because the two countries had different enemies. Britain was preoccupied by the possibility of a war with Russia, while Jordan's enemy was Israel. It seemed to me that it would have been better to explain this more frankly. Britain was pledged to come to Jordan's assistance in the event of an Israeli attack on her, and Jordan conversely was pledged to join Britain in the event of war with Russia. This was a perfectly honourable alliance. Yet it was never sufficiently plainly enunciated. British politicians or newspapers who sympathized with Israel were constantly making pronouncements which seemed to suggest that Britain could never fight Israel. This enabled hostile Arab opinion to throw doubts on Britain's sincerity.

Jordan was greatly handicapped all this time in her relations with the Western world, because nearly all important Western newspapers maintained correspondents in Cairo and Tel Aviv only. Accordingly nearly all news reaching the West presented either the Egyptian or the Israeli point of view—and both were hostile to Jordan.

Indeed, it seemed to me also that Britain was lacking in understanding of Jordan's tragic plight. In 1940, after the fall of France, Trans-Jordan alone in the whole world voluntarily declared war on Germany and sent her tiny army to fight, when Britain stood alone. Neither of the giants—the U.S.A. or Soviet Russia—had thrown down the gauntlet until they were attacked. The sublime defiance which caused tiny Trans-Jordan to step into the lists at such a moment would have been laughable if it had not been so heroic. It is not fair to say that that was not Trans-Jordan but King

Abdulla. In that case it was not Britain who won the war but Winston Churchill.

In 1948, Trans-Jordan became involved in hostilities with Israel. She did not want to do this. She intended only to occupy that part of Palestine awarded to the Arabs, but the Jews were already in the Arab area when the Arab Legion arrived. Not only did Britain not come to Jordan's assistance, but a few days later, Britain blockaded her ally. It is true that Britain did so in accordance with a UNO resolution. But, as the Jordanians pointed out, if obligations to UNO took precedence of obligations to her allies, then Britain was not much use as an ally. Then again, when Israel was known to be receiving considerable quantities of arms from Czecho-Slovakia, in spite of the blockade, Britain (it seemed to Jordan) made little or no protest. The least she could have done would have been to denounce Czecho-Slovakia (and Russia) and to state that, unless Russian and her satellites ceased to arm Israel, Britain would abandon her blockade of Jordan.

*   *   *   *   *

Meanwhile, the frontier situation with Israel continued to deteriorate. On January 23rd, 1953, an Israeli company attacked the Jordan hamlet of Falama, which contained only thirty men. Fortunately, we had just previously erected a barbed-wire fence round this tiny village. The Israelis were unable to get into the houses. Some days later they returned with a battalion group, and a party of engineers with torpedoes, for use to blow a passage through the barbed wire. Inside the village was one corporal of the Arab Legion and fifteen villagers trained as National Guards. The Israelis mortared Falama heavily before their attack. Even so, their infantry failed to get into the hamlet. There were casualties on both sides.

On January 28th, the Israeli army attacked the Jordan village of Rantis. Some men were killed, but again the Israelis failed to get into the village. The training of the National Guard was obviously progressing. In February, we commenced a programme of putting frontier villages in a state of defence.

*   *   *   *   *

The disturbing factor was that the Israeli government seemed to have adopted a new policy vis-à-vis Jordan ever since the beginning of 1953. Infiltration into Israel had been going on for four years. Throughout this period, the statistics of infiltration had maintained a remarkably steady average. The last three months of 1952 had, however, been exceptionally quiet.

In January 1953, the Israeli government turned on the propaganda. The surprised Jordanians were suddenly told that the situation was critical, and that tension was mounting rapidly. Statistics revealed no increase in incidents. The border seemed quieter than usual. Those familiar with Israeli tactics concluded that Israel was about to do something. A few days later came the attacks on Falama and Rantis. In both cases, the Israelis retired rather hastily, leaving considerable quantities of ammunition and equipment, and in one case a dead Israeli soldier. Usually the Israelis took great trouble to remove their dead. Both the British and United States governments protested strongly to Israel.

The Israelis were incensed at the failure of their attacks on Rantis and Falama. Thenceforward their propaganda became more and more exaggerated and wild. An "Israel Army Spokesman" began to make frequent releases to the Press, stating that ten, fifteen or twenty "Arab marauders" had been killed. Stringent police enquiries in Jordan failed to discover anyone to be missing. More remarkable still was the fact that no corresponding complaints were made by Israel to the Mixed Armistice Commission. Moreover, everything that occurred was reported as the activities of "para-military raiders" from Jordan. A caravan of smugglers was caught by the Israelis near Gaza. They were all natives of Gaza, not Jordanians. The Israelis knew them to be smugglers, because they captured their caravan of pack animals laden with rice and sugar. Yet the incident was reported as concerning "para-military raiders from Jordan". On every border in the world there are smugglers, people in pursuit of gain. Nowhere but in Israel is the existence of smugglers regarded as a *casus belli* against another government.

One of the most dangerous aspects of this unrestrained propaganda was the effect which it seemed to be having on the Israeli public. They complained that the inhabitants of their frontier colonies could not sleep at night. This is scarcely to be wondered at, if they read the Israeli Press, which daily described the most bloody (but fortunately often fictitious) battles. Nevertheless, we were aware of the problem, and were most anxious to solve it.

But the Israeli thesis, that the responsibility for infiltration rested solely on Jordan, did not seem to us tenable. To begin with, the Israelis had created the problem, by driving all these people from their homes. Secondly, on no frontier in the world is a government held responsible that its subjects do not leave their country—even if we assume that the refugees, who with their ancestors had lived for centuries in what had now become Israel, had become automatically Jordanians and not Israelis.

If an Englishman enters France illegally without a passport, the British government are not thereby held to be guilty for not having prevented his leaving Britain. If France does not want the man, it is for her to keep him out. Jordan, however, did not use this argument. She declared that she would do her best to prevent persons crossing from Jordan into Israel, but she asked the co-operation of Israel. The Israeli authorities frequently adopted the thesis that Jordan alone was to blame.

Such an argument, however, was in reality indefensible. Jordan would only really have been guilty if she had been organizing, or at least conniving at, infiltration. This therefore was the proposition which the Israelis were chiefly anxious to prove. As a result, every infiltrator was described by them as "the para-military forces of Jordan". A man who crossed the line to pick an orange in his own garden, another to search for a missing relative, a third to smuggle a load of hashish to Gaza, all were classified as "para-military forces from Jordan". One factor, however, cannot be too much emphasized. Whereas Israeli aggressions were all carried out by the Israeli army, not a single planned action of a similar nature was ever carried out by the Arab Legion.

At 5 p.m. on Wednesday, April 23rd, Israeli troops suddenly opened fire all along the line in the city of Jerusalem. The firing was done almost entirely by snipers with rifles, picking out individuals in the crowded streets of the city, overlooked by tall buildings on the Israeli side. We were taken by surprise. We had always considered that Israel would not use violence in Jerusalem, for fear of reviving the demand for internationalization.

No sooner was the first shot fired than every Israeli civilian seemed to vanish from the streets. By a curious coincidence, eight days before, the Israeli authorities had held a rehearsal, giving an alarm and clearing the streets of civilians. The Jordanians had not rehearsed, and consequently ten were killed and twelve wounded before civilians took cover. At the subsequent inquiry, the Mixed Armistice Commission decided that they could not establish which side had fired first.

People who have not lived in Palestine will be at a loss to understand the reason for such incidents. Arab hatred is more easily explicable. The Arabs had lost their country, been driven from their homes and had become wanderers and vagabonds. Despairing of life, they sought only to vent their hatred on those responsible for their ruin, whether Jews, British or Americans. But the Israelis were victorious. It was surely in their interest to settle down, to make peace with their neighbours, and to enjoy the fruits of their success. Great numbers of Israelis undoubtedly thought so too. But many more were afraid. In spite of their victories, they knew that they were only a tiny beach-head on the seashore. In face of this situation, two alternatives presented themselves. The first was to be conciliatory and try to obtain peace, even by some concessions. The second policy was that adopted. Its advocates claimed that Arabs understood no argument but force. To survive, Israel must terrorize her neighbours. Force was their only guarantee of survival.

Yet, in Jordan at least, they were not striking terror. They were merely increasing hatred, hastening Arab unity, fanning fanaticism and making peace more and more remote. In 1949, they might have paved the way for peace—by 1953, peace was out of the question. Time is probably on the side of the Arabs. Some day they will co-operate and then they will endeavour to wreak a terrible revenge. Generations may pass before this problem is solved, but it is difficult to believe that Israel can finally solve it by force. She must either conciliate Asia or, sooner or later, Asia will overwhelm her.

* * * * *

In May 1953, tension with Israel increased. There were fourteen incidents in four days. Jordan invoked the Anglo-Jordan treaty. In an official statement, the Jordan government claimed that 200 attacks had been delivered by Israeli troops from January 1st to May 25th, resulting in the deaths of 165 Arabs, mostly women and children. Ninety-five others were wounded.

Meanwhile, on the Jordan side, a new phenomenon had appeared. Hitherto, almost all the infiltration by refugees had been of two kinds only—"innocent" that is, to contact a relative, visit an old home or cross to Gaza—or with the object of theft. The Israelis made great play with the subject of looting and marauding. It is interesting to note that, from official figures, Jordan had 677 head of cattle stolen by Jews in 1952, whereas Israel lost only 539. Of the 677 stolen from Jordan by Israelis, 357 were returned and 320 were not. Of those stolen by Jordanians from Israel, 362 were returned and 177 were not. Thus in 1952, the Jordanians lost 320 head of cattle to Israel, while the latter suffered only to the extent of 177 head! Yet the world was convinced that Arab looting was a severe economic problem for Israel.

In the summer of 1953, however, appeared a new feature—infiltrators who went only to kill. The new pattern gradually became apparent. Infiltration for stealing had been greatly reduced by the activities of the Jordan police and troops. Now, at occasional intervals, two or three Arabs would appear in Israel and shoot one or two people at night, or throw a hand grenade into a window. These parties were all armed with new Sten guns and hand grenades. The tactics they used were always the same. A new factor had obviously appeared.

Investigation soon revealed the identity of the new movement. It originated with a group of refugees in Damascus, all of them former terrorists employed by the Mufti in Palestine. The Saudi Arabian government was arming and subsidizing these men to infiltrate through Jordan into Israel and kill Jews. The Saudi government had not hitherto shown any great enthusiasm to fight Israel. But there was no doubt of the Saudi jealousy of the Hashemites. As one of the leaders of this Damascus movement explained, when recruiting terrorists: "Ibn Saud does not wish the Hashemite family to rule Jordan in peace."

The Saudi King, who lived a thousand miles from these tragic scenes of bloodshed, was in a peculiarly happy position. By organizing raids into Israel, he was able to pose as a patriot. If the Arabs were killed—well, they were only Palestinians. If Jews were killed, were they not the enemies of his race? And whichever way it turned out, the reprisals would be directed against his enemy, the King of Jordan.[1]

The organization of these murder attacks was not easy and few such incidents occurred, but their brutality infuriated the Israelis, and provoked more violent reprisals than before. The politicians, in and out of Jordan, were not slow to blame the new Jewish reprisals on Britain. The usual charges of treachery or negligence were directed against the Arab Legion.

Meanwhile, public security in Israel left a good deal to be desired. The Jewish *Palestine Post* for Sunday, May 31st, 1953, reported that the Israeli police had unearthed an Israeli terrorist organization, which used sub-machine guns and grenades for its crimes. This Jewish gang, consisting partly of former Stern Gang terrorists, was said to be inspired by resentment against some of the internal administrative methods of the existing Israeli government. Bombs had been placed in the Israeli Parliament, and in the Ministry of Education. Arms caches had been found in Jerusalem. The Israeli police had perhaps found it convenient to attribute every serious offence committed in Israel to infiltrators. On one occasion, in an Israeli law court, the judge had referred to the too-easy solution of every crime problem by claiming that it was committed by unknown Arab infiltrators.

As usual, Jordan and the Arab Legion were under attack from every direction. To meet the further deterioration of the border, the East Bank was denuded of a large part of its police force. Arrests of known terrorists were made. Barbed wire and pickets were obtained from the British in Egypt to strengthen the defences of frontier villages. The United Nations Truce Supervision Organi-

---

[1] Since this was written, the wisdom of the Hashemite monarchs and of King Saud seems to be leading to a reconciliation and co-operation between the two dynasties—a consummation greatly to be desired.

zation was urged to persuade the Israelis to conclude an agreement for the co-operation of Israeli and Jordan police officers on both sides of the border.

*   *   *   *   *

In April 1953, the King attained eighteen years, which was the royal coming of age according to the constitution. He returned to Amman, to be inaugurated King. His youth, his good looks, sympathy for the misfortunes of the royal family and hopes for a return of prosperity and stability, united to make him universally loved. In so far as lay within my power, I encouraged King Husain to tour the country, to visit all units of the army, and to show himself to the people. Everywhere he received enthusiastic ovations. I suggested also that he should get to know the officers of the army personally, and many visits to units were arranged. The King also invited officers to the palace. Jordan had always remained stable, owing to the devotion of the army to the throne; the continuance of this devotion seemed to me the best guarantee of stability for the future. I told the King my opinion whenever the opportunity offered.

In the spring of 1953, we were assailed by another enemy. Swarms of locusts arrived from Central Arabia, threatening the crops which were the life-blood of the country. As usual, the government appealed to the Arab Legion. The equivalent of a whole brigade of infantry was employed. Destruction of locusts is comparatively easy with the new poisons now available. The mature locusts arrive in flying swarms, which, however, eat comparatively little. They then bury their eggs in the ground and die. When the eggs hatch, the tiny locusts cannot at first fly. They can only hop, and they are voraciously hungry. It is at this stage that they devour everything, leaving a green countryside as brown and bare as a board.

The art of fighting the locusts is to locate these swarms of hoppers, not always an easy task in an area nearly the size of England. When a swarm was located, the troops moved against it with their supplies of bran soaked in poison. The infantry extended in open order, each man carrying a can or sack full of poison, which he scattered on the ground in front of the advancing swarm of hoppers. The latter devoured it greedily and died within a few hours. The task of reconnoitring for the swarms, pin-pointing them on the map, reporting back the locations by wireless and then moving troops and supplies to the map references received, constituted quite a military operation.

I flew out with the King and landed in the desert to watch a

battalion—it was the 3rd Regiment, of Jerusalem fame—which
was fighting locusts.

At the end of the day, when I took my leave, the young King
thanked me charmingly.

"Pasha," he said, "wherever I go in Jordan, I find the Arab
Legion doing everything. The whole country seems to depend on the
Arab Legion alone. I have no words to express my thanks to you
and the army."

I was deeply touched.

"The army and myself are always in Your Majesty's service and
in that of the country," I replied.

And I meant every word I said.

*   *   *   *   *

That summer of 1953 was indeed overwhelmingly strenuous.
There were the arrangements for the King's inauguration (or
coronation as it would be called in England), and for the ensuing
ceremonial review. Apart from the brigade in the desert fighting
locusts, there were new flare-ups on the Israel border. We dealt
with these by reinforcing the police and by constantly following up
all cases of infiltration. We continually urged the government and
the civil administration to take stronger action. Israeli reprisals
actually made it more difficult for the Jordan government to punish
infiltrators. Opposition politicians were enabled to raise an outcry
that, whereas Jews were allowed to slaughter Jordanians with
impunity, any poor refugee who went to see his old home was
immediately put in prison.

The measures adopted were, however, on the whole successful.
After a series of incidents in April, May and June, there was a great
diminution in complaints about infiltration in July, August and
September. We began to feel happier. Our measures were obviously
proving effective.

On the night of August 11th, however, the Israeli army delivered
attacks on three villages—Wadi Fokeen, Sureef and Edna. They
used two-inch mortars, medium machine guns, mines and
torpedoes, and attempted to blow up houses. The attacks were not
uniformly successful. We could not understand the reason for these
attacks, as we were straining every nerve to reduce infiltration,
which had in practice become much less frequent.

*   *   *   *   *

On October 13th, 1953, the Israelis complained that three
Arab infiltrators had crept up to a house in the village of Tirat
Yehuda and had thrown a grenade in at a window. The Israelis
alleged that a woman and two children had been killed. It was a

horrible crime, and we immediately took every possible measure to find the offenders. It was obviously a killing raid, of the new type. The Israelis sometimes used police dogs for tracking. We suggested their employment in this case. We also said that if the dog brought a scent up to the demarcation line, it could come on over the line with its Jewish trackers, in the hope that the trail could be taken on to a specified camp or village. We offered every possible assistance we could think of. The dog brought the trail a short distance over the line into Jordan and then lost it.

At 9.30 p.m. in the evening of October 14th, two Arab watchmen in the olive groves outside the village of Qibya were suddenly overpowered and their hands bound by a party of Israeli soldiers. One of them, however, succeeded in getting away in the dark and warned the village. Qibya was a mile and a quarter inside Jordan. The National Guard stood to, and manned their trenches. Soon they heard sounds of movement in their front and a message was sent back to that effect. Mortar and rifle fire was opened on the village shortly afterwards. The National Guard replied and the shooting continued from 10.30 to 12.30. By this time the National Guard had fired off most of the ammunition in their pouches. They carried only twenty-five rounds per man, but there were several boxes of reserve ammunition in the house of the headman. These were never used, and were discovered later under the ruins of the house, which was blown down. Presumably the reserve ammunition was forgotten in the heat of battle.

At about 10.30 p.m. a message was handed to "Teal" Ashton, who was commanding the brigade, stating that Qibya was being attacked. Such signals were received almost nightly, both because the Israeli army was constantly shooting and patrolling right up to these villages, and also because most of the villagers were nervous and often gave false alarms.

There was a section (ten men) of the 10th Regiment in Budrus village, about a mile and a quarter away. The brigade commander told the brigade major to signal the section in Budrus to send out a patrol, and report if anything was going on in Qibya. He then went to bed, telling his staff to wake him up if any more signals came in. The section in Budrus went out, but became involved with considerable numbers of the enemy. Meanwhile a heavy bombardment had been turned on the two neighbouring villages of Budrus and Shuqba.

Soon after midnight, the Israelis broke into Qibya, which had, in any case, been defended by only forty National Guard. The Israeli infantry entered, firing indiscriminately with sub-machine guns, as could be seen the next day by the number of bullet marks on all remaining walls and buildings. Behind the infantry came sappers, each carrying an explosive charge especially made into a pack to fit on a man's back. Each man placed his charge against a house. Only the National Guard had been out of doors trying to repel the attack, and as the Israelis broke into the village, the National Guardsmen withdrew through the surrounding gardens. The old men, the women and the children were cowering in their houses, amidst the din of battle. The Israeli soldiers fired at anybody who attempted to leave his house. Then the charges were fired, and forty-two houses were blown up, burying their occupants under the ruins. The village school was also completely wrecked. When a great part of the village had been reduced to heaps of rubble, with the inhabitants buried beneath the ruins, the Israelis withdrew, after throwing incendiary bombs.

At dawn the next day, the brigade major drove down to Qibya, not feeling happy about the various disjointed signals which he had received during the night. He found a few dazed villagers wandering about the heaps of debris.

By nine in the morning, signals began to reach Amman, and it was soon evident that we were in face of a major massacre. Nothing like this had ever happened before, in all our many frontier skirmishes. I left with the Minister of Defence and at about twelve o'clock we were driving down the twisting narrow road leading to Qibya. Here we met the district governor coming away. He urged us not to go. He told us what had happened. Early this morning, he said, the villagers had begun to dig amongst the ruins to extricate their relations. Then two lawyers had arrived from Ramallah, and began to make speeches. They had worked the villagers up into a frenzy, by telling them that the British had urged their friends the Jews to destroy them.

"The Arab Legion is commanded by British officers," they said. "Of course they left you undefended. They knew that their friends the Jews were coming to massacre you, and disposed their troops so as to ensure that they could not save you."

XIX

Battle and Murder

That fatal drollery called a representative government.

BENJAMIN DISRAELI

XIX

BATTLE AND MURDER

SIXTY-SIX people had been killed in Qibya, of whom nearly three-quarters were women and children. A large part of the village had become mounds of rubble. The Israelis quoted, as their excuse, the incident in Tirat Yehuda two days before, when a Jewish woman with her two children had been killed. They omitted to mention that we had done everything in our power to detect the perpetrators of that crime. The murderers formed part of the refugee terrorist organization, of which the headquarters were in Syria and which was subsidized by Ibn Saud. Thus Jordan once again was being crushed between the upper and the nether millstones.

In practice, it would seem very unlikely that the attack on Qibya was planned after the Tirat Yehuda murders. The Israelis have always been extremely painstaking at rehearsing their raids in advance, as they were when they raided the British Army in the years from 1944 to 1948. The attack on Qibya was probably carried out by a battalion group, supported by sappers and extra artillery or mortar fire. The operation must have taken considerable preparation. The village and surroundings must have been carefully reconnoitred. All the explosive charges were specially prepared for carriage on men's backs. To lay these charges while other soldiers were shooting all civilians showing themselves, and then to fire the charges without injuring one another, must have necessitated considerable drill and practice.

My own guess—and it is only a guess—is that this massacre was prepared several months before, in April or May, when there were many incidents and acute tension. Then the energetic measures taken by Jordan put a temporary end to infiltration, and there was no excuse for the proposed operation. When the woman was murdered in Tirat Yehuda, the Israeli army jumped at the chance.

The Arab politicians also seized the opportunity. Since the loss of Lydda and Ramle, no such occasion had been offered them. The schoolboys were soon out in the streets. In Nablus, in Jerusalem, in Ramallah, in Jericho and in Amman itself, crowds surged through the towns, shouting slogans and throwing stones. But, curiously enough, most of the slogans were not against Israel but against Britain, America and the Arab Legion. The politicians could turn everything to serve their own ends. As I sat in my office in Amman, the crowds collected outside, shouting: "Down with the Arab Legion! Down with the Arab Legion!"

One lawyer wrote an article for the Press in which he stated that it was a common saying in the study of crime, "*Cherchez la femme.*" A woman was at the bottom of every crime. In the same manner, it was possible to say of every crime in Jordan—"Look for the Anglo-American imperialists." I had been on a short leave in England in August. Some of the politicians did not hesitate to say that, while on leave, I had arranged the attack on Qibya with representatives of the Israeli government.

Many factors combined to increase the violence of the demonstrations. Perhaps for the first time, Communist agents mixed with the crowds, shouting: "Down with the British! Down with Glubb Pasha!"

At the same time, politicians who were not extremist or anti-British encouraged the disturbances in the hope that the Cabinet would resign, and that they might obtain office.

I could not help remembering a sentence used by an English writer in the reign of Henry VIII. Referring to the members of King Henry's long parliament, he described them as "lightly furnished with either learning or honesty". Historians may be interested to know that the type still persists in some countries, if not in England.

The Palestinians were certainly a difficult people to serve. Everything of their country which had been saved, had been saved by the Arab Legion. For five years since 1948, the men of the Arab Legion had spent half their time in trenches, out every night on patrol in all weathers, separated from their wives and families for months on end. But at the least mishap, it was always "Down with the Arab Legion!"

It was indeed true that Qibya had been a tragedy. The fact was that brigade and battalion headquarters were too familiar with frontier skirmishes. Village reports had always been exaggerated. If troops were sent to every alarm, two divisions would not have been enough. By ill luck, the Qibya reports were true, whereas in so many previous cases exactly similar reports had been merely false alarms.

But to some extent, the fault had been ours in headquarters. The fact, of course, is that the whole Arab Legion, which at this time was 17,000 strong including base units, was not nearly enough to defend nearly four hundred miles of front. Then, in the summer of 1953, so many things had happened at once—the King's inauguration, the locust campaign, the frontier tension in the spring—and no units had done any training at all. When July, August and September had proved so quiet, we had withdrawn some of the troops from the front line for training, and were exceptionally weak when this sudden attack was delivered. Nor had the National Guard in Qibya offered the resistance expected of them. None had been killed or wounded, and the reserve ammunition had not been used. Falama, the previous January, had repulsed two Israeli attacks with fewer men than Qibya.

The Jordan government itself was anxious to find scapegoats. A ministerial court of inquiry visited the site. In the end, Brigadier "Teal" Ashton had to leave the Arab Legion. The Jordanian battalion commander was placed on pension. It was sad that "Teal" should fall a victim. Of all the British officers in the Arab Legion, he was the one most emotionally committed to the country. He was utterly devoted to the Palestine cause. All the British officers in the Arab Legion, with very few exceptions, were deeply attached to their troops and intensely proud of the Arab Legion. But "Teal" Ashton, apart from soldiering, was deeply enamoured of the country and the people. He had taught himself Arabic, he was an amateur expert in Palestine archaeology, he loved visiting the villages, he constantly had about him groups of poor boys for whom he was caring. He hoped to build a house, and pass the rest of his life in the country.

*　　*　　*　　*　　*

The Arab League Political Committee held an emergency meeting in Amman after Qibya. There was a good deal of violent talk. West Bank members of Parliament and lawyers wrote a memorandum to the Committee, claiming that Britain and America had ordered the Jews to massacre the people of Qibya. To some extent, the meeting of the Arab League Political Committee assisted us, for they promised two and a half million pounds for the National Guard. In practice they paid only a million spread over two years, but that million was a great help in the purchase of weapons and ammunition.

When a fortnight had elapsed after Qibya, a mild reaction set in. So volatile and passionate a people are at times inclined to have a swing-back after a great burst of emotion. Some of the local newspapers even reminded their readers of the services rendered by the Arab Legion in the past. Most of the newspaper editors in Jordan were my friends, but they were unwilling to publish anything contrary to the prevailing mood of the public. They made little attempt to tell the truth or to guide public opinion. They followed it, admitting with engaging candour that if they wrote anything not in harmony with public emotion at the time, the people would not buy the paper—"and we have to live," they added. In general, they swam with the stream. At times, however, they would publish special articles in return for payment. And as they received money from Ibn Saud, no criticism of the Saudi government ever appeared in the Press. In Jordan, the newspapers were jealous of the rights of citizens and the strict observance of the laws. If a man were arrested without a warrant, the Press was ready to raise an immediate protest. In Saudi Arabia, there was not only no *habeas corpus*, but no laws at all, no law courts, no budget, no constitution. But oil royalties were adequate to secure the silence of the Press on such delicate subjects.

*   *   *   *   *

The year 1953 had been a difficult one. For two years after the murder of King Abdulla, things had seemed to go on as before, in spite of the insanity of King Tellal. In 1953, the first signs of disintegration became apparent. But the young King Husain seemed a splendid boy and he was universally loved. We still hoped that the situation could henceforward be retrieved.

Incidents had increased in number and in savagery on the Israeli border, culminating in the unprecedented massacre of Qibya. On the Arab side, Ibn Saud began to subsidize refugee terrorists in Damascus, in order that they should infiltrate into Israel from Jordan, and thereby bring down Jewish reprisals on Jordan villages, and the resulting internal disturbances in the country. Moreover, the weakening of the position of the throne had emboldened subversive elements. For the first time, Communists began to play an active part in political life.

As against all these alarming factors, the positive gain was the steady build-up of the Arab Legion in both numbers and efficiency. While General Sir Brian Robertson had been Commander-in-Chief in the Middle East, he had given us immense assistance. The divisional organization was virtually complete and we were well ahead with creating an armoured corps. The necessary workshop organization had also been built up, so that henceforward tanks, armoured cars, trucks and guns could be maintained and repaired. But more than the increase in numbers, the steady rise in the standard of professional soldiering was heartening. Schools, courses, examinations, exercises—nobody who has not had to do it can have any idea of the immense amount of detailed labour involved in the creation and build-up of a new army, especially in a country where no army has ever existed before.

In some ways, the Arab Legion was even more thorough than the British Army itself. For one thing, there was always a waiting list for recruiting, with the result that recruiting officers were able to select only the best candidates. The character and antecedents of every recruit were checked by the police before his acceptance. Then again, in the Arab Legion, a confidential report was sub-

mitted on every officer and man every year. Every N.C.O. or private
soldier had to pass an examination before he could be promoted.

While this intense effort was being devoted to render the Arab
Legion professionally competent, an entirely new army was being
built up by (and side by side with) the Arab Legion. This army was
the National Guard. Originally consisting merely of armed peasants
in villages liable to Israeli raids, the National Guard had now
become country-wide. In rear areas and in Trans-Jordan, it was
being built up into a territorial army, each unit of which served for
two months a year in an annual training camp. The money promised
by the Arab League was to be spent on weapons and ammunition
for this territorial army.

The front-line villages were also becoming organized, and every
six or eight villages were grouped to form a frontier regiment. The
Israeli front-line villages were organized in much the same manner,
but with an immense difference—the Israelis had money and we had
none. On December 29th, 1953, the *Daily Telegraph* published an
account of a visit by their military correspondent to a group of
Israeli front-line villages. He described how he saw the village
armouries, stocked with light and medium machine guns, two-inch
and three-inch mortars, Piats, rifles, mines and military equipment.
The settlements, he alleged, contained deep concrete dug-outs,
command posts, wire entanglements and minefields.

On our side, where everything was on a no-cost basis, we could
not afford such luxuries. No other Arab country made during these
years anything remotely resembling the military effort put forth by
ruined and bankrupt Jordan. Officers and men alike were fully
aware of this fact, and were intensely proud of what they had done
and were doing.

One of the reasons for the lack of appreciation of their army by
the Palestinian part of the population was their own ignorance
of everything military. Even Cabinet ministers—let alone the man
in the street—were unaware that training or organization were
necessary. They believed that, if ten thousand rifles were handed out
to a camp of refugees, the army would thereby be increased by
another division. They saw no need for highly trained officers—let
alone for British officers. They believed that anyone could be an
officer, particularly if he had a university degree.

*   *   *   *   *

The first two months of 1954 passed uneasily, with numerous
frontier incidents, the nature of some of which had changed with
the appearance of the subsidized gangster, paid by the Syrian or
Saudi governments to go and kill Jews. To prevent these incidents,
both sides increased their forces deployed on the demarcation line,

with the result that the two armies began to fire at one another across the line!

On March 17th, 1954, an Israeli bus was coming up the long road from Eilat[1] towards Beersheba (see the map on page 248). At the top of a long ascent, a place called by the Israelis "Scorpion Pass", some Arabs, lying in concealment, opened fire on the vehicle. The driver was killed instantly and the bus ran backward until it was stopped by a bank beside the road. The Arabs then emerged from hiding and continued to fire on the bus. Eventually two of them climbed into the vehicle and finished off the survivors at point-blank range.

In an official statement issued by the Israeli government, the following paragraph appeared:

"The Government of Israel expresses its revulsion and horror at the murderous attack by an organized Arab force on a passenger bus in the Negev,[2] which was carried out as a military operation, and which resulted in the cold-blooded killing of eleven men, women and children and the wounding of three others."

Men never will remember that those who take the sword perish by the sword. *Mutatis mutandis*, the same expressions could well have been applied to the Israeli attack on Qibya. Both were abominable cold-blooded massacres.

The news of this horrible incident, and the violence of the Israeli reaction, threw the government and the diplomats into intense activity. I was summoned to give an explanation.

I was almost completely convinced that we had nothing to do with this crime. To begin with, the incident took place in the desert, too far from the village area to be the work of ordinary refugees, or even of the gangs from Damascus. This was the work of nomad or semi-nomad tribesmen. The Israelis, of course, always attempted to depict every crime as being committed by regular troops of the Arab Legion. If such had been the case, it would have "balanced" the raids of the Israeli army against Jordan villages. But of course no such incident ever occurred.

Assuming that the bus outrage could only have been carried out by tribesmen accustomed to the desert, there remained three possibilities—bedouins from southern Trans-Jordan, the few bedouins still left in the Beersheba area under Israel, or tribesmen from the Sinai desert. I was able almost to guarantee that no Trans-Jordan bedouins were involved—I knew them too well. There remained the few bedouins still in Israel. The passengers in the bus had not been

---

[1] Eilat was the name given by Israel to the new settlement which they founded on the Gulf of Aqaba, west of Aqaba village.

[2] Negev is the Hebrew form of the Arabic Neqeb.

robbed, although some of them had been carrying both money and jewellery. It was therefore a crime of revenge, not of robbery. It was, of course, possible that some bedouins in Israel had been killed by the Israeli army or police, and had sought this means of revenge. The theory was, however, unlikely, as the Israelis would obviously have wreaked a terrible revenge on any tribe camped within their boundaries if the identity of the murderers had been discovered. Thus by far the most likely solution was that the attackers were from a tribe in Sinai. It so happened that there was a nomadic tribe in Sinai which had a bitter feud with Israel—the Azazma. This tribe was native to the Beersheba area but had been driven out by the Israelis and had taken refuge in Sinai. Several armed clashes had occurred between the Israeli forces and the Azazma. A number of members of the tribe had been killed.

Having worked the case out in this manner, I reported to the Jordan government, which, on March 18th, boldly declared that the attackers of the bus were not Jordanians. The Israelis replied by handing in the names of three persons, alleged to be Jordan tribesmen, who were the criminals. Investigation failed to trace any such persons.

Meanwhile Israel insisted on an immediate emergency meeting of the Mixed Armistice Commission. When it assembled, the Israeli delegate demanded the condemnation of Jordan, in an impassioned speech. The chairman, Commander Hutchison of the United States Navy, a peculiarly calm and courageous individual amid these storms of passion, urged a postponement to allow of further investigation. The Israelis would have none of it, and insisted on a vote. As has already been explained, the Mixed Armistice Commission consisted of two Israelis and two Jordanians, with a UNO chairman, and as the Israelis and Jordanians obviously voted on opposite sides, the chairman always held the casting vote. Commander Hutchison gave it as his opinion that Jordan's guilt was still not proven. The Israelis lost their case. They walked out. This result produced a wave of intense and passionate resentment in Israel. On March 25th, the Prime Minister, Moshe Sharett (formerly named Shertok), made a statement in the Israeli Parliament. "It was the patent truth," he said, "that the perpetrators of the crime had come from Jordan. No amount of quibbling could cover it up."

Mr. Sharett then expressed his opinion of the Mixed Armistice Commission in no measured terms. He said:

"As to the Israel-Jordan Mixed Armistice Commission, which has failed to carry out its responsibilities and betrayed our confidence, we have come to the conclusion that there is no sense in our continued participation. Accordingly the Israeli delegation announced yesterday at the meeting of the Commission that it will no longer participate in its work."

It was said of the great Dr. Johnson that if you were not convinced in argument by the pistol of his wit, he finished you off by clubbing you with the butt. Mr. Sharett had employed similar tactics. Commander Hutchison had not exonerated Jordan. He had merely said that the proof submitted was not conclusive, and had asked for time for further investigation. The Israeli Prime Minister had replied with a torrent of emotional oratory, in which he had produced no proofs. He had merely stated that Jordan was obviously guilty and, on that assumption, had given vent to an impassioned denunciation, both of Jordan and of the Mixed Armistice Commission.

The situation was still profoundly disturbing. Technically, Jordan had escaped condemnation, but Jewish publicity agencies would doubtless persuade a great part of the world that we were guilty. Israel was seething with excitement and some reprisal raid on the lines of Qibya was more than probable. Should a further Qibya take place, not only would Israel be triumphant, but our Arab rivals, our opposition politicians, the Communists and the refugees would rise once more in their wrath denouncing "Arab Legion treachery".

It was obvious that mere denials were unconvincing. We must find out who did do it. I accordingly despatched a number of independent persons to Gaza, Beersheba and Sinai in an attempt to discover the truth. In due course our efforts were crowned with success. The names of the assailants of the bus, a full story of the crime and statements of witnesses were collected. The criminals, as we had guessed, were from the Azazma tribe, camped in Qusaima in Sinai. The whole case was gathered into a file and handed in to the United Nations Truce Supervision Organization. The Chief of Staff, General Bennike, informed us that Israel had complained to the Security Council. He had accordingly, he said, sent the case-file to the Security Council, where it would be produced when the case was heard.

But events moved too swiftly. Further incidents and outrages followed. The Security Council never gave the bus incident a hearing, and our case-file presumably disappeared in the archives of Lake Success. Thus Jordan never received the public vindication which she had earned. Most people now have forgotten about the Scorpion Pass incident. But if any remember it, they probably still believe it to have been an abominable outrage committed by Jordanians.

*   *   *   *   *

The Israelis were so convinced of Jordan's guilt at the Scorpion Pass that they had no hesitation in putting in the reprisal attack.

It took the form of an attack on the village of Nahhaleen, at midnight on the night of March 29th–30th, 1954. We had done a great deal of work since Qibya, five months before. It was obviously unsound to have regular troops distributed in little detachments in every frontier village. The only reasonable course was to locate them in centrally situated reserve positions behind the line, ready to reinforce any village which was attacked. The National Guard would have to defend the village until regular reinforcements arrived.

At Nahhaleen a company of Israeli infantry entered the village unopposed. The National Guard had made the elementary mistake of wiring only the western side of the village, which faced the enemy. All the sentries, moreover, were on this side. The Israeli force made a detour and entered the village unnoticed from the rear.

In each frontier village, there was now one N.C.O. from the regular army, who trained and commanded the National Guard. In Nahhaleen, a small village, there was a lance-corporal.

It so happened that at midnight on the night in question, this lance-corporal set out to walk round the village and visit his sentries. The first people he encountered were a company of Israeli infantry. Whipping out the Sten gun which he was carrying, the lance-corporal slipped behind the corner of a house which commanded the entrance to the village street, and opened fire. The Israelis had occupied eight or nine straggling houses at the east end of the village, but had not reached the main street. The lance-corporal alone held the entrance to the village against a company of the enemy. The fire fight which developed roused the rest of the village, and soon a National Guardsman appeared with a Bren gun, then three more with rifles. Thus a little front line was built up, which pinned the enemy to their ground. In the dark, they may have thought that a stronger force was barring their way.

The nearest regular troops to Nahhaleen were a platoon of infantry four kilometres away. There was a wireless set in the village with a regular Arab Legion operator. He immediately signalled the platoon. The platoon commander decided to reconnoitre. He took six men with him, in a 15-cwt. truck and a Land Rover, and drove rapidly in the dark down the rough country track towards the village. The platoon remained standing by, in wireless touch with their commander on his reconnaissance.

Of course the Israelis had reckoned that Arab Legion reinforcements would arrive. Two kilometres from Nahhaleen they had stretched a trip wire across the road, attached to a mine, and posted ten men with a Bren gun to cover the mine. The 15-cwt. truck duly hit the trip wire, the mine was detonated, and the truck was blown right off the road. The platoon sergeant who was in the truck was killed, and a soldier with him was made unconscious by the concussion. As soon as the mine exploded, the Israeli soldiers poured an intense rifle and Bren-gun fire on the two vehicles. The platoon commander was wounded. One corporal and one private in the Land Rover still survived. The corporal jumped out of the Land Rover and single-handed ran to attack the Israeli section and Bren gun team. He was killed only two yards before reaching the gun.

But although this little reconnaissance party was exterminated, its gallantry had saved the village. For the Israeli company, which was still in action against the lance-corporal and his four National Guardsmen, heard the detonation of the road mine. "The Arab Legion is coming," they thought. Within a few minutes their fire had slackened—then ceased. They had slipped away and were making tracks for the border. The gallant little lance-corporal with his Sten gun was left in possession of the field.

The previous evening, the National Guard of Nahhaleen had sent a standing patrol under a regular Arab Legion N.C.O. to ambush the path from the border, a few hundred yards west of the village. The Israelis had avoided the ambush in their advance, because they had not approached the village from the west. In their more hasty retreat, however, they ran into the ambush from behind, and suffered casualties in a confused night battle in the dark. Better still, the National Guard in the next village of Jeba' had heard the fighting in Nahhaleen. Led by their regular N.C.O., the Jeba' National Guard had gone out to intercept the retreat of the attackers of Nahhaleen, and had also run into them before they crossed the border. On the whole, the action had been satisfactory. Although a number of Arab Legion soldiers and National Guards were killed, the enemy failed to enter the village, except for the few isolated houses to the east.

In one respect, the Israelis varied their Qibya tactics. They did not bring large explosive charges and demolish whole houses. Instead, they were carrying small charges which they placed against the front doors and blew them in. Immediately the door was blown in, Israeli Sten-gunners stepped inside and sprayed the interior of the houses with sub-machine gun bullets, killing men, women and children indiscriminately in the dark. In a few seconds they had moved on to the next house. The eight houses captured were treated in this manner. As usual with all Jewish raids, every detail of this drill must have been carefully practised in advance.

The military correspondent of the Israeli newspaper *Jerusalem Post* commented that the Jordan government was responsible for the Nahhaleen incident, "because it could have stopped bloodshed long ago by preventing its citizens from crossing into Israel with murderous intention. From this village must have come the murderers who killed the watchmen in Mahasea two months ago and in

Kessalon on Friday night. . . . It is assumed that members of the
National Guard do most of the political killing in Israel."

It is hoped that my readers will have realized that we were, and
had been for a long time, straining every nerve to prevent infiltration into Israel. Half the men in prison in West Jordan were serving
terms of imprisonment for infiltration. Half a million destitutes and
a frontier nearly four hundred miles long made it impossible to
guarantee that no party of two or three infiltrators would ever cross
the line on a dark night. In any case, the infiltrators were scarcely
ever normal Jordan citizens. They were the refugees whom the Israeli
government had driven from their homes. The political murderers
were, of course, the terrorist organization from Damascus, former
Mufti terrorists subsidized by the Saudi government. The assumption that members of the National Guard did nearly all the political
killing was only a newspaper claim. The Israeli government had a
pre-eminently efficient intelligence system. They must have known
better.

In point of fact, neither the inhabitants nor the National Guards
from frontier villages advocated infiltration, because the reprisal
raids by the Israelis fell on them. The infiltrators came from refugee
camps many miles from the border—in some cases from as far afield
as Damascus. This indeed was what made the Israeli attacks both
brutal and unsuccessful in preventing infiltration. The punishment
fell on the innocent and was no deterrent to the guilty.

*   *   *   *   *

Our troubles were principally due to the fact that one-third of the
people in Jordan were destitute refugees, without possessions, without
work and without houses to live in. The best way to realize what this
meant is to consider it in terms of the country one knows best. In
Britain, the same proportion would have meant eighteen million
destitutes, living in ragged tents or under the trees. In the United
States, one-third of the population would have been fifty millions. If
either of these countries had suffered such a proportion of destitutes,
revolution or anarchy would have resulted in a matter of weeks.
And yet Jordan endured this condition for year after year, with only
an occasional murder or robbery effected against the Israelis, who
had driven these refugees from their homes.

Care of the refugees had been assumed, in 1948, by the International Red Cross, an organization, surely, to which humanity
owes an immense debt of gratitude. But this was in the nature of an
emergency measure. The United Nations Relief and Works Agency
assumed responsibility from the Red Cross. The activities of
UNRWA were twofold. Its first duty was to keep the refugees

alive by collecting them in camps, issuing tents, supplying rations, and providing medical services, schools and other essential amenities. Its second duty was to resettle them in life—in other words, to provide homes and the means of earning a livelihood.

UNRWA was remarkably successful in its first duty, particularly in the direction of health. The rate of mortality amongst refugees was alleged to be, in some cases, lower than that of the original settled inhabitants. The rations issued appeared barely adequate, but had obviously been carefully calculated to provide sufficient nourishment, as none of the refugees looked hungry.

A cynic once said to me: "It is a mistake to interfere in the processes of Nature. If this had happened in former ages, the disaster of 1948 would have been followed by a year of intense tragedy. Tens of thousands—perhaps hundreds of thousands—of people would have died of cholera, plague, dysentery and other epidemics. But two, or at most three, years after the disaster, the population would have been reduced to the numbers which the country could support. Thenceforward everyone would have had a home and a job, peace and stability would have returned and the ravages of war would soon have been forgotten. All the United Nations have done by keeping these people alive is to prolong the agony, to leave us all facing an insecure future and immensely to increase the volume of human hatred."

Few will agree that the unfortunate refugees should have been left to die. But the remarks of our cynic do emphasize an undoubted fact—namely, that UNO tends to apply palliatives and no more. In just the same manner, the United Nations supported a precarious armistice in Palestine, unwilling to leave the protagonists to fight it out to a conclusion, but unable to bring the dispute to a final settlement. This dilatoriness would indeed seem to be a characteristic of modern democracy—of government by assemblies and committees, and by political parties in office, which change every few years. "Peace in our time"—"Avoid a crisis" are the perhaps inevitable outcome.

The fact remained that, eight years after the 1948 disaster, the number of refugees was still increasing. This was largely due to natural increase, under the efficient care of the UNRWA medical organization. The number of children born was greater than the number of refugees who died or were settled. The excuse put forward for this failure was that the Arab governments wished to keep the refugees destitute, in order to maintain the Palestine problem as a live political issue. This charge may or may not have been true of some Arab governments in whose countries the number of refugees was negligible. It was certainly not true of the Jordan government as long as I knew it.

There was, however, a good deal of talk of this kind amongst extremist politicians, who liked to explain that Britain and America were anxious to settle the refugees, not for humanitarian reasons, but in order to protect Israel from demands to permit their return. Consequently, they deduced, to settle the refugees in other Arab countries was to help Israel. Needless to say, the most enthusiastic advocates of this policy were themselves comfortably established in houses.

In practice, the result of the continued maintenance of the refugees in a destitute condition was extremely injurious to Jordan. It condemned that country to live with one-third of its citizens embittered and discontented, and, what was worse, bred up a new generation of children in sordid surroundings, accustomed to idleness and discontent.

But, to be just, it must be admitted that the United Nations themselves were also to a considerable extent responsible for the non-settlement of the refugees. That organization was too centralized in America. Local projects were all referred to New York, involving endless delays. The brief given to UNRWA appeared also to be too narrow. The funds available could be spent only on settling refugees, and the original inhabitants of Jordan were not thereby to profit. Such a proviso may seem wise and necessary, in order to avoid misappropriation of the funds, but in reality it rendered settlement almost impossible.

For example, let us say that there was an opening for a certain industry in Jordan. If a complete industry could have been started, staffed solely by refugees, such a scheme might have been possible. In practice, however, a small Jordanian company might already be engaged in the industry. A capital loan to this firm would have enabled it immediately to extend its activities and employ (let us say) a hundred refugees. Such a loan could not, however, be made, because the existing business did not belong to refugees. I was personally of the opinion that no progress could be made on so restricted a basis. The way to settle the refugees was so to raise the economy of the whole country that a demand for labour would be created, and then the refugees would disappear imperceptibly into the economic life of the community. Such a method would, moreover, have overcome the political difficulties, for the refugees would have been absorbed one by one into different fields of employment. For, whatever the politicians might say, the refugees did not wish to be idle—they were always ready and anxious to find work.

The solution which I believe would have been successful would have consisted first of all in decentralization. The best and most capable man obtainable should have been delegated to undertake the task, and given the money and a free hand, without the necessity of constant reference to New York. He should have encouraged and expanded every industry (principally of course agriculture), which seemed likely to be successful. In most cases, these would be industries already existing, and which were paying their way and possessed experienced staff. They would merely have been helped to extend their operations and engage more labour. No mention whatever of the refugees need have been made—if Jordan became prosperous, the refugees would gradually disappear.

But UNO, as in so many other fields, was divided, lacking in drive and lethargic. It is conceivable also that some of the officials were not over-anxious for a settlement, which would mean the termination of their appointments, for UNO was paying very high salaries, in hard currency and exempt from income tax.

In addition to UNRWA, both Britain and the U.S.A. gave money for development. The American plan was that known as Point IV. It was neither very popular nor very effective, though it brought in money, which in itself was a valuable service in so poor a country. But the theory of Point IV was that it would supply expert advice rather than funds. Jordan was desperately in need of money, but was not particularly anxious to receive advice. Point IV did indeed supply the funds to build a hospital and certain schools, which were badly needed, even if not productive of increased revenue. Point IV assisted me personally with funds for schools for bedouin boys, which the Jordan government had never done. It also enabled us to make some charming American friends.

Curiously enough, the most successful development work in Jordan was accomplished by an annual contribution of about a million pounds paid by Britain. For this money was given to the Jordan government to spend. Its outlay was controlled by a specially constructed Development Board, of which only one subordinate member was a British official. The Board made small advances to farmers for specific development schemes on their farms, visited each project and personally made sure that the funds were expended on the purposes for which they had been sanctioned. The Jordanians made good use of this money, because they themselves had the spending of it.

Many Americans are genuinely imbued with deep suspicions of Britain and her attitude to the people of Asia. Yet in Jordan Britain gave her money to the Jordanians to spend, whereas Point IV funds were spent directly by American officials, not by the Jordan government.

For the rest, the British funds were spent in detail, in the form of small advances to individual farmers. For Jordanian agriculture was in the hands of peasants. To Americans, a peasant economy is perhaps strange, or at least unrewarding. They tend to be impatient of petty items and to long for vast projects, a single one of which may suffice to revolutionize the country.

I have always been an advocate of Anglo-American co-operation. It is the great tragedy of our times that we can be so like one another, and yet so constantly divided by misunderstandings and unfounded prejudices. Which only shows how inadequate is human nature to the opportunities which lie before us.

Some people would have us believe that American Big Business is deliberately endeavouring to oust Britain from all Asia and Africa, in order itself to be able to exploit these countries without a competitor. It is certainly striking how often the U.S.A. seems to lead the attack on Britain's position in some Eastern country—it is even more remarkable how often the U.S.A. and Russia speak with one voice in attacking Britain.

The American people are, as I have said, suspicious of British "colonial methods". They have grown up in the belief that Britain oppressed the American colonies, and it is only natural that they should suspect that she is still doing the same to the peoples of Asia and Africa. Americans have little or no appreciation of the immense amount of love and benevolence which thousands and thousands of Englishmen have devoted to many Eastern races. I am glad to say that it was an American missionary who told me that Britain had done more than any other nation to spread the Gospel. If, in reality, big American financial interests are striving to destroy Britain's position, will their "exploitation" be in reality more benevolent?

I have never served in the British Empire. My life has been spent in the service of independent Asiatic states. During my last few years in Jordan, there were more Americans in the country than British, and they were interfering more in the government than were the British. Whereas the British were inclined to work through the Jordan government, the Americans were more in the habit of doing everything themselves. Certainly I do not think that one could say unreservedly that the Americans were more devoted or idealistic than the British.

If indeed certain power groups in the U.S.A. are deliberately trying to supplant Britain in many parts of the world, I do not believe that this is done with the cognizance and approval of the American people. I have never been to America, but I have always loved the idealism, the generosity and the hospitality of Americans, wherever I have met them. I do not believe that they would consent to a plan to undermine and destroy their nearest ally.

In the Arab countries, America is believed to be Britain's worst enemy. I remember well a prominent Arab personality saying to me that he could not understand why Britain was always worrying about Russia.

"Believe me, Pasha," he said, "Britain has only one enemy in the Middle East, and that enemy is the U.S.A. The Americans will never rest until they have destroyed Britain's position."

What then is the end of the whole matter? To me, it is this: that the world is extremely complicated; that generalizations are usually wrong. No two countries and no two peoples are the same. Every problem requires intense and special study. The theorists of London, Washington and Lake Success are nearly always wrong, because they do not know enough. My second conclusion is that we are all too swift to see the mote in each other's eyes.

When I was young, the founder of the Legion of Frontiersmen, Roger Pocock, wrote a little book called *Horses*. In it he said: "When my horse goes badly, I examine my conduct to see what I have done wrong." What a pity that some of our political theorists cannot follow so wise and humble a maxim. When the world goes wrong, let us each examine our own conduct, rather than our neighbour's, and see what we have done wrong.

XX

Reprisals

Stand firm like a smitten anvil under the blows of a hammer; be
strong as an athlete of God, it is part of a great athlete to receive
blows and to conquer.   IGNATIUS LOYOLA

Give us courage and gaiety and the quiet mind.
                                       ROBERT LOUIS STEVENSON

XX

REPRISALS

THE year 1954, which had such a troubled beginning on the Israel border, continued to be one of constant alarms and outbreaks. May and June passed in a continuous succession of incidents, recriminations and threats. "Further clashes on Israel border." "Arab harvesters fired on by Israelis." "Four Arabs shot at work." "National Guard killed by Israeli patrol." "Israelis attack Kherbet Illin"—and so on day after day. In the second half of May, Israel complained to the Security Council on the subject of thirty-seven alleged "incidents".

Most of these incidents involved no particular hostility to Israel. An increasingly frequent cause of Israeli complaints was that farmers were ploughing across the demarcation line. Doubtless in some places they had done so ever since 1948, but the attention of the Israeli authorities had only recently been drawn to the fact, with the result that they observed the line with increasing care. What appeared to us a trying feature of Israeli tactics was that they did not normally complain at the time of ploughing or sowing. They waited until the crop was ripe and the Arabs went in to harvest it, and then fired on them. In many cases, Arab farmers were not clear where the line was, to within 100 or 200 yards. In some cases, they probably knew, but could not resist the temptation to plough 50 or 100 yards beyond it. It must be remembered that all the land was their personal property, and had been the property of their ancestors for generations.

In the north of Samaria, between Tulkarm and Jenin, there were several villages still inhabited by Arabs just across the border line. These were in the strip of land surrendered by us at Rhodes. Naturally many people living on our side of the line had friends or relatives living on the Israeli side, and every now and again slipped across to see them. The village of Berta'a was bisected by the line, and, curiously enough, the headman of the village was recognized by both governments. This privileged personality was liable to be summoned to Tel Aviv to discuss the affairs of the west end of the village, and to Nablus or Amman regarding the concerns of the east end.

In Arab villages and tribes, the women still wore long black clothes and veils. No such garments could be bought in the shops in Israel. As a result, the husbands and fathers of these ladies were obliged to "infiltrate" into Jordan to buy their clothes.

I accidentally came across an Arab boy at school in Nablus, whose parents lived just across the demarcation line in one of these villages. He lived in Nablus in term time, but he "infiltrated" into Israel for the holidays, and back again to Nablus at the beginning of the term. Doubtless every frontier in the world has complications of this nature, which are comparatively simple to handle. Where, however, the two governments are competing to produce causes of complaint, even the most innocent escapades can be used to add to the number of "flagrant breaches of the armistice agreement".

At about 8 o'clock in the evening of June 30th, 1954, I was called to the telephone to speak to divisional headquarters. They told me that heavy firing had broken out in Jerusalem. The Israelis had started it, for no apparent reason. A little later, the telephone rang again—it was Lieutenant-Colonel Peter Young, who commanded the 9th Regiment, which at the time was holding Jerusalem.

"Can you hear me, sir?" said a distant small voice. "I'm speaking from the walls of the Old City, over the Damascus Gate. There's rather a lot of shooting. I have pretty well succeeded in stopping our chaps shooting, but the Jews are giving us all they've got. Can you hear me?"

I could not only hear him, but I could hear high explosive bursts too. "Can we shoot back, sir?" went on the thin, small voice. "Troops are getting annoyed. Can you hear me?"

"You know the orders," I said. "Shoot back on a less scale than the enemy, but enough to keep up morale. Use the same calibre and weapons they are using. Is there any sign of movement? Any chance they are going to attack?"

"I don't think so," replied he. "Haven't seen any signs of an attack. They seem to want to get rid of their surplus ammo."

Peter Young had been in the commandos in the war and had a D.S.O. and an M.C., and had commanded a brigade. He liked battles and sounded jovial—if not facetious.

"Have you spoken to UNO?" I asked. "I suggest you ring up Commander Hutchison."

"All right, sir!" he said. "I'll do that."

A few minutes later the telephone rang again.

"Is that Glubb Pasha? This is Hutchison. I'm in the middle of one hell of a big battle here. Noise is deafening."

Hutchison, who seemed to disregard his personal safety, lived with his wife in a house on the edge of no-man's-land, almost between the two armies.

"I want to fix a cease-fire at twenty-one hours," he said. "Could you please impress on your people to stop then?"

At twenty-one hours (9 p.m.) the Arab Legion ceased fire, but the Israelis carried on until 9.40. Firing slackened until 11.30 p.m., when the Israelis began again, first with rifle and automatic fire and then with a three-inch mortar bombardment of the Old City. Fourteen Israeli mortar bombs fell in the Citadel of the Old City, where we had a company of infantry. The Israelis continued firing spasmodically until half an hour after midnight.

On the morning of July 1st, the Israeli army again opened fire from 11.20 a.m. to 11.50 a.m. This time the Arab Legion did not reply. On July 2nd, however, shooting recommenced and the same procedure followed—fixing a cease-fire time—fire recommenced—fix another cease-fire, and so on.

The Israelis immediately proclaimed to the world that this outburst of shooting was a Jordan attack, carefully planned at the highest level. The Israeli Press claimed premeditation to be proved, because firing began all over the city simultaneously. It was not a case of an accidental shot that caused other shots and thus gradually built up into a battle.

We had noticed the same thing, but it was not we who began. Peter Young, commanding the battalion in the line, was in his bath when the shooting commenced. He certainly did not know. As the firing was said to have begun simultaneously in many places, the only assumption, if the Arab Legion did begin it, was that the 9th Regiment was mutinous, and had arranged a battle unknown to its commander. Anyone who knew the Arab Legion in those days—and especially the 9th Regiment—realized that such an idea was ridiculous.

The Israelis claimed that the Arab Legion had been heavily reinforced two days before the shooting. Not only was this not the case, but no reinforcements were sent to Jerusalem the whole time—the support and reserve companies of the 9th Regiment were not even deployed throughout the whole duration of the incident.

As soon as the situation had returned to normal, General Bennike, head of the United Nations Truce Supervision staff, initiated an inquiry as to who fired first. He finally issued a statement to the effect that it was impossible to prove which side had been the aggressor. No other investigations were carried out. We suggested that inquiries might be made into other aspects, such as the Jewish three-inch mortar bombardments of the Old City, which was packed with shrines, churches and holy places. Nineteen Israeli three-inch mortar bombs had fallen on the Armenian Convent, three on the roof of the Armenian Cathedral of St. James. Seven bombs broke the windows of the Anglican Christ Church. One fell near the Holy Sepulchre, and another on the Russian Convent. The Arab Legion had not used three-inch mortars. Nearly all the Jordan casualties were from these Israeli three-inch mortars. As soon as the shooting began, civilians took cover from bullets. But they could not protect themselves from the mortar shells. The one that fell near the Holy Sepulchre killed three civilians and wounded eleven. But UNO were unwilling to follow the matter up further.

My mother, who was ninety-one years old in 1954, was living at the time in the American Colony. Her bedroom window looked out over Israel, and she received a burst of Israeli machine-gun fire through it. When I hastened over to Jerusalem to see how she was, she told me that all was well now.

"I've moved my bed to the other side of the room," she said. "Now I can't be shot through the window."

The habit of firing indiscriminately with all weapons except artillery, into the streets of a crowded city, was outrageous. The soldiers of the two armies were by now well-established in concrete bunkers or solid defences, and could fire down the streets filled with civilians at no risk to themselves. Nearly all the casualties of the Jerusalem shootings were civilians. If any soldier was hit, he was not on duty, but walking out to look at the shops, or returning from leave. This shoot cost Arab Jerusalem hundreds of thousands of pounds in tourist cancellations. All the Jerusalem and Bethlehem Holy Places were on the Jordanian side. Until this summer of 1954, the tourist traffic had been increasing steadily since 1948, and the city was beginning to look more prosperous. This wanton shooting outrage put everything back once more.

* * * * *

I have always remembered Cromwell's saying that a soldier fights better when he knows what he is fighting for. Ever since I commanded ninety men in the first Desert Patrol in 1931, I have constantly collected all those under my command and explained to them every detail of the situation in which we have found ourselves. I have then invited questions and discussion.

When the Arab Legion grew to ten thousand and then twenty thousand men, I could not talk with them all. But I constantly visited units and gave talks to all officers and N.C.O.s. I always told them that an army is a band of brothers, that a soldier is no good if he only carries out orders without understanding them. Every man in the Arab Legion was himself a partner in the great enterprise in which we were engaged, and every man must understand our situation, our objective and the reasons for our actions. I would then give a perfectly true summary of our situation, stating correctly the strength of the Israeli forces, the other Arab armies and other essential factors. There was, to some extent, perhaps, a security risk in talking so freely. But in general the Israelis knew more about us than the ordinary Jordanian did, so there was much to explain which the Israeli General Staff undoubtedly already knew.

Discussions were usually frank. I remember an occasion when a corporal in the 2nd Regiment asked the question:

"Why does Britain always help the Jews and never the Arabs?"

"That's a very important question," I said. "Who was it who saved what is left of Arab Palestine from the Jews?"

"We, the Arab Legion, did," he replied.

"And who pays for the Arab Legion?" I asked again.

"Britain," he answered.

"Well, then," I said. "It doesn't seem that Britain helps only the Jews."

He smiled. "I never thought of that," he said.

But these talks of mine conflicted with a viewpoint which was almost universally held, at least by the Levantine Arabs and Egyptians. This generally held opinion was that morale must be kept up by telling lies—or we may perhaps state it more fairly by saying that it is unwise to tell the common people all the truth. Possibly this belief was reinforced by the weak politicians' desire to buy peace, even if for a short time, by pretending that everything was going well.

This unwillingness to say anything unpleasant seemed, indeed, to be deeply engrained in the Arab character. When our neighbours took their little boy to the dentist, they told him that he was going to the cinema, until he was actually in the chair. If a patient is dying in hospital, the relatives will be assured that his health is improving. When, therefore, I told the truth to officers and men of the Arab Legion, the politicians considered that I was undermining the morale of the troops. In their opinion, I should have minimized the strength of the enemy and exaggerated our own, so as to draw a more cheerful picture.

Such were the views of the politicians with whom I worked. But it was not a very long step from them to the intriguers, the agitators and the discontented. They explained that I was intentionally undermining the morale of the army, on secret orders from London, in order to facilitate the Israeli conquest of the rest of Jordan. How little did these embittered and cynical intriguers appreciate the loyal freemasonry and the happy brotherhood which bound me heart and soul to these men. For I was in an extraordinarily happy position, which falls to the lot of very few commanders.

I had served twenty-four years in the Arab Legion, which when I joined it was only 800 strong. I had commanded it for fifteen years. Many of the men in it were already sons of the men who had served with me twenty-four years before. I was already commanding the Arab Legion when the young officers of 1954 were still infants. Some of them I had known as children. I had myself taken a hand in the education of not a few. The officers promoted from the ranks had served with me as soldiers and as N.C.O.s. I do not suppose that any general in the British Army has even been in so fortunate a position.

The same question of depressing morale arose in connection with civil defence. This subject in most governments is dealt with by the Ministry of the Interior, but as no action whatever had been taken, I had advised the Prime Minister several times of the importance of considering the matter. Eventually he paid me back by ordering the Arab Legion to do it.

The civil police were still under the command of Arab Legion headquarters and we accordingly sent police officers to England for training. But when they returned, the Prime Minister would not sanction air-raid practices. He feared that the public would be alarmed and think that there was a danger of war. My reply to all these arguments was that people get used to any idea. They would be frightened for a week or two. Then, when no war came, they would recover their normal mentality and thenceforward we could carry out regular air-raid precaution training without any further difficulty. Israel, I told him, already had a most elaborate air-raid and civil-defence system. But he was adamant and no training was carried out.

In the case of the army, the situation was different. It was impossible to plan or train at all if we were to pretend that we were stronger than Israel and would attack all along the line. The situation of Jordan vis-à-vis Israel was in reality reasonably favourable, if we faced facts and planned realistically. For Jordan, with all the Arab countries as her allies on the one hand and Britain on the other, was in the long run stronger than Israel, if she played her cards wisely. There could be no doubt that, if Israel did launch a full war against Jordan, we should have a hard time for some days. But if we survived that period of crisis till all our allies could come to our help, the final result could not be in doubt. The army understood this, but the fact that I said it was constantly used against me. The majority of the politicians preferred to live in a world of dreams. They saw visions of a mighty united Arabia pouring its vast armies into Israel to overthrow and annihilate it. But in the interval, they took scarcely any practical measures to ensure that end.

In the eight years from 1948 to 1956, the Arab Legion increased in strength from 6,000 to 23,000. Behind this army an even more numerous National Guard was being steadily and methodically built up into a reserve or territorial army. Such an immense military effort would have done credit to any nation. It was all the more meritorious in that it was done with scarcely any money. Nearly all the training of the National Guard was voluntary and unpaid. Only

PLATE 21

King Husain presenting a medal for gallantry to a warrant officer
of the 2nd Infantry Regiment, Arab Legion

The author with a group of young officers of the Arab Legion artillery after lunching in their mess

PLATE 22

when away from their homes in a two months' camp did the men of the National Guard receive £2 a month. At the same time, in Jordan, an unskilled labourer could earn £6 a month.

To create an army requires years and years of detailed, monotonous and steady labour, but of this, as I have said, the Arab civilian was unaware. Politicians still constantly urged the issue of rifles to refugees "to reconquer Palestine".

* * * * *

Nineteen hundred and fifty-four appeared to be the worst year we had yet experienced with Israel since 1948. Moreover, her boycott of the Mixed Armistice Commission and the Local Commanders' Agreement[1] meant that we no longer had any contact with her. Since Israel could no longer protest to the Mixed Armistice Commission, she began to announce her complaints through the so-called "Israel Army Spokesman". She had lost, by this method, the opportunity of securing the Mixed Armistice Commission's endorsement for such of her complaints as investigation proved to be justified. But, on the other hand, as the Israel Army Spokesman's claims were not investigated, she was able to make the most of them without fear of exposure.

We noticed at this time a feature which seemed somewhat sinister, from the Jordan point of view. The revolutionary government had already seized power in Egypt, and frontier incidents in Gaza were increasing. Of ten incidents complained of in the first week of September 1954 by the Israel Army Spokesman, nine were close to Gaza and only one, a rather nebulous one, was near the Jordan demarcation line. Yet, when it suited their book to do so, the Israelis ceased to differentiate and denounced ten Arab incidents. They then proceeded to carry out reprisals against Jordan.

On the night of September 1st to 2nd, the Israeli army attacked the Jordan village of Beit Liqya, four kilometres on the Jordan side of the demarcation line. The Israeli force was divided into four portions.

A force of between one and two companies of infantry attacked the village itself after dark. The village National Guard, commanded by a regular N.C.O., defended the village and repulsed the attack. The retreating Israelis abandoned considerable quantities of small-arms ammunition, hand grenades and explosives.

The Israelis realized that Arab Legion reinforcements might come

---

[1] The Local Commanders' Agreement was designed to decentralize the settlement of local frontier incidents, by allowing Israeli and Jordanian local commanders to meet at specified points on the demarcation line and settle minor disputes direct. Jordan constantly pressed for decentralization, whereas Israel wished all disputes to be handled centrally by the Mixed Armistice Commission in Jerusalem. Experience proved that such local agreements did relax tension, but Israel continued to oppose them.

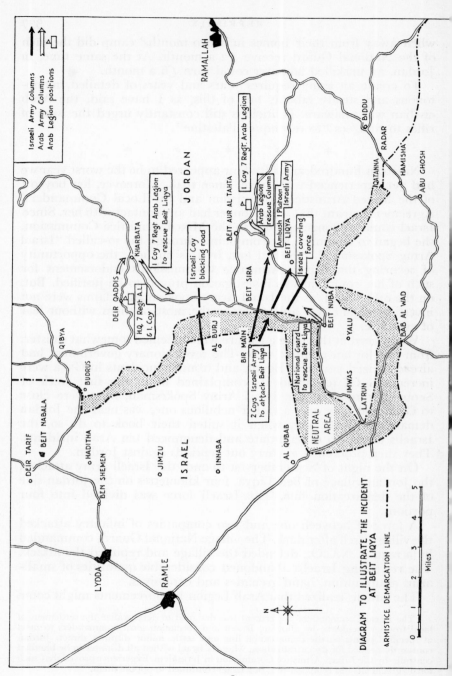

DIAGRAM TO ILLUSTRATE THE INCIDENT
AT BEIT LIQYA

either from Beit Aur al Tahta or from Deir Qaddis. They accordingly mined the road from Beit Aur al Tahta and placed a platoon in
ambush covering the mine. In actual fact, as soon as the attack on
Beit Liqya developed, a platoon of the Arab Legion came down
this track to rescue the village. The leading vehicle was blown up
by the mine. Two Arab Legion soldiers were killed, one wounded,
and three, in a dazed condition after the explosion, were captured
by the Israelis.

A company of Israeli infantry was placed astride the road from
Deir Qaddis. A force of Arab Legion coming from Deir Qaddis
engaged this company which, after a brief exchange of fire, retired
across the demarcation line.

The National Guard at Beit Nuba heard the battle at Beit Liqya.
Led by their regular N.C.O., a section of National Guardsmen set
out to help Beit Liqya. They ran into an Israeli covering force, and
engaged them. The regular Arab Legion N.C.O. was wounded.

Judging from the quantities of ammunition, hand grenades and
explosives abandoned by the retreating Israelis, a major destruction
raid on Beit Liqya was intended, possibly on the lines of Qibya.
From one point of view, the Beit Liqya action was most encouraging.
Firstly, of course, the Israelis (with a regular battalion) failed to get
into a village defended only by the National Guard. Although the
Arab Legion had suffered casualties, the fact that the enemy attack
on the village failed meant victory. In addition, all these small Arab
Legion and National Guard detachments had taken action without
awaiting orders. All had gone out on a dark night to look for the
enemy.

At an emergency meeting of the Mixed Armistice Commission,
Israel was condemned for a flagrant breach of the armistice agreement.

In Beit Liqya, one old woman was wounded in the hand. Otherwise all the casualties were Arab Legion. They had given their lives
or suffered wounds to save the civilian inhabitants of the village.
That was as it should be.

*　　*　　*　　*　　*

In a debate in the Israeli Parliament following on the Beit Liqya
incident, the Israeli government admitted for the first time its policy
of reprisals. It had in reality already followed this policy for four
years, but had hitherto attempted to deny or conceal it. Public
opinion in the United States and Britain was shocked by this
admission.

There were doubtless many people in Israel who believed that
reprisals provided the only means by which Israel could live. If an
Israeli is murdered, they said, and Arabs are not immediately

murdered in revenge, then the Arabs will go on murdering us until we are exterminated. Superficially, this argument may sound logical, but in reality the world does not run on these lines. Hate only breeds more hate.

In so far as Jordan was concerned, however, the situation was different from that between Israel and Egypt. For the Egyptian revolutionary government was already organizing infiltration and sabotage in Israel, and was beginning to boast of the fact. In Jordan, on the contrary, the government was making every effort to prevent it, despite being hampered in its measures against infiltration by several factors I have already explained: firstly, the presence of half a million destitute refugees, made such by Israel herself; secondly, the fact that extremist organizations in Syria, Lebanon and Egypt, in some cases subsidized by the Saudi government, were actively supporting and fomenting infiltration into Israel through Jordan. The unjust result of the Israeli policy of reprisals was that the Jordan frontier villages suffered, whereas nearly all the infiltrators were refugees, living in camps out of reach of Israeli attack.

Between these two fires, the Arab Legion, army, police and National Guard alike, toiled day and night. The whole frontier was covered with a network of patrols, pickets, and ambushes. These faced both ways—to resist Israeli reprisal raids from the west, and to prevent and arrest Arab infiltrators coming from the east. All ranks of the Arab Legion and an increasing number of civilians (particularly from the frontier villages) took a realistic view of their situation. One and all regarded Israel as their bitterest enemy and oppressor, but at the same time they realized that she was immensely stronger than Jordan, probably than all the Arab armies together. This strength was due to money, financial support from world Jewry and particularly remittances from the United States. Jordan, barren, bankrupt and burdened with refugees, could not hope to match Israel's immense superiority.

In view of this situation, to encourage infiltrators to murder an occasional Jew was ridiculous. Such pin-pricks could do Israel no serious harm, but might well give her a pretext to attack Jordan in overwhelming strength. Were that to happen, only Britain could save Jordan from destruction. But if Jordan had deliberately encouraged pin-prick raids, then British support might not be forthcoming. The only reasonable policy to follow, therefore, was to work for a quiet border, to rely on British help if Israel should attack, and to hope for better days.

It may of course be argued that Jordan should have made peace. Such a course was for her impossible. It was the irony of Jordan's position that she almost alone endured the material damage inflicted on the Arabs by Israel. She was by far the poorest of the major

Arab countries and had the smallest population. She had been cut off from the sea and had lost all power to trade. She had half the refugees. Yet the bigger Arab countries, who had suffered no injury except to their pride, denounced Jordan as lukewarm, while doing little or nothing to help her—in some respects deliberately trying to destroy her. If Jordan had attempted to make peace, the other Arab countries would have turned upon her, if only by urging the refugees to rebel against the traitor.

One-third of the people in Jordan were destitute refugees, kept alive by the United Nations, who issued them with rations and provided schools and medical care. Many Jordanians believed that UNO paid for these people only because it was afraid they would otherwise cause trouble, or even war. But if peace were concluded, it was feared, UNO would be relieved of anxiety and would cease to pay for the refugees.

Israel could possibly have obtained peace from Jordan in 1949 or 1950, if she had been prepared to make any gesture of concession. But King Abdulla could not make peace, against the opposition of the other Arab States, unless he had valuable gains to show for it.

Ever since then, Israel, on the international stage, claimed that she held out the hand of peace to the Arabs. But at the same time her politicians assured the Israeli public that no concessions would be made. The Jordanians saw no use in incurring the resentment of the other Arab States, if they did not thereby derive any advantage.

Finally, Israel herself complained that her economy was stunted by the Arab trade boycott, and that lack of money prevented her from further expanding her armed forces. The Jordanians concluded that to make peace with Israel, and agree to trade, would thereby enable Israel yet further to increase her armed strength, already so greatly in excess of that of Jordan.

In brief, the benefits of peace were so questionable that it seemed to Jordan to be folly further to exacerbate her relations with the other Arab States, in the hopes of securing them.

*   *   *   *   *

In a certain sense, Israel's attitude was comprehensible. Although, in 1954, she was still militarily stronger than all the Arab States put together, she was apprehensive of the future. Year by year, she was intensifying Arab hatred against herself. Even non-Arab Muslim nations, such as Persia and Pakistan, were becoming alienated from her. How long could she retain her precarious foothold? Yet, while all Israelis agreed in desiring long-term security, they were sharply divided on the question of how to obtain it. Israeli speakers were probably sincere in claiming that Israel desired peace, but they stipulated that it must be peace on their terms. There was no indication of her willingness to compromise in order to attain it.

Meanwhile, however, the needs of day-to-day security, in the opinion at least of Mr. Ben Gurion and his party, necessitated a policy of vigorous—not to say ruthless—reprisals. "Force is the only argument which Arabs understand" was constantly proclaimed as an axiom in Israel.

There is no race in the world which understands only force as an argument. It is ironical to think that such a statement should be made in Palestine, where the Sermon on the Mount was pronounced.

* * * * *

A constant source of irritation throughout the years from 1948 to 1956 was the Israeli position in the Hadassa Hospital and the Hebrew University. It will be recollected that the massive buildings which housed these institutions were built on Mount Scopus, a low ridge overlooking the Arab city of Jerusalem from the north-east. (See the map on page 122.)

I have already related how the Jordan government, in 1948, had been warned that any attempt to attack them would provoke indignation in America. It will be remembered that Count Bernadotte had arranged for the area to be demilitarized and handed over to the sole control of the United Nations, although the Israelis were permitted to leave a party of civil police to prevent pilfering. The Count promised shortly to replace them by United Nations police, but after his murder UNO lost its authority.

We soon discovered, from intelligence sources, that the men in Hadassa were not police at all, but a company of infantry. An Israeli prisoner of war, captured in a frontier incident, gave a detailed statement. He told how the infantry company to which he belonged had been brought to police headquarters in Jerusalem, where they had been dressed in police uniforms. They had then been sent as "civil police" to relieve the garrison of Hadassa. (Reliefs took place once a fortnight on a convoy which passed through our lines.) The "police" in Hadassa, the prisoner admitted, were always a company of regular infantry. Then one night a platoon of Israeli infantry endeavoured to infiltrate through our lines to the Hadassa. Ten men of this platoon were acting as armed escort, while the remaining twenty were carrying three-inch and two-inch mortar ammunition in packs on their backs. The party ran into an Arab Legion patrol, an engagement took place in the dark, and the Israelis retired hurriedly back to their front line, having dropped most of the mortar ammunition. Next day, the United Nations observers were taken to see it.

The Hadassa was supposed to have been demilitarized—that is, stripped of weapons, except those of the "police". If there were no mortars in the buildings, why did the Israeli army want to smuggle in the ammunition?

The garrison were alleged to be constructing defences, although they were supposed to be civilian police, whose sole duty was to prevent pilfering. We asked the United Nations Chief of Staff to make a personal inspection of the area, but when he arrived to do so, he was refused admittance.

"This is Israeli territory," said the commander of the police. "I cannot admit you without an order from the Israeli government."

We and the United Nations held copies of the agreement, signed by the Israeli commander in 1948, admitting that the Hadassa area would be under the sole jurisdiction of the United Nations. This result produced considerable bitterness in Jordan and in the Arab Legion. It would have been comparatively easy to capture the place in 1948. We were tricked into not doing so by the plan to demilitarize the area and hand it over to the sole jurisdiction of UNO. As a result of the weakness of the latter, the position remained a military fortress behind our lines, garrisoned by Israeli infantry, who made little or no attempt at concealment. They frequently fired rifle shots, or bursts of Bren gun, into the Arab city, and were still doing so at intervals when I left Jordan in 1956.

XXI

Seditions at Home

Democracy is on trial in the world, on a more colossal scale than ever before.
Dole

When Tzu Lu asked what constituted a man's duty to his prince, the Master said: "Never deceive him and then you may boldly withstand him."
Conversations of Confucius

XXI

SEDITIONS AT HOME

INTERNAL political strife was to end the year 1954, which had begun with increased tension with Israel. Soon after the King's inauguration in the spring, he had appointed Fawzi Pasha al Mulqi to be Prime Minister. When the King had been at Sandhurst, Fawzi Pasha had been Jordanian Ambassador in London, and had thus become His Majesty's friend and confidant. He was a comparatively young man, and was studying at Liverpool University at the beginning of the Second World War.

Fawzi Pasha had modern ideas about democracy. He was in favour of freedom of speech, freedom of the Press, independence of the judiciary and all those basic principles on which British freedom is founded. Not only did he approve of these principles, but he set himself to pass laws depriving his own, and any future, government of the right to deny them.

No word in human speech has aroused more enthusiasm or commanded more profound devotion than the word "freedom". But it is always risky to transfer the customs of one nation bodily to another, without regard to local conditions. In a country where the masses are almost entirely ignorant of the world at large, and where everybody (even the rulers) are lacking in experience, unexpected results may ensue from the application of what, in England, would be regarded as the most elementary human rights.

In the Arab countries, there is no tradition of public service. Anybody who enters politics does so with the sole aim of achieving personal gain or advancement. There is nothing dishonourable in such aims—most men enter business or a profession with no other objects. But a true democracy requires also numbers of responsible citizens who are prepared to engage in political activities in order to serve their country alone, and for no personal motive. Where such do not exist, politics become the monopoly of a small class of professional politicians. Such people are only too often apt to forget the public service in the struggle for their personal advancement.

This was the situation in Jordan when Fawzi Pasha introduced his reforms. Freedom of speech and of the Press did not act as a safety valve to enable the public to give voice to their complaints, but merely emboldened the Communists and the fanatical elements to attack all existing institutions. Not that the government had hitherto repressed speech or censored the newspapers. But they had the legal power to do so if it became necessary, and the mere knowledge of this fact did something to restrain the violence of the extremists. Fawzi Pasha's changes, therefore, were in the nature of depriving the government of those reserve powers which they had hitherto possessed in the event of an emergency.

All the extremist parties made great advances during Fawzi Pasha's tenure of office. The Communists, although in theory the party was banned, gained considerable influence. A small number of persons were avowed Communists, and lived underground. They issued a secret newspaper called *Popular Resistance*. This periodical used the violent and abusive language commonly employed by Moscow. The government, but particularly myself, were bloodthirsty criminal reactionaries, ruling by barbaric methods of tyranny, floggings, beatings and shootings. It was couched in such violent terms, and so ridiculously unlike the truth, that it was difficult to believe that it could impress anyone living in Jordan.

A far more insidious approach was that of the fellow-travellers. Britain and America, they pointed out, had created Israel and would inevitably continue to support her, to the final ruin of the Arabs. Why not try Russia for a change? Why not at least frighten the Western Powers by introducing Russia into the Middle East? By playing the Great Powers off against one another, the Arabs could dictate terms to both. Fear of Israel and the question of what to do with half a million Arab refugees were the two problems which dominated life in Jordan. Britain and the U.S.A. had taken no effective action to deal with either. Perhaps Russia would.

In April 1954, as a result of propaganda of this nature, the Jordan Chamber of Deputies unanimously voted to send a telegram of thanks to Mr. Vyshinsky, the Russian representative, for supporting the Arab cause in the United Nations. Political memories are notoriously short. Nobody now remembered that in 1948 Russia and the U.S.A. had recognized Israel within a few hours of the end of the mandate. When the United Nations prohibited the sale of arms to both sides in May 1948, Russia and her satellites had smuggled arms into Israel. At the close of the fighting in 1948, Mr. Ben Gurion had acknowledged that, without Russian help, Israel might well have been overrun. Not only was the shameless opportunism of Russia not appreciated, but by 1954 it was a recognized "fact" that it was the Western Powers which had helped Israel in 1948. This inversion of the truth was possible because Russia worked unceasingly at disseminating her propaganda. Britain never replied, although these libels could have been confuted with ease.

In May 1954, the rapid deterioration of the internal situation had alarmed King Husain. He dismissed Fawzi Pasha, and invited

Taufiq Pasha once more to form a Cabinet. The new Prime Minister was asked to restore the damaged prestige of the government.

The Jordan constitution was modelled on that of Britain. The King had the power to invite any politician to form a government. In Britain, however, the Sovereign is in practice compelled to invite the leader of the strongest political party in the House of Commons. Should the Sovereign invite anyone else, the new government would immediately be defeated in the House and be compelled to resign again. In Jordan, however, there were, properly speaking, no parties. This gave the King considerably more latitude. He might, of course, choose a Prime Minister with whom the Chamber of Deputies refused to work. But here another factor affected the situation.

In the absence of a party system, there were no party funds. Many members spent a great deal of money in the effort to be elected. They hoped to recover their losses, and make a profit, during their period as members. For this purpose, they hoped that Parliament would run its full term. Thus, if the Chamber of Deputies refused to co-operate with the Prime Minister chosen by the King, the latter was able to threaten Parliament with a dissolution. In the present instance, Taufiq Pasha asked the King to dissolve Parliament. A general election was fixed for October 16th.

During the past years a new political factor had appeared in the field, in addition to the Communists and their extreme Nationalist associates. This new element in the struggle was the extreme Muslim religious groups. The "Muslim Brethren" was originally an Egyptian political group, which demanded a return to a primitive Muslim religious government. It was fanatically anti-foreign and anti-Western, and had spread to some extent into other Arab countries. A second, and even more extremist religious group, was called the "Freedom Party". It had been founded by a Palestinian religious teacher, Shaikh Taqi-al-Din al Nebhani. It was narrower and more bitter in its xenophobia than were the Muslim Brethren. Being both advocates of somewhat similar policies, the two parties were not a little jealous of one another. At times, rival preachers contested the right to preach in the same mosque, and the mutual exchange of recriminations during public prayers created scenes by no means edifying to the worshippers. If anything the Freedom Party, being the more violent of the two, tended to steal the thunder formerly wielded by the Muslim Brethren. Both were intensely bitter in their denunciation of the Western Powers, whom they accused of a plot to destroy the Muslim religion.

The Freedom Party seemed mysteriously to be in possession of funds, although it did not collect money in Jordan. Many Jordanians believed that the U.S.A. supported it financially, under the impression that religious fanatics would oppose the Communists. It seems more probable that the Russians were financing it, if indeed it was subsidized. Russia has often supported rival parties at the same time, merely in order to produce anarchy.

Taufiq Pasha took careful measures to ensure the election of the candidates of whom he approved. To some extent, he proposed to "rig" the elections. In reality, of the forty members of Parliament, about thirty-two or thirty-three were always re-elected. They were men with local influence, and the Jordanian elector is more interested in personalities than in politics. Indeed, candidates rarely attempted to offer political programmes to the approval of their constituents. It was over the seven doubtful seats that the contest was to rage.

It is scarcely possible to arrange an election in Jordan in which there will not be foul play. The cheating takes place either at the ballot boxes or during the count. If the government remains absolutely neutral, the extremist parties will make great efforts to secure the appointment of their adherents to take charge of the ballot boxes and to be on the counting committee. If the government proposes to intervene, it will select the officials with care from those it trusts.

The officials on the ballot boxes can work by several different methods. Some of the electors are illiterate, and the officials in charge of the boxes fill in their papers for them. At times, officials on the ballot boxes provide themselves with several thousand papers filled up in favour of the candidates whom they support. An opportunity will almost certainly occur to slip these into the box. Some voters, on the other hand, are undecided, and are pleased to accept the advice of the official.

The procedure for counting also provides an opportunity for cheating. Taufiq Pasha was anxious to secure the election of his candidates, and informed the responsible officials of the fact. I do not think he did more than that. For that matter, senior administrative officials, themselves alarmed at the increase of fanaticism and the loss of prestige of the government, were anxious to secure responsible members of Parliament, and to exclude extremists.

A more complicated issue, from my own angle, was that Taufiq Pasha wished to take advantage of the votes of men of the Arab Legion. There had been some question of debarring soldiers from voting, and I myself tended to favour such a measure. But legal opinion was that such a step would need a change in the constitution. It was accordingly arranged that troops would vote in their barracks or camps. It was obviously not possible to allow all the troops to join the crowds at the polling booths during the election. The country would have been without an army for twenty-four hours. The Prime Minister wished all soldiers to vote for his candidates.

I protested against such a suggestion. Eventually we compromised. It was agreed that soldiers voting would be shown a list of candidates, on which the government's candidates would be marked. No pressure would be used to make them vote for the government's candidates. It is possible that a number of soldiers voted for Taufiq Pasha's men when they saw them marked "Government Candidates". Very few soldiers were interested in politics. The loose employment of the word "government" in Western democracy is always perplexing to Eastern peoples, who have only a vague idea of the working of the whole system. The "government" can mean the cabinet in office at the time, and it can also be used of the whole machinery of government, including the permanent officials and the services. To some simple soldiers, to oppose the government may, by a confusion of thought, have appeared like mutiny.

The results, however, showed that, in most units, no compulsion was used. As was to be expected, such units as workshops voted for rather left-wing candidates, not Taufiq Pasha's nominees. A few soldiers voted Communist. One explained that he did so because the Communist candidate was a doctor who had treated his sick child.

The Jordanian constitution provided for candidates to represent minorities. In certain areas where there was a number of Christians, one or two Christians had to be elected. In Amman, there was a considerable colony of Circassians.

In 1877, hostilities had broken out between Russia and Turkey, and a small war ensued, commonly called the Plevna Campaign. As a result, Russia annexed part of the Caucasus. The inhabitants of the area thus surrendered included both Circassians and Shaishans —two racial groups of the Muslim faith. Some of these refused to remain under the Christian government of the Czar, and migrated to Turkey. The Turks were in constant difficulties in endeavouring to extend their authority over the Arabs. The Caucasian refugees were therefore settled in Syria and Trans-Jordan, in the hope that they would constitute, in these wild Arab tribal areas, a community loyal to Turkey. A number of Circassians settled in Amman, which, in the 1870's, was an uninhabited ruin.

Since Amman became the capital of Trans-Jordan (and then of Jordan), it grew to be an Arab city, but the Circassian community still remained and was entitled to two Circassian members of Parliament to represent it. For many years, Saeed Pasha al Mufti had been leader of the Circassian community, and had sat in Parliament as one of the Circassian members. Most unfortunately, a few days before the election, Taufiq Pasha quarrelled with Saeed Pasha. The Prime Minister sent for me and asked me to delete the name of Saeed Pasha from the list of government candidates and substitute that of another Circassian candidate. From our point of view, this made no great difference. Saeed Pasha remained on the list of candidates and soldiers were free to vote for him or not. All that happened was that the designation of government candidate was removed from his name and appended to that of another Circassian. The result, as will be seen later, was unfortunate.

Taufiq Pasha was convinced that the measures which he had taken would ensure his success at the polls. His predecessor, Fawzi Pasha, had made considerable capital out of his support of the right of free speech; Taufiq Pasha was consequently unwilling to limit this right during the period before the election. The only people who profited were the Communists. Their candidates, especially in Amman, had no chance whatever of being elected. But untrammelled free speech for three months was a priceless opportunity for subversive propaganda. As Communism was still illegal, the Communists called themselves the "National Front".

The cleverest and most active member of the party was a doctor, originally from Damascus, called Abdul Rahman Shgair. Psychologists may trace the reason for his intense bitterness to the fact that he was a partial cripple. This man made speeches daily in Amman. In fiery tones, he denounced the wicked, greedy and brutal imperialists, as represented by the U.S.A. and Britain. He advocated almost unmeasured violence, and every speech was an incitement to rebellion. Loudspeakers had been fitted outside his headquarters in Amman so that not only those who attended his meetings heard his speeches. His remarks were broadcast in stentorian tones all over the crowded shopping centre of the city. I was returning one evening by car from a day with the troops and, driving through Amman, found such a meeting in progress. A dense crowd of refugees and workmen blocked the street. Abdul Rahman Shgair was speaking on the flat roof of a house, but a loudspeaker in the street was blaring out his words in almost deafening tones. As I drove slowly through the crowd, he was shouting to his audience to drive out or exterminate the brutal colonizers. His words were punctuated by loud outbursts of applause from the crowd in the street.

Many people represented to Taufiq Pasha the dangers of allowing free rein to Communist agitation, especially in a country containing half a million refugees. But he was deaf to their advice. He was confident that Abdul Rahman Shgair would not be elected, and thought therefore that he could gain credit for allowing free speech, without any injurious result.

The day of the elections, October 16th, duly dawned. We had brought two infantry regiments from Zerqa and had concealed them in a fold in the hills outside Amman in case of trouble. There were no government forces in the streets except the civil police.

PLATE 23

The author with the officers of the 9th Infantry Regiment, Arab Legion

PLATE 24

King Husain on his throne on the occasion of the opening of the
session of the Jordan Parliament, October 21st, 1954

Somebody had told Saeed Pasha al Mufti that Taufiq Pasha had ordered the army to vote against him. As already narrated, this was not correct, but presumably Saeed Pasha thought that it meant that he could not be elected. Sooner than suffer defeat, he announced the withdrawal of his candidacy, claiming that he had information that the election results in Amman were to be falsified. Following his example, most of the opposition candidates in Amman also withdrew. In a completely free and open contest they would probably in any case have been defeated. To withdraw on the grounds of foul play thus provided them with an excuse to cover their discomfiture.

The chief misfortune was the quarrel of Taufiq Pasha with Saeed Pasha, for the latter was an eminently moderate and reputable public man, and one greatly loved and respected in the town. The violence of personal feuds amongst these passionate people, quite apart from political opinions, is illustrated by what followed. For politically, Taufiq Pasha and Saeed Pasha held similar views.

Shortly after Saeed Pasha announced the withdrawal of his candidacy, two or three rifle shots rang out in the town. Who fired these shots was never established, but it was strongly rumoured that Saeed Pasha's supporters were responsible. Other shots followed at intervals. Arabs have a habit of firing their rifles into the air. Perhaps this was what they were doing, merely to create tension or panic.

The police had appeared in the streets to ascertain the cause of the shooting, when suddenly a hail of stones and rocks poured down on their heads from the flat roofs of the tall buildings in the centre of the city. Within a remarkably short time, barricades of rocks were being erected across the streets at various places in the town. In most cases the barricades were erected at points where there were high houses on either side of the street. The roofs of these houses were suddenly seen to be manned by men armed with stones, which they were prepared to throw down at the police advancing to remove the barricades. We were unexpectedly faced with what was evidently a most carefully planned and deliberate insurrection. Subsequent investigations revealed that heaps of stones had been previously accumulated at certain key points. While the riot was in progress, trucks laden with stones were seen driving in from the country to the centre of the city. It was no coincidence that when police called at the house of Abdul Rahman Shgair, he was not to be found. Two days later we heard that he was in Damascus. There could be no doubt that he had organized the whole outbreak and escaped across the border just before the trouble began.

As soon as the first shots rang out in the town, I spoke on the wireless to the two waiting regiments, and ordered one company of infantry into the city. While, however, they were coming, the barricades were erected and the stone-throwing from house-tops began. We then called for the remainder of the two regiments. The first company drove into the city in its vehicles across the main square and into the narrow street called Wadi Seer Street. On one side of this street lay the massive buildings of the General Post Office, on the other a large block of buildings containing shops and flats. On both sides of the street, the buildings were four storeys high. Suddenly a hail of rocks rained down on the troops. Unable to see an enemy, they could not use their weapons. They were glad to take refuge in the General Post Office.

Taufiq Pasha had been on the telephone several times in some agitation. "Where is the army? What are you doing?" he asked. "Everything is in confusion."

"We have ordered them in," I replied. "They will soon be here. Nothing can be done till they come. Then we will soon restore order."

Taufiq Pasha was obviously in great anxiety. He kept ringing up. We could only assure him that the troops were on the way. The central square of Amman and the main streets and shops lay at the bottom of a steep narrow valley. High buildings, near-skyscrapers, filled this valley and dominated the narrow streets. The police and first infantry company were in these streets, the rioters on these skyscrapers. But the hills on either side of the valley commanded the skyscrapers. The brigade commander, to whom belonged the two regiments, had been at Arab Legion headquarters since early morning, and had watched all these developments. He now spoke to his regiments by wireless and ordered them to occupy the hills overlooking the valley. Suddenly the rioters on the roofs in the valley looked round and saw troops lining the hills looking down on them, just as they were looking down on the police in the streets.

Within a few minutes the rioters were flying in panic. Shots continued to ring out at intervals. It was impossible to tell whether they came from the troops or the rioters. Within twenty minutes order was restored. Fortunately, the rioters had not attacked the polling booths. The police succeeded in guarding all the ballot boxes. The election proceeded, and was completed by six o'clock in the evening.

When the results of the elections became known, the claim that the government had falsified the voting did not appear to be fully confirmed. In Nablus, a Communist ("National Front") candidate was elected, in spite of strenuous government opposition. In Tulkarm, a member of the extreme Muslim Freedom Party was successful. One extremist in Irbid, one in Jerusalem, and one in Ramallah, were not elected, whether by falsification or not could not be ascertained. In Amman, the usual candidates were elected, with the exception of Saeed Pasha al Mufti, who had withdrawn. Had he not withdrawn, he would probably have been elected also.

If, therefore, the government did falsify the elections, they thereby gained only three seats in a Chamber of forty members. In practice, probably very little falsification, if any, took place. But the charge of "rigging" the elections was a godsend to the extremists, the Communists and the unsuccessful candidates. An intense propaganda campaign was launched to besmirch the honour of the new Cabinet and Parliament.

* * * * *

The bedouins have a story which they love to tell, and which they call "The man who feasted in two villages". The most important Muslim feast of the year is that called "The Feast of Sacrifice". On it, Muslims eat a kind of semi-ritual meal, as people do in England on Christmas Day. And, as in England, some eat it at midday and some in the evening. The hero of our story worked out a plan by which he hoped to have two "Christmas dinners" on the feast day.

He accordingly arrived just before lunch at a certain village, where he had heard that they usually ate their feast at midday. To his chagrin, he was told that that year they had decided to have it in the evening.

He had already decided to dine at a neighbouring village, where it was customary to celebrate the feast in the evening. Arriving there at sunset, he was disappointed to hear that, on this occasion, they had held their festive dinner at midday. Thus he had no dinner at all, but the reputation he acquired for greediness made him the butt for everyone's laughter. The narrator of the story always ends up by remarking sagely, "He gained no good but received all the blame."

The same remark might indeed be applied to Taufiq Pasha and his allegedly "falsified" election, which produced a Parliament almost identical with the one dissolved. The Prime Minister indeed had gained no good, but he duly received all the blame.

Taufiq Pasha, however, was too agile a politician to allow matters to rest at that. The story that all soldiers had been ordered to vote for government candidates received wide circulation. Moreover, the army had come in and dispersed the rioters by opening fire. Ten persons had been killed—whether all by fire from the troops was uncertain. In both these cases, the Arab Legion was involved. The Prime Minister was widely blamed for ordering the Arab Legion to vote for his candidates, and for the alleged brutality of the soldiers in firing at civilians. He soon developed a technique of smiling deprecatingly, and saying, "You know who commands the army." He would then relapse into silence, as though he was unwilling to say more. In this way was built up the tradition that it was I who falsified the elections, and then ordered savage soldiers to massacre the crowd. Newspaper articles to this effect enjoyed quite a vogue in Beirut and Damascus, where the fugitive Communist Abdul Rahman Shgair never tired of telling the tale.

Taufiq Pasha was the best Prime Minister Jordan produced. His mind was clear and he had a firm grasp of the essentials for the peace and security of the country. He, almost alone of Jordan Prime Ministers, had firmness, and a certain quality of moral courage. As a national leader, his great fault was that he was all intelligence, with no emotions. He disliked meeting people, never went to social functions and never visited the out-districts. There was something cold and calculating about him. To command devotion, warmer and more human qualities are necessary.

From my own point of view, he had the disadvantage that, when he made a mistake, he always placed the blame on his subordinates. In 1948, he had agreed that we could not defend Lydda and Ramle, but when they fell he had passed on the blame to the Arab Legion and myself. He himself had checked every word of the Rhodes armistice agreement before authorizing its signature. When, however, there was a public outcry, he professed to have known nothing about the terms, and suggested that the Arab Legion had acted alone—perhaps on orders received by me from London. Now in the matter of the elections, he repeated his old technique. I bore him no ill will—he was a politician, I was a soldier. These were presumably the tricks of his trade.

Yet perhaps I was too philosophical on the subject. Everybody knew that, if I had done all these things, I had no personal axe to grind. My actions were therefore attributed to secret orders from London. This theme was admirably suited to the Communists, who were thereby enabled to depict me as the tool of imperialism. For that matter, Taufiq Pasha had no hesitation in excusing his own actions by dark hints of "foreign pressure"—usually understood to be British interference. In practice, the British government never interfered in Jordan's affairs and scarcely ever even made a suggestion. Indeed, Britain also was not unlike the man who wanted two Christmas dinners—she failed to protect her interests but was blamed for everything which went wrong.

*   *   *   *   *

The fact that the troops opened fire on October 16th, 1954, broke a record of thirty-three years. From the creation of Jordan in 1921 to the elections in October 1954, no soldier or policeman in Trans-Jordan or Jordan had ever fired a single shot at a civilian crowd. In

Palestine, in Lebanon, in Damascus, in Baghdad, in Cairo riots, *coups d'état* and revolts were endemic. Syria and Saudi Arabia had suffered complete rebellions. Palestine was in chaos from 1936 to 1939. But in Trans-Jordan there had been none of this. During the thirty years from 1921 to 1951, the stability had been due to the personality of King Abdulla; for three years after his death this tradition survived. From October 1954 onwards, Jordan was to become just one more unstable, passionate, blood-stained Arab country.

XXII

Planning for Wars

Can loyalty refrain from admonition?   Confucius

Advice is seldom welcome: and those who want it the most always like it the least.   Lord Chesterfield, *Letters to his Son*

To lead an untrained people to war may be called throwing them away.   Confucius

PLANNING FOR WARS

W E devoted a great part of our time to planning. We had so many possible crises before us, were surrounded by so many enemies. On a length of nearly four hundred miles on our western border, an aggressive Israel was an ever-present menace. Syria on our north, and Egypt to the south regarded us with constant suspicion and jealousy, because we did not keep step with their emotional nationalism. Not that Jordan was any less patriotic than the others. But we endeavoured to keep our feet on the ground, and follow a prudent and practical course amid so many dangers. On the south-east, Saudi Arabia regarded us with envy and hostility, because the Saudi and Hashemite dynasties were rivals for supremacy. To the east, Iraq should have been our ally, but seemed to offer singularly little practical support. Neither France nor the United States was particularly cordial towards Jordan. The former was anxious to regain influence in Lebanon and Syria, while America favoured the rival Saudi dynasty. Britain was indeed Jordan's only reliable ally, but she was under constant attack by Palestinians as having been the cause of the ruin of their country.

Generally speaking, we appeared to be threatened by three possible forms of attack.

Firstly, a major war, involving Russia, in which the attack on Jordan would probably come from Iraq or Syria.

Secondly, a full-scale war with Israel, aiming at the destruction of Jordan.

Thirdly, the day-to-day frontier raid or incident.

I had never before taken a leading part in technical military planning, and the results achieved were to me a revelation. There is indeed no profound science needed for the purpose. It is merely the product of care and method. But I found it nevertheless extraordinary that the relative value of alternative plans, which could be the cause of heated debate before the planning stage, should emerge so plainly after it.

Planning consists firstly in appointing a planning staff who have nothing else to do. They will then methodically sit down and list all the eventualities liable to arise. Then they write down the possible protagonists—allies and enemies—with the military, air and naval potentials of each in detail, possibly followed by their financial and economic assets. Courses open to ourselves and our allies, and the alternatives open to the enemy, must then be considered. By this time, certain main features of the situation are probably beginning to appear. Before the whole process is completed, in almost every case, it will become obvious that one course, and one alone, is the correct one. Hard facts and figures will have destroyed the many other alternatives so heatedly debated before the main study was carried out. The final stage of the process is to hold a war-game in which officers, acting as the enemy, are detailed to make the plan with which the other side will confront our own. Many omissions or errors of detail are often revealed in this practical test.

The extraordinary clarification of thought which resulted from this detailed planning amazed me. I have, since then, never ceased to marvel at the fact that the great democracies seem so often to be caught unawares by an international crisis, which any technical planning staff would surely have foreseen. As a result, each of the Western allies reacts differently, because no previous plans had been concerted between them. Chaos, a defeat for the free world, and a new triumph for Moscow, have again and again resulted.

*   *   *   *   *

We were less concerned in our planning with a third world war than with a war with Israel. In a world war, our part would be secondary. Moreover, a great war would be unlikely to come overnight. On the other hand, we knew that Israel had perfected extremely detailed plans for secret and rapid mobilization. The smallness of her country, and the fact that most of the inhabitants lived in cities, with excellent road and telephone communications, made it possible for her to mobilize, with almost complete secrecy, in a matter of hours.

Jordan was a far bigger country. Nearly all reservists and National Guards lived in rural districts—some in nomadic tribes. Road communications were only moderate and the telephone system was inadequate. Thus we might well be faced with a major invasion from Israel at only a few hours' notice, whereas we would require several days to mobilize.

The outstanding consideration, in meeting an Israeli invasion, was that the area which we held on the West Bank was a salient connected to the East Bank by a narrow neck (see the map on page 248). The obvious course for Israel to follow was to drive down the Jordan valley from Beisan to Jericho. To facilitate the advance of the Beisan column, parachute troops could be dropped in advance on the Jordan bridges. The Israeli numerical superiority was so great that they could simultaneously have launched a major attack in the city of Jerusalem, which, if it had broken through, would have descended to Jericho and joined the Beisan column and the parachutists.

To meet this decisive threat to the neck of the salient, it was essential to keep a large mobile operational force in the Jordan valley neighbourhood. But as the Jordan valley was more than a thousand feet below sea-level, it was, for a great part of the year, unhealthy and unpleasant to live in. To hold this main reserve force back in Zerqa was nearly as central and was far better for health and training. Moreover, there was also the threat of an Israeli advance to Irbid, and thence through Mafraq to Amman by way of Zerqa.

The antithesis of this full-scale war was the day-to-day series of incidents. The frontier villages were under the constant threat of Israeli night attack. The depots of the Israeli army were only four, five or six miles from the demarcation line, across a dead flat plain, intersected by many first-class roads. The Arab Legion was farther back, in a country of mountains and valleys, connected with many frontier villages only by narrow earth tracks.

Naturally the frontier villages were nervous. Each village demanded a regular company to defend it. But there were two hundred such villages, requiring more companies than existed in the Arab Legion. In any case, even if a company had been placed in every village, Israel still had the initiative. There was nothing to prevent her from attacking a selected village with a brigade. In such circumstances, with all the Arab Legion deployed on the basis of one company per village, no reinforcements would have been available to rescue the doomed village from the fate of a second Qibya. In addition, the deployment of the whole Arab Legion along the demarcation line would have been extremely tempting to Israel. The neck of the salient would have been unguarded.

The policy decided upon was necessarily a compromise. Half the Arab Legion was left in Zerqa, to be ready to hold the neck in the event of a full-scale war. The other half was stationed on the West Bank. Here the greater part of the troops were located near road junctions some miles behind the line, so that they could go to the rescue of any village attacked. A few detachments were placed actually in the front line, at points particularly vulnerable or of special importance. The day-to-day defence of the front-line villages was the duty of the National Guard, under regular Arab Legion officers and N.C.O.s.

This technique of keeping the reserves back from the line, to rescue whatever village was attacked, encountered a special Israeli method of action. Before attacking any village the Israelis sent detachments under cover of darkness to move round behind the objective, and to mine all roads or tracks leading up to the village in question from the rear. Detachments were then posted in ambush, covering the road mines with fire. Only then was the attack launched on the village. When the Arab Legion relief column came driving down the road to rescue the villagers, the leading vehicle was blown up, and any survivors killed by fire from the ambush. It was necessary for us to accept this risk. To have dismounted and examined the road would have involved too much delay, during which the Israelis could have captured the village.

Such was the general outline of the plan, providing at the same time for either a full-scale war or a frontier raid. One problem only remained, and it was eventually to prove our undoing. The dispositions adopted on the West Bank to meet raids on villages assumed the demarcation line to be the "front line", where the enemy would be engaged. But throughout a great part of the front line the demarcation line was in the coastal plain. In the event of a full-scale attack all along the line, any attempt at static defence would allow the Israelis to encircle and annihilate the few isolated detachments in the front line along the plain, then roll up and cut off large portions of the army. In such circumstances, disaster might overwhelm us in three or four days, and Jordan would cease to exist before help could arrive.

It was accordingly decided that should a full-scale Israeli attack be made, our front-line detachments would withdraw to the best line of resistance. A few miles back from the demarcation line in the coastal plain rose the steep rocky slopes of the mountains, the roads running from the plain to the top of the mountains passing through narrow defiles between rocky and tree-clad slopes. Here the regular Arab Legion sub-units would be reinforced by the National Guard, and would take up an organized line of defence, which they would have to hold for perhaps a week. We hoped that, by this time, the intervention of Britain, the other Arab States, the U.S.A. or the United Nations would have turned the scale against Israel.

The principal danger which faced us in executing this plan was the volatile and emotional nature of the people of Palestine. Not only, moreover, were they emotional, but hostile propaganda had done all it could to convince them that we were disloyal; indeed, that we were probably trying to help the Jews. At the same time, they were utterly ignorant of war. When, therefore, our front-line detachments withdrew to their main defensive positions, it was almost certain that the political extremists would convince the public that we were abandoning the country to the enemy from motives of treachery. It was probable that civil disturbances would break out in Jordan, that our line of communications would be cut by rioting mobs, and that our soldiers would be attacked and roughly handled by our own people.

At the same time, the defensive plan depended more and more on employment of the National Guard. But this force did not consist of regulars. It was a citizen army. Would its morale survive an outbreak of popular fury against the regular army?

If the crowds were to riot in Amman, we could spare no troops to restore order. They might overthrow the government, or storm the royal palace, while we were engaged in a desperate battle with the Israeli army. Thus, by an extraordinary irony, the passions of the so-called patriotic extremists were likely to play an important part in giving victory to Israel, the very result to prevent which they claimed to be devoting all their energies.

*　　*　　*　　*　　*

In every modern country the government is aware of and approves the main outline of the military plans prepared by the services against the possibility of war. In 1948, I had contented myself with explaining them to the Prime Minister and the Minister of Defence. When, however, the fall of Lydda and Ramle had provoked public indignation, the Prime Minister evaded all responsibility. The rage and fury of the crowds were directed against the Arab Legion and myself. It therefore seemed to me that if we were in the future to be subjected to a far severer test, it would be advisable to secure the prior approval of the King and Cabinet to the military plans.

I several times asked Taufiq Pasha whether he could arrange for a Cabinet meeting to enable me to explain the outline of our plans. Each time he agreed in principle, but excused himself on the grounds that he was too busy. Months dragged by. It was evident that Taufiq Pasha was not interested—unless, indeed, he preferred not to know, so that he could escape responsibility in the event of a military reverse.

It seemed to me curious that although Jordan was probably in more imminent military danger than any other state, neither the ministers nor the politicians manifested the least interest in the military aspect of the situation. The fact is, I became convinced, that people are interested in varying subjects—money—politics—pleasure—soldiering. When a man has spent many years absorbed in one pursuit, his brain has set in a mould of such thought. He is physically incapable of devoting serious thought to any other subject. Every thought of the politicians was absorbed in politics. They could think of nothing else.

King Husain's eight months at Sandhurst had, however, interested him in military matters. I decided to try with him. At my next audience, I asked His Majesty if I could come to the palace one day with the maps and explain our military plans to him. The proposal seemed to hang fire for a fortnight. Then I enquired again. The King agreed. We discussed who should be present. We agreed on the Prime Minister and the Ministers of Defence and Finance. I emphasized the need for secrecy and that no unauthorized persons should be admitted.

It so happened that the day before that fixed for the discussion of our plans at the palace, the King spent the day with us. We flew early in the morning to Jerusalem airport, and spent the day on the border west and north of Nablus. We visited units and discussed defence problems. I drove in the King's car all day. He chatted cheerfully. When we arrived back at the palace, he thanked me most charmingly and said how much he had enjoyed the day.

Next morning we assembled in the palace, hung up our maps and prepared our papers. The King came in, accompanied by the Cabinet ministers agreed upon. An officer from our Intelligence Branch then gave an appreciation of the Israeli army.

I stood up to explain our plan. When I had spoken for a few minutes, the King suddenly exclaimed: "I had forgotten. Excuse me a minute," and left the room. We waited for his return. A few minutes later he re-entered, accompanied by two young A.D.C.s, some palace officials and a few others.

"Please carry on," he said to me, when these individuals were seated. Such was the result of my exhortation to secrecy.

I concluded my explanation, which occupied a little over an hour, and then sat down. There was a short silence, then the King himself rose, and stepped out in front of the audience.

"I want to say a few things," he remarked. He took a piece of paper from his pocket and began to read, rather nervously.

"I do not agree with any of the plans we have heard," he began. "I will never surrender one hand's-breadth of my country. The army will defend the demarcation line. Then we shall attack. I will sanction no withdrawal." He proceeded to denounce many other "mistakes" in the command of the army. He claimed that officers' promotions were not properly handled, that we were wrong in planning to build a new headquarters, and other points of detail.

"Finally," he said, "we are grateful to the Chief of the General Staff for all the work he has done, but I think now it is time for him to enjoy a rest."

When His Majesty finished his speech, the A.D.C.s and palace officials clapped loudly. There followed a minute or two of tense silence. Then Taufiq Pasha said:

"May I have the text, sir? I will have copies typed, and we will see what action can be taken." We rolled up our maps and papers and withdrew.

* * * * *

This extraordinary scene struck us like a thunderbolt. The King had always been charming to me. Never had he expressed to me a word of criticism. It is true that we had heard stories. When he was in England he had met with students from other Arab countries. He had made a few remarks to various people, seeming to indicate a certain resentment against Britain, but, on the other hand, he seized every opportunity for a holiday in England.

After the King's speech I allowed two days to pass to think it over. I then called on the Prime Minister and asked him what course I should take. He advised me to do nothing, and said that he would discuss the matter with the King.

A few days later, I saw the King myself in the palace. I had made a note of the points to which he had referred in his speech, and I asked his permission to explain each in turn. His attitude was now transformed. He was smiling and friendly. He cut me short and remarked deprecatingly that they were small matters, of no importance.

In practice, his facts were wrong in all his minor criticisms. It was, however, a perplexing feature of the situation that the King obviously listened to rumours or complaints made by junior officers. He assumed such stories to be true, but never asked me for an explanation. I was therefore unaware of what he had heard.

I doubt if any army ever took as much trouble in selecting officers for promotion as did the Arab Legion. Not only were promotion examinations held and confidential reports submitted. In addition, every officer was required to pass successfully a number of courses before each step in rank. Special reports were required from commanding officers. In some doubtful cases a vote was taken of previous commanding officers under whom the officer in question had served.

One major difference of opinion did, however, exist between us and the class of politicians and lawyers in general. The army in Jordan was so new that there was no class of middle-aged educated men in retirement who had served in the army. The educated classes consisted of the professions—doctors, lawyers, schoolmasters, pressmen and, of course, politicians. These were all people whose lives had been passed studying abstract subjects or theories. All were strongly of opinion that a man's value consisted solely in his educational qualifications. There was a strong feeling in the country amongst these intellectuals that the only qualification for the acceptance or promotion of an officer should be his academic standard. This unpractical idea was widely held in Arab countries. In Syria, I was told, all the army officers had university degrees. Why could not we attain the same standard, I was often asked. My reply that the Arab Legion had never lost a battle and the Syrian army had rarely won one was brushed aside.

The King's criticism was partly based on this illusion. To the political theorist such qualities as leadership, bravery, endurance or loyalty did not exist. Two remarkable examples of this fact occurred in 1948. Before the fighting began there were only two officers left in the Arab Legion who were practically illiterate. They were about to be discharged. But once heavy fighting began, one of them, Ghazi al Harbi, was the hero of Jerusalem, the man who led the desperate attacks on Notre Dame de France.

The enemy had occupied Mount Zion immediately after the end of the mandate and before we reached Jerusalem. Our troops, when we arrived, occupied a few buildings on the slope of the hill, completely overlooked by the Israelis. The other uneducated officer, Lieutenant Sari Awwadh, was here in command. When Sari had been three weeks at his front-line post, he was relieved. The next night, however, there was a good deal of shooting and the new relief officer spent all night telephoning for reinforcements. Next day, the battalion commander put Sari back. Such actual experiences of battle persuaded us that university degrees were not the sole qualification of an officer. In confidential reports and re-commendations for promotion knowledge gained only half the marks possible. The other half were allotted for leadership, courage, loyalty and other soldierly qualities. Thus young officers proud of their educational qualifications were annoyed that others of lower academic standards should be promoted with them. In the Arab countries, where education is so new and so rare, intellectual pride is a common and unattractive quality of the young secondary school graduate. It is a form of snobbery which never inspires loyalty in fighting men. When the King complained that the best officers were not always promoted, I realized that he had received complaints from the young intellectuals.

My chief justification for my methods was that they worked. Almost everyone admitted that the Arab Legion was by far the best Arab army. But the politicians were unwilling to admit that this result was due to the methods we employed.

The most important issue at stake, however, was that the King had rejected our plans, and insisted on the deployment of the whole army in a thin line all round the frontier, with orders to every man to die in his place but never retreat. It would, of course, have been possible for us to comply with His Majesty's orders. But if Israel had then attacked, they would have broken through in one or two places and occupied the whole country, while the army still sat deployed in its static positions on the frontier.

It is difficult to visualize a countryside from a map, even for experts. A visit to the ground always proves enlightening. We decided that careful examination of the ground would convince the King that his plan was impossible. To have deployed the whole army along the demarcation line would have meant one soldier about every fifty yards.

King Husain agreed to spend three days in the field. We deployed a considerable number of troops in their battle positions and then took him round to see how they looked. After three exhausting days His Majesty admitted that he was convinced. He never referred to the subject again while I was in Jordan. After my departure, however, he told the Press that my plans for the defence of the country were unsatisfactory—that he had ordered me to change them, but I had refused.

* * * * *

One of the curious features of Palestine, and indeed perhaps of all the northern Arab countries, is the remarkable difference between the people of the towns and the rural population. The tribesmen and villagers make excellent soldiers—the townsmen are rarely martial. Many other surprising contrasts between the two communities strike the observer. Perhaps the fact that these countries, and particularly Palestine, have been so frequently invaded, conquered and garrisoned by other nations, largely accounts for these differences. For foreign rulers usually garrison, and live in, the cities. Thus the urban populations are of mixed descent, while the peasants go on, century after century, intermarrying amongst themselves. A curious contrast in social outlook is revealed in the fact that countrymen in Jordan who become rich, tend to move to the towns and live there. In England, city dwellers who grow wealthy go and live in the country.

The Arab Legion was almost entirely enlisted from countrymen, with the exception of a few specialists like clerks, and a proportion of signals operators and mechanics. The National Guard, perhaps to an even greater extent, consisted of villagers. It had been noticeable that in 1948 many villagers—almost unarmed and completely untrained—had fought with considerable determination against the Jews, but that few, if any, town dwellers had done any fighting.

By law, every Jordanian between twenty and forty was liable to training in the National Guard. But, for lack of money, we could only arm, clothe, feed and equip a very much smaller number. It seemed, therefore, unnecessary and inadvisable to use compulsion— there were always more volunteers than we could train. The volunteers, however, were nearly all countrymen. It was rare for a city dweller to volunteer. The city populations constituted only about one-fifth of the people of Jordan—four-fifths were countrymen.

Ironically, the imitation-British democracy, which was the political system in force, placed almost all political power in the hands of the cities. It was a system strange to the traditions of the country and one in which success depended, to a great extent, on skill in writing and speaking. As a result, the government tended to fall into the hands of lawyers, a profession more inclined to produce theorists than practical men of action. The army was everywhere popular with the rural population from which it was recruited.

I constantly visited the villages and rural areas, both to watch the training of the National Guard, and because nearly four hundred miles of the demarcation line ran through rural areas. Moreover, the loyalty and co-operation of the villages were essential to us for purposes of recruiting. Arab hospitality is often embarrassing. It was difficult to visit a village unless one consented to eat a large meal which occupied two hours and made it difficult to do any work. About once a week, however, I used to lunch in a village, in order to get to know the people and their opinions. I always had a waiting list of invitations. I would usually be accompanied by the district commander of the police, and possibly by the commander of a near-by unit of the Arab Legion or the National Guard. More often than not, the district governor would also be invited. In Palestine, most of the villages are built on hilltops for purposes of defence, and have been in the same place for many thousands of years. The houses are huddled close to one another for the same reason. Isolated houses in the country are rarely to be seen.

The village would probably be approached along an earth track, roughly metalled in places, climbing and twisting across the rocky hills. Sometimes it would pass through olive orchards, and steep hillsides cut in terraces only three to four yards wide, and planted with vines and fig-trees. Round some rocky spur we would come in sight of the village, perched on a little hillock, a jumble of grey stone houses on top of one another, scarcely distinguishable from the weathered grey rocks of the hillside from which the building stone had been quarried. The cars usually had to be left before entering the village, where the houses were so close to one another that the lanes between them were too narrow for vehicles.

In Palestine, most of the men would be crowded round the entrance to the village, with the *mukhtar* or headman standing in front of them. Everybody would want to shake hands, with the result that much shoving and pushing and laughing resulted. In Trans-Jordan, on the East Bank, the proceedings were often less formal. Eventually the *mukhtar* would call "Enough! Enough! Let the guests pass!" and we would be led through the crowd up and down narrow alley-ways between old stone houses to the *mukhtar*'s house.

A heavy wooden door would probably lead into a courtyard,

where hens would be pecking and a horse or cow be tethered by a heap of straw. In a room across the yard women flitted about, smoke bellied out from an unglazed window and a rattle of dishes heralded the approaching meal. We would perhaps be led up an open-air stone staircase to the guest-room, probably the only room on the first floor. While the crowd surged into the yard below, we could snatch a minute to look away over the village and its grey-green olive orchards, over the terraced spurs of the mountains, and across the narrow coastal plain, to where a white line in the distant haze marked the shore of the Mediterranean.

But our host has arrived and is bowing us into the guest-room. *"Sharafu! Sharafu!"* he keeps repeating. "Do us the honour! Do us the honour!"

Arabs are very particular about precedence. The most important person has to sit in the top place, and the other guests arrange themselves down the sides of the room in order of seniority. The senior position has usually been carefully marked by the host before-hand, either with a special chair or a heap of gaudy cushions. In spite of this, however, we make a modest attempt to sit down elsewhere, only to be prevented by the host, who insists on our taking the places of honour. If the district governor is present, he and I can indulge in a little bowing and smiling, each en-deavouring to persuade the other to accept the seat of honour.

Eventually the guests are seated, but meanwhile all the villagers have disappeared. It must, I imagine, be a relic of Turkish days—the custom of leaving important government visitors alone. Petty bureaucrats were perhaps unwilling to debase themselves by ming-ling with mere peasants.

"Where are the village people?" I ask the *mukhtar*.

"They are in another room. Your Excellency can now rest."

"I don't want to rest. I could rest at home. We have all come here to talk with the village people. If they don't come, we won't have any lunch."

Eventually the *mukhtar* gives way, and, thrusting his head out of the door, shouts:

"Ya abu Ahmed!—O father of Ahmed!—Ya abu Suleiman! Ya Hajji Mustapha!"

One by one the elders of the village come in and sit down. The next step is to get them to talk.

"Is it true that this season is going to be bad for the olives?"

Sometimes the conversation would become animated and general, and from talking about crops we would pass on to discussing the National Guard and how to prevent Jewish raids. Sometimes the villagers would be shy or suspicious. In earlier years, I used often to sleep in such villages, and found that, in the evening after dinner, tongues were loosed and life-long friends were made. But after 1948 it was rarely possible to be away from headquarters for a night.

Soon the lunch would begin to appear, whether (in the more simple households) in the form of a mountain of mutton and rice carried on a single great dish—or (amongst the more aspiring) a quantity of varied concoctions on small plates. When all was ready the villagers would stand back to watch us eat and a further struggle would be necessary to persuade them to join us.

"They are standing at your service," the *mukhtar* would explain.

"By Allah, we will not eat unless you eat with us!" we would expostulate. At last the *mukhtar* would give way once more, and nominate some of the older men:

"O father of Salama! O Hamdan! O Hajji Mahmoud!"

After lunch the atmosphere would be freer. The room would perhaps be crowded, requests and complaints would be brought forward.

"O father of Faris! God prolong your life! My son here has passed the sixth class, and wants to be a —— What is it you want to be? . . . Where's the boy gone—here, Mehdi, what is it you want to be? An electrician? An electrician, O father of Faris."

"O father of Faris! There is here an old woman whose son was killed by the Jews! The government will not give her money. By Allah, she has no dinner!"

"O father of Faris! There is here an orphan boy. The Jews killed his father and mother at Ramle. (God destroy their houses!) If possible, could you put him in an army school?"

Now the ice has thawed. Everybody is crowding round, smiling and pushing. The more timid thrust forward pieces of paper bearing their petitions. "O father of Faris! O father of Faris!" But alas! it is already time to go. It will take us three hours to get back to Amman, and I know that four boxes of papers will be awaiting me at home. But when we rise to go, we are greeted by loud protests:

"It's still early! We are all enjoying ourselves!"

At the car, the hand-shaking recommences. Smiling faces throng round us. Some enquire when we shall come again. Others remind us of their various cases:

"O Pasha! Don't forget my son Mehdi!"

"O Pasha! Remember the orphan who wants to go to school!"

At last we get into the car, the *mukhtar* gives us a final hand-shake, the escort shouts: "Make way, O people!" and once more we are winding through the olive groves, and looking out over the hills and valleys to where the evening sun will soon be setting in a golden glory over the calm Mediterranean Sea.

XXIII

Egyptian Leadership

Thou trustest upon the staff of this bruised reed, even upon Egypt, on which if a man lean, it will go into his hand, and pierce it.

II Kings xviii. 2 1

The practice of politics in the East may be defined by one word— dissimulation.

BENJAMIN DISRAELI

Man is a creature who lives not upon bread alone, but principally by catch-words.

ROBERT LOUIS STEVENSON

XXIII

EGYPTIAN LEADERSHIP

FOR more than two hundred years, Britain has regarded as a vital interest the power to come and go across the Middle East. Her need for free transit originated with her growing interests in India. It increased as time went on, and she not only acquired interests also in Malaya and China, but sister nations came into existence in Australia and New Zealand. Britain had no interest in the Arab countries themselves. She was happy that Turkey should rule them. She was afraid only that some hostile Great Power might occupy them and bar her passage. Lord Palmerston had expressed the attitude of his country in a famous speech in the House of Commons:

"We do not want Egypt or wish it for ourselves," he said, "any more than any rational man with an estate in the north of England and a residence in the south would have wished to possess the inns on the North Road. All he could want would have been that the inns should be well kept, always accessible, and furnishing him, when he came, with mutton chops and post horses."

If Britain thought this right of transit to be vital to her, other Great Powers likewise believed that to block this route would ruin her. In every great war, her enemies tried to destroy her by occupying the Middle East and denying her passage. Britain, a small over-populated island, has been obliged for more than two hundred years to live on commerce and navigation. Without these, the British Isles cannot support their population. Thus to her, more than to any other country, it is important that the trade routes of the world be free and open. For the greater part of the period, she kept them open herself with her fleet. But it is one of Britain's chief services to the world that her power was never used exclusively for her own interests. The trade routes which she kept open were free to all.

Her understanding with Turkey was to the mutual benefit of both parties: without British support, Turkey would have been partitioned by other Great Powers; in return, to offer transit facilities to Britain across the Middle East cost her nothing. It was not until the beginning of the present century that this amicable understanding came to an end. Britain, out of fear of an aggressive Germany, allied herself with Russia, the hereditary enemy of Turkey. The latter, in turn, joined Germany. As a result, Britain entered the First World War in the situation which she had sought so long to avoid—

with Germany, a major enemy Power, dominant in the Middle East. No sooner did Turkey declare war, than a Germano-Turkish army advanced from Palestine to seize the Suez Canal.

As soon as Turkey entered the war, Britain opened negotiations with the Arabs, through the Sherif Husain of Mecca, a lineal descendant of the Prophet Muhamad. In December 1915, an agreement was concluded, in which Britain promised after the war to support the creation of a great Arab State.[1] The object of this agreement was doubtless to perpetuate, with the new Arab State, an understanding similar to that which had so long been in existence with Turkey. It was an arrangement which, had it succeeded, would have been equally beneficial to both parties. The new Arab State would have been in need of much help and advice which it could have obtained in exchange for the right of transit, which would have cost the Arabs nothing.

It was a broad and statesmanlike conception. Such an Arab government, could it have been created, would have been strong enough with our support to resist domination by Germany or Russia. To create it would have required much technical assistance, which Britain could readily have supplied. This wise far-seeing plan was ruined by the introduction of the Jews to Palestine, and the French conquest of Syria.

In 1945, Britain hoped to return to a similar policy by creating a bloc of Arab States in treaty relations with her. The Arab League resulted. In this instance, Egypt, which was not included in the Arab countries in the agreement with Sherif Husain, was accepted in the Arab League. Indeed, not only was she accepted, but she succeeded in establishing herself as the leader. The Arab League charter included a clause that the headquarters of the League would be in Cairo and its Secretary-General would be an Egyptian. Under Egyptian leadership, the Arab League attacked Israel, and once again the Jewish problem destroyed any hope of co-operation with the West.

The U.S.A. and Britain had then attempted in unison to build up an organization which they had named M.E.D.O. (Middle East Defence Organization). It was to be a group of Middle East governments agreed to resist Communist infiltration or domination from Russia. But the Arab League, under Egyptian leadership, was more concerned with Israel than with Russia. They stipulated an acceptable solution of the Palestine problem, as a pre-condition to co-operation with the West. But Jewish influence, particularly in the U.S.A., was apparently too strong to enable the Great Powers to coerce Israel into giving up anything she had conquered.

If, however, Egypt, Syria and Jordan were more concerned with

[1] See Chapter I, page 24.

Israel than with Russia, the dangers of Communism were better appreciated in Iraq. The reason was geographical. The northern frontier of Iraq is only 140 miles from the frontier of Soviet Russia.

In February 1955, Iraq signed an agreement with Turkey, designed to enable the two countries to co-operate to resist Russian domination. Later on, Persia, Pakistan and Britain herself, were to adhere to what was to be known as the Baghdad Pact.

Just as geography led Iraq to sign a defensive pact against Russia while Egypt held back, so geography also had for thousands of years made Egypt and Iraq potential rivals. A great part of the Old Testament consists of an account of the struggles between Assyria or Babylonia (both names for what we now call Iraq) and Egypt. Israel, Judah, Lebanon and Syria, the smaller Middle East countries, were merely incidental to this struggle. Their position indeed resembled that of Belgium, Holland and Luxembourg, when France and Germany were at war. Egypt and Iraq are still, as in the Old Testament, the biggest of the northern Arab countries, and geography has made them competitors for leadership of the group.

When therefore Iraq, on her individual initiative, signed the Baghdad Pact in 1955, the Egyptian government was immediately roused to resentment. Egypt was jealous that Iraq should have dared to take an independent course, without awaiting the lead from her. The Egyptian radio stations poured forth a stream of invective against the Iraqi Prime Minister, Nuri Pasha Saeed.

It so happened that, in April 1955, a conference was held at Bandung in Indo-China, called the Conference of Asian and African Nations. The two greatest figures on the occasion were Mr. Nehru of India, and Chou En-Lai, the Communist Prime Minister of China. Jordan amongst others also sent a delegation.

When the Jordan representatives returned from Bandung, one of them gave it as his opinion that we must expect trouble.

"Jemal Abdul Nasser," he said, "was frequently closeted with the Communist Chou En-Lai. I think we shall soon see ominous developments in Egypt."

Colonel Nasser, it would appear, went to Bandung in a spirit of irritation against Iraq. Egypt may well herself have been seriously considering a defensive pact with the West. But now that Iraq had signed one, Colonel Nasser was unwilling to do so—he might be accused of following the lead of Iraq. A new and spectacular policy was necessary to enable Egypt to trump the Iraqi move. At Bandung, Chou En-Lai suggested an Egyptian agreement with the Communist bloc.

Colonel Nasser is personally charming. He is delightfully frank and sincere in appearance, but he is nearly always telling lies. For three or four months after Bandung, the United States and Britain

were deceived by cordial and sincere meetings between their ambassadors and Colonel Nasser. In September 1955, the Czech arms
deal was announced. Czecho-Slovakia had agreed to supply arms to
Egypt. Soon it became apparent that Russia also was contributing.
Colonel Nasser had succeeded in trumping the Baghdad Pact.

It is easy to be wise after the event, but even before 1955 there
were some who deprecated the keenness shown by Britain and
America to secure signatures to a Middle East defence agreement.
A peace-time co-operation against Communist propaganda and
infiltration would have been useful, though such co-operation might
perhaps have been inaugurated without signatures. But a military
alliance with such small countries was of doubtful value. In the
event of another world war, they could scarcely be expected to resist
a Russian invasion alone. If British and American forces arrived in
time, then they would meet the Russian attack, and would be assisted by the local governments, even if no military alliance existed.
Thus many people contended that such agreements, in so far as a
major war was concerned, were valueless. The smaller States would,
in an emergency, bow to whichever Great Power first reached the
scene in sufficient strength.

As against this argument, however, there was a military factor
of vital importance. The smaller States would indeed bow to the
Great Power which first arrived in strength. They had no other
course. The problem then was not so much one of signatures, as one
of planning how to get there quickly.

In former times, when armies moved overseas, they did so accompanied by their weapons and administrative requirements. Today,
the transport of personnel and the transport of material are widely
different problems. The men of whole armies can be flown over seas
and continents in a matter of days, if not hours. But the material
which they need has never before been so difficult to move. The
problem of transporting tanks, guns, vehicles and heavy ammunition
is immense. Not only so, but the maintenance of these weapons in
the field requires an extensive organization of workshops and
stores. If, therefore, either side can pre-position its heavy material
in peace-time, in the theatre of possible operations, so that only the
personnel need be flown out, then that army will be the first in
action when war begins.

But, it may well be argued, even a Great Power will not be able
to afford to pre-position quantities of heavy material in another
country, unless it has an agreement with that country to guard it.
So a signed peace-time agreement may be necessary, not to ensure
that the small power will resist a Russian invasion at the beginning
of another world war, but to ensure that the small country will
receive and guard the heavy material pre-positioned by the Great

Power. This indeed had been the basis of our agreement with Egypt over the evacuation of the Suez Canal Zone. We withdrew our men on condition of leaving our heavy material in the Canal Base.

This is one of those many situations in which insistence on open diplomacy places the free nations of the world at so immense a disadvantage. For Russia has greatly improved on our technique in this direction. When Britain wishes to pre-position heavy material overseas, open diplomatic negotiations are undertaken. If agreement is reached, the exact terms are made public. If any doubts remain as to exact figures, a question in the House of Commons or the indiscretions of an enterprising journalist will almost certainly inform both the British people and the Russian government of the exact details of the agreement. The terms agreed to between Russia and her allies are difficult to ascertain. In several cases, at least in the Middle East, such agreements have remained unknown to the Western Powers for months. Even when the existence of such relations are known, the exact numbers and details are rarely ascertainable. Thus the Communist Powers invariably have the advantage of surprise.

There is little doubt that the policy of Jemal Abdul Nasser was re-orientated to the Communist side at the Bandung conference. The Western Powers, however, seemed to be unaware that anything had happened until the Czech arms deal in September 1955. Even then the Egyptian government succeeded in explaining that also. Another year was to elapse before the U.S.A. and Britain realized that Egypt had really gone over to Russia.

* * * * *

The Egyptian government of the revolution, when it came into power, announced many internal and economic reforms. But such measures are easier to promise than to execute. Dictators and revolutionaries, however, must always be doing something spectacular. War with the Jews appeared to be a less intricate matter, and certainly more useful as a slogan. For a great part of the Arab world—and more especially one million Arab refugees—were intensely embittered over the problem of Palestine.

Jemal Abdul Nasser appeared as the shining hero, who was to drive Israel into the sea, and conduct the refugees back to their homes. The majority of the educated people in Jordan were aware of the skill which has always characterized the Egyptians, when it is a matter of talking. They knew also that the Egyptians are not good soldiers, and that the idea of their leading a war against Israel was unrealistic. But to the emotional masses, talking was enough.

When the Czech arms deal was announced in September 1955, there was an outburst of wild enthusiasm, not only in Egypt, but in

Jordan, Syria and Lebanon. The fervour with which the agreement was greeted was due to certain errors in the Arab appreciation of military matters.

It was Egypt which had insisted on fighting Israel in 1948. She had, as a result, suffered a humiliating defeat. The weapons and ammunition were defective, they claimed, owing to the corruption of King Farouq's régime. And there were not enough modern weapons, because the Western Powers would not sell them to the Arab States. On the contrary, they were secretly arming Israel. Either owing to this propaganda, or likewise to explain their own inadequacy in 1948, emphasis in all Arab countries was laid on weapons alone. Efficiency was rarely mentioned. The tradition was built up that the Arabs had been unsuccessful because the Western Powers starved them of arms. If only they could get arms, Israel would soon be defeated.

Thus the Czech arms deal seemed to the Arabs the magic solution of all their troubles. Lack of weapons, they believed, had been the reason for all their defeats. Colonel Nasser had opened the door to a new and unlimited source of supply. Henceforward all their troubles were over.

The whole history of war goes to emphasize that—no matter what weapons are or are not available—men are more important than machines. Even with the best of human material, months and years are required to build an army. Discipline, morale, devotion—*esprit de corps*—the moral qualities are even more important than the military training. The general public in the Arab countries was utterly unaware of any of these factors. They expected an Egyptian attack on Israel to follow the arrival of the Czech arms in a few weeks, if not in a matter of days.

*   *   *   *   *

The Egyptian government encouraged the hopes of their admirers by intensifying the incidents on the frontier. From 1948 to 1954, the majority of the incidents on the Israel borders had been on the Jordan sector. This indeed was natural enough, for Jordan had nearly 400 miles of border with Israel, of which 220 miles ran through densely populated country. Every yard of this part of the line lay in fields, gardens, orchards or even villages. The Egyptian sector was 160 miles long, and only 40 miles of this—the Gaza strip—was inhabited. The remaining 120 miles were desert. Moreover, nearly all infiltrators were refugees, and Jordan had two and a half times as many refugees as Egypt.

From 1954 onwards, however, the incidents in the Gaza strip became far more numerous than those on the Jordan front. This was due firstly to the fact that the Jordan government had nearly mastered infiltration, and secondly, that the defences were better organized. The Israeli battalion attack on Beit Liqya in 1954 had failed.

On the Gaza strip, however, the Egyptian revolutionary government were desirous of incidents, for they were posing as the great military power which was about to defeat Israel. The Israelis, it must be admitted, were no less aggressive and temperamental, and constant outbursts of shooting kept the sector in a continual state of tension throughout the year 1955.

Apart from shooting at one another across the demarcation line, the tactics of the two sides differed. The Egyptians organized and despatched infiltrators into Israel, either to kill people or to lay mines on roads. The infiltrators being principally Palestine refugees from the Gaza strip, the Egyptians were able to gain a reputation for patriotism, whereas the casualties were suffered by the Palestinians. Against these constant pin-pricks, the Israeli army periodically organized a reprisal operation.

Mr. Ben Gurion had been out of office for fourteen months, and Mr. Sharett had been Prime Minister of Israel. But in February 1955, Mr. Ben Gurion returned to office as Israeli Minister of Defence. He was the original sponsor of the policy of armed retaliation. His return to office was thought to have been due to the numerous incidents in the Gaza strip. It portended a more aggressive Israeli policy, which was indeed ushered in by a major "retaliation raid" against Gaza on the night of February 28th. Forty-two Egyptian soldiers were reported killed, and thirty wounded. Mr. Ben Gurion admitted officially that Israel would follow a policy of reprisals.

After the Israeli attack, the refugees in the Gaza strip rioted, attacked United Nations officials, and destroyed stores of food accumulated by the United Nations Relief and Works Agency for issue to the refugees themselves. An Egyptian spokesman stated that Communist agitators were active amongst the refugees.

* * * * *

The Egyptian revolutionary government did not limit their activities to the Gaza sector. They made great efforts to create incidents on the Jordan front also. Egyptian agents visited the refugee camps in Jordan, and offered money and weapons to any refugees who would carry out sabotage raids into Israel. The headmen of villages near the demarcation line were sent for by the Egyptian Embassy in Amman, and offered money to facilitate raiding into Israel. Some of the people thus approached reported to the Jordan police, and gave sworn statements as to what had passed between them and the Egyptian Embassy.

An officer and five other ranks of the Arab Legion were approached by the Egyptian Embassy and asked to organize raids into Israel. They were given a sum of money, but they were afraid to organize any raids. Eventually they confessed and gave sworn statements of the proposals made to them by the Egyptian diplomats.

In general, the Jordan villagers were fully aware of the real facts on the subject of infiltration. They realized that to administer small pin-pricks to Israel, as long as the latter was militarily stronger than Jordan, would serve no purpose. Our task was to build up our military strength until it was more equal to that of the enemy. The Arab Legion, of course, entirely understood the logic of our policy, and the necessity for vigilance day and night to prevent incidents. It was not always possible, however, to ensure that no infiltrators got through. One party even arrived by taxi from Damascus, the capital of Syria, crossed over into Israel the same night, blew up a house, returned to Jordan and drove straight back across the border into Syria. By the time the police investigation was under way, the offenders had left Jordan.

In the spring of 1955, the Jordan Minister of Defence visited Egypt for a conference. I asked him to see Jemal Abdul Nasser and complain to him about the efforts of the Egyptian Embassy to organize raids into Israel. On his return, he informed me that he had obtained an interview with Colonel Nasser and had made the complaint.

"Jemal Abdul Nasser," said the Minister to me, "was very surprised. He told me that he had never heard of such a thing. He said that he found it difficult to believe that such incidents could be happening without his knowledge. He assured me that he would institute an immediate enquiry and promised that I need have no further cause for anxiety."

I thanked the Minister and said I hoped that things would now be easier. In practice, however, no improvement resulted—on the contrary, Egyptian attempts to organize infiltration increased.

Three months later, the Jordan Prime Minister was about to visit Egypt. I called upon him and asked whether he would be seeing Jemal Abdul Nasser. If so, I suggested that he ask him to prevent the Egyptian Embassy in Amman organizing raids into Israel. He promised to do so. I called on the Prime Minister again after his return to ask what success he had achieved.

"Jemal Abdul Nasser," said the Prime Minister, "received me most cordially. He was very surprised at what I said about the activities of the Egyptian Embassy. He told me that he had never heard of such a thing. He said that he found it difficult to believe that such incidents could be happening without his knowledge. He assured me that he would institute an immediate enquiry and told me that I need have no further cause for anxiety."

I thanked the Prime Minister for taking so much trouble, and asked him if he would compare his text with that of the Minister of Defence three months before. Colonel Nasser was all smiles—nothing was too much trouble—no-one need be anxious any more—but Egyptian attempts to organize raiding increased.

But our difficulties with Egypt did not mean that things were any easier with Israel. The Israeli army remained extremely aggressive. A new procedure which they developed was to fire bursts of machine-gun fire across the line into Jordan villages. Sometimes the procedure was varied by shooting three-inch mortar bombs. When we protested to the Mixed Armistice Commission, the Israeli delegation replied that they were sorry, but the troops had been on manoeuvres. A week or ten days later, another similar incident would occur, and again our protests would receive the same reply.

Eventually I asked for an interview with General Burns, who was the principal United Nations officer in the Middle East. His designation was Chief of Staff of the Truce Supervision Organization. He agreed to see the Israeli authorities, and ask them not to hold "manoeuvres" within a thousand yards of the demarcation line.

Next time I saw General Burns, I asked him what progress he had made. He told me that he had called on the Israeli Minister of Foreign Affairs and had asked him to arrange for "manoeuvres" to be held not less than one thousand yards from the line.

"General," the Minister had answered, "you can go and give orders to the Canadian army, but not to the Israeli army."

Israeli "manoeuvres" continued to fire into Jordan villages.

General Burns was a man of remarkable placidity and tenacity. To be in theory the representative of an embryo World Government, and in practice obliged to submit to rudeness and insults, without adequate support from Lake Success must have tried his patience considerably.

* * * * *

In April 1955, King Husain was married to his cousin, the Amira Dina. The new Queen, in addition to being young and attractive, had won a degree at Cambridge. Two days after the wedding, His Majesty held a ceremonial review of the Arab Legion. Only a few days before had occurred that scene in the palace, when the King, in the presence of a number of persons, had told me that he disapproved of all our plans. As I stood behind him on the dais at the saluting base, I could not help wondering whether this would prove to be my last Arab Legion review.

The ceremonial reviews of the Arab Legion had gained a reputation which had reached distant countries. There were, of course, those who considered all ceremonial parades as playing at soldiers, an occupation far removed from the crude realities of the modern world. But my own experience led me to believe the contrary, for soldiering is a profession which depends on spirit more than on material. A great parade is a deeply stirring event.

In addition to the emotion aroused by the ceremony, however, the men of the Arab Legion were made aware of the admiration and enthusiasm produced in the many foreigners present. Their pride in their own army was intensely stimulated by the obvious surprise and emotion of the spectators.

In the Arab Legion, perfection was the lowest standard acceptable. Whether in drill, in training for war or in actual battle, we never accepted the second best—and I say advisedly "we", for officers and men evinced the same enthusiasm.

It was during this summer of 1955 also, that the Arab Legion massed bands did a tour of Great Britain. People who imagined Arabs to be wild desert camel riders were surprised to see the massed bands beating retreat on the Horse Guards' Parade, or the Arab Legion pipes and drums marching down Princes Street, Edinburgh. It was our swan song—within eight months the Arab Legion had ceased to exist.

* * * * *

Meanwhile in Jordan, the stability the country had enjoyed for thirty-five years was becoming daily more precarious. Taufiq Pasha had taken office in the spring of 1954, with orders from the King to strengthen the authority of the government, and put an end to subversion, Communism and insecurity. He was the firmest and most realistic of the possible Jordan Prime Ministers. In May 1955, King Husain dismissed him from office, and asked Saeed Pasha al Mufti to make a government.[1]

Saeed Pasha was a Circassian. He was universally popular, perhaps even beloved. He was also a rich man, and was recognized to have no desire or incentive for personal gain—a rare quality indeed. But he was not young, and his health was uncertain. Frequently he would be indisposed and unable to leave his house— and the government would drift without leadership, perhaps for days.

On November 2nd, as the climax of a summer of shooting on the Gaza sector, the Israeli army again attacked and overran an Egyptian position at Sabha, on the armistice line south of Gaza. This action was, in a peculiar manner, memorable. A few hours after the Israeli attack, the Egyptian authorities announced that the Egyptian army had delivered a counter-attack, great numbers of Israeli soldiers had been killed, and the positions lost had been

[1] Taufiq Pasha committed suicide four months after my dismissal.

recaptured. It was only gradually, from the United Nations observers, that we discovered that no such counter-attack had taken place.
The Egyptian communiqué had been a complete fabrication with
no foundation whatever in fact.

In Britain, people believe that honesty is the best policy. They
repeat the proverb that truth will out, but I have not found it so.
Perhaps, to a limited extent, history gives a truer verdict when the
fires of controversy have subsided. But there is some truth in the
statement that history is the propaganda of the winning side.

Apart from history, however, I have not found in the Middle
East that truth can be relied upon to emerge. Modern means of
publicity offer unequalled facilities for the dissemination of lies, and
a great part of this immense output of falsehood is permanently
believed, and builds up between nations those barriers of hatred and
mistrust which so largely poison our lives today.

Perhaps in the West lies are more liable to exposure than in the
Middle East, because people are more sophisticated and have more
varied sources of information. But in the Middle East, the gullibility
of the masses is unending. The Egyptian radio stations broadcast
unending lies, no less blatant than that of the counter-attack at
Sabha. But even if each lie be exposed, the new lie will be believed.
The explanation of the unending credulity of Middle East crowds
lies perhaps chiefly in their emotions. For Arab politics are more
guided by passion than by reason. To be believed, it is not necessary
to be truthful, or even to be reasonably plausible. It is important
only to say that which will arouse passion, and to say it in the most
emotional manner.

I trust that Britain will never tell lies, because to do so is wrong
and undermines the moral character of the liar. But I have not
found that, in Middle Eastern politics, honesty is the best policy.
Over a period of the last three or four years, persistent, flagrant and
shameless lies seem to have met with unadulterated success. Perhaps one day, such a deliberate policy of falsehood will meet its
Nemesis.

*   *   *   *   *

When he was at Harrow and Sandhurst, King Husain had acquired
a liking for the pleasures of European capitals. When he ascended
the throne, he made a practice of taking a long annual holiday in
London, Paris, Switzerland and Rome. Ali abu Nuwar, it will be
remembered, was military attaché in Paris. I have already related
how he tried in vain to get the ear of King Tellal for his political
views, but that the King had refused to receive him. His chance
came when King Husain visited Paris. He constituted himself the
King's guide to the sights of the city.

After the King's visit to Paris in the summer of 1954, I had received a private letter from Ali. He told me that he had heard that I had been told that he had intrigued against me with the King.

"I would never intrigue against my own chief in his absence," Ali had written. "I am sure that you will believe me." I had heard no such reports, but I realized from Ali's letter that he had been speaking against me to the King. *"Qui s'excuse, s'accuse."*

On the King's return from a visit to Paris a year later, he asked me whether Ali could not be posted to Jordan. I temporized at first, replying that the posting of a military attaché was usually one of three years' duration, and that Ali had not been in Paris so long.

Eventually, in the autumn of 1955, the King spoke to the Prime Minister on the subject. The latter asked me if there was any objection to the return of Ali abu Nuwar, as His Majesty was most anxious to secure him as an A.D.C. I replied that the only objection was that Ali was a political intriguer. If he returned, he would make trouble between me and the King. The Prime Minister admitted that Ali held extreme political views.

"His Majesty is devoted to him as long as he is far away," he said. "If he comes back, the King will probably get tired of him."

The whole basis of my position was that I was a servant of the Jordan government. I could not defy the King and the government. I had already told the King that, if he did not want me, I was ready at any time to resign.

"As your Excellency orders," I said, smiling, "I am afraid that Ali may make trouble, but I will certainly not oppose his posting if His Majesty and your Excellency desire it."

Two days later, I met King Husain at a lunch party. He thanked me most kindly for posting Ali abu Nuwar to be his chief A.D.C.

* * * * *

We were aware that the presence of British officers in the Arab Legion was only a temporary phase. In this respect, however, the Arab Legion was in a peculiar position.

Firstly, it had been only a police and gendarmerie force from 1926 to 1940. During this period, it was largely staffed by officers who had served under the Turks before 1918. The few new officers admitted were trained solely in police duties. In 1940, under the stress of the Second World War, young officers were admitted, and received a military training. Thus in 1956, the most senior Jordanian officers with military training were thirty-three to thirty-six years old.

After the end of the Second World War, the strength was cut down to 6,000, but between 1948 and 1956 it rose to 23,000. In addition, the National Guard of 30,000 was created, which also took its officers from the Arab Legion. Thus the number of officers increased fivefold in the period from 1948 to 1956, rising from 300 to 1,500. The 1,200 officers admitted in these eight years were of two almost equal categories—schoolboys of eighteen or nineteen years who entered as cadets, and non-commissioned officers who were given commissions. In 1956, the average age of the first category was about twenty-four. The former non-commissioned officers were older, but in most cases their lack of education rendered them unsuitable for high rank. Thus the whole officer structure was extremely precarious. There were immense numbers of lieutenants and second-lieutenants, some of them of excellent quality. But good captains were scarce. Battalion commanders could be found only with great difficulty, and senior staff officers did not exist, much less brigade or divisional commanders.

It must also be remembered that the Arab Legion was unfortunately unable to take part in operations in Europe in the Second World War. Israel, however, had several hundred officers who had taken part in the war in Europe, either in the Jewish Brigade, or in the American or European armies. The Arab Legion was therefore at an immense disadvantage. It had no senior officers and virtually no officers over thirty-six capable of promotion. It had also no officers with war experience, except of the fighting in Palestine in 1948. In these operations, there were virtually no air force, no artillery and no armour. The British officers seconded to the Arab Legion, on the other hand, had nearly all held similar commands in the Second World War. The British brigade commanders had commanded brigades against the Germans and the Japanese, and the battalion commanders had corresponding war experience.

If Jordan had not been threatened with attack by Israel, the British officers could have been greatly reduced at once, even at the cost of a drop in efficiency. But Jordan was constantly threatened by such a danger. If we had drastically reduced the number of British officers, and Israel had attacked and defeated the Arab Legion, there can be no doubt that the politicians would have cried out against British treachery. Logically there were only two courses open—the first was for British officers to remain in sufficient numbers to make the Arab Legion efficient. The second was for British officers to be reduced to any degree the Jordan government wished, but not to be responsible for any military operations.

A third course would, of course, have been to make peace with Israel, but this Jordan was unable to do.

However, although we unwillingly decided that, for the present, the British officers were necessary to ensure efficiency, we prepared extremely detailed plans for their replacement. As a result of my personal intervention, we secured two entries a year at the British Staff College, Camberley. Calculating in considerable detail the ages of all officers, their qualifications and the output of the

Staff College, we produced a plan according to which the last British officer would leave in 1965. The senior Jordanian officer, who would assume command as a lieutenant-general, would then be forty-five years old. But although the last officer would not leave for ten years, about half of them would leave in the first three years.

This plan was submitted to the King, who accepted it and proclaimed himself satisfied. Later on, we produced a modified plan for a period of six years for the take-over. This proposal would have entailed a considerable drop in efficiency, as it would not have been possible in that time to produce officers qualified for all the posts which would be vacant.

The King accepted our proposals without comment or criticism. Had he or the government asked for a shorter period, we should have revised the scheme in any way they desired, while pointing out the possible dangers. The Anglo-Jordan treaty placed Britain under an obligation to supply such officers as were asked for by the King of Jordan. The latter was under no treaty obligation to have any British officers.

Our difficulties in this connection were twofold. Firstly, the Cabinet and the public were both ignorant of, and indifferent to, military matters. It was always an effort to persuade any minister, even a Minister of Defence, to read or listen to any detailed plans of this nature. In reality, they were not convinced that there was anything difficult in raising or commanding an army, or that officers required any particular training. Our second difficulty arose from the intense propaganda which was circulating, to the effect that the Western Powers were unscrupulous and deceitful. The East tends naturally to consider that politics are a competition in duplicity, but this normal opinion had been intensified by Communist and Nationalist propaganda. Cabinet ministers with whom I had worked for many years were aware of our complete sincerity, but other politicians, particularly from the West Bank, were inclined to scent a plot in everything.

This indeed seems to be a possible key to the King's action. We had again and again submitted our plans to him and received his approval. Finally, he dismissed almost all the British officers without notice and in a manner calculated to inflict the greatest hardship and indignity on many officers who had served him with single-minded devotion.

He had had frequent opportunities to ask for a reduction of officers, but had always said that he wished to retain them. Presumably he thought that our requests for his approval to our plans were just a trick to ascertain his views. Or, alternatively, he had really wished to retain them, but acted suddenly in dismissing them in a moment of irritation.

XXIV
Mob Violence

Then I said, I have laboured in vain, I have spent my strength for
nought, and in vain: yet surely my judgment is with the Lord, and my
work with my God.   *Isaiah* xlix. 4

Fire and People do in this agree,
They both good servants, both ill masters be.
                                            GREVILLE

And each dweller, panic-stricken,
Felt his heart with terror stricken,
Hearing the tremendous cry
Of the triumph of Anarchy.
                                    P. B. SHELLEY

XXIV

MOB VIOLENCE

KING ABDULLA had paid a state visit to Turkey not long before his assassination. King Tellal, after his abdication and a brief and uncomfortable stay in Egypt, was living in a villa on the Bosphorus, where King Husain and the Queen Mother had visited him more than once. Then King Husain himself had paid a state visit to Turkey. It was time for the Jordan royal family to return this hospitality. The President of the Turkish Republic, Mr. Jellal Bayar, was invited to pay an official visit to Jordan. November 2nd, 1955, was fixed for his arrival.

The visit did not meet with the approval of the Egyptian government. Egypt's passion for leadership had haunted Arab politics like a witch's curse. She was bitterly jealous of the possibility of Iraq disputing the pre-eminence with her, and she was no less apprehensive of Turkey. Iraq had little more than a quarter of Egypt's population, but her economy was expanding and she also was an Arab country, and therefore capable of nationalist appeal. Turkey on the other hand had no nationalist appeal, but she was immensely more powerful than any Arab country. Should Turkey, therefore, enter into agreements with any Arab governments, Egypt might be almost completely eclipsed.

Consequently Turkey had frequently been the victim of attack by Egyptian propaganda. A commercial agreement was in existence between her and Israel, and the Egyptians had constantly represented her as the devoted ally of that country.

The announcement of the impending visit of the Turkish President produced an outburst of criticism from Egypt. The Jordan government, in reply, issued a statement to the effect that the visit was purely a return of hospitality by the Jordan royal family, and that no political subjects would be discussed. Nevertheless the visit caused us some anxiety lest attempts be made at political assassination.

The President paid a visit to Jerusalem, accompanied by His Majesty, but very detailed precautions had been taken and no untoward incidents resulted. The royal party lunched with an Arab Legion unit north of Jerusalem. In a short speech, Mr. Jellal Bayar stated that he would not be surprised one day to see Turkish soldiers fighting beside the Arab Legion in Jerusalem. The next day, the King and the President inspected a brigade group of the Arab Legion in battle order. The troops looked splendid.

The Turkish President, accompanied by the acting Foreign Minister, Mr. Fatin Rüstü Zorlu, had, it appeared, been discussing politics with the King and the Jordan government, although such a possibility had not at first been envisaged.

On the evening of November 7th, I was summoned to King Abdulla's former winter residence, at Shuna in the Jordan valley. I found His Majesty in conference with the Prime Minister, Saeed Pasha al Mufti, and with Mr. Jellal Bayar and the Turkish Foreign Minister. When I had seated myself near the King, he whispered to me that he thought the Arab Legion should consist of three infantry divisions and one armoured division, and enquired if I agreed. I whispered back that such a force would be magnificent, but that it would take some time to carry out such an expansion, amounting to a threefold increase. The King nodded. Then he looked up at the company and began to speak.

"We have heard all your arguments in favour of our joining the Baghdad Pact," he said, "and we were impressed by them. But Jordan is in a peculiar position, living in constant fear of an aggressive and powerful enemy. Moreover we are also economically ruined. We have half a million refugees without work. We want more money for development schemes."

The Turkish President replied in carefully weighed sentences.

"If you are in need of money," he said, "I am afraid that Turkey cannot help you. We ourselves are in the throes of a financial crisis. But we understand the difficulties which beset you. The British have helped you hitherto. They are our friends also. I suggest that the Jordan government write to the British government to ask for the additional help you need. We at the same time will write to the British and support your case."

The matter was left in this state. The next day the Turkish President left for home.

As soon as the Turkish guests had taken their leave, the Jordan government began work on a memorandum to Her Majesty's Government. In it, the course of the negotiations with the Turks was briefly related, and a note of Jordan's needs was appended. The list was largely compiled by the King, and included considerable air forces and a navy. The note was handed to the British Ambassador in Amman on November 16th, 1955. It referred also to previous negotiations for the revision of the Anglo-Jordan treaty, and indicated that Jordan's admission to the Baghdad Pact would be a suitable moment for the completion of the revised treaty.

Early in December 1955, General Sir Gerald Templer, Chief of the Imperial General Staff, arrived in Amman. On presenting his credentials he explained that he had come as a plenipotentiary, not as a general. He had been chosen instead of a diplomat because so many of Jordan's requests had been connected with military assistance.

Ever since the signature of the Baghdad Pact by Turkey and Iraq in February 1955, the British government had refrained from suggesting that Jordan might join the pact. Britain appreciated Jordan's position, placed as she was between Egypt and Iraq, and constantly menaced by Israel, and did not wish to embarrass her. But when Jordan herself suggested her adherence, the British government welcomed the step.

The increases in the Arab Legion offered by the British government were substantial. They included a 4th Infantry Brigade. We had, at the time, an infantry division of three brigades, so that this offer represented a twenty-five per cent increase in infantry. In our circumstances at that time a 4th Brigade would have been of especial value because we were obliged to keep two brigades deployed in West Jordan along the Israel demarcation line, leaving only one brigade in reserve and for purposes of training. Had we possessed four brigades we could have had two deployed and two on training. With the two brigades deployed and one in reserve, the standard of training required for war could not be maintained.

The Arab Legion had one regiment of tanks. A second regiment was to be formed. The Arab Legion was disproportionately weak in armour, and this addition would have been most valuable. There was also to be a medium artillery regiment—a long-felt requirement. It had been a weak point in our organization that we possessed nothing heavier than field artillery. A number of other units were also included, in order to make the new force properly balanced in transport, workshops, signals, administrative units and all the complicated ramifications of a modern army. It was estimated that the hitting power of the Arab Legion would be raised some thirty-five per cent by these increases.

The Arab Legion subsidy was £10,000,000 in 1955. If the new increases were authorized, the cost for the first financial year would be £16,500,000, and for each subsequent year £12,500,000.

There was also a promise to form a jet fighter squadron immediately and to continue the expansion of the Jordan Air Force, as fast as pilots could be trained.

It was true that King Husain had asked for three infantry divisions, but the Arab Legion had already increased from 6,000 to 23,000 (or fourfold) in eight years. A further threefold increase would have required eight or ten years to consummate, unless the army was to degenerate into a mob. There was already an acute shortage of senior officers and N.C.O.s.

To take one example alone, the Arab Legion in December 1955 contained about 1,500 officers. To treble it in size would require

3,000 new officers. The output of the cadet training school was 100 officers a year, requiring thirty years to produce 3,000. Perhaps the output of the cadet school could have been doubled, but, even so, fifteen years would have been necessary.

In practice, from a purely military angle, the increases in the Arab Legion were the least part of the proposals. The most essential gain was a military alliance with Turkey, Persia and Pakistan, all countries with large armies. Jordan already had a treaty with Iraq, the fourth member of the pact.

Especially vital was the treaty connection with Turkey. For whereas Jordan had one division and an armoured brigade, Egypt had three to four divisions and Israel perhaps the equivalent of five or six (though of varying categories and efficiency). Turkey had some twenty-four divisions. In a similar manner, Israel had something less than two hundred combat aircraft, but Turkey had more than two thousand.

In other words, the power of Turkey, Persia and Pakistan was vastly in excess of that of Israel and the Arab governments. Thus, if Jordan had joined the Baghdad Pact, her safety from any attack by Israel would have been absolutely assured. She was already allied to other Arab governments by the Arab League Collective Security Pact and to Britain by the Anglo-Jordan treaty. Israel was possibly stronger than all the forces the Arab governments could put in the field. The Arabs professed suspicion of the Anglo-Jordan treaty. Britain, they claimed, was too friendly with Israel, and would never fight against her. But the addition of Turkey, Persia and Pakistan would have made Jordan's position unassailable.

I endeavoured to point this out to the Cabinet ministers, but they were not greatly interested. They were pleased with the increases in the Arab Legion, because they meant more money and employment in the country.

In reality, however, the government were almost solely concerned with the political aspects. Egypt was determined to prevent Jordan joining the Baghdad Pact, thereby in her view, abandoning the Egyptian faction and rallying to the Iraqi party. The Egyptian broadcasting stations, particularly "Voice of the Arabs", poured forth a stream of propaganda, incitement and abuse. The Egyptian newspapers, which arrived by air every day, carried heavy banner headlines with the same slogans. The Egyptian Embassy in Amman worked day and night, interviewing politicians, threatening and cajoling and distributing literature and propaganda. Saudi Arabia was still (in its jealousy of the Jordan royal family) an ally of Egypt. The Saudi Embassy paid money freely to the Jordan newspapers, members of Parliament, agitators or anyone else from whom they hoped for help.

The principal item of Egyptian propaganda was that the Baghdad Pact was a trick to help Israel. If Jordan adhered to the pact, "Voice of the Arabs" explained, Israel would then be admitted, and Jordan would find herself tricked into being an ally of Israel, without any chance of border adjustment or of a solution of the refugee problem, which were essential to her. To this General Templer replied by pointing to the charter of the Baghdad Pact, which stated that new members could not be admitted without the unanimous consent of the existing members. Thus if Jordan were to join, she could veto the admission of Israel. This reply satisfied the ministers, but it scarcely reached the fringe of the general public, who were listening avidly to "Voice of the Arabs" from Cairo.

Egypt then declared that the object of the Baghdad Pact was to break up the Arab Security Pact. Accordingly a clause was added to the effect that nothing in the new agreement should interfere with Jordan's obligations under the Arab Security Pact.

The system of bilateral treaties between Britain and individual Arab countries, which had been in vogue since 1930, had come to be regarded by the latter as making the Arab country in question in some way subservient to Britain. King Husain had for some time been anxious to change this form of relationship, although Jordan of course still needed the British subsidy.

An even more vicious report from Egypt was to the effect that Britain had secretly agreed with Israel and Iraq to dismember Jordan, her ally. Israel would be given the remainder of Arab Palestine (that is, the West Bank), while the East Bank would be annexed to Iraq.

Fantastic and ridiculous as such stories might seem, the ignorant and inexperienced masses were ill-qualified to distinguish between what was probable and what was absurd. No Iraqi government could venture to conclude a secret pact with Israel to partition another Arab country. The Egyptians were in the habit of branding their rivals as secret allies of Israel. Egypt alone was the staunch maintainer of the Arab cause!

Meanwhile the Jordan government continued to vacillate. The West Bank members suggested that the proposal for Jordan's adherence be first submitted to the Egyptian government or the Arab League for approval. It was obvious that Egypt would bitterly oppose the agreement. The King agreed to send the agreement to Egypt, after signature, explaining the reasons for Jordan's adhesion.

I was personally present at one only of the meetings between General Templer and the government. It was in the palace, and the King presided. The Prime Minister and two or three Cabinet ministers were present. Details of the new weapons were discussed. The King was extremely anxious to conclude the agreement, and he even offered to sign for Jordan if the Cabinet were afraid to do so. General Templer replied that His Majesty was a constitutional monarch, and that it would be most rash for him to take on such a responsibility and expose himself to intrigue.

I felt a deep affection for the young King, so courageous, so entirely deprived of disinterested advisers and plunged in such a vortex of intrigue, falsehood and power politics. It occurred to me that, if he could survive until he reached forty-five years old, he might well become another King Abdulla. For King Husain's grandfather also had been headstrong and impetuous in his youth; it was only when his hot-headedness became cooled with age that he became a great ruler.

Meanwhile, General Templer had agreed to all the Jordan government's requests. They admitted that the terms offered were most advantageous. They could see no drawbacks to the plan—but still they vacillated. Saeed Pasha al Mufti was an ageing man in bad health. Besides which he was a Circassian, and feared that the Arab Nationalists would accuse his community of treachery if he took the lead in a courageous political *démarche*.

There was nothing more to be said. The negotiators had agreed on the terms. The Jordan government could think of no more concessions they wanted. The real point at issue was whether the ministers had the courage to take a decision which they believed to be for the good of their country, but which might well expose them to popular clamour, or to a campaign of calumny by the Egyptian propaganda machine. The Egyptian and Saudi Embassies were working day and night, both negotiating with politicians and stirring up excitement in the bazaars. Certain West Bank Cabinet ministers were said to have been seen calling at the Egyptian Embassy.

Then, suddenly, on December 13th, the four West Bank members of the Cabinet tendered their resignations. Saeed Pasha, secretly relieved to have found a way to avoid making up his mind, hastened to the palace to inform the King that he could not continue in office.

Why the four ministers resigned was not finally established. Two days before, they had admitted that they could think of nothing else to ask for from Britain. All their objections had been met, all the concessions had been granted. Some people opined that they had been threatened with assassination, others that they had received some form of inducement. Whatever were the actual motives which caused them to resign, they were perhaps not such as they desired to admit. When asked for their reasons, therefore, they tended to assume a noble posture and reply, "Do you want me to betray my country?" or "The salvation of Palestine is more important than imperialist alliances." It was curious that, if treachery to their country were the obstacle, they had not expressed their opposition to it during the long fortnight through which the negotiations had dragged on.

The resignation of the West Bank ministers, however, produced a sudden and catastrophic change in public opinion. Hitherto, the majority of the educated people in Amman had favoured adherence to the pact. Enough of the negotiations had leaked out to convince them that the conditions were extremely favourable to Jordan. Even on the West Bank public opinion was calm, if not favourable. But whatever may have been the reasons for the resignations of the four ministers, they were all sufficiently good politicians to realize that political capital could be made out of it. By hints, asides and half-confidences to their friends, they let it be understood that it was true—the whole thing was an imperialist plot—they were not the men to betray their country.

The King, who was still determined to join the Baghdad Pact, sent for Hazza Pasha al Mejali, and asked him to form a new government. Hazza Pasha was a young man who had been a minister in the previous Cabinet. King Abdulla had regarded him with especial favour. He was a member of a family of tribal shaikhs in Kerak, not a city dweller as were the other ministers.

Hazza Pasha set himself to form his Cabinet. There had been an unwritten agreement since 1950 that half the Cabinet ministers should be from the East Bank and half from the West. It was easy enough to find the East Bank ministers, but the four West Bank ministers who had resigned had made it difficult for any others to take office. By claiming that they had resigned for "patriotic" reasons, the retiring ministers had proclaimed that any who took office in their place were traitors.

Eventually Hazza Pasha formed his Cabinet. He stated openly that he had come to office to sign the Baghdad Pact. Some of the shiftier politicians advised him to make a contrary announcement, and allow the agitation to settle down. "After that," they said, "you can sign the pact without trouble." But Hazza preferred to adopt a more honest and courageous policy. In this, he was strongly supported by the King, who was still quite determined. As a result, the Egyptians and the Saudis redoubled their efforts. Hazza was a tool of the imperialists, screamed "Voice of the Arabs"; he was selling Palestine to the Jews. In Amman, the Egyptian military attaché was active, summoning people to his house and urging revolt and sedition.

All over the Arab countries, students and school-children were the tools of politicians. When Communist infiltration first began, the earliest converts were small schoolmasters. Such of the latter as were not Communists were extreme Nationalists. In many government schools, pitched battles took place between Communist and Nationalist pupils, each side egged on by rival teachers. Successive governments, anxious to gain popular applause, increased the number of schools, and of classes in each school. The standard of teaching declined, because teachers of the necessary academic standards were not obtainable—let alone teachers with the necessary moral qualifications. Parents complained that their children learned nothing at school but a variety of political creeds, each one more fanatical and destructive than the other. Children who on the orders of their parents refused to join political parties in their schools were made to fail in their examinations and were passed over for promotion to a higher class. All responsible men in the country were aware that the government schools were producing an ignorant and fanatical younger generation, but no minister had the courage or the public spirit to attempt a purge. It was for this reason, and at the urgent request of the officers and men, that we in the Arab Legion established our own schools for our Arab Legion children, where politics were forbidden and we attempted to teach religion and a spirit of service.

Every riot in Jordan, and indeed in the whole Middle East, was initiated by school-children. When the schoolmasters received the word from the extremist politicians, they turned all the children into the streets, boys and girls, primary and secondary schools, young and old alike. On some occasions, the teachers had written on pieces of paper the slogan which the children were to call out. A mass of children, shouting and singing, waving flags and throwing stones, blocked the traffic. Shops closed their shutters lest their windows be broken by stones. It was difficult for the police to disperse crowds of big girls, or even of little boys and girls of ten or twelve years old. When sufficient confusion had been created, the roughs, the refugees and the discontented took over the riot.

On December 16th, 1955, this process began in Amman. The school-children started it, but soon large crowds blocked the streets. The Egyptian military attaché was in the town and was reported by the police to have accosted individual police constables and told them not to disperse the crowds. "If you lose your jobs," he was alleged to have said, "the Egyptian government will pay you pensions enough to support your families."

Hazza Pasha, the Prime Minister, gave orders to disperse the crowds, opening fire if necessary. A battalion of infantry had been brought into the town, but told not to intervene unless the police reported that the crowd was out of control. Meanwhile, the Minister of the Interior, unknown to us, had ordered the police not to disperse the crowd. A great mass of people surged up the road and on to the

waiting troops, who took no action because the police had not
reported the crowd to be out of hand. The whole town was closed
down, crowds packed the streets, the police stood aside. "Voice of
the Arabs" blared out wild appeals to the people of Jordan to rise in
rebellion.

Abdul Rahman Shgair, the Communist organizer of the election
riots the year before, was back at work once more. A short time before,
he had appealed to the young King's mercy, and promised not to
take part in politics again. The King, touched by his appeal, told
the government to allow him to return. He arrived just in time to
organize the new riots. As at the time of the elections the year before,
there was evidence once more of planning and leadership. Barricades
suddenly appeared in the streets. Trucks loaded with stones could
be seen arriving from the country.

This first day of rioting was chaos. But gradually we settled down
to a kind of routine. The main shopping centre of Amman was in
the bed of a narrow valley. Overlooking the town centre stand four
steep hills, which form the residential areas, in which the foreign
embassies and legations are situated. An infantry brigade was
moved in and occupied the four dominating hills. All exits from the
valley were blocked by cordons of troops. Thus the crowds were
confined to a narrow space in the shopping area in the centre of
the town. Here they paraded endlessly up and down the barred
and shuttered streets, shouting and chanting. Occasionally they
came up against one of the cordons, and the troops fired one or
two shots at their legs. A man fell wounded and the crowd surged
back again into the town. A European diplomat came to see me.
He had been in an embassy in Eastern Europe. "I have seen
a Communist revolution in Europe begin exactly like this," he
said.

I had been careful during the negotiations to pay periodical
visits to army units and explain to the officers what was going on.
They were, therefore, fully aware of the details of the Baghdad
Pact negotiations, the offer of increases in the Arab Legion, and the
support of Turkey, Persia and Pakistan in the event of an Israeli
attack. They were aware that the Egyptian propaganda was untrue
and sprang merely from jealousy of Iraq and Turkey.

It was heart-breaking work for the troops. Many stood for ten
hours a day in cordons on the streets. They were abused, periodically
stoned and called Jews and traitors. Yet whenever they were obliged
to fire, they showed perfect steadiness and discipline. The officer
in charge would give a quiet command, two or three single shots
rang out, one or two men fell, and the incident was over. Nearly
all the wounded were injured in the legs—proof of the calm discipline with which the soldiers aimed. Only soldiers who have them-

selves faced an excited, screaming crowd can realize how much discipline such calm action required.

Amman was not the only city affected. In Jerusalem, the crowds attacked the French, British, American and Turkish Consulates. The riots were directed by the Egyptian Consul in Jerusalem, while the Saudi Consul supplied the cash to encourage the rioters and control the newspapers.

Everything now depended on the firmness of the government. From the very first day, the Minister of the Interior had no stomach for the fight. On the evening of December 18th, I was called to a Cabinet meeting. Hazza Pasha was still determined. It was suggested that we go over to the offensive, and arrest the principal rioters, or the promoters of the disturbances. But the Minister of the Interior and two others hesitated. The police produced a list of the organizers of the riots. The Cabinet began to discuss each name in detail. The Minister of the Interior argued with the police, objecting in turn to the arrest of each one. In spite of everything, a few names were agreed to, and the police arrested them. Abdul Rahman Shgair, as before, had slipped away to Damascus.

All day on December 19th, the crowds again surged through the streets, but there were slight indications that the town was getting tired of it. That evening, however, the Minister of the Interior and two other ministers resigned. The crowds during the day had been chanting: "No more imperialism after today." Some were heard to call out: "No more monarchy after today."

We had found some old tear-gas bombs in stores, and this day we tried a few on the crowd. The result was highly satisfactory. The crowd dispersed almost immediately, without more ado.

The resignation of four ministers a week before had brought Saeed Pasha's Cabinet down. When three of Hazza Pasha's Cabinet gave way, he decided that he could not continue. At 9 p.m. I was called to the palace and shown into a room where Hazza Pasha was sitting. He told me that his plan was that he would resign and the King would dissolve Parliament. A caretaker government would be in charge until the new general election in four months. He could not continue, he said, if no Cabinet would stand by him. The King came in. The tension must have been unbearable for him. He was by nature highly strung; he could not sleep at night, he smoked continuously. Everyone in the Palace was pale and drawn. At last Hazza Pasha's plan was accepted. *"Khair in sha Allah,"*[1] said King Husain.

* * * * *

Jewish propaganda had long sneered at the Arabs for being "feudal". The expression is not very apt. The feudal system was an

---

[1] "May it be for good if God wills."

PLATE 25

King Husain and the Turkish President at the saluting base during an Arab Legion march past. *Left to right:* Saeed Pasha al Mufti, Prime Minister of Jordan; Mr. Jellal Bayar, President of Turkey; King Husain; Mr. Zorlu, acting Turkish Minister of Foreign Affairs

PLATE 26

The President of the Turkish Republic, Mr. Jellal Bayar, with King Husain, inspecting a brigade group of the Arab Legion in battle order, November 4th, 1955 arrangement by which tenants rendered military service in return for land—a system never followed in Arabia. But the Arabs had for centuries been accustomed to autocratic rule. Suddenly autocracy had vanished, and they had slid into anarchy and mob rule, scarcely even pausing at the intermediate stage of democracy. For democracy needs generations—perhaps centuries—to build up.

XXV

Order Restored

If you can keep your head when all about you
    Are losing theirs and blaming it on you,
If you can trust yourself, when all men doubt you,
    And make allowance for their doubting too;
If you can wait and not be tired by waiting,
    Or being lied about, don't deal in lies,
Or being hated, don't give way to hating,
    And yet don't look too good, nor talk too wise:

If you can dream—and not make dreams your master;
    If you can think—and not make thoughts your aim;
If you can meet with Triumph and Disaster
    And treat those two impostors just the same;
If you can bear to hear the truth you've spoken
    Twisted by knaves to make a trap for fools,
Or watch the things you gave your life to, broken,
    And stoop and build 'em up with worn out tools....

RUDYARD KIPLING

"Que dites vous? C'est inutile? je le sais!
Mais on ne se bat pas dans l'espoir du succés!
Non! Non! C'est plus beau lorsque c'est inutile!"

ROSTAND, Cyrano de Bergerac

ORDER RESTORED

W E passed a rather strained and unhappy Christmas, amid so much hatred. "Voice of the Arabs" continued to pour forth its daily stream of lies and hate. We sent an officer to England to purchase the necessary equipment for jamming it, and early in January we succeeded in doing so, without any great difficulty.

The Anglican Church in Amman was next door to our house, so that I could sometimes slip out to early morning Communion through our back door. Sunday was a working day with us, as Muslims use Friday as their weekly day of rest. But I nearly always managed to go to Communion and to Evening Prayer on Sundays. I had been a churchwarden of the Anglican Church for several years, Donald Blackburn being the chaplain. For two or three years, I had been acting as a lay-reader and taking services when needed. We had built a small church in a hut in the camp at Zerqa, and I often drove out there to take an evening service for British officers and other ranks. It was a peaceful and happy reaction to days of passion and anxiety, to spend an hour in the quietness of our little camp church.

One day I came upon this passage from Evelyn Underhill: "A saint is a human creature devoured and transformed by love: a love that has dissolved and burnt out those instinctive passions— acquisitive and combative, proud and greedy—which commonly rule the lives of men."

*   *   *   *   *

The December riots had revealed that we had not devoted enough time to training for action in the event of civil disturbances. For eight years, the Arab Legion had concentrated almost entirely on preparation for defence against external attack.

It was obvious now, however, that the city mobs had tasted power. They had overthrown two governments in ten days. A final trial of strength could not be long delayed. We accordingly issued a directive on the use of troops to aid the civil power, and units were given training in dealing with rioting crowds. The first essential, however, was to come to an understanding with the civil authorities.

On the resignation of Hazza Pasha, the King had asked Ibrahim

Pasha Hashim to form a government. Ibrahim Pasha was an old man, who in the past had often been Prime Minister, but who had now been many years in retirement, though he was still Speaker of the Upper House or Senate. He was a man of integrity, with an unspotted reputation and a high character. But he was old. A humorist in the bazaar named the new government—The Resurrection of the Dead.

I conferred with Ibrahim Pasha, and we agreed that, if further rioting were to develop, the Arab Legion would be given a free hand to deal direct with him. Individual ministers would not then be empowered to interfere, or to telephone orders to the troops or the police.

Early in January a legal point arose. The royal decree dissolving Parliament had been signed by the Prime Minister alone, and then confirmed by the King. It appeared that the Minister of the Interior should have signed also. He had not done so, because he had already resigned before the royal decree was drawn up. A special court was appointed to interpret the constitution, and it ruled that the dissolution of the Parliament was invalid. Meanwhile, the King and the government had reconsidered the question of a dissolution. They had begun to doubt whether it was advisable to face a general election at a moment when feeling was so inflamed.

On January 8th, we received information that there were going to be "street demonstrations" to protest against the court ruling that the dissolution had been illegal. I consulted Ibrahim Pasha. He told me to take no action, and to show no troops in the town. He did not think that the public felt deeply about the dissolution. It was only an agitation by the professional politicians. The public had not been worked up by subversive agitation on this subject, as they had been about the Baghdad Pact. Indeed, outside the cities, there had been something of a reaction against the rioters. From rural districts, particularly, many village headmen and tribal leaders had come to Amman to protest their loyalty to the throne and the government.

The demonstration began as usual with crowds of school-children. It dragged on throughout the day, blocking the traffic in some of the roads, but no violence was used. The police alone were unable to disperse the crowd, but they succeeded in keeping it within reasonable bounds.

At 3 o'clock I left the office and returned to my house. The police telephoned almost immediately to say that the crowds were increasing in numbers. I rang up the Prime Minister, but he ordered me to take no action. "It is nearly evening," he said. "They will disperse at sunset and go home to dinner."

"Very good, sir," I replied, but I took the precaution to warn a battalion in the camp to stand by—it was the 2nd Regiment, the men of Jerusalem and Latrun in 1948.

A minute later the telephone rang. It was the Amman police. "This is the police duty officer," the voice said. "The crowd are blocking the Salt Road. They are getting ugly. They have broken into the offices of the Department of Agriculture."

"Thank you," I said. "Keep me informed of what happens."

Two minutes later the telephone rang again. It was Ibrahim Pasha. "The crowd is getting dangerous," he said in an impassioned voice. "They are burning the town. Call the army at once."

"Shall we disperse the crowd?" I asked him. "Do you order the troops to open fire if necessary?"

"Yes! Yes!" he answered in an agitated tone. "Disperse them at once! Open fire! They will burn down the city."

"When they are dispersed the army must remain in charge. We must have a curfew tomorrow. Does your Excellency agree?"

"Yes, I agree to a curfew tomorrow," he replied. "Only bring the army quickly now!"

"Good," I said, "I will do as your Excellency orders."

I lifted the army telephone, and asked for the Abdulli camp.

"The crowd is in the Salt Road," I said. "They are said to be looting and setting fire to buildings. The 2nd Regiment will send one company down the road and disperse the crowd. They should begin by using their gas bombs, but may open fire if necessary. When the streets are cleared, we will enforce a curfew. Get the company down quickly."

"Very good, sir," came the reply.

I leaned back in my chair and lit a cigarette. I used to be a heavy smoker, but have given it up. Still, however, in moments of strain, I instinctively light one. I find it relaxes the tension.

The telephone rang again.

"Where is the army?" shouted the Prime Minister. "They have set alight to some more houses! They will burn down the town. Please be quick!"

"The army will be there in a few minutes, your Excellency," I replied.

Both telephones rang at once. The first was the police.

"Sir," said a voice, "the crowd have set fire to the offices of the Veterinary Department. The fire engine came to put it out and the crowd attacked the fire engine and burnt it. It is still in flames. How can we put out the fire?"

"I don't know," I said. "The army will be along in a few minutes, and they will disperse the crowd."

"If God wills," said the policeman in an anxious voice.

The other telephone was still ringing.

"Is that you, Pasha?" said an English voice. "This is Foster of the Bank. I am in the house opposite the Ministry of Agriculture. There's a huge crowd here. They seem to have gone mad. They have set fire to several buildings. They are coming across the road to this house with burning torches. They are going to set fire to this house. Pasha, can't you do something?"

Both telephones were now ringing incessantly. Suddenly the door opened and my son Godfrey looked in. He was home for the Christmas holidays.

"I say, do you know what happened to that book—"

"I'm afraid I'm busy now," I said. "There is a riot on."

"Sorry," he apologized, "I didn't know." He shut the door again.

I picked up the telephone again.

"Where is the army?" called the Prime Minister. "They haven't arrived. The rioters will destroy the city."

"They'll be along any minute now," I said. "I'll find out and inform your Excellency."

The telephone from the camp rang. "One company, 2nd Regiment, left camp two minutes ago," said a brisk voice.

"Thank you," I answered, but before I could ask for the Prime Minister the telephone rang again. It was an Arab woman's voice.

"The army!" she screamed. "*Wein al jeish, ya Pasha?*—Where is the army, O Pasha?—Help! Help!"

Then an English voice:

"Pasha! This is the British Bank! The crowd are breaking in the doors! Can't you send troops?"

I got up and walked up and down the room. I lit another cigarette. Too many things were happening at once. Would one company be enough to disperse so large a crowd? Why did they take so long? I rang the camp again. "Where is the commander of the 2nd Regiment?"

"With the company that has gone into the town."

"Has he got his wireless truck? . . . Good, send one more company in support, and inform the C.O. on the wireless that it is coming."

A large crowd was wedged into the Salt Road. People were running along with burning torches throwing them into houses. This was a new technique. We had not planned for riots at night with the town on fire.

Looters were already at work. People were running out of houses carrying boxes, chairs, tables and curtains.

Suddenly three trucks appeared coming down the road. It was already dusk. The fires were glowing in the burning Ministry of Agriculture. The trucks stopped two hundred yards short of the crowd. Soldiers in battle order, with steel helmets and gas masks, jumped out. They formed up across the road. Then they began advancing steadily towards the crowd—one hundred men, silent, steady, determined, orderly. In front of them, a howling mob of six or seven thousand, screaming, shouting, looting, throwing burning torches.

The troops advanced steadily. They seemed completely calm, regular, impassive, precise. They glanced right and left to ensure that the leading rank was in dressing. An officer blew his whistle and held up his hand to halt. He waved to the crowd to disperse. His voice was inaudible in the noise and pandemonium which prevailed.

"Gas!" shouted the officer, and in a matter of seconds every soldier was transformed into a hideous pig-like figure with a ghastly green snout.

"Two gas bombs—throw!" yelled the officer, above the noise of the crowd. Two soldiers came forward through the front rank. They stood with their feet apart, they swung their bodies back, right arms straight and slung two small black balls into the crowd. A minute elapsed, and suddenly the crowd was in confusion. Some sought to run away, hands to their eyes, some fought with others to escape.

The troops resumed their slow and deliberate advance. The front rank moved forward with fixed bayonets in front of them at the ready. The bomb-throwers came behind them, then the reserve platoon. In the rear came the wireless truck, its long, whippy aerial waving right and left.

Now the crowd was running, some down the main road, others up side streets to right and left. Soon the main road was clear, except for smouldering debris, abandoned heaps of loot and the gutted fire engine. The troops moved slowly forward into the town. There had been no casualties.

The telephone rang again. It was police headquarters.

"Another crowd is attacking the Philadelphia Hotel," said the duty officer. "They have thrown stones and broken the windows. They are forcing the doors. The hotel is full of foreign tourists."

I picked up the telephone again.

"The crowd is now attacking the Philadelphia Hotel. Tell 2nd Regiment to send another company to disperse them."

It was all over in about twenty minutes. I told the Prime Minister that order had been re-established. He asked me to come round to his house. There he wrote out an order, addressed to me, establishing a curfew for the next day. He spoke to the governors of the districts, telling them to impose curfews. It was the Orthodox Church Christmas Day, with the result that we could not impose a curfew in Jerusalem, which was full of pilgrims. It was imposed there twenty-four hours later.

Next day when I drove to the office, the curfew in Amman was complete. Only here and there, a patrol of soldiers moved along the silent streets. We not only imposed a curfew, but we also occupied the telephone exchange in Amman, and operated it with Arab Legion operators. After two days, we lifted the curfew for two hours for shopping. By the fourth day, the town was begging to be allowed to resume work. The municipal council passed a resolution condemning riots and political demonstrations. We gradually released the curfew, and normal life returned. This time the government had been victorious, and had to a great extent re-established its prestige.

While we had stopped these disturbances by using the curfew, we had not enough men to keep order all over the country. The village of Remtha, on the Syrian border, had cut the road and held up vehicles. Some villages in Ajlun had attacked an American mission house. The large refugee camps in the Jordan valley had rioted wildly and taken to looting. We had not had enough troops to impose a curfew in Hebron, and the people of the town had been giving trouble.

Meanwhile, Ibrahim Pasha had assumed office only on condition that he was to form a caretaker government, pending new elections. Now that the dissolution had been declared illegal and there were to be no elections, he resigned. Sameer Pasha Rifai formed a new government. Sameer Pasha had been in office when King Abdulla was murdered. In Jordan, he had the reputation for being unlucky. Something disastrous always happened when he was in office.

I held a conference with Sameer Pasha about the refugees and the villagers. Now that the government had re-established its position, it seemed to us advisable to take action against people who had taken advantage of our preoccupation to indulge in disorder or looting. We agreed to form a small mobile force to visit the villages and refugee camps one after the other, arrest the ringleaders of the disturbances, recover looted property and assess the damage. This little operation was completely successful. It was carried out entirely under the command of Jordanian officers, to avoid any political complications.

King Husain, on several occasions, expressed his thanks to the Arab Legion for their work in restoring order and stability. I think that he really was grateful. I accompanied him on a visit to all the units in and around Amman which had assisted in quelling the riots. In each unit, he spoke a few words of thanks to officers and men. Then we did the same in Zerqa. The troops had really done splendidly, in a task most distasteful to all soldiers. They deserved the thanks of their King and their country.

"Voice of the Arabs" conceded that the "enemies of the Jordan people" had won. The tactics used by the Egyptians had failed. They had devoted all their efforts to raising the masses in revolt, in the hope of overthrowing the throne and making Jordan an Egyptian satellite. Their efforts had proved vain, solely owing to the discipline and loyalty of the Arab Legion. They decided to concentrate on securing my dismissal and on undermining the loyalty of the Arab Legion. "Voice of the Arabs" switched from popular agitation to denunciation of me.

Curiously enough, after the abortive riots in January, the Communists announced in Ramallah, apparently with complete confidence, that I should be dismissed within three months. They proved to be right. My dismissal took place six weeks later. As this narrative will show, it was the King, and he alone, who removed me. It is scarcely to be imagined that the King confided his intention to the Communists six weeks in advance. Perhaps it was merely a coincidence. The Communists undoubtedly make use of a policy of announcing their triumph in advance, in order to lower the prestige of their enemies and strike fear into their supporters.

*   *   *   *   *

No sooner were the riots at an end than we turned once more to defence against Israel. We regarded the summer of 1956 as a period of special danger, and issued a warning order to all commanders that a major Israeli offensive was likely between March and November 1956. The Israelis still enjoyed a military preponderance over all the Arab armies put together, in addition to which the Arab States had never been more disunited. But heavy shipments of Soviet arms to Egypt were causing Israel alarm for the future. It was not unlikely that Israel would decide to strike first. It seemed to us risky for Israel to attack the Egyptian army, leaving the Arab Legion so near Tel Aviv. We consequently visualized the possibility of a sudden Israeli attack on Jordan, with a view to moving the frontier to the Jordan river. If this could be done, the Israelis would have overcome the strategic danger which arose from the narrowness of the coastal plain. It was possible, however, that Israel might attack the Egyptian army first, leaving holding forces to defend their line against Jordan.[1]

In such an operation, we calculated that the Israelis could destroy the Egyptian army in Gaza and Sinai in five or six days, and be back with their full army facing us in a week.

The irony of the situation was that we could not discuss these possibilities with the Egyptian army, because the Egyptian government had embarked on a full-scale propaganda attack on the Arab Legion.

Another irony lay in the fact that the Arab Legion had a very full programme of defence works and training, in readiness for a possible

[1] This actually occurred in November 1956.

Israeli offensive in the summer. The whole programme was delayed and most of it abandoned owing to the riots. Yet the alleged reason for the riots was that we were said not to be sincere in our measures to defend Jordan against Israel. Was there ever a more insane situation?

It had become a custom for the Arab Legion to hold a conference in February of each year, to discuss defence measures for the forth-coming summer campaigning season. It was possible to carry out an offensive in winter in the desert conditions of the Gaza–Sinai area, but it was thought unlikely that the Israelis would embark on a winter offensive in the mountains of Samaria and Judaea. Thus a February planning conference enabled all commanders to be briefed just before the campaigning season began. Our 1956 defence con-ference had to be postponed owing to the riots. It was fixed for the 3rd to 5th March. As I was dismissed on March 1st, no conference ever took place.

*   *   *   *   *

In 1952, an Arab Legion officer in the Supply and Transport Corps had been dismissed the service for financial dishonesty. In-tent on revenge, he went to Beirut, where he printed a number of pamphlets directed against myself, and signed them "Free Officers". We obtained information of the activities of this ex-officer through the Lebanese police. He was warned, and no further pamphlets appeared.

In 1955, pamphlets began once more to appear with the signature of "Free Officers". For the moment we were perplexed. The pam-phlets were sent by post to various addresses. They bore an Amman postmark. Then two incidents drew our attention. One pamphlet contained a number of military terms used in the Egyptian army. The Jordan names for the same things were different. Obviously, therefore, the pamphlets were not, as was pretended, written by Arab Legion officers.

Then they made another mistake. A copy of one of these pam-phlets was reproduced in an Egyptian newspaper, with an article alleging that the pamphlet had been sent to the editor "by a corres-pondent in Jordan". But this pamphlet had not yet been circulated in Jordan! It arrived a day or two later. We sent a man to Egypt to investigate. He reported soon afterwards that a copy of the pam-phlet had been sent to the newspaper by the Egyptian Ministry of National Guidance, with orders to publish it with a leading article commenting on the disloyal movements among Arab Legion officers. Thus the plot stood revealed. The Free Officers were the Egyptian government, the pamphlets were printed in Cairo. We suspected that they were sent to the Egyptian Embassy in Amman by diplomatic bag, but we could not prove this—anyhow, they were smuggled in. They were posted in Jordan.

In February 1956, the Egyptian Ministry of National Guidance excelled itself. One morning, we received in Arab Legion head-quarters several letters from different units, enclosing envelopes and pamphlets. All bore the rubber stamps of different Arab Legion units. Thus the 5th Infantry Regiment had received by post sub-versive pamphlets signed "Free Officers" and bearing the office stamp of the 3rd Brigade headquarters. The Engineers had received them stamped "Headquarters Nablus District", and so on. The recipients were alarmed and had written hastily to inform head-quarters that there obviously must be a group of disloyal officers in the other unit, the office stamp of which had been on the pamphlets they received.

We called in all the office stamps of the units concerned. As soon as the stamps on the envelopes and pamphlets were compared with the original office stamps, it was obvious that the stamps used on the pamphlets were forgeries. We issued a circular to all units to explain this. The incident is of interest in showing the lengths to which Egyptian propaganda would go in order to undermine the morale of an allied army, itself intent on preparing to resist attack by Israel, "the common enemy".

A curious situation indeed had arisen owing to the fact that the United Nations has concentrated so much of its attention on the prevention of open, armed conflict. The art of subversion, or creating confusion and rebellion in another country, has attained a remarkable degree of skill. Such action, though intensely hostile, is not regarded as aggression, though it may lead to civil war, refugees and an immense extension of hatred and human misery. A country attacked in this manner, as was Jordan, has no redress, although these methods can do as much damage as active warfare. If the Egyptian army had attempted to invade Jordan, it would have been defeated. By propaganda, lies, forgery and calumny, the stability of Jordan was destroyed.

Failing an appeal to a supernational authority, the only reply would appear to be retaliation of a similar kind. For moral reasons, a rival campaign of lying and forgery cannot be accepted as the solution. The possibility of countering such a campaign by energetic and widespread publicity, telling the truth, does not appear to have been adequately tried. In face of libel, the British government remains silent and aloof, or, at rare intervals, issues a laconic com-muniqué to the effect that a certain statement is completely untrue. The statement is rarely repeated more than once, and includes no proof.

The righteous, says the Sermon on the Mount, are the salt of the earth. They are to be as wise as serpents, though as harmless as doves. Why is it that British virtue has so monotonous a tendency to be dull? The reply to libellous propaganda should be well seasoned with salt. It must always be true, but it must at the same time be copious, witty, vivacious, pathetic, sarcastic—perhaps tragic—but always entertaining. And, above all, it must have a few simple themes which anyone can understand which emerge incessantly under innumerable forms and as the point of every joke or story. "Britain and America stand for personal freedom" might do for one. No more than two or three should be on the programme at any one time. The great masses of the human race cannot grasp abstruse speculations. They like the points to be plain, but noble and worthy.

* * * * *

Throughout February, the Egyptian propaganda campaign was almost wholly directed against the Arab Legion and myself. The Syrian newspapers followed suit.

Inspired as I was by deep affection and loyalty to the King and people of Jordan, the feature of this propaganda which I found most trying was the constant attribution of evil motives to our every action. By this method all human affection and mutual confidence could be undermined. One instance of this caused me an especial pang.

Immediately after we were married in 1938, my wife had taken a great interest in the barefooted little boys who used to run errands and carry parcels for shoppers in Amman. She rescued many of these boys, and we took an empty house for them, looked after them and engaged a schoolmaster to teach them. Several of them did very well, though a few were failures. One or two eventually became officers in the Arab Legion, one even going to Sandhurst. Others became N.C.O.s or soldiers. A lame boy who had suffered from polio was set up as a shopkeeper in Kerak. We enabled another cripple, whom my wife found begging, to open a shop in Amman. When we had several children of our own, my wife was obliged to give up this work, but we maintained affectionate relations with most of these boys when they were established in the world. They often looked in at our house, irrespective of their rank, when they happened to pass through Amman. They came to tell us of their little affairs—one was married, another had a baby, a third had been promoted to sergeant.

It was at the end of 1955 that one of these boys was sitting with a group of civilians in Amman. They were discussing the riots and one of those present made a derogatory remark about me. The boy whom we had brought up agreed with the denunciation of me. Another man present, however, protested.

"You ought not to say anything against the Pasha," he said. "After all, you owe everything to him."

"I used to think that myself," our boy replied. "But now the whole matter has been explained to me. I realize now they did not care for me at all—it was all clever politics. That was why they helped me. We don't want any foreigners in this country."

In this way, everything we said or did was interpreted as deceit or trickery, done with a selfish object. By such means were friendship and confidence transformed into hatred and suspicion.

I have mentioned that, during these disturbances, villagers in Ajlun attacked the house of some American missionaries. When order was restored, an Arab told certain Americans that I had connived at these attacks because I wanted to get rid of them. This report made quite a stir among the American community. Eventually the Ambassador of the United States, Mr. Mallory, held a meeting, at which he explained the falsity of such rumours.

It is a striking fact that Britain and France were allies for thirty years in Europe, but at the same time regarded one another with intense hostility in the Middle East. Now the same situation exists between the British and Americans—always in disagreement in the Middle East, but united elsewhere. These facts are not coincidences. The Middle East politicians are experts at playing one nation off against another. They will tell one man how much they love him, but will complain to him of the conduct of another. They then go off to the second one with protestations of affection, but complain to him of the first.

Thus the British believe that the Arabs like them but hate the Americans, and *vice versa*. The vanity and simplicity of Westerners cause them to be constantly deceived by these tactics, and friction and resentment result.

XXVI

Nunc Dimittis

And king Rehoboam consulted with the old men, that stood before Solomon his father while he yet lived, and said, "How do ye advise? . . ."
But he forsook the counsel of the old men, which they had given him, and consulted with the young men that were grown up with him.

I Kings. xii

Above all, believe it, the sweetest canticle is "Nunc dimittis".

FRANCIS BACON

XXVI

NUNC DIMITTIS

I WAS so used to personal vilification that I was not greatly distressed by the February campaign. Besides which, the people with whom I dealt day by day all knew me personally. The effect was more intense in countries where I was not known in person—Egypt, Syria and Lebanon, and perhaps the more distant Arabic-speaking countries like Libya, the Sudan and the Yemen. Yet these other Arab countries, impressed by the propaganda, produced a reflex reaction in Jordan.

Between the two world wars, when Palestine, Lebanon and Syria were mandates, Trans-Jordan had felt herself in the lead of Arab independence. The British scarcely interfered at all in her internal affairs. Now Egypt and Syria were constantly taunting Jordan with being still a colony, while they were free. Young Jordanians visiting neighbouring countries were asked why they tolerated the continued dictatorship of a brutal British general. Even though they knew that I was not a brutal dictator, they felt hurt and humiliated at these jeers. The East- or Trans-Jordanians regarded me as one of themselves—not as a British general. Many Palestinians were my friends, even if they did not regard me quite as one of themselves, as the Easterners did. But I had few friends amongst the refugees, who were deeply penetrated by propaganda to the effect that I had sold Lydda and Ramle to the Jews.

Perhaps my principal handicap was the fact that I was British. Before 1948, the Trans-Jordanians had forgotten this and I had become one of them. The family of a distinguished politician from a neighbouring Arab country visited Petra in 1947, and, owing to weather conditions, was obliged to take refuge in a nearby police post. In the course of conversation one of them asked the police:

"How do you like having a British officer to command you?"

"How do you mean?" answered the police sergeant, puzzled.

"Why, Glubb Pasha, of course," was the answer.

"Glubb Pasha isn't a British officer," cried the men indignantly. "He is one of us."

It was what I had promised King Abdulla.

These intimate relations were not appreciated by other Arab countries, and indeed not entirely so by the Palestinians. The politicians, whether Egyptian, Syrian or extremist Palestinians, delighted to describe me as a dictator. Some European newspapers even repeated these charges. Military dictators are so numerous today that the expression is a common term of abuse. Even the reputable Jordan politicians, however, could not, at times, resist the temptation to put the blame on me when they were in difficulties.

I had no powers of arrest and never, in all my service in Jordan, gave an order to arrest anyone (except in my early years when acting as a magistrate in the desert, to put an end to raiding). Ministers and district governors had certain powers of arrest in addition of course to magistrates. When, however, they had ordered an arrest, they sometimes forestalled criticism by hinting that they were not free agents or that Glubb Pasha was angry. Many people who believed this, but knew me not to be normally an irascible individual, concluded that these actions were secretly ordered by the British government, and consequently thought that the system was in reality somewhat "colonial". These speculations were entirely unfounded. I had no official connection with the British government at all, nor did the latter ever attempt to interfere or give orders. Many of the actions of the Jordan government were by no means popular with the British government, but the latter did not protest.

In reality, most Jordan Cabinets after 1951 suffered from vacillation. Sometimes they ordered a few arrests, but then their hearts would fail them and they would release the persons arrested, who had thereby merely acquired enhanced notoriety. Although the politicians did not always hesitate to put the blame for the arrests on me, they were quick to claim for themselves the credit for the releases.

Knowing that the propaganda was depicting me as a British dictator, I was particularly careful to be absolutely correct, to limit my actions strictly to the duties of a chief of staff, and to take no action outside these duties without an express order from the Prime Minister or the Minister of Defence. I was, I sincerely believe, more punctilious in my obedience to the government than were the Arab chiefs of staff of the armies of the neighbouring countries, a fact admitted on more than one occasion by the ministers concerned.

In fact, I myself was, to a great extent, in the position of the man who tried to have two Christmas dinners. For I was blamed for being a dictator, but in reality had no power (outside the army, of course—of that I was constitutionally the commander); I "derived no benefit but suffered all the blame".

From the point of view of the revolutionary government of Egypt, they had, perhaps, no alternative but to attack me. For their whole policy was founded on the thesis that Britain was the enemy, the oppressor and the exploiter of the Arabs. The existence, in a neighbouring country, of a British chief of staff voluntarily employed by an Arab government to command their army, therefore directly disproved their basic theory. They were logically obliged to claim that this officer was maintained in his appointment by British colonial power, and that the Jordan government did not want him there—or else they had to persuade the Jordan government to get rid of him.

The King had seemed to be very grateful after the suppression of the abortive disturbances in January. One evening he suddenly walked into our house and drank coffee in our drawing-room. On another occasion I was asked to a dinner at his uncle's house, and we dined together in privacy. Some senior Arab Legion officers noticed the change, and remarked that the riots had done at least one good thing if they had reconciled the King to the Pasha. Not that His Majesty had ever been unfriendly to me. Except for the one occasion of his speech at the palace conference on our plans, he had never uttered one word of criticism in my presence. Usually he was extremely cordial and pleasant. I frequently suggested that he should tour towns and villages, and visit Arab Legion units, in order that he might be more widely and personally known to his subjects. Often I went with him.

A year before, I had assured King Husain that I was his servant, not that of the British government.   If he ever wanted to get rid of me, I said, he only had to tell me so, and I would immediately resign.

But the situation was not entirely reassuring. Several Cabinet ministers informed me that Ali abu Nuwar was endeavouring to influence the King against me. Whenever I went to the palace, Ali was in evidence. He was always extremely cordial, perhaps a little too much so. If I had to wait for an audience with the King, he invited me to his room for coffee. He expressed anxiety at the situation, and indignation at the many intrigues directed against Jordan. But certain Arab Legion officers told me that they had been approached by Ali on the necessity of getting rid of me. Ali was not a person who was intrinsically of any importance. He was not much respected in the army. The key to the situation was the young King himself, and the problem was whether Ali could dominate him or convince him.

After the abortive January riots, I had hastily toured tribes and villages in East Jordan. Town dwellers could only riot, and the curfew seemed to be the answer to their activities. Tribesmen and villagers, however, could make rebellions, but ninety per cent of these were behind the throne. The situation seemed to me to be comfortably in hand.

On my return from my tours, however, I was told that certain politicians had informed the King that I had toured the tribes in order to strengthen their loyalty to myself and seduce them from their allegiance to the throne. Of course, the reverse was the case; all my life in Jordan had been spent in the service of the royal family. The intention of the intriguers, however, was to arouse the King's jealousy—to tell him that he would never be really a king as long as I remained in the country.

I accordingly informed His Majesty that I had heard stories to the effect that he had been told that I toured the tribes to seduce them from the throne. I was sure, I added, that he knew that, on the contrary, I had spent a great part of my life in the service of his grandfather, his father and himself. King Husain replied that no-one had told him that I was seducing the tribes. Then, after a moment's silence, he added:

"You know, Pasha, there are people in this country who are trying to make trouble between you and me."

I replied that I knew it, and that we must make sure that they did not succeed. Then we discussed arrangements for a projected visit by His Majesty to Hebron, on which I was to accompany him ten days later. I withdrew after a particularly pleasant and cordial interview.

At nine o'clock the same night I received a telephone call from the palace. It was Ali abu Nuwar speaking. He asked if I would be in Amman the next day. I replied that I had planned to go to Zerqa in the morning but would be back by twelve.

"Does His Majesty want to see me?" I asked.

"It will be all right if you are back by twelve," he replied. "We can get in touch with you then."

Since the end of the riots I had paid frequent visits to Arab Legion units and had explained to officers and men every step in the negotiations. I had also told them that Jordan had now rejected the Baghdad Pact, which was no longer practical politics, because we could not incur the resentment of the other Arab countries. (Admittedly the policy of the government had changed so quickly that it was difficult to keep pace. Until December 18th, King and government had been determined to enter the pact at all costs. Now the official policy was on no account to enter it.)

On the morning of March 1st, I spoke to the officers of the 1st Armoured Car Regiment. I left Zerqa at 11.30 a.m. to return to my office. As we drove through Amman and passed the Prime Minister's office, I noticed the King's car and escort outside the building.

"There must be a meeting of the Council of Ministers," I said casually to an officer with me. "I see our lord's car outside the Prime Minister's office."

I went to my office and started to work on the papers on my table.

Officers came in and out. Then the telephone rang. The Minister of Defence was speaking.

"Could you come down to the Prime Minister's office for a minute?" he said.

"Certainly," I answered. "Do you want me now?"

"Yes," he said, "please come now."

I got into my car and drove to the white stone building of the Prime Minister's office. I was shown into his private room. There was no one there.

"His Excellency is in conference with the Council of Ministers," said the orderly.

A few minutes later the door opened and Sameer Pasha, the Prime Minister, entered, followed by Felah Pasha Medadha, the Minister of Defence, a stout jovial party and rather a friend of mine. Sameer Pasha seemed nervous.

"It is very sad for me to have to say this to you," he began. "His Majesty came here this morning and he said that he thinks it is time you had a rest."

I realized, of course, the meaning of this tactful approach.

"Has anything happened?" I enquired. "What is the reason?"

"I don't know anything about it," said the Prime Minister, obviously relieved that I seemed to be taking it calmly. "The King asked me to summon the Cabinet this morning. When the ministers arrived, he walked into the room and said you were to be dismissed. 'These are my orders. I want them executed at once,' he said. I hope you are not upset," Sameer Pasha added.

"You need not worry about me," I said. "I will not intrigue or make trouble. I have lived most of my life in Jordan. I shall never create difficulties for her or the King."

"I daresay it's only a temporary phase," said Sameer Pasha. "Perhaps in a few days we'll all be welcoming you back. I've been Prime Minister several times, then I have been dismissed, and now I'm back again."

"That may apply to politicians," I said, smiling, "but I don't think it can apply to me."

"Perhaps you think that I should resign sooner than agree," continued the Prime Minister. "I thought of that, but if I did so, the King could easily find another Prime Minister who would be willing to carry out his orders. So it would not help you if I did so."

It occurred to me that some people resign in protest at what they consider unjust, even though obviously someone else will succeed them.

"I would not suggest what course your Excellency should follow," I replied.

I felt no particular emotion. When something happens suddenly to change one's life, one cannot realize it at once. There was a box of cigarettes on the table. I took one and lit it.

"To whom do you want me to hand over, and when do you want me to go?" I asked.

"Can you leave in two hours?" enquired the Prime Minister.

"No, sir!" I said with emphasis, "I cannot! I have lived here for twenty-six years. Almost all my worldly possessions are here, to say nothing of my wife and children."

"You could go and leave your family behind," he hazarded.

"I am afraid I can't do that either," I said.

Eventually we agreed that I would leave at seven o'clock the next morning. We rose and moved to the door. The two Ministers shook hands with me; I had worked with them both, on and off, for twenty years or more.

I went back to my office. I collected a few personal things. The heap of files on the table had grown taller while I was out.

"You can lock up," I said to my orderly. "I shan't be coming back."

When I got home, my wife was in the drawing-room. As I came in, she jumped up smiling.

"Hullo!" she said. "How nice! You're back earlier than usual. Were things slack today at the office?"

"My dear," I said, "the King has dismissed me. We leave Jordan at seven o'clock tomorrow morning—and we shall never come back."

She looked at me for a moment with wide eyes. She turned away from me and looked out of the window. On the dusty hill opposite to us, on the other side of the valley, I could see the little cemetery where our second son was buried. It was nine years now since I had stood there, with only five Arab companions, and had lowered that tiny body into the soil of Jordan. I remembered how I had thought that perhaps I should be buried there too, amongst the simple Jordan folk whom I loved.

My wife turned and looked at me.

"We'll have some tea now," she said. "Then I'll put the children to bed early, and we'll pack all night."

"Thank you, my dear," I said, and she walked past me out of the room.

I glanced round our little drawing-room. It was so small it could only contain the piano, a sofa and three chairs. I had lived for twenty-four years in that room. Eighteen years before I had brought my wife here as a bride. It was a chilly evening in November, and we arrived after dark. I remembered how we had walked into the drawing-room, where my old Sudanese cook had already lit a fire and laid the table for tea. And how my little bride had laughed happily and said: "Isn't it lovely and cosy in here?"

When the children were in bed and asleep, we began to pack. We were to go in an Arab Legion aircraft and could take only a suitcase each. The problem was what to put in. Our inclination was to take the things we loved, rather than what was useful. I packed my father's and my own medals, and the family miniatures, and a few pieces of silver, presentations to my great-grandfather and silver cups won by my father.

* * * * *

The British Ambassador came in late in the evening. He had had an audience with the King and had asked him in vain to delay action. A telegram for King Husain had arrived from Sir Anthony Eden, asking for time to consider the situation. The King, however, had been warned by his friends to beware of the wiles of the British, and to say nothing to the British Ambassador.

Various reasons have been given why the King took his sudden decision. A few days before he had asked me for a return of ammunition in stock. An officer had prepared a list and a covering letter. In the letter it was explained that our target had been to accumulate ammunition for so many weeks of war. The number of weeks was based on the estimated time required to acquire fresh stocks after war had commenced. We had to hold enough ammunition in reserve to bridge the time gap between the outbreak of war and the arrival of fresh stocks in wartime. The covering letter explained this and said that the attached list showed the deficiencies which had still not been made up. In actual practice, ammunition stocks were almost complete, according to the agreed holdings. As a result, the list of deficiences was extremely short, and showed only a few rather subsidiary kinds, such as red and green shells for mortars, smoke shells for artillery and a few similar items. It subsequently came to light (after I left Jordan) that His Majesty and Ali abu Nuwar did not read the covering letter, but only the list attached to it. They jumped to the conclusion that the list represented the total ammunition held in store, not the deficiencies. They were naturally shocked at the idea that the commander of the army, threatened by an invasion, had provided only coloured lights and smoke with which to repulse the enemy.

Another immediate irritant had been an article which appeared in an English periodical. This had implied, though not in so many words, that I was the real ruler of the country, while the King had little power. This of course was what the intriguers had been telling the King. He was incensed at seeing the same idea reproduced in an English paper.

The King had been enthusiastically determined to enter the Baghdad Pact, and had thereby incurred the hostility of Egypt and of the Jordan extremists. The policy had failed. It was pointed out to him that he could regain his popularity with these extremely vocal enemies at one stroke. To perform some act of defiance towards Britain and to dismiss me would immediately re-establish his popularity with the noisy politicians at home, and would quieten the active hostility of Egypt. At the same time, however, the King's mind and imagination had been genuinely fired by Arab Nationalism, precisely at the age when young men are most susceptible to the appeal of what appear to them to be idealistic causes.

We nearly all act from mixed motives. The King was probably influenced partly by the illusion that I had neglected to provide ammunition, partly by a desire himself to exercise authority unfettered by a middle-aged and cautious adviser. He also believed that to defy Britain would restore his popularity and, finally his imagination was fired by the idea of being the hero of his country.

But while these may or may not have been the immediate reasons for the King's sudden resolve, he had been considering whether or not to get rid of me for at least a year. Eleven months had elapsed since his speech at the conference of war plans at the palace. Probably he himself had varied. Sometimes he trusted and relied on me, sometimes he resented or suspected me. Perhaps the difference in age was the greatest obstacle. I was nearly a contemporary of his grandfather. He was twenty years old, and I was fifty-eight.

During General Templer's visit to Amman three months before, he had been accorded a private audience with King Husain, and had specifically asked him whether he wanted to retain my services, and that of his other British officers. The King had answered that he did.

* * * * *

A number of Arab officers came in after dark. They were all from Arab Legion H.Q. or near to me. Units outside Amman did not hear of my dismissal until the next day.

Several officers were in tears. One drew his revolver and said he would avenge me, until I succeeded in quietening him down. The men of my escort came to say good-bye. Many burst into tears and fled from the room. Without them, I would probably have been murdered long before. We lay down at midnight. At half-past four the alarm clock went, and we finished our packing, and then woke our children. Our old cook (he was with me twenty-five years) gave us coffee, with the tears running down his face.

During the night, we had received a telephone message to say that our aircraft would leave at six, instead of seven o'clock. We accordingly set out at six, but at the gate there was an officer whom I did not know.

"It is forbidden to leave the house," he shouted—so we went back.

In a subsequent Press interview, Ali abu Nuwar told a pressman that I had tried to escape at six o'clock, in order to take refuge with the R.A.F.

At twenty minutes to seven, a car arrived bringing the King's Chamberlain and the Minister of Defence. They stated that they had come to escort me to the airport. They protested when I said that I would follow with my family, in my own car. They pressed me to come in their car and to sit between them. Perhaps they also had been told that I might try to escape.

I do not think that it was from discourtesy or hatred that the King wanted me to leave at two hours' notice. His young advisers had told him that I would probably call the Arab Legion to march on Amman, dethrone the King and establish a dictatorship. It was perhaps how they would have behaved. The telephones to the houses of British officers had been cut the evening before—presumably to prevent this. In practice, one or two units did contemplate action when they heard of my dismissal. In every case it was the British officers who prevented incidents.

Many accounts of my dismissal have been published. The majority attributed it to a military *coup d'état* by the Arab Legion. This was not the case. The King was the originator of the order. Ali abu Nuwar and two other young A.D.C.s were the King's advisers. Three other young officers, friends of the A.D.C.s, were also aware of what was afoot. The names of all six officers were known to us as being intriguers. But they were friends of the King.

My dismissal was perfectly legal. I was ordered to leave by the King and the Cabinet in office. I was a servant of the Jordan, not of the British, government. I was subsequently told that the Cabinet had voted whether to dismiss me or not, that the votes were equally divided and that the Prime Minister gave the casting vote for dismissal. I do not know whether this was so or not.

In my interview with him, the Prime Minister had told me that the King's order had been a complete surprise to him. Another cabinet minister subsequently told the British Ambassador that this was untrue, and that His Majesty had discussed the matter with several Cabinet ministers a few days previously.

Sameer Pasha had visited Egypt shortly before. There were people who claimed that he had settled it with the Egyptian government. We shall never know the truth—nor does it matter. The essential fact is that my dismissal was perfectly legal. It was not a revolution, or a mutiny.

* * * * *

I chatted with the Chamberlain and the Minister on the way to the airport. One armoured car was our sole escort. The Chamberlain presented me with a portrait photograph of the King in a silver frame. His Majesty had written across the photograph in his own handwriting:

"With our acknowledgment of the good services and untiring exertions and with our best wishes for His Excellency General Glubb Pasha. 1/3/56. Husain Tellal."

I asked the Chamberlain to thank His Majesty.

At the airport were the British Ambassador, Mr. Charles Duke, and six or eight people. It was a chilly March morning, with light clouds. It had been raining, and there were pools of water here and there on the tarmac. I spoke to a few people while our suitcases were loaded. Then I said good-bye to my escort, my orderly and my driver. We shook hands with the Ambassador and Mrs. Duke, the Chamberlain and the Minister of Defence. The children and my wife ran up the steps into the aircraft. At the door I turned to wave goodbye; then we sat down.

As the aircraft rose into the air, I could see the city of Amman below us. I had first seen Amman in 1924, when I arrived on a camel, having ridden across five hundred miles of desert from Baghdad. Then it was a little village. Now it was a city of a quarter of a million inhabitants.

"You are a founder member of this kingdom," a former Prime Minister had once said to me.

For twenty-six years I had watched the country grow up. From a handful of policemen, I had seen the Arab Legion grow to an army of 23,000 men and a National Guard of 30,000. When reservists were called out, they could put nearly 60,000 men in the field.

Now, in a few hours, twenty-six years of work had been destroyed. For I had not handed over to anyone. The British officers were virtually under house arrest. All the Jordanian commanding officers had been deprived of their commands by the King's orders. No army could survive such a purge.

Already Jordan had faded into the blue distance of the horizon. We swung to the west as we passed over Damascus, leaving the snowy crest of Mount Hermon on our left. Soon we skimmed over the ridges of Lebanon, splodged with patches of snow, and headed over the calm blue Mediterranean. Fascinated, I watched the Arab coast fade into the blue mist.

I turned away and laughed.

"I expect the children will want a second breakfast by the time we get to Cyprus," I said.

Epilogue

Dost Thou not know, my son, with how little wisdom the world is governed?   COUNT OXENSTIERNA

Si jeunesse savait; si vieillesse pouvait.   HENRI ESTIENNE

For I know this, that after my departing shall grievous wolves enter in among you, not sparing the flock. Also of your own selves shall men arise, speaking perverse things, to draw away disciples after them.   *Acts* xx. 29, 30

EPILOGUE[1]

AFTER my departure, King Husain was hailed by the extremists as the saviour of his country. Much of the extremist bitterness injected into Jordanian politics from 1951 onwards had been due to a Damascus political party called the "Ba'th", founded after the Second World War. (Its full name was Al Ba'th al Arabi meaning The Arab Renaissance.) In internal politics, the Ba'this were supposed to be left-wing socialists, but these European labels mean little in Arab politics. What is more important is that they were intensely nationalistic, and that, since about 1954, they had made common cause with the Communists.

Communism as an ideology has few genuine adherents in the Arab countries, but extreme nationalism and xenophobia can command wide support, particularly among the young. The Ba'this were of course left-wing republicans, whereas, in 1951 to 1954, the Hashemite royal family seemed to be firmly established. As a result, Ba'thi emissaries in Jordan were instructed to state that the party was prepared to work with either a monarchical or a republican régime, Arab Nationalism being their sole concern. Since 1955, another party appeared in Jordan calling itself the National Socialists. There was little apparent difference between the Ba'this and the National Socialists, both being left-wing near-Communists, and both willing to co-operate with Russia. The Communists, receiving their orders from the Soviet Embassies in Beirut or Damascus, were content for the moment to hang back, and allow the Ba'this and their friends to make the running.

Ali abu Nuwar, when he became politically active after King Abdulla's death, was a member of the Ba'th. The latter having signified its readiness to work with a monarchical régime, and the Communists being willing to keep out of sight, Ali abu Nuwar and his six young officer friends were able to win over King Husain, who, fired with youthful nationalist enthusiasm, became their willing but unconscious tool.

Ever since 1954, the Ba'this had made my dismissal one of their principal objectives. I have already mentioned that, six weeks before my departure, the Communists were saying that I would leave the country before three months had passed, a fact which may show how closely the King's Nationalist supporters were sharing their plans with the Communists. But the Ba'this and the

[1] The Epilogue was written June 1st, 1957.

Communists were a minority in the country, and had, in those days, no influence in the army. Their stroke of genius was to win the King to their side. In the end, of course, they intended to get rid of him also, but they were willing to use him until they had further undermined the loyalty of the country, and particularly until they could seduce the army. As soon as this was done, they believed that King Husain would be at their mercy. The King was thus inveigled into leading a revolution against the throne.

Sameer Pasha, the Prime Minister who informed me of my dismissal, was himself dismissed by King Husain a few weeks later. He was too middle-aged and conservative to be acceptable to the left-wing parties, and was suspected of favouring the United States. The King agreed to dissolve Parliament, and hold another election. A caretaker government was appointed to supervise the elections, and the King himself gave strict orders that the elections were to be free. An extremist left-wing government took office after the elections, consisting of a coalition of the Ba'this and National Socialists, and including one Communist minister—the usual National Front which has preceded Communist revolutions in so many countries all over the world. But the King and the extremists could not fail to be uneasy bedfellows, for the new government was relying more and more on Egypt and Russia. Neither could be expected long to tolerate a monarchy.

If previous moderate Jordan governments had, from weakness and vacillation, failed to put a stop to Communist agitation, the new government set itself to promote revolution by every means at its disposal, including active efforts to seduce the army from its loyalty to the throne. It assumed office a week before the Franco-British landing in Port Said. The Communists and the Ba'this made great capital out of the action by France and Britain. Under the pretext of supporting Jordan in case she also were attacked by Israel, both Saudi Arabia and Syria sent troops into the country. What would have happened if the Israelis had attacked it is difficult to imagine. Bits and pieces of different armies without a common system of training, and with diverse types of arms, are unlikely to be effective in battle. The Syrians later brought their families, and took over a Jordan army cantonment at Mafraq and appeared to have the intention of remaining permanently. Not for the first time, under the pretext of patriotism, they were preparing to grab what they could for themselves.

In Jordan, both the new Prime Minister, Suleiman al Nablusi, and the chief of the general staff of the army, Ali abu Nuwar, were privy to the plot to overthrow King Husain. Ali had been the King's closest friend and confidant, who had persuaded him to break the long-standing alliance of Jordan with Britain. Six years earlier,

Abdulla al Tell had been the recipient of similar favours from King Abdulla, and had betrayed him in the same manner.

The Anglo-Jordan treaty was terminated on March 14th, 1957, and as a result British financial aid, which had amounted to some £12,000,000 a year, also came to an end. Egypt, Saudi Arabia and Syria undertook to pay Jordan this amount. Such an arrangement obviously placed the country entirely under the domination of its new paymasters. It may be argued that she had previously been a servant of Britain in the same manner, but in reality the two situations were different. Britain paid Jordan a subsidy as a long-term investment to ensure stability in the area. She rarely if ever interfered, even when the Jordan government pursued a policy different from that of, and distasteful to, the British government. Egypt was to prove less forbearing.

Friction between the King and the government continued to increase. The latter gave permission for the publication of a Communist newspaper, although the Communist party was still officially proscribed, and although the paper openly demanded a republic and a treaty with Soviet Russia. On January 31st, the King dispatched a letter to the Prime Minister, instructing him to put an end to Communist agitation. The letter was published, but the government took no notice. It became obvious to the public that the King and his government were at cross-purposes. Soon their hostility was undisguised. The King was frequently in consultation with members of the opposition. The government spoke disrespectfully of the King and endeavoured even more actively to turn the army against him.

The net had almost closed on Jordan and on King Husain alike. The conspirators had cut off Jordan from her ally Britain, and had deprived her of her source of funds. Both the Prime Minister and the chief of the general staff of the army were in the plot. It is scarcely to be wondered at that they decided that the time had come for the *coup de grâce*.

It was alleged that Ali abu Nuwar had met the Soviet Ambassador to Syria, and had secured his support for a *coup d'état* in Jordan. A plan was agreed upon with the Syrian army, for the latter to intervene in support of the proposed revolution, the Syrian infantry brigade being still conveniently placed in Jordan territory.

Meanwhile, during the period of one year for which Ali abu Nuwar had been chief of the general staff, a large number of loyal officers of the Jordan army had been discharged, pensioned or sidetracked. Promotion had been governed solely by political considerations. The government had been actively engaged in infiltrating extremist and pro-Soviet personnel into key positions on the staff or in commands, as well as into the rank and file. Young officers of

Ali abu Nuwar's party had been promoted two or three times within the year, and given important commands and appointments.

Fourteen officers, including those who had persuaded King Husain to dismiss me a year earlier, were engaged in organizing the plot. Each of these officers was secretly receiving from Egypt a monthly salary ten times as great as his army pay. In addition, extra funds were available for use in political propaganda within the army, and in persuading other officers to join in the intended revolution. It was believed that the loyalty of some sixty officers had been undermined by these methods, to a greater or lesser extent. Considering that the Arab Legion, when I left, had included some 1,500 officers, it would appear that only some 4.5 per cent. had become disloyal, in spite of the passage of more than a year under the command of a political intriguer, constantly endeavouring to seduce them.

Every detail of the proposed new Jordan Republic seems to have been planned. Even the republican flags had been prepared and were subsequently found in Ali abu Nuwar's desk.

Meanwhile, however, a number of loyal army officers had pretended to join the conspiracy and had warned the King that a military *coup d'état* would take place on April 7th, 1957. Early that morning, he received a telephone message from Zerqa, warning him that a force of armoured cars was leaving the camp by the road leading to Amman. The King telephoned the Prime Minister and the Minister of Defence to ask the meaning of these troop movements, but both professed ignorance. He then rang up Ali abu Nuwar, who replied that the troops were engaged in a training exercise. Both the Egyptian military attaché and the Syrian army staff from Damascus were in constant telephone communication with Ali abu Nuwar, and indeed seemed to be directing the operations.

Meanwhile the armoured column from Zerqa had reached Amman, and a force of armoured cars had surrounded the King's palace. Another detachment had surrounded the residence of the Queen Mother, on the other side of the town. It was rumoured later on that the commander of the column had the King's abdication in his pocket, and that he had been instructed to order the King to sign it. Had he done so, he was to be flown immediately to Cyprus, and an announcement of his abdication and departure was alleged to have been ready for issue to the Jordan broadcasting station. If these reports were correct, it is not evident how the plan miscarried. It appears that the King sent for Ali abu Nuwar, and ordered him to tell the troops to return to barracks, which they did. Presumably the chief of the general staff lost his nerve. Perhaps the position of the conspirators was weakened by the fact that the rank and file of the armoured car regiment were unaware of the object of the operation, and that therefore the King could not be coerced by force. If such an attempt had been made and the troops had discovered what was afoot, they would probably have rallied to the throne.

This fiasco was of great service to the King, for it destroyed his last doubts about the young officers, whom for the previous year he had supported, favoured and promoted. He knew now that he was himself to be their next victim. As a result he exchanged secret communications with a number of loyal officers, who had taken no part in the activities of Ali abu Nuwar and his young friends. The King's brother, the Amir Muhamad, and his cousin, the Amir Zeid, visited the camp in Zerqa and warned loyal units of the plot against the King.

Meanwhile the government decided to challenge the King openly. It prepared a list of a number of senior officials known to be loyal to the throne, decided on their dismissal and sent the list to the palace for the King's approval. This was apparently intended to be an act of defiance. The King replied on April 10th, 1957, by inviting the government to resign. Had it refused, he had the constitutional power to dismiss it.

Tension rose to fever point after the resignation of the government. The three parties, the Ba'this, the National Socialists and the Communists announced that they would oppose the formation of any other government. This was no idle threat. Ever since the elections in the autumn of 1954, they had improved and made frequent use of the street riot. By directing their most active propaganda at school-teachers, they had obtained almost complete control of the schools and could produce student demonstrations at short notice. The refugees had been deeply penetrated by Ba'thi and Communist propaganda and were always ready for trouble. Desperate and embittered, they had nothing more to lose.

It will be recollected that they had used this weapon in December 1955, when Jordan had proposed to join the Baghdad Pact, and they had thereby compelled two governments to resign office within a week. In January 1956, it is true, the Arab Legion had defeated the rioters and restored the prestige of the government, but it was a result that was unlikely to be repeated, because this time the chief of the general staff of the army was himself one of the conspirators.

Meanwhile the three extremist parties produced great numbers of pamphlets, which were distributed far and wide all over the Kingdom. These declarations warned the people of Jordan against American imperialism, and against "Eisenhower the Colonizer", who was plotting with "reactionary elements" against the freedom of Jordan. But here the King found himself not without allies. The religious parties, particularly the Muslim Brethren, had been alarmed by the progress of Communism. They in turn distributed pamphlets calling for support for the King. Meanwhile, with the excitement rising and rioting apparently imminent, the King could find no one willing or able to form a new ministry. Five days passed thus in tension, rumours, excitement and expectation of a violent outbreak. The King never left his palace. He knew now that his throne and perhaps his life might at any moment be forfeit.

Several units of the Arab Legion had, in my time, been enlisted principally from tribesmen, many of them nomadic bedouins. The conspirators regarded these regiments with fear and aversion. The bedouins were hardy simple men, with a straightforward and un-questioning belief in God, even if they were not pious. They were but little corrupted by foreign influences, still regarded the Hashemite dynasty with reverence as descendants of the Prophet Muhamad, and were not fertile soil for Communist propaganda. The con-spirators could not hope to win over these units, but they had appointed one of their party, Lieutenant-Colonel Maan abu Nuwar, the cousin of Ali, to command them.

On April 13th, Maan abu Nuwar gave orders to these bedouin-recruited units to go out on a night exercise. The royal palace, however, as already narrated, had communicated with these units secretly and had warned them of the probable imminence of another attempt against the King. Suspecting a trap, the troops refused to parade for the exercise. Unable to influence them, Maan abu Nuwar appears to have consulted a group of artillery officers, who were privy to the conspiracy. Although the artillery officers in question were involved in the plot, it appears that the N.C.O.s and soldiers were not. It is alleged that the officers of the artillery told their men that the bedouin infantry were mutinying against the King and ordered them to attack them. Whether this version be correct or not, fighting broke out between the different units and resulted in two killed and twenty-five wounded. To such a pass had a year of plotting reduced this once splendid little army.

King Husain was informed, in his palace in Amman, that fighting had broken out between units of the army, twenty miles away in Zerqa. The King, as was his wont, decided to go himself. (Whenever there had been an incident on the Israeli frontier in my time, the King had almost invariably wished to go to the site. Two or three times I had accompanied him, praying that the shooting would be over before we arrived. Royal visits are not always welcomed by military commanders in the middle of a battle.) The King's visit to Zerqa, however, was to result in a triumph. At this moment of crisis, King Husain showed that he possessed the same physical courage as had characterized his grandfather, King Abdulla.

Ordering his traitorous and now alarmed general, Ali abu Nuwar, to accompany him, the King set out for Zerqa. Before reaching the camp, they met a column of troops driving towards Amman. The young King's heart may well have stood still for a moment—were they the traitors who had come to kill him, or the loyalists who had risen to defend his cause? A rumour, it appeared, had reached the cantonment in Zerqa to the effect that the King had already been murdered. The troops, wild with excitement and largely out of control, had set out for Amman to find out the truth. On the way, they met the young Husain himself. Frenzied with enthusiasm, they surrounded the King, cheering excitedly. Then they recognized General Ali abu Nuwar in the car and began shouting "Kill him! There is the traitor!" It was with difficulty that the King rescued his former adviser and sent him back to Amman. Then King Husain drove on to Zerqa, where he visited one unit after another, receiving everywhere a wild ovation. It was a gallant performance, worthy of his grandfather and of his race.

His Majesty returned to the palace in triumph, accompanied by a volunteer escort from the Armoured Car Regiment. When he arrived he found Ali abu Nuwar grovelling. The King permitted him to leave the country, and the next day he crossed the frontier to Damascus. King Husain personally ordered the arrest of the other officers, whom he knew to be of Ali abu Nuwar's party.

Scarcely had this day of passionate emotion drawn to a close, than reports were received in Amman that the Israeli army was concentrating on the frontier. To meet this new peril, the King summoned a meeting in the palace, to which he invited the members of both Houses of Parliament, ex-ministers, and other notables. The conference assembled on April 15th. The King delivered a speech before the meeting, explaining the reports of Israeli military activity, and appealing for unity in face of this danger. Eventually agreement was reached to form a national ministry of neutral politicians, under the premiership of Doctor Husain al Khalidi of Jerusalem. The Israeli threat never materialized.

Both Egypt and Syria were deep in the plot to dethrone King Husain and to create in his place a left-wing republic entirely subservient to themselves. On the day of the crisis, the Syrian troops in Jordan left their camp at Mafraq and occupied strategic points all over the northern province of Ajlun. It was claimed afterwards that the Syrian government had planned to annex this province to Syria, as soon as the King had been dethroned. A subsequent communiqué issued by the Jordan government alleged that, on the day of the crisis, the Syrian army had cut all telephone communications between Jordan, Syria and Iraq, and had established control over all internal telephone communications in the northern province of

Jordan. It was further stated that Syrian officers had armed large numbers of bandits in Jordan, and urged them to commit breaches of the peace. The Syrian army was accused of holding meetings with Communists, and of distributing pamphlets calling for the overthrow of the Jordan government, which they had ostensibly come to support against a possible Israeli attack. As against these Syrian activities, however, King Husain received offers of support from King Saud and from Iraq.

It is extraordinary now to remember that only a few years ago, when King Abdulla was alive, Syria and Saudi Arabia lived in fear of Jordan; and Egypt, with fourteen times her population, viewed her with anxiety as a rival. So immense can be the power and influence of one man.

Meanwhile courts of inquiry had assembled to investigate the plot for a military *coup d'état* and a number of officers were placed under arrest, while others fled to Syria. These proceedings were not at all to the taste of the Ba'this, the National Socialists or the Communists, who had pinned their hopes on the seditious elements which they had encouraged in the army. They foresaw that if the courts of inquiry were allowed to complete their investigations, the conspirators would be eliminated from the army. They accordingly decided to proclaim a general strike and organize riots.

At the same time, the three extremist parties presented their demands to the palace. The first of these was for the cancellation of the army courts of inquiry, the release of all officers under arrest, the return of all officers who had fled to Syria and their reinstatement in their former appointments. They also demanded the rejection of the so-called Eisenhower Plan embodying the policy of the United States, and conformity with the policy of Egypt and Syria. These demands were presented to the King on April 23rd by a deputation of left-wing members of Parliament. They were obviously intended as a challenge to the throne. At the same time, the three parties threatened openly that, unless their demands were accepted, they would raise rebellion all over the country. Faced with such a threat, the "neutral" government of Doctor Husain al Khalidi hastily tendered its resignation. The crisis had already lasted nearly three weeks when this final battle was engaged.

The King summoned the old supporters of the crown in the days of King Abdulla. Ibrahim Pasha Hashim, the octogenarian, became Prime Minister, supported by Sameer Pasha Rifai. Riots broke out in all the cities, but particularly in Amman and on the West Bank. We had fought and won this battle once before, in January 1956, but on that occasion it was the King himself who had thrown away our victory. Now the methods which we had used were applied again, but this time even more drastically. Curfew was imposed on all the towns where rioting was taking place, the army assumed control, martial law was declared, all political parties were abolished, Parliament was dissolved and the constitution was suspended. These drastic measures were quickly effective, and order was restored with the army firmly in control. On April 27th, the government turned its attention from purging the army to dealing with the political parties. Several hundred arrests were made, from among the Communists and the left-wing extremists.

It is extremely difficult to foretell the future of Jordan. For the moment, the King appears to be firmly in the saddle, supported by the army. But Soviet Russia, the Communists, the left-wing extremists, the refugees, the Egyptians—none of these can be expected tamely to accept defeat. A number of the Jordan extremists and conspirators escaped to Syria, whence they will doubtless continue to conspire against their country. King Husain has personality, courage and initiative, but he has hitherto been lacking in experience. It is too early to deduce whether he has now gained experience and will in future persevere in his present course. For the moment, he aspires himself to rule. Will he later on be able to return, even if only partially, to democracy and a parliamentary constitution?

If he succeeds in surmounting these political obstacles, his financial troubles remain. Jordan, cut off by Israel from the Mediterranean, can neither import nor export, except at prohibitive prices by a long land haul through Lebanon and Syria or through the Red Sea and Aqaba. Thus, through no fault of her own, she finds it difficult to live. In addition to this, she is burdened with half a million refugees—one-third of her population. Ever since Trans-Jordan came into existence in 1921, Britain has made up the deficit in her annual budgets. With the termination of the Anglo-Jordan treaty, this financial support has ceased. Jordan now raises money where she can—from Saudi Arabia, the U.S.A., Egypt, Iraq or Britain. But such sources are precarious, in comparison with a single ally bound by a treaty. On the other hand, the system according to which a small country depends on a single Great Power has, rightly or wrongly, become discredited in Asia. At least it permits the sneer that the lesser of the two partners is "only a colony" of her greater ally. Jordan may in future be saved from some of these taunts, even if the economic situation remains thereby insecure.

Many of Jordan's problems are at present unanswerable, especially as her troubles are neither spontaneous nor local. These violent convulsions are only one other aspect of the struggle between Russia and the West, which is bringing so many misfortunes on the human race.

If Britain and America had co-operated in the Middle East as they do in Europe, Communism would not have been able to penetrate the area. To British eyes, the United States seems to follow a double policy. In Europe, she co-operates whole-heartedly, in Asia she often acts against Britain, even joining hands with Russia to oppose her. In a world divided into two ideological camps, such schisms may well prove fatal. The world today is all one piece. Europe cannot be treated as if it were a water-tight compartment, for Europe depends for its strength on commerce and raw materials from other continents. American misunderstandings with France and Britain have resulted in extensive Russian penetration into Asia.

The disastrous manner in which the Suez Canal question was handled by the Western Powers must surely contain for us many lessons. The soldier of today has learned in the hard school of war to foresee, and plan for, every situation which could possibly arise. The practice has not, it would appear, been adopted by the foreign services. While many residents in the Middle East had foreseen a Suez Canal crisis, it was painfully obvious when the emergency arose, that the governments of the Western Powers had not considered such an eventuality and still less had they consulted one another on the subject. Each government reacted differently. Having been thus taken by surprise, however, they still appear to have failed to co-operate.

At the midday Press conference on July 19th, 1956, the London Foreign Office spokesman told the reporters that Britain intended to fulfil her promise of a £5,000,000 grant for the Aswan Dam, provided that the World Bank continued its support and that the United States made its proposed grant. On the same day, a few hours later, the Egyptian Ambassador in Washington called on Mr. Dulles and was told that America had cancelled the grant. The next day the British Foreign Office was obliged to cancel its grant, an embarrassing situation in view of the fact that, twenty-four hours before, the official spokesman in Downing Street had reaffirmed Britain's intention to pay. British relations with Egypt at the time appeared to be improving, an Egyptian trade mission was at the time negotiating in London, and the Cairo radio stations had considerably modified their anti-British broadcasts.

Mr. Dulles does not appear ever to have claimed that he consulted Britain before cancelling America's grant to Egypt. It is essential, moreover, to remember that the Suez Canal is of vital importance to Britain and France, but only of minor importance to the U.S.A. To the outside observer it would appear that America, by an arbitrary action taken without consulting her allies, inflicted on those allies a very serious injury.

It has been claimed that the United States government cancelled the loan to Egypt because she decided that the latter was irretrievably committed to Russia. But if this were the case, why did she give Colonel Nasser her almost passionate support when Britain and France endeavoured to overthrow him by force by landing at Port Said? If the United States did not think that Egypt was committed to Russia, was not her conduct somewhat irresponsible when she precipitated the Suez crisis, by cancelling the proposed loan?

Few things are more difficult than to judge the relative truth of different ideals. Suffice it to say that, in areas where British and Americans work side by side, the superior moral standards of the latter are not always universally recognized. In the Middle East, the United States, while publicly denouncing Britain, seems often to adopt methods remarkably similar to those previously adopted by the British. The United States government, for example, explained at the time why she opposed the landing at Port Said. American policy, it was stated, was guided by a high standard of idealism—she would never use force as Britain had attempted to do. Yet four months later, when the new crisis arose in Jordan, the United States Sixth Fleet was sent to the Eastern Mediterranean. If the American government had declared the landing at Port Said to be unwise and ill-timed, many people would have agreed whole-heartedly. It could then have justified the despatch of the Sixth Fleet as being more timely and more efficiently carried out. But condemnation of the Port Said landing was not on these lines, but was based almost entirely on the moral principle of the wickedness of the use of force. If morality is to be the touchstone, why was it wicked to send the British and French fleets but wise and righteous to send the Sixth Fleet?

We must be careful, in our mental processes, that our complaints are not caused by jealousy of the rapid rise of America to power. It is a mistake to imagine that Britain was once supreme in the world, and that the United States has now taken her place. Britain has always been a small country. At the time of the Spanish Armada, the power and resources of Spain were vastly greater than those of England. Napoleon's France had a population four times as great as that of the Britain of those days. It is quality not quantity that counts.

The inability of Britain and America to co-operate in Asia has been largely due to the opinion, widely held in the United States, that British foreign policy is of a lower moral quality than that of America. Such a belief is obviously genuine and sincere, but it may possibly be founded on incomplete knowledge. Living in a vast country still only partially developed and containing immense resources, Americans have hitherto had little inducement to wander over the face of the globe. As a result, they have little conception of the immense amount of loving service and devoted idealism which great numbers of British men and women have expended on other races all over the world. When the Pharisee thanked God that he was not as other men are, he undoubtedly spoke from conviction, but his estimate of his own moral superiority was based on an incorrect appreciation of the facts. In spite of his obvious sincerity, he was less highly commended than the poor publican.

Both countries are doubtless to blame for their misunderstandings. We are too near to these events to be able to judge them impartially, but the historian of a thousand years hence may well be amazed that the statesmen of the United States and Britain, the two great protagonists of democracy, should have been unable to overcome their petty differences in the interests of human freedom all the world over.

*   *   *   *   *

The reverse suffered by Communist and Egyptian policy in Jordan in April 1957 was soon followed by another damaging revelation. A plot was discovered to assassinate King Saud of Saudi Arabia, and it was stated that the conspiracy had been directed by the Egyptian military attaché in that country. This incident emphasized another aspect of Egyptian policy, which had been evident since 1954. Egyptian ambassadors in the Arab countries had in many cases been elderly men, who constituted respectable diplomatic figures, often not in entire sympathy with Colonel Nasser's revolutionary régime. In each Embassy, however, the military attaché was a young army officer and a close associate of the Nasser group. His duties were twofold. The first was to report to the Egyptian government on the words and actions of the ambassador. The second was to organize subversive propaganda, terrorist activities and assassinations in the country to which he was accredited. Reference has already been made to the Egyptian military attaché in Amman urging the Jordan police not to disperse rioting crowds. On the night of the 11th May, 1957, the Jordan broadcasting service claimed that the Egyptian military attaché in Amman had received a sum of money to organize the assassination of King Husain. The same broadcast claimed that the Egyptian assistant military attaché in Beirut had been a member of a committee of which the Russian vice-consul and the Soviet assistant military attaché were members, to organize the *coup d'état* in Jordan. Already in 1955, the Egyptian military attaché in Baghdad had been discovered to be organizing terrorist activities, and similar incidents have occurred in Libya.

For forty years, Arabia has been split by the rivalry between the Saudi and the Hashemite dynasties. I remember twenty years ago, at a meeting with the Saudi Arabian frontier inspector, the Amir Abdul Aziz as Sudairi, remarking that the development which I most desired would be a real Saudi-Hashemite reconciliation. "If

God wills, they will be reconciled," the Sudairi had remarked piously. Their dynastic rivalries were to continue until 1957. Perhaps the growing threat of Communism and Russian domination, combined with Colonel Nasser's attempts to assassinate all the Arab kings, may at last effect such a reconciliation. Moreover, Iraq and Saudi Arabia both command the financial resources to pay the Jordan subsidy should they wish to do so.

Meanwhile a general election was due to take place in Lebanon. The Egyptian–Syrian–Communist front employed their usual tactics. Syria was particularly well placed, and Syrian arms and rioters easily infiltrated into Lebanon. On May 30th, 1957, rioting began in Beirut on precisely the same lines as had been used again and again in Jordan and elsewhere. The same passionate appeals for revolt on the Egyptian radio, the same distribution of money, the threats and terrorism, the Soviet and Egyptian Embassies organizing subversion. Even the tactical methods used by the rioters were identical—the erection of barriers across the streets, the posting of men on the flat roof-tops with a supply of stones to throw down on the police. There is no attempt at originality in the Egyptian-Communist technique; the same blue-print is everywhere in use.

Perhaps the crudeness of Egyptian methods, the violent propaganda and the attempts to assassinate their Arab rivals, may eventually discredit Colonel Nasser's régime. But such a development would not detract from the alarming potentialities of mass emotional propaganda campaigns. The German people eventually discovered the truth about the propaganda of Herr Goebbels, but not until many millions of human beings had been killed, crippled or driven from their homes. Colonel Nasser will eventually disappear, and Egypt will obtain another government, but we cannot foresee what sorrow, losses and confusion will have been caused before then.

Mussolini was perhaps the first politician to introduce passionate emotional propaganda as a means of exploiting the masses for his own political ends. Hitler and Goebbels immensely improved on their Italian model. Moscow has inherited these diabolical arts. The basis of this type of propaganda may be summarized in a few lines:

Firstly, always to appeal to passion, never to logic or reason.

Secondly, to remember that negative passions are more easily aroused than positive—hatred, jealousy and resentment are more powerful for the destruction of rivals than are attempts to win loyalty or affection for Russia or Egypt themselves. To provoke hatred, a villain is necessary. Russia's or Egypt's enemies must be labelled as the villains and hatred against them fanned into flame.

Third principle—human nature is more interested in people than in ideologies. Therefore, where possible choose individuals and make them objects of hatred. Regardless of truth, load them with abuse as traitors, butchers, cruel, corrupt, greedy, immoral—it does not matter much what you say, some of the mud will stick. (I personally was the victim of a campaign of this type.) Finally, the public will believe anything if they hear it often enough. Constantly repeated catch-words and slogans form a never-ending theme.

Britain herself is today the victim of such psychological campaigns all over the world. Tyrants in past ages could only torture or destroy our bodies. Now they can dominate and distort our minds, and deliberately inspire us with jealousy and hatred for our fellow men. It is essential for us to study what methods can be adopted to protect mankind from evil thoughts, false beliefs and vile suggestions deliberately projected into their unthinking minds by wicked men.

For the rest, we should all be happier if every nation were to seek to improve itself, rather than spend so much time and breath in denouncing others.

It is related of the famous Curé d'Ars, that an admirer asked him how he managed to exercise so great a degree of spiritual control over his parishioners. He is said to have replied: "By always being very hard on myself and very lenient to others."

It is a lesson which might well be learnt by those politicians who seek to win the applause of their supporters by pointing out what other nations have done wrong.

If I had my way, I would write in golden letters on the wall of the office of every Foreign Minister in the world, the words of the Divine command: "Judge not that ye be not judged." How vastly improved international relations would be if we were all to follow such a maxim.

*   *   *   *   *

So much of this book has been devoted to fighting between Jews and Arabs, that it would be wrong to omit all mention of the subject in a final summing-up. There is no golden road to peace in Palestine, but undoubtedly the settlement of the problem of a million Arab refugees is an essential preliminary to stability. For the rest, a policy of bloody reprisals and counter-reprisals is disastrous for all. Israel will have to make some concessions if she is to live in amity with her neighbours, to whom she has caused so much suffering. The Arabs have constantly made mistakes, but the fact that a million Arabs have lost their homes and their country cannot be gainsaid.

Meanwhile, however, progress is rendered infinitely more difficult by the fact that it is in Russia's interest to perpetuate confusion. In her present mood, she can be relied upon to nullify any constructive attempt at a solution. Though she was the champion of Israel in 1948, she now claims to be the defender of the Arab cause. Colonel

Nasser also, like all dictators, finds it in his interest to breed hatred. To upstart rulers, successive crises are a useful expedient for the maintenance of their power.

* * * * *

I began my book with Jordan, and will end it on the same note, for Jordan has been my country, almost as much as Britain.

Some people claim that Jordan was an artificial creation and that there is no need for her to survive. For that matter, nearly all the nations of the world were artificial creations produced by the political expediency of their time. By living as one nation, peoples of varied origin have become a single entity with a national individuality.

From 1920 to 1953, Trans-Jordan (and then Jordan) developed many peculiarities of her own. She alone of the Arab countries seemed to have discovered the secret of success. The Arabs could not progress without European help, yet they feared to accept that help lest it lead to European domination. In some cases, doubtless Western help was given in a tactless, supercilious or dominating manner. Some of the Arabs reacted by refusing the help—and remaining backward and chaotic.

In Jordan alone, under the influence of King Abdulla, was the assistance whole-heartedly accepted, yet without submission. Of all the Arab countries, perhaps Jordan was the only one which benefited to the full by cordial co-operation with Britain, while always remaining an equal.

Under the King's wise guidance, she developed a broad and statesmanlike attitude to the world, a genial welcome to foreigners and a stalwart common sense, qualities so often conspicuous by their absence in the narrow and embittered politics of the Middle East today.

The fact that Jordan for thirty years found the secret of benefiting from Western aid, without losing her own character or dignity, presents us with a tantalizing vision. For the rest of Arabia— indeed the rest of Asia—was all this time travelling in the opposite direction. Jordan alone was too small to turn the tide. If only some greater Asiatic country had been able to set the example by achieving the same Asio-European harmony, the history of the world might have been different.

To me, it is a sad thing that the special relations between Jordan and Britain have come to an end. Not indeed that British material interests need thereby suffer. The object of British policy was merely that the country be stable, peaceful and friendly—conditions which necessitated it remaining outside the Communist camp. An alliance with the U.S.A. or with Iraq and Saudi Arabia may perhaps produce the same result, and save the British taxpayer the cost of the subsidy.

My regrets are less materialistic. Indeed, apart from my personal love for so many of my friends, it seems sad to me that so long and intimate a relationship should come to an end—a relationship not limited to a political alliance between the two governments, but which embraced the people of the two countries and, to an extraordinary degree, a close comradeship between all ranks of their respective armies.

I do not think that we should allow these political vicissitudes to cloud our memories of the Second World War and of Trans-Jordan's heroic stand by Britain's side in 1941. We must remember also that they, but even more the Palestinians, have suffered a grievous wrong. I trust that the British government will continue to render all possible support to King Husain. In my opinion he deserves such help, not only for the sake of his grandfather, but because he is a man of character and courage, who may render great services to the Middle East if he survives these uncertain times. It cannot be denied that he has made mistakes, but God rarely creates an old head on young shoulders. Most of us have to gain our experience the hard way.

Finally, let us remember that from the soil of what is now Jordan (with a slight extension southwards down the shores of the Red Sea, with which the history of the Hashemite family is so intimately connected) sprang the three greatest religions of mankind, Judaism, Islam and Christianity. This little tract of country has done more to bring the human race to God, than have all the vast continents by which it is surrounded.

Index

Index

To reduce the size of the index without loss of usefulness, a system of code letters has been adopted for the longer entries. Below is shown how these letters are related to the eight periods into which the narrative has been divided for this purpose. The main events listed under each heading will, it is hoped, provide the additional advantage of a chronology for the general information and reference of the reader.

a From ancient times to the First World War

b The First World War   1914–1918

    Sherif Husain of Mecca rises against the Turks (1915) and is recognized by the Allies as King of the Hejaz   1916

    The Balfour Declaration (letter from A. J. Balfour, British Foreign Secretary, to Lord Rothschild, chairman of the British Zionist Federation)   Nov. 2nd, 1917

c From the beginning of British administration of Palestine to the Second World War   1918–1939

    British military administration of Palestine   1918

    British civil administration of Palestine   July 1920

    Creation of Trans-Jordan as an independent State under Amir Abdulla   Mar. 1921

    Haj Ameen al Husaini elected Mufti of Jerusalem 1921

    Britain given Palestine mandate by League of Nations   July 1922

    Mass immigration of Jews into Palestine since 1920 leads to Arab riots in Jerusalem, Hebron and elsewhere   1929

    Palestine Arabs in rebellion against British mandatory government   1936–1939

d The Second World War   1939–1945

    British and Free French forces occupy Syria; British forces occupy Iraq   1941

Formation of the Arab League (Egypt, Iraq, Lebanon, Saudi Arabia, Syria, Trans-Jordan and the Yemen), supported by the Indian Muslims

Mar. 22nd, 1945

e From the end of the Second World War to the withdrawal of the British from Palestine   1945–1948

Anglo-Trans-Jordan treaty, Amir Abdulla assuming the title of King   Mar. 22nd, 1946

Anglo-American committee recommends immediate immigration of 100,000 Jews into Palestine

Mar. 29th, 1946

UNO partition plan for Palestine   Nov. 29th, 1947

Heavy fighting between Jews and Arabs in Palestine

British withdraw from Palestine, leaving UNO to implement partition plan   May 14th, 1948

f From the withdrawal of the British from Palestine to the Israel-Jordan armistice   1948–1949

Arab forces enter Palestine   May 15th, 1948

The battle for Jerusalem and the road from Tel Aviv

Count Bernadotte appointed UNO mediator in Palestine   May 20th, 1948

The first truce   June 11th, 1948

Renewal of hostilities   July 9th, 1948

Israeli offensive   July 9th–18th, 1948

The "shooting" truce   July 18th, 1948

Assassination of Count Bernadotte by Stern Gang

Sept. 17th, 1948

Successful Israeli offensive against Egyptian army in the Neqeb   Oct. 15th–22nd, 1948

Israeli siege of Egyptians in Falluja

Oct. 22nd, 1948 to Feb. 24th, 1949

Palestine Arabs decide upon union with Trans-Jordan   Dec. 1st, 1948

Israel-Egypt armistice   Feb. 24th, 1949

Israel-Lebanon armistice   Mar. 23rd, 1949

Israel-Jordan armistice signed at Rhodes

Apr. 3rd, 1949

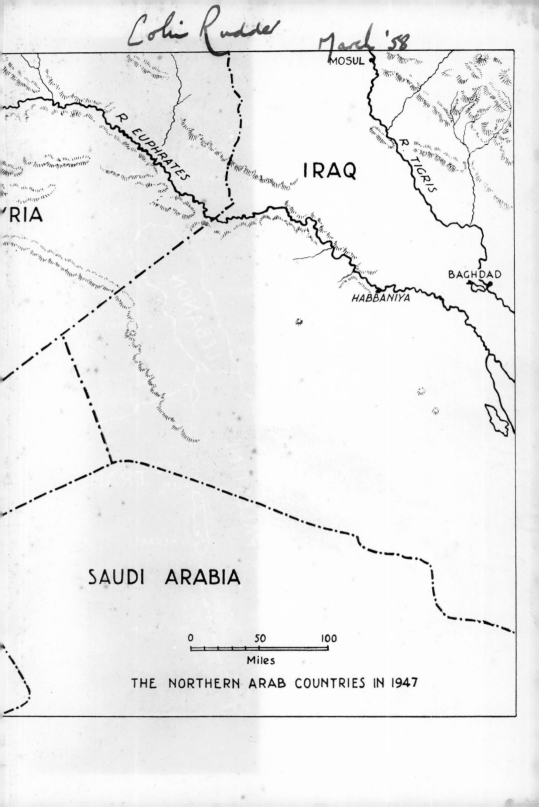

THE NORTHERN ARAB COUNTRIES IN 1947